DENOMINATIONS:
FROM GOD OR MAN?

Volume Two

JOHN F. LUGGER

authorHOUSE®

AuthorHouse™
1663 Liberty Drive
Bloomington, IN 47403
www.authorhouse.com
Phone: 833-262-8899

Published by AuthorHouse 06/20/2024

ISBN: 979-8-8230-2103-6 (sc)
ISBN: 979-8-8230-2104-3 (hc)
ISBN: 979-8-8230-2102-9 (e)

Library of Congress Control Number: 2022922880

Print information available on the last page.

Note: Per Thomas Nelson's Preface, "Words or phrases in italics indicate expressions in the original language that require clarification by additional English words, as was done in the King James Version.

(Italicized words within all Scriptural quotations indicate words that were added by the translators for clarity purposes).

FOREWORD

When I learned that my brother John was writing a five-volume set of books based on a religious theme, I was amazed and proud that he was transferring his considerable intellectual and organizational talents to a work that could be shared with many people.

We both started out in the Lutheran faith, but as he describes in his books, he made the transition to the Church of Christ, yet gives a fair review of all of the other major religions which I find both an ambitious and tremendous accomplishment in a five-volume set of books.

There is a wealth of reference to the Scriptures— to both the Old and New Testaments. People of all religious faiths should find these books thoughtful and provoking, often prompting one to review one's own religious convictions as it did for me.

As communicated to me, the author's intent is not to offend anyone or their faith; rather to read these books with an open mind and heart: studying the Scriptures one's self to verify what is written there.

To this end, I found these books to be excellent, absorbing, and thought-provoking explorations of both difficult and wide-ranging topics.

The examinations and contrasts of the major religions in this particular format—-augmented with reference to Biblical books and topics— was most interesting and helpful; and surely may prompt the reader to re-examine their own religious ideations.

I believe this is a superior read, having much to offer those of any religious preference. Significant notations and documentations of the Scriptures further enhance the interest and value of these books.

Dear reader: Enjoy!

Jerry L. Lugger M.D. F.A.C.S. (Retired)
Lt Col U.S.A.F. MC (Retired)

CONTENTS

INTRODUCTION

As a continuation of the first volume concerning our study on Denominationalism, the original premise by which we began needs to be restated here in the form of two questions: (1) Who are the Lost? referencing Jesus's words as recorded in Luke 19, verse 10, "For the Son of Man came to seek and to save what was lost" and (2) Does God approve of denominations? (Is one church or denomination as good as any other in one's search to correctly serve and worship the God of heaven, or does Scripture describe a particular church that is acceptable to God, to the exclusion of others?). In attempting to answer these two questions in Volume 1, I examined Denominationalism as a chapter topic in and of itself, then proceeded to look at the church established by Christ as described in the New Testament, "The Church of Christ," followed with an examination of the first denomination to break away from Christ's church—the Roman Catholic Church.

Several assumptions were also stated in Volume 1 which need repeating here. First, it's assumed the reader honestly seeks truth, wherever that truth may lead. Jesus stated, "I am the way, the truth, and the life." (John 14:6), therefore His teachings are the truth we must follow, and none other. Second, it's assumed the reader recognizes, or at least has an open mind as to, the fact that the Scriptures are the inspired Word of God and the sole standard for authority. Paul, speaking to Timothy, stated, "All Scripture *is* given by inspiration of God, and profitable for doctrine, for reproof, for correction, for instruction in righteousness, that the man of God may be complete, thoroughly equipped for every good work." (2 Timothy 3:16–17).

In addition to the above, Paul, speaking by inspiration, told the Colossians, "And whatever you do in word or deed, *do* all in the name of the Lord Jesus" (Col. 3:17). By that example, whatever we do religiously, we must do "in the name of," or by the authority of, Jesus. Also, concerning the worship assembly, Paul told Timothy, "These things I write to you … that you may know how you ought to conduct yourself in the house of God, which is the church of the living God" (1 Tim. 3:14–15).

The importance of these passages cannot be overstated; as we've seen already with the Catholic Church and will continue to see moving forward with other denominations, much liberty has been taken with interjecting man's ideas into what the Scriptures clearly instruct. If, in the reader's mind the Scriptures and Jesus's teachings are irrefutable, they will stand as the authority to judge all other doctrines; however, if they are under any suspicion, or if the reader feels they've been compromised in any way, it undermines their credibility for speaking truth.

To lend credibility, I included an appendix at the end of Volume 1 dealing with the inspiration of Scripture. This second volume also contains an appendix to help build confidence in the Scriptures, which is entitled "Translation of the Scriptures," and which gives insight into this process from Old Testament to New. These appendixes go to great lengths to provide arguments and, yes, even proofs that the Scriptures are what they claim to be – every word to be true, factual, non-contradictory, and in accordance with God's will. Should further evidence be desired, the reader is encouraged to consult the references given, particularly Apologetics Press (www.apologeticspress.org) [1], as a source specializing in this subject.

The purpose of this volume, as with the first, is not to insult or otherwise discredit sincere believers of one denomination or another, but rather to appeal to Scripture for direction on this subject. God's Word does indeed describe a church established by Christ, giving insight and examples on how we are to serve and worship our God. It speaks of a simple, unpretentious plan by which we may be saved from our sins; five distinctive "acts" that God has expressed in his Word, that He desires we incorporate into our worship to Him; and direction on how we are to conduct our daily lives to help us remain faithful until Jesus' return.

The reader is encouraged to simply pick up the Bible and read it (just as the Bereans did in Acts 17, comparing and testing Paul's words with the Scriptures) to verify all that is claimed within these volumes concerning the Scriptural arguments are factual. If one were to forget all denominational ties and influences and simply read the Bible, cover to cover, one would come away with a correct understanding of what God desires on this subject. The Scriptures are not difficult to understand, regardless of what some denominational teachers may indicate; God created us with the ability to comprehend His instructions through His Word, and certainly, translators over the years have aided in making the Bible accessible for all to read and understand. I touched on this earlier in Volume 1 with the Roman Catholic Church, where pastoral leaders not only lift themselves up spiritually with their doctrine of apostolic succession, creating a separation from the "laity," or common people of the congregation but also instill this false notion that God's Word is just too difficult for the laity to understand on their own, thus requiring special help and interpretation from those who have been "educated" on such things, creating even more separation and dependence upon the clergy.

In this volume, we'll continue with an examination of three additional denominations. The first two, the Orthodox Church and the Anglican Church—or, as it is known in the United States, the Episcopal Church—hold doctrine very similar to that of the Roman Catholic Church, with some variations. Within the Orthodox study, we'll look at the early ecumenical councils, which helped form and clarify doctrine in that era and continue to maintain authority and influence today. The final denomination of study in this volume, the Lutheran Church, represents the first protestant body to depart from Catholicism—as part of the Reformation movement. Breaking from much of the "formality" and doctrines of the parent church, Martin Luther, founder of this body, held wide appeal, as many denominations would soon follow; although with various doctrinal differences, these groups split from this body into multiple denominations.

The same format will be followed here as with the first volume, that being to include an introductory overview of each denomination's prominence within the United States and around the world today, followed by a look at the origin, organization, recognized authority, and primary beliefs and doctrines of each group. In addition, a look at a typical worship service, giving the reader further insight into the public focus with each, will be examined. Comparison to Scripture and to Christ's church as described in the New Testament (Chapter 2 of Volume 1), will be infused throughout these topics as the benchmark for truth. Final thoughts of each chapter will include questions the reader might consider asking those of that particular denomination they may find themselves in conversation with (or, if the reader is a member of the denomination under discussion, questions they may consider themselves), concerning these matters.

To help the reader reference the formation of these various denominations, two charts that were introduced in Volume 1 are repeated here. The first, entitled "Apostasy of the Church—Tree of Denominations 1" shows the events leading up to the first denomination to separate from the Lord's church as recorded in Scripture, the Roman Catholic Church, which in turn split in A.D. 1054 into similar yet independent denominations: the Western Roman Catholic and Eastern Orthodox Churches. The second chart, entitled "Apostasy of the Church—Tree of Denominations 2," reveals a number of denominational splits originating from the Roman Catholic branch that were formed as a result of the Protestant Reformation initiated in Europe and the English Reformation—both of which spread to the United States over time, where additional denominational division took place.

Apostasy of the Church—Tree of Denominations 1

(Events Leading to the Formation of the Catholic and Orthodox Churches)

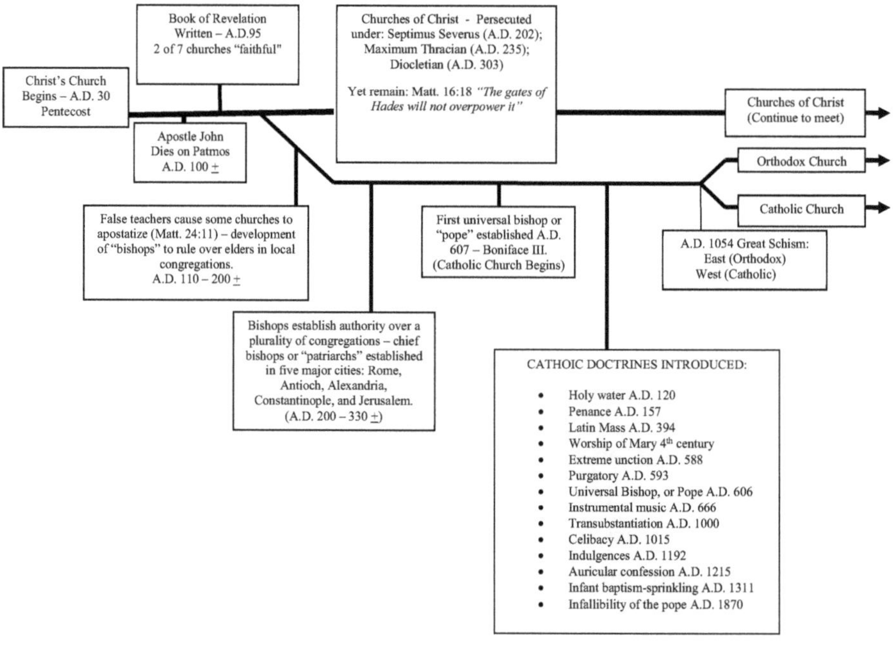
Book of Revelation
Written – A.D.95
2 of 7 churches "faithful"
Churches of Christ - Persecuted under: Septimus Severus (A.D. 202); Maximum Thracian (A.D. 235); Diocletian (A.D. 303)
Yet remain: Matt. 16:18 "The gates of Hades will not overpower it"
Christ's Church Begins – A.D. 30 Pentecost
Churches of Christ (Continue to meet)
Apostle John Dies on Patmos A.D. 100 ±
Orthodox Church
Catholic Church
False teachers cause some churches to apostatize (Matt. 24:11) – development of "bishops" to rule over elders in local congregations. A.D. 110 – 200 ±
First universal bishop or "pope" established A.D. 607 – Boniface III. (Catholic Church Begins)
A.D. 1054 Great Schism: East (Orthodox) West (Catholic)
Bishops establish authority over a plurality of congregations – chief bishops or "patriarchs" established in five major cities: Rome, Antioch, Alexandria, Constantinople, and Jerusalem. (A.D. 200 – 330 ±)
CATHOIC DOCTRINES INTRODUCED:
Holy water A.D. 120
Penance A.D. 157
Latin Mass A.D. 394
Worship of Mary 4th century
Extreme unction A.D. 588
Purgatory A.D. 593
Universal Bishop, or Pope A.D. 606
Instrumental music A.D. 666
Transubstantiation A.D. 1000
Celibacy A.D. 1015
Indulgences A.D. 1192
Auricular confession A.D. 1215
Infant baptism-sprinkling A.D. 1311
Infallibility of the pope A.D. 1870

Apostasy of the Church—Tree of Denominations 2

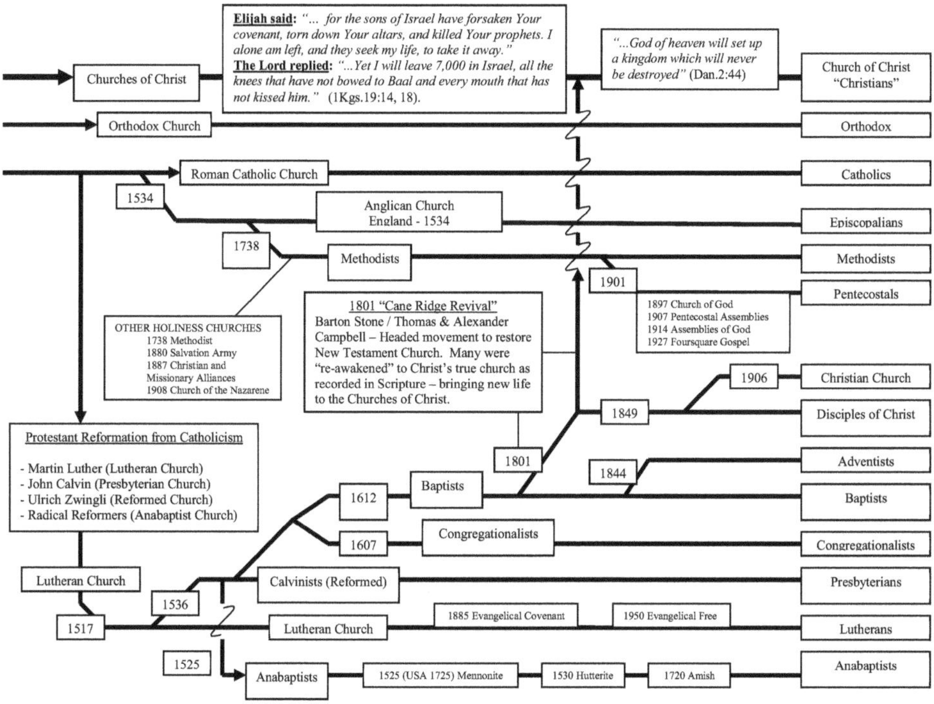
Churches of Christ
Elijah said: "... for the sons of Israel have forsaken Your covenant, torn down Your altars, and killed Your prophets. I alone am left, and they seek my life, to take it away." The Lord replied: "...Yet I will leave 7,000 in Israel, all the knees that have not bowed to Baal and every mouth that has not kissed him." (1Kgs.19:14, 18).
"...God of heaven will set up a kingdom which will never be destroyed" (Dan.2:44)
Church of Christ "Christians"
Orthodox Church
Orthodox
Roman Catholic Church
Catholics
1534
Anglican Church England - 1534
Episcopalians
1738
Methodists
Methodists
1901
Pentecostals
1897 Church of God
1907 Pentecostal Assemblies
1914 Assemblies of God
1927 Foursquare Gospel
OTHER HOLINESS CHURCHES
1738 Methodist
1880 Salvation Army
1887 Christian and Missionary Alliances
1908 Church of the Nazarene
1801 "Cane Ridge Revival"
Barton Stone / Thomas & Alexander Campbell – Headed movement to restore New Testament Church. Many were "re-awakened" to Christ's true church as recorded in Scripture – bringing new life to the Churches of Christ.
1906
Christian Church
1849
Disciples of Christ
Protestant Reformation from Catholicism
- Martin Luther (Lutheran Church)
- John Calvin (Presbyterian Church)
- Ulrich Zwingli (Reformed Church)
- Radical Reformers (Anabaptist Church)
1801
1844
Adventists
1612
Baptists
Baptists
1607
Congregationalists
Congregationalists
Lutheran Church
1536
Calvinists (Reformed)
Presbyterians
1517
Lutheran Church
1885 Evangelical Covenant
1950 Evangelical Free
Lutherans
1525
Anabaptists
1525 (USA 1725) Mennonite
1530 Hutterite
1720 Amish
Anabaptists

CHAPTER 1

THE ORTHODOX CHURCHES

Introduction

The Orthodox Church—predominately the Eastern Orthodox churches, including Greek Orthodox, Russian Orthodox, Syrian Orthodox, Serbian Orthodox, and Romanian Orthodox—claims to be the second-largest Christian community in the world after the Roman Catholic Church, and though they claim separation from Roman Catholicism, the Orthodox Church holds many of the same beliefs and practices.

Numerical estimates range from 150 million to 350 million adherents worldwide. Eastern Orthodox is the largest single religious faith in Belarus (89 percent), Bulgaria (86 percent), the Republic of Cyprus (88 percent), Greece (98 percent), the Republic of Macedonia (70 percent), Moldova (98 percent), Montenegro (84 percent), Romania (89 percent), Serbia (88 percent), and Ukraine (83 percent). In addition, there are significant Orthodox communities in Africa, Asia, Australia, and North and South America. The percentage of Orthodox adherents among the worldwide population is approximately 14 percent, and in the United States population, it's roughly 2.5 percent. [1.]

This chapter contains quotations from official online resources of the Orthodox Church (including Greek Orthodox Archdiocese of America [www.goarch.org], Orthodox Church in America [https://oca.org], and Orthodox Christian Information Center [http://orthodoxinfo.com].

Origin of the Orthodox Church

The Eastern (Orthodox) and Western (Roman Catholic) churches, for all intents and purposes, were one and the same throughout the first few centuries following the time of Christ and the apostles. The Orthodox Church thus joined Catholicism in a slow departure from the divine example.

Hints of a separate denomination (from Catholicism) came as early as A.D. 325 when the Roman emperor Constantine the Great convened the First Ecumenical Council in Nicea, the first of seven such councils convening between the years 325 and 787. These councils, by proclaiming and clarifying doctrine via consensus, marked a departure from the Western (Catholic) practice of papal dictates alone, though prior to the East–West Schism in 1054, the bishop of Rome (the pope) did attend and had influence as "First among Equals" [2.] at these early councils. Differences between Western (Catholic) and Eastern (Orthodox) beliefs emerged, however, as a result of this consensus-versus-individual protocol. The councils were convened by ruling emperors or by patriarchs of Alexandria, Antioch, and Constantinople and were attended by anywhere from 150 to 500 bishops. The proclamations of these councils are held to be on par with Scripture itself concerning their authority and early influence on the formulation of Orthodox theology and doctrine.

In addition to these seven councils, a number of other significant councils (though not recognized as ecumenical) occurred between 1484 and 1672 to further define Orthodox doctrine. In A.D. 330, Emperor Constantine renamed the city of Byzantium as Constantinople, which became the city of the leading patriarch in the Great Schism of 1054. Today, this city is known as Istanbul, Turkey.

Below is our timeline, once again highlighting this major split between the two Catholic churches in 1054. One could make a case for the origin of the Orthodox Church as either the move to rename Byzantium in 330 or this later recognized split in 1054. Certainly, the definitions of separation began in 330, shortly following the First Ecumenical Council meeting, which ultimately culminated in 1054.

Founding of the Orthodox Churches
Split from Catholicism, AD 1054

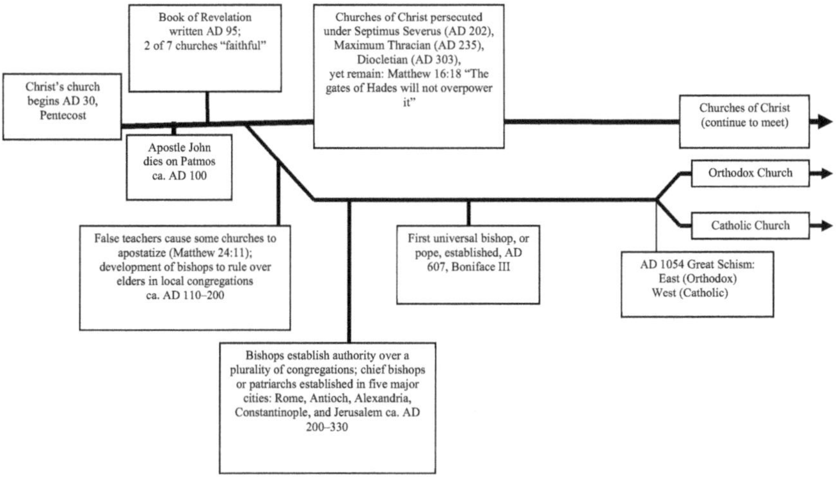
Christ's church begins AD 30, Pentecost
Book of Revelation written AD 95; 2 of 7 churches "faithful"
Apostle John dies on Patmos ca. AD 100
Churches of Christ persecuted under Septimus Severus (AD 202), Maximum Thracian (AD 235), Diocletian (AD 303), yet remain: Matthew 16:18 "The gates of Hades will not overpower it"
Churches of Christ (continue to meet)
Orthodox Church
Catholic Church
False teachers cause some churches to apostatize (Matthew 24:11); development of bishops to rule over elders in local congregations ca. AD 110–200
First universal bishop, or pope, established, AD 607, Boniface III
AD 1054 Great Schism: East (Orthodox) West (Catholic)
Bishops establish authority over a plurality of congregations; chief bishops or patriarchs established in five major cities: Rome, Antioch, Alexandria, Constantinople, and Jerusalem ca. AD 200–330

The Orthodox Church claims to have descended from Christ's original church and has upheld the teachings of Christ and His apostles, maintaining a "continuity of faith" [3.] through apostolic succession to the current day. "Reverend [sic]" [4.] Thomas Fitzgerald, in his "Teachings of the Orthodox Church," for instance, confirms this continuity with the apostolic community and notes, "Orthodoxy believes that she has preserved and taught the historic Christian Faith, free from error and distortion, from the time of the Apostles. She also believes that there is nothing in the body of her teachings, which is contrary to truth." [3.] Another confirmation comes from the Orthodox Church in America website concerning "The Original Christian Church," with these words: "We Orthodox believe that we are the continuation of the ancient Orthodox Christian Church, that we trace our history back to Christ and the apostles, and that the Church was 'formally' established on the day of Pentecost. The Roman Catholic Church placed itself outside of the fellowship when it broke off communion with us in the 11th century." [5.]

Adding to the gifts and authority of the apostles through apostolic succession, Vladimir Berzonsky, in his work, "Thoughts in Christ," acknowledges another avenue of authority: "Apostolic succession is a phrase describing those Christian communions that can claim to be descended from the earliest apostles… But for us it's more than that – it's the inheritance of sacred tradition that identifies the bearers and grateful heirs of spiritual gifts that flow in the Church through the centuries." [6.]

This "sacred tradition" is identified as the teachings of the church fathers, particularly the ecumenical councils, whose doctrine was so revered and reverenced that those who did not believe these writings were declared "anathema" (cut off from the church and salvation).

George Bebis, Ph.D., in his article titled "Tradition in the Orthodox Church"; subhead, "The Ecumenical Councils," made this statement "These Ecumenical Councils became instruments for formulating the dogmatic teachings of the Church … In the Fourth Ecumenical Council of Chalcedon, it was stated that: 'The Fathers defined everything perfectly; he who goes against this is anathema; no one adds, no one takes away.'" Later in this same article, under "The Living Tradition of the Eucharist," Dr. Bebis stated, "By adhering to the teaching of the Scriptures, the Ecumenical Councils, and the Patristic writings, by observing the canons of the Church, by frequently participating in the Eucharist, where Tradition becomes an empirical reality, we are members of the Body of Christ and are led to the "'contemplation of God.'" [7.]

As previously noted in Volume One, this idea of apostolic succession is not supported by the Scriptures; nor can the pronouncements of ecumenical councils or patristic tradition be added as authoritative revelation to the Scriptures. Passages such as 2 Timothy 3:15–17, Jude 3, and Acts 20:27 simply will not allow this.

The same Scriptures referenced with the Roman Catholic Church (as a prophecy given in the New Testament, warning of a coming departure from the Lord's true church) also apply here, as the Roman Catholic and Eastern Orthodox Churches were one and the same at this point. This includes Paul's exhortation to the Ephesian elders in Acts 20:29–30, where he warns them that after he leaves, "savage wolves will come in among them," and that these would be men who would rise up from among their own brethren, "speaking perverse things" in order to "draw away the disciples after themselves."

Paul also warns Timothy of some of the doctrines that would be espoused by those advocating this departure, first in 1 Timothy 4:1–4: "In later times some will depart from the faith, giving heed to deceitful spirits and doctrines of demons … forbidding to marry, *and commanding* to abstain from foods which God created." Later, Paul warned Timothy again, this time in his exhortation to encourage him to persevere in his preaching: "Convince, rebuke, exhort, with all longsuffering and teaching." Why? "For the time will come when they will not endure sound doctrine, but according to their own desires, *because* they have itching ears, they will heap up for themselves teachers; and they will turn *their* ears away from the truth, and be turned aside to fables" (2 Timothy 4:2–4).

The Thessalonians were told of the reality of this departure as well, and "the man of sin" will be exalted to a position "displaying himself as being God": "Let no one deceive you by any means, for *that Day will not come* (the coming of our Lord Jesus Christ) [8] unless the falling away comes first, and the man of sin is revealed, the son of perdition, who opposes and exalts himself above all that is called God or that is worshipped, so that he sits as God in the temple of God, showing himself that he is God" (2 Thessalonians 2:3–4).

Various postulations have been put forth as to the identity of this man of sin, including Satan, Judaism, a Roman ruler, or possibly the Antichrist, but nothing fits all details of this prophecy more precisely than the religious departure from New Testament teaching, as found in Catholicism, including its associated branches of Greek Orthodoxy and Anglicanism (Jackson 2012, 441–443). [9.]

Although the man of sin spoken of in 2 Thessalonians is singular in this prophecy, as is other verbiage used in this passage, such as "**son** of perdition … exalts **himself** … **he** sits as God," [10] and it lends itself to the idea of the pope of Catholicism, as Jackson points out, this prophetic phrase "man of sin" indicates a broader meaning, including the associated denominations of Catholicism, Eastern Orthodoxy, and Anglicanism (the American Episcopal Church), to name a few. The Orthodox Church is organized under patriarchs, who govern much the same as popes, except they have control over geographical areas, rather than a single pope governing the entire denomination. Similarly, the Anglican Church is set up with archbishops, acting as patriarchs, governing large provinces. All three of these denominations are similar in their theology; as mentioned, the Orthodox and Catholic Communions were one and the same until the split of 1054, and the Anglican Church split from Catholicism via King Henry VIII of England in 1534. The common factor with these three churches to this man of sin, identified as a man or men or theology, most closely resembling the religious departure from New Testament teaching, as described in 2 Thessalonians, at least in this author's view, seems to be apostolic succession.

Apostolic succession and its enactment by the clergy of this denomination (and others) have created a human-made elevation for certain clergy, giving them gifts supposedly carried forward from the apostles (even exceeding the attributes of the apostles, in some respects), to be employed in these denominations today. The gifts include the ability to receive confession and forgive sin, to heal the sick, to intercede in prayer, and to stand before the congregation through the Spirit in place of Christ.

As previously mentioned in Volume I, one of the church fathers, Ignatius of Antioch, said: "Take care to do all things in harmony with God, with the bishop presiding in the place of God, and with the presbyters in the place of the council of the apostles, and with the deacons … entrusted with the business of Jesus Christ … It is necessary that you do nothing without the bishop, and that you be subject to the presbytery, as to the apostles of Jesus Christ." [11.]

The OCA confirms this idea in their official doctrine of Holy Orders: "Christ is present now, always, and forever in his Church. The sacramental ministry of the Church – the bishops, priests, and deacons – receive the gift of the Holy Spirit to manifest Christ to men … As the apostles received the special gift of God to go forth and make Christ present to men … so the clergy of the Church receive the gift of God's Spirit to maintain and manifest Christ's presence and action in the churches." [12.]

It's not only the upper echelon of clergy who take on this role as Christ in the Spirit to men; any bishop or priest who asserts his apostolic prerogative may do so. This seems to fit into what Paul was warning of in 2 Thessalonians 2:4—a departure in which one "opposes and exalts himself above all that is called God or that is worshipped, so that he sits as God in the temple of God, showing himself that he is God." In some instances, the highest of clergy (pope, patriarch, or archbishop) will accept worship, something even the apostles never dared to do. This is not what Jesus had in mind or what He set up as His church (an almost complete separation between clergy and laity). The Lord's church is to be led by elders or overseers, with deacons as servant leaders, and each body is to be autonomous. These three denominations are governed by popes, patriarchs, and archbishops who reside far from their individual congregations and who exert authority well beyond what Scripture allows.

Organization of the Orthodox Church

The government of the Orthodox Church has a hierarchy similar to the Roman Catholic Church, except for a variation in the top position. According to "Father [sic]" [13] Vladimir Berzonsky, in his article "Thoughts in Christ—One Shepherd, Many Flocks," published December 26, 2004, on the Orthodox Church in America (OCA) website:

> The original transmitters of the life and resurrection of Christ were the apostles. They established parishes wherever they went, ordaining by laying on of hands bishops, presbyters or priests, and deacons. The continuity of the Church was marked by apostolic succession; but that also is seen in two ways. One is that a single bishop is understood to be the successor of the apostles, while another tradition is that Christ is the only head of the Church, and His authority is received and promulgated by the assembly of bishops open to the work of the Holy Spirit within the gathered body. [14.]

The Greek Patriarch - Israel

The "single bishop" idea undoubtedly refers to the Catholic pope, while the second, claiming an "assembly of bishops" to be preeminent in the church, is the position taken by the Orthodox Church. Additional support for this is evident in the OCA online Q&A document "On this Rock I will build my church." [15.]

Although claiming no single pope, the Orthodox Church recognizes the patriarch of Constantinople as the "First among Equals" [2.] (An honor bestowed on him from the Great Schism forward), reflecting both this individual's administrative leadership and his spiritual elevation among the churches. Unlike the Catholic pope, however, this person does not proclaim doctrine; nor does he claim to be infallible. Whereas the pope asserts himself as the vicar (substitute) of Christ on earth, this person and many of the archbishops and others who exert apostolic privileges present themselves as being "Christ in the Spirit"—not exactly the same, but if asked to give a difference between the two, one would be hard-pressed for an answer.

The Orthodox Church is set up territorially, with a hierarchy of governors or clergy to rule each territory. In descending order, from the First among Equals, there are patriarchs, archbishops or metropolitans, bishops, priests or presbyters, and deacons.

- A patriarch is head over a large geographical area or country, including all dioceses contained therein.
- An archbishop, or metropolitan, is the leading bishop of the chief city or capital of a region, which usually contains other bishops, each with his own particular diocese.
- Bishops are responsible for a number of churches within a region; all bishops are said to be equal in authority and cannot interfere with each other's territory. The territory governed by a bishop is called a "see" or a "diocese."
- In a similar fashion to the Catholics, along with the regular ranks of Orthodox clergy, there are parish priests or presbyters who govern the individual congregations (comprising the laity); deacons, who usually assist the priests in liturgical services; subdeacons; and a host of monastic orders.

The development of this hierarchy is explained in several sections of the document *The History of the Orthodox Church*: "Early Administrative Structure," "Heresies and Ecumenical Councils," and "The Pentarchy." The document begins with a statement from the "Early Administrative Structure" that once the apostles founded a community, they would depart, leaving behind others to administer the new congregation, mainly to function as presiders over the Eucharist, or Lord's Supper, and to baptize. Within this structure, a hierarchy developed to include a presiding officer for the community called the "*episcopos*," or "bishop," who was assisted by priests and deacons. This was based upon the Last Supper (the first liturgy), which "could not have taken place without the Lord's presiding presence ... the existence of a presiding head was taken for granted by the Church. This establishment of a local 'monarchical' episcopate is still at the very center of Orthodox ecclesiology." [16.]

Under "Heresies and Ecumenical Councils" we learn by the fourth century, a provincial system had developed, grouping churches by province and following the Roman government structure. Greater honor was afforded larger cities, whereby the metropolitan, or bishop, of a capital city was given special precedence. At first the presiding bishop of the three largest cities in the empire—Rome, Alexandria, and Antioch—was ranked as the most important by common consensus (without any ecclesiastical legislation to support it). This problem was rectified in 325 when the bishops of the First Ecumenical Council sanctioned these dioceses. Constantinople soon emerged as the new capital of the empire, and by the fifth century, the pentarchy, or system of five sees, with an understood order of precedence, was established. Finally, under "The Pentarchy" is stated, "This system of patriarchs and metropolitans was exclusively the result of ecclesiastical legislation; there was nothing inherently divine in its origin. None of the five sees, in short, possessed its authority by divine right. … The determining factor was simply their secular status as the most important cities in the empire … each of the five patriarchs was totally sovereign within his sphere of jurisdiction … the bishop of Rome was simply vested with the presidency, as the senior bishop, the first among equals." [16.]

Christ, as the affirmed head of the church, is said to be personified within the Orthodox clergy and those clergy alone (as distinguished from other members or laity of the church). This is the premise upon which the above statements are based, where an episcopos, or bishop, elevated above a priest or elder (as the Orthodox view the Scriptures), was established and given authority to preside first over a community of congregations in a given area, and later over larger cities and provinces. Below are a few more quotes confirming the Orthodox ideology that their clergy do indeed have divine sanction and responsibility to lead their respective congregations as Christ personified:

> All members of the Church are called to "lead a life worthy of God" (1 Thess. 2:12), but in a complementary way, the Church is distinguished between clergy, laity, and monastics. The clergy trace their descent by uninterrupted succession from the apostles and through them from our

Lord Jesus Christ. (An Outline of the Orthodox Faith, 8/25/90). [17.]

As the apostles received the special gift of God to go forth and make Christ present to men … so the clergy of the Church receive the gift of God's Spirit to maintain and to manifest Christ's presence and action in the churches. It is the doctrine of the Church that the clergy must strive to fulfill the grace given to them with the gift of the "laying on of hands" in the most perfect way possible. (OCA Vol. II – Worship; The Sacraments; "Holy Orders"). [12.]

Bishop Irinej, bishop of Eastern America Diocese

The Orthodox Church claims that its clergy have received special gifts, including God's Holy Spirit, through apostolic succession by the laying on of hands. These gifts allow them to impart the presence of Christ in all aspects of their ministries to the laity. The clergy includes the *bishop* (*episkopos* in Greek), the leading Church ministry, overseeing particular churches or dioceses as well as the Universal Church to their constituents. "A bishop of the chief city of a region which has within it other bishops with their own particular dioceses is usually called the metropolitan or archbishop. "Metropolitan" merely means "bishop of the metropolis," the main city. The title of archbishop means "leading bishop" of an area. The title of patriarch belongs to the bishop of the capital city of a region containing other metropolitanates and dioceses. Today this usually means a national church." [12.]

Next in line is the *priest*, also called the *presbyter*, who is called to assist the bishop in his work. Priests act as pastors of the local churches or parishes, presiding at the celebration of the Eucharist, exercising the ministries of forgiveness and healing, along with teaching, preaching, and counseling. "The priests in the Church are assigned by the bishop and belong to the specific congregations which they serve. Apart from his bishop and his own particular parish community, the priest has no "powers" and, indeed, no services to perform. Thus, on the altar table of each Christian community headed by the priest as pastor, there is the cloth called the antimension signed by the bishop which is the permission to the community to gather and to act as the Church of God. Without the antimension, the priest and his people cannot function legitimately, and the actions of the assembly cannot be considered as being authentically "of the Church." [12.]

Finally, the third of the Orthodox clergy rankings, the *deacon*, who in times past functioned only to serve the bishops and priests in the service of divine liturgy or eucharist, "the diaconate … may now not only assist the priest and bishop in liturgical services, but will often head educational programs and youth groups, do hospital visitation and missionary work and conduct projects of social welfare."[12.]

"The bishops, priests, and deacons of the Church have no other function or service than to manifest the presence and action of Christ to his people." (OCA Vol. II – Worship; The Sacraments; "Holy Orders"). [12.]

The only organization to be found in Christ's church is in the local churches, where Scripture sanctions oversight by a plurality of elders within each local congregation. Each congregation is seen as autonomous, independent from, and nonaccountable to any other church body, group, or individual, except for Christ and His teachings:

> And when they had preached the gospel to that city and made many disciples, they returned to Lystra, Iconium, and Antioch, strengthening the souls of the disciples, exhorting *them* to continue in the faith, and *saying*, "We must through many tribulations enter the kingdom of God." So when they had appointed elders in every church, and prayed with fasting, they commended them to the Lord in whom they had believed. (Acts 14:21–23)

> For this reason I left you in Crete, that you should set in order the things that are lacking, and appoint elders in every city as I commanded you. (Titus 1:5)

Neither the establishment nor the development of the Lord's church, as described in Scripture, matches what the Orthodox Church has done. In the first place, the apostles never "established parishes wherever they went, ordaining by laying on of hands bishops, presbyters or priests, and deacons." The Scriptures indicate the apostles appointed elders in every church, in every city; they did not "lay hands on them" to pass on divine gifts. That's simply not what the Scriptures say. There were times—for instance, in Ephesians 4:11—when our Lord gave, from His ascended residence in heaven, special gifts, including to elders, for the equipping of the saints for a period of time, "till" proper unity of the faith was reached; and the apostles did pass along the Holy Spirit on occasion—for instance, in Acts 8:14–17, where the brethren in Samaria needed a special portion of the Spirit, and Peter and John "laid hands on them" to supply them with this gift. That's not, however, what we're talking about here. Regardless, passages such as 1 Corinthians 13:8 simply preclude these "gifts" from being carried forward from the apostles to now; this passage says, "They will fail … cease … vanish away."

In addition, the word for "elder," "*presbyteros*," is connected to the same individual in Titus 1:5–7 as "bishop" or "episcopos" which also means "overseer." And "elder," "overseer," and "shepherd" (or "*poimen*"), also meaning "pastor," are tied together in both Acts 20:17, 28 and 1 Peter 5:1–2. The Orthodox have added a third position here (similar to the Catholic Church): an overseeing bishop, or episcopos, and under him, what they perceive as an elder or priest—and under him, a deacon. These are all specialized clergy, supposedly ordained by other bishops and clergy—all without Scriptural mandate.

This episcopos is supposedly justified, as Jesus presided at the Last Supper (what they consider the first liturgy) as presiding head, giving license to a single monarchical episcopate being established. Tying this to their theology of apostolic succession, whereby their clergy maintain a direct link back to the divine gifts of the apostles and, in turn, the presence of Jesus Himself, this position thus was established. Not only was it established for one congregation; it was established for a community, which could involve multiple congregations. The Scriptures tell us elders are to be appointed. With the initial congregations of the Lord's church, the apostles did this, but subsequent to this, up to and including today, elders are appointed by the Christians within each congregation, according to a list of qualifications outlined in Scripture (1 Timothy 3:1–7; Titus 1:5–9). Also, deacons are to be appointed within each congregation; again, qualified men are submitted from among the Christians within each congregation of the Lord's church to meet a list of qualifications (1 Timothy 3:8–13) and appointed accordingly.

This whole idea that individuals within the clergy can receive divine gifts through apostolic succession by the laying on of hands simply cannot be supported by Scripture. The miracles we see in the first century were done predominately to confirm Jesus as the Christ, the true Son of God. The several examples we see in Scripture, including Luke 4:40, where Jesus heals the sick by the laying on of hands; Acts 8:17, where the Holy Spirit is bestowed by the apostles; and 1 Timothy 4:14, where Timothy receives special gifts to help in his ministry, also by the laying on of hands, are all examples of things done to confirm Jesus and the validity of His church to an unbelieving world at that time.

As stated previously, these miracles ceased (along with the miracle of divine gift-giving via laying on of hands) toward the end of the first century, as the church was established and confirmation of Jesus by this method was no longer necessary. Any argument that Peter (as the first supposed pope, envisioned by the Catholic Church) or an assembly of bishops (as envisioned by the Orthodox Church) initiated this supposed divine succession cannot be supported.

The development of the Orthodox Church from the first century onward is also foreign to New Testament mandate. Upon altering the Scriptural pattern of individual congregations to be under the leadership of appointed elders assisted by appointed deacons into one of a senior bishop presiding over multiple congregations and ordaining other priests or elders and deacons, these congregations evolved into a hierarchy, creating separation and dependency between clergy and laity within each congregation. As well, the clergy, particularly the bishops, were ranked according to secular conditions, including city size. According to the document "The History of the Orthodox Church," the church was aware that such ranking of one bishop versus another was done by common consensus and without any ecclesiastical legislation to support it. The problem was solved by the fathers or bishops of the ecumenical councils, who later sanctioned this ranking.

Because the Roman Catholic and Orthodox Churches were essentially one and the same through the first millennium, this development applies to both: a bishop or group of bishops first established control over a small group of congregations (community), then a larger geographical area (city or province); finally, a universal bishop was considered First among Equals, or pope in Rome. All of this falls outside of what we see in Scripture. This hierarchy, being ultimately sanctioned by the First Ecumenical Council of 325, is also a non-Scriptural event; these councils do not have Divine authority.

Scripture attests that Christ is the head of His church (not a First among Equals, not a pope, not a patriarch of a country, not a bishop or archbishop of a portion of that country). Jesus stated, "I also say to you that you are Peter, and on this rock [Peter's confession that Jesus was indeed the Christ, the Son of the living God] I will build My church …" (Matthew 16:18). Paul affirms in Ephesians 1:22: "And He put all *things* under His feet, and gave Him *to be* head over all *things* to the church."

In addition, individual Christians are not without knowledge and thus totally dependent upon Orthodox clergy, who profess to be their exclusive pathway to Christ. In fact, the Scriptures teach that as one repents, confesses, and is baptized into Jesus, one receives the gift of the Holy Spirit: "Then Peter said to them, "Repent, and let every one of you be baptized in the name of Jesus Christ for the remission of sins; and you shall receive the gift of the Holy Spirit" (Acts 2:38).

Also, Paul, speaking to the Christians in Rome, explains that not only the Spirit but Christ is in them, which discounts this idea altogether: "But you are not in the flesh but in the Spirit, if indeed the Spirit of God dwells in you ... And if Christ *is* in you, the body *is* dead because of sin, but the Spirit *is* life because of righteousness" (Romans 8:9–10).

One last point before we leave this section – the assumed power of the bishop to sanction a church assembly to meet or not meet based on his blessing. As mentioned above, each local congregation must have either a bishop present or a cloth called the antimension, draped over the altar of that church, signed by the priest – otherwise, the church does not have "permission" to meet or function! Where, might I ask, can one find this stipulation in Scripture? We're talking about God's desired worship of Him, which no man has a right to preclude! Do you suppose these bishops, even with the power of apostolic succession (presuming upon the original apostles' powers they believe they possess), realize that Jesus's apostles would not accept worship themselves, (Acts 10:26) and to our point here, they set up churches to function on their own without the apostolic presence or any "cloth" signed by an apostle to allow them to continue worshipping God as Christ's church (Acts 14:23)?

Authority of the Orthodox Church

St. Basil's Cathedral
Moscow, Russia

In addition to the above-mentioned authority vested within its clergy (perceived as divine gifts through apostolic succession), the Orthodox Church recognizes other sources of authority, all of which can be included in what they call Holy Tradition (similar to Roman Catholicism's Divine Tradition). According to Orthodoxy, "Among the elements which make up the Holy Tradition of the Church, the Bible holds first place." [18.] However, other elements that hold high importance to tie this body of authority together include the church's liturgical life and prayer. This would bring in the interpretation of those Scriptures, prayer, and the exercise of apostolic gifts by the clergy during worship services, along with the observance of the Eucharist, where the clergy are indispensable, as well as the dogmatic decisions and acts of the churchly councils (these would include the first seven ecumenical councils, which further defined and clarified Scriptural concepts). The first and second of these seven councils developed the Nicene Creed, another authoritative doctrine, as a testament to the Orthodox faith. This creed is so honored the Orthodox Church stated this, "The Nicene Creed, which was formulated at the Councils of Nicea in 325 and of Constantinople in 381, has been recognized since then as the authoritative expression of the fundamental beliefs of the Orthodox Church. The Creed is often referred to as the "Symbol of Faith." This description indicates that the Creed is not an analytical statement, but that it points to a reality greater than itself and to which it bears witness. For generations, the Creed has been the criterion of authentic Faith and the basis of Christian education. The Creed is recited at the time of Baptism and during every Divine Liturgy." [19.]

There are also the writings of the church fathers, those individuals living alongside and after the apostles, who, according to patristic tradition, took what the apostles preached, both as found in Scripture and, in addition to what was later canonized as Scripture, being successors to the apostles themselves, they kept, treasured, interpreted, and explained to the church those Scriptures, as well as leaving extra writings for the church's benefit – held to be authoritative. "Taken as a whole, the writings of the Fathers which are built upon the biblical and liturgical foundations of Christian faith and life have great authority within the Orthodox Church and are primary sources for the discovery of the Church's doctrine." [20.]

Holy Tradition also encompasses the lives of the saints, as recorded in history, canon law (surrounding Scripture), and inspired forms of artistic works, defined as iconographic tradition, together with music and architecture. "None of these elements stands alone … All come alive in the actual living of the life of the Church in every age and generation … As the Church continues to live by the inspiration of the Holy Spirit, the Holy Tradition of the Church will continue to grow and develop" [18.] Holy Tradition is further defined as "the deposit of faith given by Jesus Christ to the Apostles and passed on in the Church from one generation to the next without addition, alteration or subtraction … Holy Tradition is that same faith that Jesus taught to the Apostles and that they gave to their disciples, preserved in the Church and especially in its leadership through Apostolic succession (Jude 1:3)." [21.]

While the Scriptures are held in high regard, it seems Holy Tradition, which is taught to embody those Scriptures, also acknowledges other elements of authority, including the teachings of the church fathers, as well as the councils, particularly the seven ecumenical councils, where further formulation of Christian doctrine, in association with these Scriptures, took place. The Scriptures are said to contain historical fact, poetry, idiom, metaphor, simile, moral fables, parables, prophecy, and wisdom literature; but they are never to be used under personal interpretation. They must be interpreted within the context of Holy Tradition. Thus, the Orthodox Christian is taught to believe in the doctrine of *sola scriptura*, which holds that all truth is to be found within Scripture, although much is too difficult for the Orthodox Christian to understand. Therefore, the only way the Bible can be correctly understood is within the teachings of the Orthodox Church and its clergy.

"Reverend [sic]" [4.] Thomas Fitzgerald had this to say concerning the Scriptures and Holy Tradition:

> While the Bible is treasured as a valuable written record of God's revelation, it does not contain wholly that revelation. The Bible is viewed as only one expression of God's revelation in the ongoing life of His people. Scripture is part of the treasure of Faith which is known as Tradition ... In addition to the witness of Faith in the Scripture, The Orthodox Christian Faith is celebrated in the Eucharist; taught by the Fathers, glorified by the Saints; expressed in prayers, hymns, and icons; defended by the seven Ecumenical Councils; embodied in the Nicene Creed; manifested in social concern; and, by the power of the Holy Spirit, it is lived in every local Orthodox parish. [19.]

The writings of the church fathers, though acknowledged as not infallible, are said to exhibit great authority within the Orthodox Church, as they are "built upon the biblical and liturgical foundations of Christian faith." [20.] The fathers are recognized as having lived between the first and eighth centuries, encompassing holy lives, ascribing to, and promoting Orthodox Christian teachings, and having church approval. They also have been categorized by the eras in which they lived: there are the apostolic fathers (those who knew the apostles); the second- and third-century fathers (ante-Nicene), or those living before the First Ecumenical Council in 325; the Nicene fathers (those who lived during the councils); and the post-Nicene fathers, or those living after the seventh Council until the eighth century.

These fathers of the church were also categorized by the focus of their writings; for instance, some were referred to as apologists (defenders against outside critics); others defended from within against heresies of the church. Still others, apart from defenders, were considered either theological (teachers of the Christian faith), pastoral (teachers of spiritual faith), ascetical (teachers focusing on the struggles of spiritual life), or mystical (those who focused on communion with God).

Some of the more universally known and praised fathers of the church include the apostolic fathers: St. Clement (30–101), St. Ignatius (35–107), St. Polycarp (69–155), and St. Justin (65–110). Of the pre-Nicene era, Origen (185–253) stands out. Although he was condemned by the Second Ecumenical Council, many of his ideas have been accepted by the Church. Fathers recognized during the council period include St. Athanasius (297–373), St. Basil the Great (329–379), and St. Cyril of Alexandria (376–444). As mentioned, though their writings are not considered inspired, they are held in high esteem. Together with the council writings and decisions, Orthodox and others come very close to making a case that they are of equal esteem to that of the Scriptures.

Fathers of the Church: (Left to Right) Erasmus de Bie, Saint Thomas Aquinas, Saint Ambrose, Saint Augustine, Pope Gregory the Great, and Jerome (contemplating the Blessed Sacrament)

With regard to the authority given the ecumenical councils, Dr. Aristeides Papadakis, in his article "History of the Orthodox Church," made this statement: "The seven ecumenical councils with their doctrinal formulations are of particular importance. Specifically, these assemblies were responsible for the formulation of Christian doctrine. As such, they constitute a permanent standard for an Orthodox understanding of the Trinity, the persons of Christ, the incarnation … they constitute an authoritative norm against which all subsequent speculative theology is measured. Their decisions remain binding for the whole Church; non-acceptance constitutes exclusion from the communion of the Church." [16.]

Expressing the authority of these councils to an even higher degree, Dr. George Bebis, in his article "Tradition in the Orthodox Church" had this to say (including a quote from Sabas, bishop of Paltus in Syria in the fifth century):

"These Ecumenical Councils became instruments for formulating the dogmatic teachings of the Church, for fighting against heresies and schisms and promoting the common and unifying Tradition of the Church … the Church Fathers who participated came from almost all the local dioceses of the Roman Empire, thus expressing the faith and practice of the Universal Church. Their decisions have been accepted by the clergy and the laity of all times, making their validity indisputable … Our Fathers who met at Nicea did not make their declarations of themselves but spoke as the Holy Spirit dictated." The OCA reinforced this statement with the following: "The dogmatic definitions (dogma means official teaching) and the canon laws of the ecumenical councils are understood to be inspired by God and to be expressive of His will for men. Thus, they are essential sources of Orthodox Christian doctrine." [22; 7.]

The Orthodox Church claims that councils began in the apostolic age with the early church. Some argue that the first "council" was the meeting of the apostles in Jerusalem to appoint seven good men to help with the daily distribution of food to the Grecian widows, as recorded in Acts 6:1–7. Others point to the meeting held to decide the conditions under which Gentiles could enter the Christian Church (Acts 15) as being the first church council. Either way, it was asserted:

"From that time on, all through history, councils were held on every level of church life to make important decisions. Bishops met regularly with their priests, also called presbyters or elders, and people. It became the practice, and even the law, very early in church history that bishops in given regions should meet in councils held on a regular basis" [23.]

Several doctrinal disputes from the fourth century onward led to the convening of these ecumenical councils, the first convening in 325 to condemn an idea of some, following the views of Arius, that Jesus was a created being and was inferior to the Father. The Second Council of 381 met to define the nature of the Holy Spirit as being equal to that of the others in the Trinity. The Third Council convened in 431 to affirm Mary as truly the birth-giver and mother of God. The Fourth Council met in 451 to affirm Jesus as truly God and truly man, without a mixture of the two natures.

The Fifth Council convened in 553 to further explain Jesus's two natures, as well to condemn teachings concerning the preexistence of the soul. The Sixth Council meeting in 681 declared that Christ has two wills assigned to His two natures, human and Divine. The Seventh Council met in 787 to affirm support for the veneration of icons, while forbidding their worship. The decisions made by these seven councils have been recognized to be Divinely inspired and essential to the formation of Orthodox Christian doctrine. An eighth council met in 879 to restore St. Photius to his see and to condemn any alteration of the Nicene-Constantinopolitan Creed of 381. Though this eighth council and future council proclamations over the centuries carry significance to the Orthodox Church, the Church places far more importance on the decisions of the first seven councils.

The Orthodox Bible contains forty-nine Old Testament books (three more than the Catholic Bible) and twenty-seven New Testament books. They hold to all of the apocryphal books as being authoritative, including Tobit, Judith, 1 Maccabees, 2 Maccabees, Wisdom of Solomon, Sirach, Baruch, 1 Esdras, 3 Maccabees, and 4 Maccabees.

The Bible teaches that the Scriptures we have—thirty-nine books in the Old Testament and twenty-seven in the New Testament—are the full and complete revelation of God to mankind for all time (2 Timothy 3:15–17; Jude 3; Acts 20:27). We are forbidden to go beyond the revealed will of Christ (2 John 9–10) or to teach anything other than the gospel revealed by the apostles in the New Testament, lest we be "accursed" (Galatians 1:6–9). Also, the apocryphal books are not to be included as inspired Scripture. The Orthodox, however, honor as authoritative the entire collection, including three more books than those observed by the Catholics.

These Scriptures, minus the apocryphal books, are the *only* source of authority to be recognized by Christ's church. Orthodoxy, however, has reduced the Scriptures to being only a "part" of God's revelation, that which is written, and though they are considered valuable, they claim "it does not contain wholly that revelation."[19.] Additional revelation to which the Orthodox refer is termed "Holy Tradition," defined as "that which is handed on, from one generation to another," including writings from the early church fathers concerning liturgy and church doctrine and clarification of doctrine, both confirmed by the decisions of ecumenical councils into canon laws and formulated by mankind into creeds, as well as emulation of the lives of saints and the veneration of icons. Along with the special gifts supposedly imparted to the Orthodox clergy through apostolic succession by the laying on of hands, all these components become the authority base, or the faith—the Holy Tradition—of the Orthodox Church.

Holy Tradition seems to be viewed differently within the Orthodox community, however. The official online source for the OCA defines "Holy Tradition" as "That which is passed on" and "given over" from one to another"; but goes on to say, "Holy Tradition is not limited to what is written … it is on the contrary, the total life and experience of the entire Church transferred from place to place and from generation to generation. Tradition is the very life of the Church itself as it is inspired and guided by the Holy Spirit."[18.] A member church, however, Holy Apostles Orthodox Church, seems to contradict this definition by defining it in a much more conservative tone, by stating Tradition is: "the deposit of faith given by Jesus Christ from one generation to the next without addition, alteration, or subtraction." [21.] (They, therefore, define Holy Tradition as not subject to change as it is passed along in time). This church, however, supports apostolic succession, ironically, by using Jude 1:3 as a supportive passage, when in fact, this passage argues just the opposite. Here, Jude is admonishing the Jewish Christians to "contend earnestly for the faith which was once for all handed down to the saints." The faith, the revelation from God, had already been handed down from God once and for all.

In addition to Scripture's self-proclaimed truth that it and it alone is the full and complete revelation of God (2 Timothy 3:15–17; Acts 20:27; Jude 3), not just the written portion of a broader revelation that God left for mankind, many passages within the pages of Scripture confirm this truth. Recognize that this does not refer to God's additional "natural" revelation—that which reveals God's very existence through nature and is evident as a result of the things God created, referred to in Romans 1:19–20.

In the Old Testament, we see the importance of God's Word when, upon finding the long-lost Book of the Law and rediscovering how God truly wished to be worshipped, Josiah (one of the few "good" kings of Judah) "tore his clothes" in humility when he heard the words of this book. Did the king seek revelation from God to confirm His will for them, other than the written words of this book?

> The king went up to the house of the Lord with all the men of Judah, and with all the inhabitants of Jerusalem—the

> priests and the prophets and all the people, both small and great. And he read in their hearing all the words of the Book of the Covenant which had been found in the house of the Lord. Then the king stood by a pillar and made a covenant before the Lord. Then the king stood by a pillar and made a covenant before the Lord, to follow the Lord and to keep His commandments and His testimonies and His statutes, with all *his* heart and all *his* soul, to perform the words of this covenant that were written in this book. And all the people took a stand for the covenant. (2 Kings 23:2–3)

The Book of the Law at that time brought about understanding and a renewal of God's authority to those people. The king made a covenant with God to live by His Word—with all his heart and all his soul—and to "perform the words of the covenant written in that book." Not only the king but "all the people took a stand for the covenant." They all recognized the authority of God and performed according to the words of that book. What has happened to that zeal for God's Word and His Word only with the Orthodox (and others)? Did Josiah search in that temple for some other form of God's revelation before realizing this Book contained all of what God desired? While the Scriptures are highly regarded and the books of the Bible are claimed to be a valuable witness of God's revelation to the Orthodox Church, unfortunately, they're not the only valuable witness being highly regarded.

In addition to the Scriptures, the writings of the early church fathers are considered authoritative (when taken as a whole), and though not generally acknowledged as inspired, they can be deceptive as being considered so by many Orthodox. Just as the proclamations of the bishops of the ecumenical councils are held in high regard, even equal to that of Scripture. As the articles above so forcefully demonstrate, "Our Fathers who met at Nicea did not make their declarations of themselves but spoke as the Holy Spirit dictated,"[7.] and "the dogmatic definitions (dogma means official teaching) and the canon laws of the ecumenical councils are understood to be inspired by God and to be expressive of His will for men. Thus, they are essential sources of Orthodox Christian doctrine."[23.] To an Orthodox Christian, differentiating between a "church father," whose writings during the first few centuries AD, are possibly inspired by God, and an "ecumenical bishop," whose writings are definitely inspired by official doctrine – can be confusing indeed. The fact is – neither is true – these notions not only violate 2 Timothy 3:15–17, Jude 3, and Acts 20:27, which preclude further revelation from being written beyond the first century, the apostolic age, when the canon of the Bible was fixed, but they elevate "man's words" to those of God, which flies in the face of passages such as 1 Corinthians 2:9–13 and 1 Thessalonians 2:13.

Turning to the New Testament, Jesus's Great Commission, given to His disciples then and to us today, makes this statement: "Go therefore and make disciples of all nations, baptizing them in the name of the Father and of the Son and of the Holy Spirit, teaching them to observe all things that I have commanded you" (Matthew 28:19–20). Where are we to go in order to learn how to teach them what Jesus has commanded? Is this knowledge to be gleaned from the church fathers? How about pronouncements from decisions made by the ecumenical councils? Can we seek information from the creeds for advice? No, no, and no - Jesus said, "Teach them to observe all things that I have commanded you." We are to consult only those things Jesus taught and that were recorded in God's Word, the Bible.

In addition, consider 1 John 2:3–6: "Now by this we know that we know Him, if we keep His commandments … whoever keeps His word, truly the love of God is perfected in him. By this we know that we are in Him. He who says he abides in Him ought himself also to walk just as He walked." This passage makes even clearer the source of Christian authority—it is found in God's Word and His Word alone. This is where we can know Jesus by learning and keeping His commandments, allowing us to abide in Him and Him in us, where we can have our love perfected, and where we can learn "to walk just as He walked." Also, notice the number of times the word "know" is used in this passage: "we know that we know Him" and "we know that we are in Him." It not only confirms God's Word as our only authority, but it also reveals the confidence and assurance we can gain by wholly trusting in His Word. John again uses this term in Chapter 5 to give confidence and certainty to his hearers (and to us, when we believe) of their eternal home: "These things I have written to you who believe in the name of the Son of God, that you may know that you have eternal life, and that you may *continue to* believe in the name of the Son of God" (1 John 5:13).

John goes to great effort to emphasize the concept that keeping Jesus's commandments is closely linked with knowing God (and God knowing us in return) and "love" – loving God and one another. 1 John 2:5 says, "But whoever keeps His word, (His commandments)[8] truly the love of God (for God and one another)[8] is perfected in him." Again in 1 John 3:19, 22-23: "And by this we know that we are of the truth, and shall assure our hearts before Him … And whatever we ask we receive from Him because we keep His commandments and do those things that are pleasing in His sight. And this is His commandment: that we should believe on the name of His Son Jesus Christ and love one another, as He gave us commandment." And finally, John's exhortation from Chapter 4, starting in verse 8, "He who does not love does not know God, (nor does God know him)[8] for God is love. In this the love of God was manifested toward us, that God has sent His only begotten Son into the world, that we might live through Him. In this is love, not that we loved God, but that He loved us and sent His Son *to be* the propitiation for our sins. Beloved, if God so loved us, we also ought to love one another." (1 John 4:8-11).

This recurring theme in 1st John, of Jesus's command to love God and one another was expressed by Jesus Himself earlier in response to the Pharisee's question in Matthew 22 as to which commandment in the Law was greatest. Jesus's answer: "'*You shall love the Lord your God with all your heart, with all your soul, and with all your mind.*' This is *the* first and great commandment. And *the* second *is* like it: *You shall love your neighbor as yourself.* On these two commandments hang all the Law and the Prophets." (Matthew 22:34-40). To know God and in turn, to be known by God is no small thing – consider the Spirit's words as written through Matthew in Chapter 7, beginning in verse 21: "Not everyone who says to Me, 'Lord, Lord,' shall enter the kingdom of heaven, but he who does the will of My Father in heaven. Many will say to Me in that day, "Lord, Lord, have we not prophesied in Your name, cast out demons in Your name, and done many wonders in Your name? And then I will declare to them, 'I never knew you; depart from Me, you who practice lawlessness!'" (Matthew 7:21-23).

The Scriptures are not simply words on a page, written as instructions that we hope will be beneficial for mankind. They are the very Words of God Himself, our Creator, written that we, His creation, might know where we came from, where we are now, and where He plans to take us in the end, if only we will read and obey His words—words He promises we can understand, words He promises will never be destroyed. His words are powerful and life-changing, not simply educational. The wisdom and authority they exhibit, if we open our hearts and minds to their truth, will humble us and motivate us into being the very people God desires.

Peter expresses these thoughts in his letter to encourage the Jewish Christians scattered throughout Asia Minor: "Since you have purified your souls in obeying the truth through the Spirit in sincere love of the brethren, love one another fervently with a pure heart, having been born again, not of corruptible seed but incorruptible, through the word of God which lives and abides forever, because … *The grass withers, And the flower falls away, But the word of the Lord endures forever.* [24.] Now this is the word which by the gospel was preached to you" (1 Peter 1:22–25).

Before looking at the councils and the various decisions and laws that the bishops who attended these meetings enacted and supposedly put into "Divine decree" status, let's consider what makes up the Bible as we know it. What allows some writings to be included as Scripture and others not? The importance of this issue cannot be overstated, as these volumes that espouse and even demand adherence to the words of Scripture alone as the benchmark for truth, superseding all other writings and doctrines, would be meaningless without the Scriptures having been proven credible.

In a work by Neil Lightfoot, titled "How We Got the Bible," the word "canon" is defined, and evidence is presented to verify that the books currently comprised by our Old and New Testaments are indeed the only canonical books we should accept. Our English word "canon" comes from the Greek word "*kanon*" and the Hebrew "*qaneh*," meaning "reed" or "cane." As a reed is sometimes used as a measuring rod, the word "kanon" came to mean "standard" or "rule," also referred to as "list" or "index" when applied to the Bible, with "kanon" denoting a listing of books accepted as Holy Scripture. Thus, canonical writings are those that are regarded as having Divine authority and are included in our Bible. Lightfoot points out, "A book's canonicity depends on its authority." [25.] In other words, the book or writing must possess and exhibit inherent authority to be considered Divinely inspired. He then uses the example of Paul's words to the Corinthians: "If anyone thinks himself to be a prophet or spiritual, let him acknowledge that the things which I write to you are the commandments of the Lord" (Corinthians 14:37).

The letter was to be acknowledged as possessing Divine authority. This letter possessed authority the moment that Paul, with the help of the Holy Spirit, wrote it; it was later canonized, being accepted because of its inherent authority. Lightfoot adds, "No church council by its decrees can make the books of the Bible authoritative. The books of the Bible possess their own authority and, indeed, had this authority long before there were any councils of the church." [25.]

There is strong evidence that by the time of Jesus in the first century, the canon of the Old Covenant was fixed. Jesus names the divisions of the Old Covenant in Luke 24:44, equating it to the Hebrew Scriptures as "the Law of Moses and *the* Prophets and *the* Psalms," and Luke 24:45 names these sections "Scriptures." This is clarified even further when Jesus chastises the Pharisees in Luke 11:51 (cf. Matthew 23:35), speaking of a time covering all of the Old Covenant period, "from the blood of Abel to the blood of Zechariah who perished between the altar and the temple." The first martyr was Abel, and the last was Zechariah (as recorded in 2 Chronicles 24:20–21; the Hebrew Bible ends with Chronicles).

In Mark 13:31, Jesus states, "Heaven and earth will pass away, but My words will by no means pass away." In this statement, Jesus makes two claims: first, His words. Every word He spoke and was recorded in the manuscripts later to be defined as the Scriptures was and is Divine. His words are canon. Second, these words will never be destroyed. This is also the same claim the Bible makes for Itself as a whole. Paul wrote in 2 Timothy 3:16–17, "All Scripture *is* given by inspiration of God, and *is* profitable for doctrine, for reproof, for correction, for instruction in righteousness, that the man of God may be complete, thoroughly equipped for every good work." At the time Paul wrote this, he understood "Scripture" as the Old Covenant canon, but the term "Scripture," as inspired Holy Writ, covers all Scripture—both the Old and New Covenants, as 2 Timothy indicates.

How do we know this? Consider the apostle Peter, who, as with all the apostles, considered the Scriptures at that time to be the Old Testament canon. In writing to the church, he said, "And so we have the prophetic word confirmed, which you do well to heed … knowing this first, that no prophecy of Scripture (Old Testament)[8] is of any private interpretation, for prophecy never came by the will of man, but holy men of God spoke *as they were* moved by the Holy Spirit" (2 Peter 1:19–20).

Peter also acknowledged that Scriptures were being written right then, confirming that all of Paul's epistles should be included as such when he wrote the following within this same letter: "Consider *that* the longsuffering of our Lord is salvation – as also our beloved brother Paul, according to the wisdom given to him, has written to you, as also in all his epistles, speaking in them of these things … which untaught and unstable *people* twist to their own destruction, as *they do* also the rest of the Scriptures" (2 Peter 3:15–16).

As the Old Testament canon was confirmed through statements by Jesus and His apostles, the New Testament can similarly be confirmed. Jesus seals His teachings as canon both directly in the Gospels and elsewhere, through His apostles: in Paul's letter to the Corinthians, where he identifies his words as "Commandments of the Lord"; in Paul's letter to the Thessalonians, where he says, "When you received the word of God which you heard from us, you welcomed *it* not *as* the word of men, but as it is in truth, the word of God, which also effectively worked in you who believe" (1 Thessalonians 2:13); and collectively in Peter's statement in which Peter acknowledges all of Paul's epistles as Scripture (2 Peter 3:15–16). Though these apostles acknowledged that the Scriptures they preached at that time were the Old Testament Scriptures, they also acknowledged that the teachings of Jesus and what the Spirit was currently inspiring them to write were also to be considered Scripture—New Testament Scripture(s) to be finalized shortly in a collection of books.

When the church of Christ was first established, the New Testament, as we know it, was nonexistent. The Bible of the church was the Old Testament and the new teachings of Christ, as confirmed through the apostles. As mentioned, other writings of inspired men were being gathered. Thus, Paul's letters were being assembled, along with the four Gospels, followed by the other writings. By the mid-second century, Christian worship assemblies were reading both "memoirs of the apostles" and the "writings of the prophets." The New Testament canon gradually took shape, and by the close of the second century, most of the books had been recognized. Origen, the well-known Biblical commentator of the third century, was one of the first to list all twenty-seven books we now have. In AD 367, Athanasius of Alexandria published a list of these twenty-seven books of the New Testament that were accepted as canon at that time. These have not changed and are included in our New Testament today.

According to Orthodoxy, the inclusion of council decisions as authoritative revelation, to which the church today is subject, began in the apostolic age with meetings, such as those recorded in Acts 6:1–7 and Acts 15, which gave precedent for continuation through the present day.[23.] This logic is erroneous on many levels.

First, as previously mentioned, the Scriptures speak only of elders (also called bishops), who are appointed to lead autonomous individual congregations with the help of deacons, who act as servant leaders, assisting the elders in carrying out the work of the church—not bishops, and under them, elders or priests, and under them, deacons. Actually, the Orthodox Church has established many oversight levels: patriarchs over archbishops or metropolitans, who are over bishops, who are over priests or presbyters or elders at the congregational level. This has enormous implications, equating all these positions as varying degrees of the position of bishop (which they claim is synonymous with the position of an apostle of the first century). Orthodoxy has created an upper class of clergy, not sanctioned by Scripture, to meet and function as the apostles did. Once again, apostolic succession is a false theology, and as such, the authority that the apostles did have (they were given special authority and gifts to help jump-start the Lord's church in the first century) disappeared along with the apostles following the first century.

Second, the meeting cited in Acts 6:1–7 was a practical problem involving a practical solution, not uncommon to a new and growing church. Luke writes, "Now in those days, when *the number of* the disciples was multiplying, there arose a complaint …" (Acts 6:1); this confirms this growth. The reason for the meeting—neglect of the daily distribution to the Grecian widows—which did necessitate the apostles to get involved and help resolve, but the fact that a growing church needed some additional guidance from gifted apostles at that time does not set precedent for future council meetings by outside authority to a local congregation to come in and solve problems or make decisions for today's congregations. This or any similar problem could and should be addressed within the bounds of any congregation today under the eldership of that local church.

The account of conditions under which the Gentiles could enter the Christian church, cited in Acts 15, is perhaps more encompassing than the previous account, as it had the potential to impact more than one congregation. The apostles met with the elders in Jerusalem (which could be considered a council at that time) and, with the aid of the Holy Spirit, came to a decision on this subject. They wrote a letter and sent it to the various congregations of the Gentiles for acceptance, which all gladly did. (Acts 15:18-35). What sets this account apart from past or current-day Orthodox councils is the special circumstances under which it took place, how the letter was written, and the manner in which it was delivered. Again, this was a unique time and situation, where even the fulfillment of prophecy took place. In this context, the fulfillment was that the Gentiles would become part of Christ's church, His kingdom:

> Now it shall come to pass in the latter days that the mountain of the Lord's house shall be established on the top of the mountains, and shall be exalted above the hills; and all nations shall flow to it. (Isaiah 2:2–3)
>
> I will also give You as light to the Gentiles, that You should be My salvation to the ends of the earth. (Isaiah 49:6) (Speaking of our Lord Jesus coming to earth to save mankind – all mankind).

In addition, the letter was presented to each church and accepted with gladness. The mandates of Orthodox councils are just that—mandates. Notice the verbiage used in the two articles above concerning acceptance of their council decisions: "Their decisions have been accepted by the clergy and the laity of all times, making their validity indisputable," and "Their decisions remain binding for the whole Church; non-acceptance constitutes exclusion from the communion of the Church." [23, 16.]

One final reason these council decisions are erroneous as authoritative revelation relates to the subject of canonicity. The New Testament books (twenty-seven in all) were fixed by the third century. They were apostolic in nature, and these Scriptures simply preclude additional revelation—period (2 Timothy 3:15–17; Jude 3; Acts 20:27)!

Since both the Catholic and Orthodox Churches have elevated the proclamations of the first seven ecumenical councils to be authoritative revelation, on par with and in addition to God's written Word, it seems appropriate to take a closer look at what these men decided and compare these decisions to the Scriptures. Were such decisions warranted as clarification, justifying such to the point where they should be deemed additional revelation, as the Orthodox Church has asserted?

Many commentaries have been authored over the years to help bring about clarity and a better understanding of the Scriptures. Take Wayne Jackson's book *A New Testament Commentary*, for example, which brings excellent insight to better understand the New Testament, particularly the interrelationship of various passages borne out by one who has devoted his life to preaching and teaching. Does that mean Jackson's work, or any other work of this nature is to be revered and elevated as *revelation?* Of course not! What sets the decisions of these councils apart from all other commentaries and works authored by men then and now? The following will endeavor to take each council's decisions and evaluate them accordingly.

The First Ecumenical Council, attended by 318 bishops, was summoned by Emperor Constantine the Great in AD 325 in Nicaea, Asia Minor, primarily to dispel a controversy that had arisen owing to charges by one of their priests (Arius) from Alexandria that Jesus Christ was created by God, thus he was denying Christ's Divinity. Arius argued that if Jesus was born, then there was a time when He did not exist; and if He became God, then there was a time when He was not God. A number of bishops followed Arius in this thinking to the point where church division was at stake. This council decreed that Jesus, the Son of God, is uncreated, ever-existent, and fully Divine. He is begotten, or generated, from the Father, not created by Him; and He is of one essence (*homoousios*) with the Father. The council encapsulated this decree in the form of a creed, known as the Nicene Creed, apparently to clarify it for future generations.

If the Orthodox Church had followed Scriptural guidelines as to church organization, this controversy likely would not have taken place! Christ, in His wisdom, instructed (along with the help of the Holy Spirit to and through the apostles) that His church was to be set up as independent, autonomous local congregations led by elders (plural) and assisted by servant leaders, called deacons. No one congregation was to have influence over another; this was by Christ's design. Here, a priest (elder) of one congregation in Alexandria came up with an erroneous theory, and instead of dealing with it within this one congregation through discussion among the other elders within that congregation and most likely solving it at a local level, as God designed, it apparently metastasized and was adopted by other priests from other congregations and overseeing bishops, to the point where multiple congregations became involved and it became a real problem. Note also, as Orthodoxy has structured their church leadership contrary to God's design, there would be no other "priests or elders" within a single congregation to consult with, making a solution nearly impossible.

Additionally, any Christian could simply go to the Scriptures and debunk this theory with passages such as John 1:1–3 and 17:5, which make clear that Jesus was with the Father in the beginning (eternally) and that Jesus was the Creator of all things. Putting this decision, which is nothing more than a confirmation of what the Scriptures have already stated, into a separate creed and then honoring such by repeating this creed at worship assemblies, baptisms, and the like as if it were authoritative doctrine, is unwarranted and unscriptural. (Neither this nor any other creed is Scripture!)

First Ecumenical Council
AD 325 Nicaea, Asia Minor

Other decisions made at this First and all subsequent councils included canons, or church regulations, again taught as inspired Holy Writ. (A complete listing of these canons, some of which as cited below, are available in a book written by Rt. Rev.[4] Mar Melchizedek, titled: "The Holy Canons of the Orthodox Church"). [26.]

As previously mentioned, "canon" is derived from the Greek word "*kanon*," meaning "list or index." If the Orthodox Church were to stop here, their interpretation of canon as "church regulations" would be more appropriate, but they add that this canon is also to be understood as inspired Holy Writ, which it is not. These Orthodox canons are more like listings of dos and don'ts, of laws and consequences. They have nothing to do with Divine writing. True New Testament Biblical canon comprises those writings that reflect an inherent authoritative nature, which cannot be made so by council decree and refers to books of the Bible written within a time frame of Jesus's teachings and the apostles' confirmation thereof, which ended shortly after the first century. All of these council decisions fail to live up to the standards of Holy Writ and fall under the category of human decisions only.

This First Council issued twenty canons, some of which confirmed the church's hierarchy or organizational structure, which had previously been instituted without ecclesiastical sanction. Canon 6, for instance, confirmed the jurisdictional authority of Alexandria over Egypt and the neighboring regions of Libya and Pentapolis, just as the Roman Catholic Church had established jurisdictional authority over Rome and the surrounding area (e.g., central Italy). It also made a blanket statement: "Likewise in Antioch and the other provinces, let the Churches retain their privileges." In other words, the prominent Church in major cities would retain full jurisdictional authority over others in the surrounding area.

Another regulation along these lines is Canon 4, which states that "a bishop should be appointed by all the bishops in the province." Again, where do we find this sanctioned within the pages of God's Word? A bishop in Scripture is synonymous with an elder; the Orthodox Church would refer to him as a presbyter. Bishops are to be appointed only within each local church, not by other leaders of other churches throughout a region. This third position was created by the false theology of apostolic succession; the position of an elevated bishop is the problem here. It's convenient for the Orthodox Church to simply dismiss passages as we've cited above, such as 2 Timothy 3:15–17, Jude 3, and Acts 20:27, by stating that the Holy Spirit was involved in these decisions (both Canons 4 and 6)—that this somehow sanctions their conflicting hierarchy. God's Word, however, stands. It does not conflict with itself, and it does not allow for human manipulation.

Much like the rationale used to dispel the initial argument that precipitated this First Council - by confirming Scripture into a creed, Canon 2 simply confirms Scripture when it states:

"Forasmuch as, either from necessity, or through the urgency of individuals, many things have been done contrary to the Ecclesiastical canon, so that men just converted from heathenism to the faith, and who have been instructed but a little while, are straightway brought to the spiritual layer, and as soon as they have been baptized, are advanced to the episcopate or the Presbyterate, it has seemed right to us that for the time to come no such thing shall be done. For to the catechumen himself there is need of time and of a longer trial after baptism. For the apostolic saying is clear, "Not a novice; lest, being lifted up with pride, he fall into condemnation and the snare of the devil." But if, as time goes on, any sensual sin should be found out about the person, and he should be convicted by two or three witnesses, let him cease from the clerical office. And whoso shall transgress these [enactments] will imperil his own clerical position, as a person who presumes to disobey the great Synod."

Unlike a creed, however, which uses Scripture as a template to formulate a man-made statement of faith, this canon goes a step further by actually co-opting the Words of Scripture, the Words of the Holy Spirit, and crediting them to the bishops of this First Council, thus giving man the glory for God's wisdom - in this case the wisdom found within First Timothy 3:6: "He must not be a recent convert, or he may become conceited and fall under the same judgment as the devil" (NIV).

The "apostolic saying" mentioned in this second canon does not mention this passage, though it uses similar verbiage without crediting Scripture. In addition, following this "fall into condemnation and the snare of the devil," a specific "sensual sin" is mentioned, which precludes continuance in the Orthodox priesthood. Does God single out sin by type? Couple these with the implications of the first and last statements of this 2nd canon - the first, "many things have been done contrary to the Ecclesiastical canon" and the last, "as a person presumes to disobey the great Synod," (statements completely ignoring the authority of Scripture, and instead, emphasizing the importance of their canons and their Synod), and one can see the focus of both rests on the elevation of man, not God.

Notwithstanding the "apostolic saying," which is vague at best, and deceitful at worst concerning the source, and claiming the words of 1 Timothy 3:6 as new words spoken through their bishops, the supposed descendants of the apostles, when in fact they are just repeating what Paul had already written in Scripture, then claiming those words as their own - amounts to nothing less than plagiarism, not from man, but from the Holy Spirt, from God Himself, who inspired Paul to write these words, which presents a serious abridgment indeed.

Church discipline and worship protocol were also stipulated in canon law. Canon 11 addressed the "lapsed"—those who had fallen away and had not partaken of Communion for an extended period of time—and conditions upon which restoration to Eucharistic Communion would be permitted. Even following repentance, Communion would be withheld from repentant sinners until they completed three stages of contrition, as outlined by the bishops at that council, lasting a total of twelve years! Canon 18 gave strict instructions on the administration of the Eucharist (precluding deacons administering to the presbyters), and Canon 20 prohibited the practice of kneeling during the church's Sunday Liturgy, as well as during the Pentecostal season. Finally, this council established guidelines for determining the date of the annual celebration of *Pascha*, or Easter.

None of these decisions have any Scriptural significance or justification; they are human ideas, nothing more. They fall under the judgment of Jesus's words in Matthew 15:9: "And in vain they worship Me, Teaching as doctrines the commandments of men."

Do we see Jesus punishing those who came to Him and repented of their sins? Jesus took the bread and broke it and said "Take, eat, this is My body which is broken for you; do this in remembrance of Me." In the same manner, *He* also *took* the cup after supper, saying, "This cup is the new covenant in My blood. This do, as often as you drink *it*, in remembrance of Me." (1 Corinthians 11:24-25). So do we see any protocol as to who should be passing the bread and the cup, and to whom? The focus here is to remember Jesus's death. Any Christian can administer (preside over or pass) the emblems of Christ's body and blood to any another Christian (deacon to elder, elder to deacon, "ordinary" Christian to elder, and so forth). The Scriptures do not restrict this function whatsoever.

Kneeling is yet another restriction levied by this council without merit. Certainly, for the Orthodox to limit the humility of oneself before God in this manner cannot be defended. Consider passages such as Psalm 95:6: "Oh come, let us worship and bow down; Let us kneel before the Lord our Maker" and Ephesians 3:14: "For this reason I bow my knees to the Father of our Lord Jesus Christ …". Finally, though Christ's Resurrection and His birth were significant events in history, if the exact dates of such were of prime importance, God would have revealed these to us in His Scriptures. What *is* of prime importance is Jesus's death and our remembrance of it (1 Corinthians 11:26)—not a date, but the event itself—and to do so weekly (Acts 20:7), so as never to forget what He has done for us.

The Second Ecumenical Council was convened in AD 381 by Emperor Theodosius I in Constantinople and was attended by 150 bishops. The main reason was to address the false teaching of Bishop Macedonios—that the Holy Spirit was not Divine (not a person of the Godhead) but rather a force, subservient to the Father and to the Son. Another reason was to condemn Apollinarianism, or the teaching by the bishop from Laodicea, Apollinaris, that Jesus was not completely human. As with the First Council, these squabbles, concerning various theological questions related to the Divinity of members of the Godhead itself, could have been avoided, had the Orthodox Church followed Scriptural guidelines concerning church organization. By placing nonsanctioned bishops in positions of authority over multiple churches, it sets up a situation where any questionable teaching by such a bishop can easily be expounded and run out of control, as occurred here. God, in His wisdom, placed multiple elders in charge of a single congregation. The chance of false teaching is thus reduced, and even if it is accepted by a single congregation, the next congregation is less likely to be influenced, as they are autonomous and led by a completely separate group of elders.

In addition to a proper organization, where such false or questionable teachings are less likely to spread, the Scriptures, which each congregation of the Lord's body relies on as its sole authority, have the answers to any such question. The Divinity and personhood of the Holy Spirit are topics readily available to discern within said Scriptures. Concerning the Divinity of the Spirit, consider Acts 5:3–4, which indicates that lying to the Holy Spirit and lying to God are one and the same. And concerning the personhood of the Spirit (dispelling that He is simply a force), one need only consider passages like John 14:26: "But the Helper, the Holy Spirit, whom the Father will send in My name, He will teach you all things, and bring to your remembrance all that I said to you."

In this passage, the Spirit not only teaches and brings to remembrance, which reveals His works as a person, but the words "He" (in Greek "*ekeinos*") and "Helper" (in Greek "*parakletos*"—some translations have "Counselor" or "Comforter") are both masculine gender pronouns, switching from a neutral-gender "Spirit" expressly to show the Spirit is a *He* and not an *it!*

The false teaching that Jesus was not fully incarnated as a human being, as taught by Bishop Apollinaris, is another topic one could easily address and dispel with a little knowledge of the Scriptures. Colossians 2:9 states, "For in Him (Christ)[8] all the fullness of Deity dwells in bodily form" (NASB). Also, 1 Timothy 2:5 states, "For *there* is one God and one Mediator between God and men, *the* Man Christ Jesus, who gave Himself a ransom for all ..." Finally, Hebrews 2:17–18 states, "Therefore, in all things He had to be made like *His* brethren, that He might be a merciful and faithful High Priest in things *pertaining* to God, to make propitiation (atonement)[8] for the sins of the people. For in that He Himself has suffered, being tempted, He is able to aid those who are tempted."

Jesus was the perfect redeemer for mankind. He had to be both fully God and fully human to fulfill His mission here on earth. Once again, elders of a single congregation would likely know these verses and be able to dispel these false ideas at the local level before they would ever have a chance to grow and become an issue for others. Not only the elders, but the members of Christ's church are, or encouraged by the elders to be, well-versed in Scripture; having a reputation as "people of the Book."

In the process of condemning these two bishops and their false ideologies, the council established the final paragraph to the creed, which was initiated at the First Council in Nicaea. This became known as the Nicene-Constantinopolitan Creed and was later simply referred to as the

Nicene Creed, a firm symbol of faith for the Orthodox Church for all time. The initial portion of this creed, which was composed during the First Council, reads as follows:

> We (I) believe in one God, The Father Almighty. Maker of heaven and earth, and of all things visible and invisible. And in one Lord Jesus Christ, the Son of God, the only begotten, begotten of the Father before all ages. Light of Light; true God of true God; begotten not made; of one essence with the Father, by whom all things were made.
>
> Who for us men and for our salvation came down from heaven, and was incarnate of the Holy Spirit and the Virgin Mary, and became man.
>
> And He was crucified for us under Pontius Pilate, and suffered, and was buried.
>
> And the third day He rose again according to the Scriptures.
>
> And ascended into heaven, and sits at the right hand of the Father; and he shall come again with glory to judge the living and the dead; whose Kingdom shall have no end. [27.]

The final paragraph that was added at the Second Council reads:

> And (We believe) in the Holy Spirit, the Lord, the Giver of Life, who proceeds from the Father, Who with the Father and the Son together is worshipped and glorified; Who spoke by the Prophets.
>
> In One Holy, Catholic, and Apostolic Church.
>
> I acknowledge One Baptism for the remission of sins.

> I look for the resurrection of the dead, and the life of the world to come. Amen. [27.]

Again, a statement of faith is harmless if treated like any other summary statement or commentary to help others better understand certain theological points. The problem arises when such a statement is elevated to a level of honor, as the Orthodox have done here, reciting it at various events, such as baptisms and particularly during worship services, in place of, and treating as if it were indeed, God's Word, which it is not.

Another similar creed was developing around this same time, known as the Apostles' Creed. The earliest known mention of this creed is in a letter dated AD 390 from a synod in Milan, where it is believed each of the twelve apostles contributed to the twelve articles of this creed.

Additionally, the Second Council introduced seven canons and affirmed them into church law. Of special note, Canon 2 reaffirmed their principles of church organization, limiting the boundaries of each bishop to his own respective region. For instance, the canon begins by stating, "The bishops are not to go beyond their dioceses to churches lying outside of their bounds, nor bring confusion on the churches; but let the Bishop of Alexandria, according to the canons, alone administer the affairs of Egypt." [28.]

This limitation is not, as Scripture delineates, to a group of elders leading a single congregation. No, this canon limits a single bishop with authority over a region—for instance, Egypt, which encompasses many local churches—and states that a bishop is not to encroach upon another bishop's region or rule over his many churches. Also, Canon 3 stipulates an organizational declaration concerning the top of the hierarchy: "The Bishop of Constantinople, however, shall have the prerogative of honor after the Bishop of Rome; because Constantinople is New Rome." [28.] In other words, the bishop of Constantinople is to be honored next after the bishop of Rome, at the very top of their organizations. Once again, if anyone is to be honored, it is Christ, and at the very least, His desires concerning His church, the one He died for—one of which is to acknowledge His desire that elders and deacons lead local autonomous congregations, with Himself (Jesus) as their only head.

The last four canons deal mainly with the acceptance or nonacceptance of certain individuals, groups of individuals, or bishops outside the Orthodox Church. Canon seven, for instance, gives conditions for a number of groups (Arians, Macedonians, Sabbatians, Apollinarians) that wish to join the Orthodox Church; joining the church was synonymous with being saved. They are to first give written renunciation of their errors, then they are sealed or anointed with holy oil, whereupon a pronouncement is given, "The seal of the gift of the Holy Ghost. The canon states, "On the first day we make them Christians; on the second, catechumens; on the third, we exorcise them by breathing thrice in their face and ears; and thus we instruct them and oblige them to spend some time in the Church, and to hear the Scriptures; and then we baptize them." [28.] This in no way resembles what the Scriptures have to say regarding God's plan of salvation for individuals. The Scriptures list five conditions, or steps, to becoming a Christian or being saved; the above cites perhaps three, and two are out of order. The "writing of their errors" *may* be considered repentance, and "spending time in Church to hear the Scriptures" *may* qualify for hearing about Jesus, but there is no indication of belief in Jesus or confession of Him as Lord and Savior. "Making them Christians on the first day" while baptizing them sometime after the third day makes no sense, according to Scripture. One is not saved and does not become a Christian without completing all four steps of hearing, believing, confessing, repenting, and then being baptized - without contacting the blood of Jesus. The other conditions mentioned, such as being anointed with oil and exorcising the incumbent are human ideas, not God's, and are totally unnecessary for inclusion into Christ's church. The anointing with oil appears to be an Orthodox belief of sealing or giving the Holy Spirit to the incumbent prior to baptism – another false doctrine (Acts 2:38). Without true belief, which is not exhibited here without a verbal confession of Jesus as Lord, and perhaps without true repentance (writing down a list of one's past errors is not the same as committing to turn 180 degrees from the past in one's heart), nor are we sure Jesus is even spoken of in that short period of time spent in an Orthodox Church) – that would mean these people have not done what God has requested to be saved – they remain in their sins. The guilt for this falls predominately on the bishops of this Second Ecumenical Council, who invented this seventh canon.

The Third Ecumenical Council, attended by two hundred bishops, was convened at Ephesus in 431 by Emperor Theodosius, primarily to condemn the doctrines of the archbishop of Constantinople, Nestorios, who taught that Jesus was two separate persons living within the incarnate Christ, as well as that the Logos, or Word (Son of God) only dwelled in Christ, as in a temple, making Christ only a *Theophoros*, or bearer of God. Also, the Virgin Mary, according to Nestorios, gave birth to a man, Jesus Christ, and not God, making Mary *Christotokos*, or bearer of Christ, rather than *Theotokos* (bearer of God). All of this was directly opposite to the Orthodox teaching, by which the incarnate Christ was a single Person, at once God and man. In the Council's rejection of Nestorios's teaching, one of the high points was the confirmation of the name "Theotokos" (bearer or mother of God) for the Virgin Mary.

The Bible nowhere implies that Mary was the mother of God, but instead that she was the mother of Jesus, the incarnation of God, the Son. In a way, Nestorios was partially correct in his idea that Mary gave birth to a human. He errored, however, in his thoughts that Jesus was also not God and human from the beginning. He envisioned the Divine Nature of Jesus coming to dwell within Jesus at some point separate from birth, which was not true. That Mary was not the mother of God is pointed out in a comparative example from the argument Jesus Himself made with the Pharisees in Matthew 22:42–45, just as David was not the father of Jesus's Divine Nature, since he called Him "Lord" yet was recognized physically in the lineage of Jesus as the "Son of David." Mary cannot be the mother of God (His Divine Nature) since she likewise called Jesus "Lord" in Luke 1:38 and again in Luke 1:46–47, yet she physically gave birth to Him. Unfortunately, this confirmation elevated Mary and set in motion a number of future false claims concerning her—for example, that she was perpetually a virgin, sinless, and cooperated in the work of human redemption. These are all man's ideas, all without Scriptural sanction.

This council also established eight additional canons,[29.] most of which continued to condemn Nestorios and his followers, and especially a group of bishops who arrived late to the council meeting, owing to unnamed circumstances, and who happened to support the views of this rogue bishop. Also of note, this third council declared it unlawful to change (to delete or add to) the creed, as written by the previous two councils, the Nicene–Constantinople Creed. (This is ironic since the Scriptures find this whole process "unlawful" on identical grounds—Deuteronomy 12:32; Proverbs 30:6; Revelation 22:18–19.) [30.]

The Fourth Ecumenical Council was convened in 451 in the city of Chalcedon, near Constantinople in Asia Minor, by Emperor Marcian and his wife, Poulcheria. With 630 bishops in attendance, it was the largest of the seven ecumenical councils and was called mainly to settle an ongoing dispute as to the two natures of Jesus (which was not completely settled at the previous council). This dispute focused on the doctrine of an Archimandrite from a Constantinople monastery by the name of Eutychius, who rejected altogether the human nature of Jesus Christ and taught that Jesus's human nature was completely absorbed in the Divine and that it therefore followed that one need only recognize the Divine Nature. This false doctrine is called Monophysitism.

The council condemned and repudiated this doctrine of Eutychius and defined the true teaching of the church in yet another creed—the Chalcedonian Definition, which basically stated that Jesus Christ is indeed the Logos incarnate, "begotten of the Father before all ages" [31.] (confirming the Nicene Creed), and affirming Mary to be the Theotokos, the mother of God, since the one born from her "according to the flesh" is the uncreated Son of God. [31.]

The council declared, "In His human birth the Word of God took to Himself the whole of humanity, becoming a real man in every way, but without sin. Thus, Jesus is one person or hypostasis in two natures—human and divine—united 'without change, without confusion, without division, without separation.' He is fully human. He is fully divine. He is perfect God and perfect man. As God, He is 'of one essence (homoousios) with God the Father and the Holy Spirit. And as man, He is 'of one essence' (homoousios) with all human beings, as the Formulary of Peace had declared." [31.]

These questions concerning the two natures of Jesus had apparently troubled the Orthodox Church for over a century by this time (and we'll see that they will continue to be problematic for many years to come), starting with the question of His Divinity addressed at the First Council; then His humanity, initially addressed at the Second Council and here again at this Fourth Council; and finally, both natures combined, His Divinity and His humanity, in the Third and again in this Fourth Council.

We might ask, if the Holy Spirit was indeed involved in these ecumenical councils, as Orthodoxy claims, would He not have solved this problem by now? The answer is clear: **He's not involved in these councils.** The Spirit had already given mankind the answers to these and many other questions through the Scriptures, long before any of these councils met!

Once again, had the Orthodox Church simply followed Scriptural guidelines, one hundred years of disputing (with more to come) could have been avoided. The Scriptures address this particular situation in two ways: first, the doctrine in dispute originated from a monastery, an institution (monastic order) set up as a suborder in the Orthodox hierarchy of clergy members, where separation and isolation encourage full devotion to God in prayer and ascetic works. The Scriptures do not speak of any such institution from an organizational level, and separation from the world is discouraged in the Scriptures (see Matthew 5:14–16 and 1 Corinthians 5:9–10). By allowing a single head of this monastery, the Archimandrite Eutychius, to teach this false doctrine unchecked, it was allowed to grow out of proportion.

Second, if this were the Lord's church as designed, with elders and deacons leading single autonomous congregations, even if one of the elders were to propose this false teaching, there's a good chance it would have been contained within that single congregation, as other elders and/or member saints would certainly search the Scriptures to find an answer. There wouldn't be one leader pushing his doctrine uncontested.

We addressed the dispute of Jesus's questionable humanity with regard to Apollinaris's claims in the Second Council. Hebrews 2:14–18 perhaps best describes that humanity and the reason for it:

> Inasmuch then as the children have partaken of flesh and blood, He Himself likewise shared in the same, that through death He might destroy him who had the power of death, that is, the devil, and release those who through fear of death were all their lifetime subject to bondage. For indeed He does not give aid to angels, but He does give aid to the seed of Abraham. Therefore, in all things He had to be made like *His* brethren, that He might be a merciful and faithful High Priest in things *pertaining* to

> God, to make propitiation for the sins of the people. For in that He Himself has suffered, being tempted, He is able to aid those who are tempted.

Jesus had to be made in all ways just as we are in order to fulfill His mission and make propitiation or atonement for our sins. He also was tempted, as we are tempted, and so can sympathize and is able to give aid to us. This clearly shows the human incarnation of Jesus, therefore, there is no need to argue over this – just accept what Scripture has said by "rightly dividing the word of truth" (2 Timothy 2:15)."

The Council of Chalcedon generated some thirty canons into Orthodox law; it also generated some controversy at this meeting. The Oriental Orthodox branch of the church did not accept the declarations of this council, as they were accused of being Monophysite; also, the Armenian Apostolic Church, which missed the council owing to a conflict with the Persians in their homelands, claimed their teaching of Monophysitism was misunderstood by the council, so they, too, rejected the decrees of this council.

Finally, Canon 28 was not accepted by the Western Church, as it elevated the archbishop of Constantinople and gave him the title of patriarch, giving him honorary precedence over all other churches, save that of Rome. It further granted this archbishop administrative rights over a number of provinces, which was rejected in the West with the excuse, "The older Eastern patriarchates should be protected." [32.]

Of the thirty canons, sixteen addressed corruption and greed that had developed among bishops and other clergy, and though not admitted within these canons, the primary reason can surely be traced to their positions of power that had gone awry—a situation that was not sanctioned by Scripture. Let's look closely at each of the problems addressed within these canons and imagine what would have occurred if the Orthodox Church had simply followed Scripture and set up their church as God designed—with single, autonomous congregations headed by two or more elders, with servant deacons to assist, rather than constructing a hierarchy, where the elder or presbyter is one of the lower-ranked clergy, and bishop, archbishop, metropolitan, and so forth, are positions of power brought about by way of apostolic succession with all positions overseeing not only elders but also multiple congregations headed by elders. Would these problems exist? Following is a very brief summary of these sixteen canons and the problems [33]:

Canon 2: Ordaining for money.
Canon 3: Using clergy rank to gain prosperity from others through devious means.
Canon 4: Clergy and leaders establishing monasteries for themselves within the cities.
Canon 6: Ordination "at large" taking place, apparently for personal gain.
Canon 8: Bishops' rule over other clergy questioned and challenged.
Canons 10, 13, 20: Prohibiting clergy from officiating at several churches under several bishops.
Canon 12: Corruption among metropolitans.
Canon 17: Outlying or rural churches subject to a single bishop.
Canon 18: Conspiracy among clergy or monks condemned.
Canon 19: Provincial meetings mandated for all bishops twice a year to settle problems.
Canon 22: Bishops' property seized by other clergy upon death.
Canon 23: Condemning excommunicated clergy seeking refuge by relocation to Constantinople.
Canon 26: Business affairs at local churches going unattended; bishops mandated to appoint stewards.
Canon 27: Fornication among clergy.

Previously, we've looked at the effects of false teaching within five of the seven churches of Christ in Asia, as recorded in the book of Revelation, and we noted the beginnings of discontentment, particularly within the churches of Pergamum, Thyatira, and Sardis, which had caused a split from within, while Ephesus and Laodicea were exhibiting attitude problems. One could almost predict this would lead to problems shortly down the road. These were churches set up under the guidelines of Scripture, not far removed from the time of Jesus, yet the majority of them were struggling to follow God's will. Is it any wonder, given the fact that the Orthodox Church abandoned the organization of Christ's church as He designed and has added forms of authority other than God's Word, that we would see this kind of corruption several hundred years later, which would prompt all these corrective canons? Remember that the

Holy Spirit is not involved here; this is simply human actions and human laws or doctrine attempting to correct those actions. Orthodoxy chooses to use the word "canon" in describing these rules or corrections, which is a word normally associated with Divine writing, as to be included within revelation and God's Word and church councils cannot legislate or decree canon of this nature. They cannot legitimize their decisions as God's Word, but we'll continue to call them canons for the sake of expediency.

Other canons of note from this Fourth Council include Canon 9, where the bishops declared that all disputes among clergy of all ranks are to be settled within the church only—not to be taken outside to secular courts. For instance, a matter between clergymen must be settled by their bishop, and if between a clergyman and a bishop, it must be settled at the province synod; if between a bishop and another bishop, an archbishop must settle, and so forth. This is not a new idea; the concept was taken directly from Scripture and modified to suit their theology. In 1 Corinthians 6:1–4, Paul tells the Corinthians that any conflict is to be handled between saints only, advising further that saints (Christians) will judge the world as well as angels. Paul continues: "I say this to your shame. Is it so, that there is not a wise man among you, not even one, who will be able to judge between his brethren? But brother goes against brother, and that before unbelievers!" (1 Corinthians 6:5)

Two other passages deal with this subject, in which our Lord gives advice: In Matthew 5:23–25, Jesus, teaching about anger, says, "If … your brother has something against you … first go and be reconciled to your brother … settle matters quickly with your adversary who is taking you to court … or he may hand you over to the judge." (NIV)

This again concerns settling disputes between Christians, and Jesus's advice is to do so without involving a third party. He also teaches us that if a brother sins against us, we should go directly to that person and first try to resolve the issue; if this fails, we are to take one or two as witnesses, "and if he refuses to hear them, tell *it* to the church. But if he refuses even to hear the church, let him be to you like a heathen and a tax collector" (Matthew 18:15–17).

To sum up, Canon 9 sets rules concerning disputes among clergy, basically to be settled by the next ranking authority, and not to involve secular litigation. The Scripture aligns with the notion of no outside courts being involved, but not with issues between clergy members being settled by higher-ranking clergy. In fact, the Scriptures say nothing concerning clergy disputes (denying even the validity of higher-ranking clergy), which gives further evidence that these canons are nothing other than man-made rules—in this case, to settle issues not sanctioned by God in the first place.

The last three canons of note focus on marriage; these are Canons 14, 15, and 16. Canon 14 was a decree prohibiting certain male members of the Orthodox clergy from marriage to non-Orthodox persons, specifically stating, "Since in certain provinces it is permitted to the readers and singers to marry, the holy Synod has decreed that it shall not be lawful for any of them to take a wife that is heterodox." This canon also had stipulations demanding that should marriage have already occurred, and any children resulted from same that they must be baptized within the Orthodox Church or suffer "canonical censure."

Once again, the Scriptures do not support this decree. Although marriage between a Christian and a non-Christian is not an ideal situation, Paul certainly does not prohibit it, and in 1 Corinthians 7:12–16, he even gives some instruction and encouragement for positive results in such a case. In addition, forcing couples to baptize their children into Orthodoxy under threat of censure is certainly not in Scripture either.

Canons 15 and 16 both preclude marriage to those who dedicate their lives to the Lord, under threat of excommunication—Canon 15 refers to women who received laying on of hands (after the age of forty) and became deaconesses to minister (presumably to other women or girls, as even to this day ordination of women is prohibited within the Orthodox Church), and Canon 16 to both men and women who have presumably committed to a monastic order. With regard to celibacy, the Scriptures have never prohibited marriage—quite the opposite. From the beginning, God sanctioned marriage for all mankind, that they might be happy and not be alone (Genesis 2:18). "Marriage is honorable among all" (Hebrews 13:4).

The Fifth Ecumenical Council was convened in 553 In Constantinople by Emperor Justinian I and was presided over by the patriarch of Constantinople, Eutychios. It was attended by 165 bishops. The Monophysite controversy was still not settled under the decrees of the previous council, as quarreling among the bishops seemed to continue unabated. Even the emperor at first favored the views of Monophysitism, only later siding with the formal Orthodox view against it. Fuel was also added to this fire by Empress Theodora, who encouraged the Monophysites by reintroducing three positions held by high-ranking, highly respected (though deceased) bishops with similar theological views. All of these views fell back to the question of Christ's humanity, as a separate and less encompassing nature to that of His Divine Nature—views that were condemned by both of the previous two councils.

This council condemned, once again, this Monophysite (or Christ's Divine taking precedence over His human nature) theology, including the three additional supportive theological views (even to the point of "anathematizing" all three), stating the Orthodox understanding: "Jesus Christ, the Son of God, is 'one of the Holy Trinity', one and the same divine person (hypostasis) Who has united personally (hypostatically) in Himself the two natures of divinity and humanity, without fusing them together and without allowing their separation in any." [34.]

This still didn't settle the matter, as we'll see that another meeting, the Sixth Ecumenical Council (convening over one hundred years later), was needed and continued to deal with yet another aspect of this issue, the human versus Divine 'will' of Christ.

This Fifth Council also condemned what they considered the problematic teachings of Origen, a sixth-century theologian whose views ran counter to Orthodoxy. For instance, Origen taught that Jesus was the only created spirit who did not become material through sin, that men's souls were preexistent, and that all of creation, including demons, will ultimately be saved by God through Christ. The Council thus decreed fifteen anathemas against Origen, citing and condemning all fifteen of his offensive teachings (this in lieu of issuance of canons, as was customary with past councils).

The Sixth Ecumenical Council convened in 680–681, again in the city of Constantinople, this time by Emperor Constantine IV, and was attended by 170 bishops. The main purpose of this council was to settle arguments, as mentioned above, concerning Christ's will. Although many, including the Monothelites, recognized Jesus as having two natures, Divine and human, they insisted He had but one Divine will. The council concluded that this view impaired the fullness of Christ's humanity and that human nature without human will would be incomplete. As true God and true man, He must have two wills, human and Divine. They therefore condemned Monothelitism with this statement: "Christ had two natures with two activities: as God working miracles, rising from the dead and ascending into heaven; as Man, performing the ordinary acts of daily life. Each nature exercises its own free will. The two distinct natures and related to them activities were mystically united in the one Divine Person of our Lord and Savior Jesus Christ." [35.]

In addition, this council anathematized as heretics a number of high-ranking clergies for their part in propagating the "heresy of Monothelitism"; these included Pope Honorius I of Rome, and Bishops Sergius I of Constantinople, Cyrus of Alexandria, Paul II and Peter of Constantinople, and Theodore of Pharan. Similar to the Fifth Council, there were no ecclesiastical canons issued with this Sixth Council, as most of the time was spent dealing with the aforementioned problems. This would be remedied, however, with the convening of an interim council between the Sixth and Seventh Ecumenical Councils, named the Quinisext, or Trullan, Council.

The Scriptural response to both the Fifth and Six Ecumenical Councils is the same as that of the Fourth and all previous Councils—wrong organization and wrong authority base continuing to be at the heart of their problems. Concerning specifics of Jesus's nature or will, nothing has changed in the response here either. Jesus's two natures are probably best revealed in Colossians 2:9, which states, "For in Him (Christ)[8] all the fullness of Deity dwells in bodily form" (NASB).

Concerning His Divine will, one need only look at passages such as John 2:4, "My hour has not yet come" or Matthew 9:2, "He said to the paralytic, 'Son, be of good cheer; your sins are forgiven you." Matthew 26:39 - "O My Father, if it is possible, let this cup pass from Me; nevertheless, not as I will, but as You *will*"—is an example of His human will, in this case in agony prior to the cross.

The Quinisext, or Trullan, Council, which was an interim council, met in AD 692, eleven years after the Sixth Ecumenical Council. Its purpose was to supplement the fifth and sixth councils with the issuance of canons pertaining to ecclesiastical government and order. This council, called by Justinian II, was attended by 211 bishops, and was convened in the city of Constantinople, in the hall under the great dome (Trullos) of the Imperial Palace. Along with the Greek for "Fifth-Sixth" (*Quinisext*), it became known as the Quinisext Trullan Council. A total of 101 new canons were generated as a result of this Council, with most being disciplinary in nature. [36.] The canons ratified per Canon 2 included all previous council canons, the so-called eighty-five apostolic canons,

canons of local synods, and the principal canons of the church fathers; all were given "Divine"/Ecumenical sanction or authority.

The disciplinary canons of this Quinisext Council were not accepted by the Western Church, including the pope of Rome, and it contributed greatly to a widening of the differences between the East and West factions of the Orthodox Church at that time. In particular, Canons 6, 13, 30, and 48 all dealt with the issue of the marital status of clergy. The East took perhaps a more correct view to Scripture by at least allowing marriage prior to ordination, whereas the West rejected the Scriptural mandate outright (that elders must be married, even with children, per 1 Timothy 3:2-5 and Titus 1:6) by maintaining clergy were to remain celibate—period; completely ignoring these passages.

No matter how one looks at it, these canons are still far removed from Scriptural sanction. Canon 6, though allowing marriage prior to ordination, prohibits it afterward and then only to sublevel clergy (subdeacons, deacons, or presbyters). Canon 13 condemned the Roman Catholic Church's practice of forced celibacy upon ordination, even if the person was already married. Canon 30 forced priests in foreign lands to live apart from their wives as well as be celibate, and Canon 48 forced the wife of one who was to become a bishop to divorce and enter a convent or monastery for the rest of her life. To even imagine that the Holy Spirit would have "inspired" the writing of any of these canons—and in so doing contradict His Own writings within Scripture, is ludicrous indeed. Just as an example: how does one reconcile Canon 48 (forced divorce to accommodate a soon-to-be bishop) with Matthew 19:6: "Therefore what God has joined together, let not man separate"? The balance of these one-hundred-plus canons is nothing more than human corrections to human actions. God is not involved in this, and these rules or laws have no authority over Christ's church.

The Seventh Ecumenical Council was convened in Nicaea in 787 by Empress Irene, widow of Emperor Leo IV, at the request of Thrasios, the patriarch of Constantinople, and was attended by 367 bishops. This council dealt predominately with a controversy that had been raging for nearly a century—the "veneration of icons" (termed the "iconoclastic controversy" [37.]). On one side, those who favored placing icons or statues and relics of Jesus, Mary, and the saints, in particular, within church buildings using the argument that they served to preserve the doctrinal teachings of the church considered these icons to be an individual's way of expressing the Divine through art. On the other side, those rejecting this veneration, so-called "iconoclasts," took the view that such was akin to worshipping idols and thus was forbidden by God as idolatry (Exodus 20:4–5).

This council decreed that the veneration of icons was not idolatry because the honor shown to them was not directed to the wood or paint but instead to the person depicted. Their doctrine stated that icons should be venerated but not worshipped. It also justified depicting Christ since He became human at His incarnation. Following the Seventh Ecumenical Council, however, this controversy reemerged under emperors Leo V, Michael II, and Theophilus and continued for over twenty-five years. The issue was finally settled by a local synod called by Empress Theodora in 843 in Constantinople when the veneration of icons was restored and affirmed as Orthodox doctrine—a decision in effect to this day.

The Scriptural response completely refutes this theology. The easiest way to reject this doctrine is to understand that "veneration," as defined in most modern-day dictionaries and even within the *Catholic Dictionary*, means "to worship." And though the Orthodox Church claims all who bow down and venerate these statues are thinking of the persons they represent, the question remains: do they? Do you suppose God, in His wisdom, refrained from asking individuals to do this because He knew some would worship the statue itself? There is no reference in Scripture advocating mankind needs a statue to better remember Jesus or anyone else; in fact, Scripture commands just the opposite: "We ought not to think that the Divine Nature is like gold or silver or stone, something shaped by art and man's devising" (Acts 17:29).

The Seventh Council also issued twenty-two canons into church law. [38.] As with other council canons, these addressed ecumenical order and corrective actions to misdeeds of the clergy, with two addressing veneration of icons: namely Canon 7, which demanded relics be placed in the sacred temples, and Canon 9, which prohibited hiding books written against the veneration of images (that they may be locked away with the other "heretical books"). The Scriptural response is also as before; these are nonbinding, nonauthoritative "laws" of man.

Regarding these Councils and their decisions made over the centuries, three facts stand out, none of which is flattering towards the Orthodox

Church. The first is the divisive nature these decisions had within the Orthodox Communion, as much turmoil resulted over the years, in particular the division between the Western Roman Catholic and Eastern Orthodox branches. This started as early as 381 with the Second Council, when the bishop of Constantinople was declared to have power that was second in line to that of the bishop of Rome, and Constantinople was established as the "New Rome." It continued to devolve at the Fourth Council meeting in 451, where Canon 28, in particular, elevated the archbishop of Constantinople with the title of "patriarch," adding additional authority over more and more provinces and churches, supplanting that of the pope in Rome. Canons 14, 15, and 16, dealing with marriage and celibacy, proved not to be forceful enough in favor of celibacy to suit the pope, as all were rejected. The Fifth Council in 553 and the Sixth Council in 680 fared no better between the two factions, as a number of the canons enacted at both were, for the most part, rejected by the popes in Rome. Tensions continued to escalate until a complete break occurred in 1054, known as the Great Schism (noted in the Tree of Denominations 1 chart).

Second, as we've said before, all of the quarreling and arguing over theological issues that precipitated these council meetings could have been prevented had the Orthodox Church simply followed Scriptural guidelines concerning church organization and established local congregations to be autonomous, with elders as shepherds, and deacons as servant leaders to the elders. Instead, they adopted the unscriptural doctrine of apostolic succession, putting bishops, archbishops, and patriarchs in charge of multiple congregations. In so doing, they created an environment where seemingly everyday problems and, on occasion, more serious issues and infractions, had nowhere to go but up and out, where multiple congregations got involved, and issues tended to grow out of control. These issues would most likely have had a much better chance of resolution if they had remained within the individual congregations, as God had intended, and had been addressed by their respective elderships, rather than escalating to other congregations.

Finally, a third fact should be considered: in addition to God's instructions concerning church organization, His Word also warns against "quarreling over words," in general. This may well be the most profound of all. In roughly 460 years of arguments over the major issues that brought these councils together, including the Divinity of Jesus, the Divinity of the Holy Spirit, Mary as the mother of God, the two natures of Jesus, and the two wills of Jesus, as well as the secondary issues as addressed in the canons issued, the Scriptures have this to say:

> *This* is a faithful saying: For if we died with Him, We shall also live with Him. If we endure, we shall also reign with *Him*. If we deny *Him*, He also will deny us. If we are faithless, He remains faithful; He cannot deny Himself. Remind *them* of these things, charging *them* before the Lord not to strive about words to no profit, to the ruin of the hearers. Be diligent to present yourself approved to God, a worker who does not need to be ashamed, rightly dividing the word of truth. But shun profane *and* idle babblings, for they will increase to more ungodliness. (2 Timothy 2:11–16)

In this passage, Paul is instructing Timothy that the gospel message is of prime importance and to remind his hearers of this and not to "strive" (the NASB uses "wrangle") about words (meaning that the hearers should not argue over words), which leads to no profit, but actually to the ruin of the hearers (compared to their salvation). Paul goes on to charge Timothy to be diligent to present himself as approved of God, to not be ashamed, and to rightly divide the word of truth. Why? In this instance, it's so he may be able to discern truth and thus shun profane and idle babblings, which will, if not stopped, increase, and spread to more ungodliness.

There's a lot to unpack here. First and foremost, this passage denounces at least 460 years of Orthodox "wranglings" over words and, for the most part, nonessential issues, where they could have been advancing the cause of Christ by focusing instead on the gospel message. Another insight from this passage is the only source to which Timothy is directed to discern truth, the only source approved by God—God's Word, the Bible. The implication for us today is that this excludes all other sources of authority (Holy Tradition, apostolic succession, creeds, and so forth).

Another passage that is supportive of these thoughts is 1 Timothy 1:3–7: "As I urged you when I went into Macedonia—remain in Ephesus that you may charge some that they teach no other doctrine, nor give heed to fables and endless genealogies, which cause disputes rather than godly edification which is in faith. Now the purpose of the commandment is love from a pure heart, *from* a good conscience, and *from* sincere faith, from which some, having strayed, have turned aside to idle talk, desiring to be teachers of the law, understanding neither what they say nor the things which they affirm."

Once again, Paul is instructing Timothy to warn his hearers against arguing and disputing, rather than "godly edification," that those who engage in such things have strayed from God's commandment of love from a pure heart and will desire "to be teachers" (have authority), though they know not what they say or affirm. Power seems to beget more power, and in the hierarchy of the Orthodox Church (and others), the "desire to be teachers of the law," coupled with the power of apostolic succession, makes for a dangerous situation where love, a pure heart, and truth many times take a backseat to winning arguments and even extending contentions over long periods of time, as occurred in the early development of Orthodox doctrine.

The Scriptures self-authenticate as the only source we need to rely on as God's authority—not bishops, who function in the place of God, purporting to have special gifts through apostolic succession imparted to them via the laying on of hands. And not Holy Tradition, encompassing additional verbal revelation from church fathers, clarification from ecumenical councils, formulated creeds, and all forms of imagined authority through liturgical doctrine, art, music, veneration of icons, and certainly not proclamations from man himself (popes or patriarchs). All are nothing more than the doctrines of men, which Jesus warned would make our religion vain (Matthew 15:8–9).

Though the Orthodox Church has recognized the Scriptures as one important source of authority, God's written revelation, they relegate it to being one of several sources, and even then, claim that it contains much extraneous information such as "historical fact, poetry, idiom, metaphor, simile, moral fable, parable, prophecy, and wisdom literature." We are led to believe this is too difficult for the common person, or laity, to understand and that it therefore must be interpreted within the context of Holy Tradition: translation—only by and through the clergy of the Orthodox Church.

This sets up a very precarious situation for the Orthodox Christian in several ways. First, access to God is limited without the Orthodox Church, as bishops and priests are essential not only to proper worship but also to participation in the Lord's Supper, as well as for access to God in prayer for, among other things, confession and forgiveness of sin. Second, these same clergy are necessary to properly understand and translate God's Word; in other words, we cannot simply read and understand God's Word on our own without the help of the clergy.

I encourage you to return to the last chapter of Volume 1 to take another look concerning the question at the end: "Can these Scriptures be understood by all men and women today, thereby allowing access to God's will for them through Jesus Christ, without the need for an institution to act as an intermediary between God and man?" The arguments and Scriptures used with regard to the Catholic Church also apply here. Is this what God had in mind? Is this what Christ died for when the curtain between the holy and most holy within the temple was torn in two upon His death, signifying a new access to God the Father (Hebrews 9:1–15, 10:19–22)? This theology of Orthodoxy is reminiscent of life before Jesus' time on earth when the Jewish people did indeed depend upon a priest to offer sacrifices for them, when the priest was the intermediary between them and God, and when they did require the priest to "interpret" the law. This covenant, however, was done away with (Colossians 2:13–14; Hebrews 9:15).

Primary Beliefs and Doctrine

Much of the information within this section has been sourced from the Orthodox Church in America (OCA) through their online outreach - oca.org. Each teaching or doctrine will first be examined in its context, followed by Scriptural considerations.

The Trinity/Theosis

Several ideas brought forth by the Orthodox Church need examination in light of God's Word. These include a perceived relationship among the Personages of the Godhead or Trinity, the relationship of individuals to the Godhead (both now and in the future), and our ultimate home with God. Though Orthodoxy teaches that the Godhead comprises three "perfectly equal" Divine Personages, in Father, Son, and Holy Spirit, it also teaches that there is a hierarchy, promoted as expressions of that Divine Nature. The Godhead is taught to have a common nature, and it is also taught that within the Trinity, "the Father alone is the source of divinity." Also, "the Son is the expression of the Father and is subject to Him," and the Holy Spirit, "of one essence and fully equal with the Father and Son, is the 'third' Person who fulfills the will of the Father and the Son." [39.]

Interlaced with the above is the concept that man is said to be slowly progressing toward a communion with the Godhead—a three-stage process starting in this life and continuing into the next, culminating in deification, or becoming as God. This process is called "theosis." Although God's essence is claimed to be unknowable and unattainable by mankind, a separation between God's essence and His energy is envisioned, the latter promoted as being attainable by mankind. Orthodoxy teaches, "God is always and forever unknowable and incomprehensible to creatures. Even in the eternal life of the Kingdom of God … men will never know the essence of God, that is what God really is in Himself." [40.] That said, it is claimed that as we "walk toward the Light Who is Christ," and we "liberate our minds from sinfulness," we "thank God for the gift of deification by cooperating as best we are able with the process of our salvation." Our lives are described as a three-stage process, moving from salvation in this life to "illumination" in the next, and finally to a "union with the energies of the Holy Trinity." [41.]

Orthodoxy teaches that for us to share in these energies, we "share in all the spiritual attributes of divinity" to become, according to the holy fathers and by divine grace, "all that God Himself is by nature." These "attributes of divinity," in addition to eternal life, include a continual and ever-increasing amount of "power, wisdom, mercy, knowledge, and love." Mankind is made to become "ever more Godlike forever." [42.]

The OCA makes the following claim: "By the Holy Spirit given by God through Christ, men can share the life, the love, the truth, the freedom, the goodness, the holiness, the wisdom, the knowledge of God Himself … the essence of Christianity is 'the acquisition of the Holy Spirit' and the 'deification' of man by the grace of God, the so-called theosis." [43.] The concept of theosis, or "becoming God," is justified, in part, by citing Psalm 82:6 (subsequently quoted by Jesus in John 10:34–36): "I said, 'You are gods, and all of you are sons of the Most High'" [44.]

In addition to the idea that humans will be deified one day, Orthodoxy teaches that mankind's ultimate home will remain on earth (heaven on earth), that the new creation spoken of in Scripture is actually a remake and purification of the existing creation here (not some faraway location). "The Orthodox Church looks not to some 'other world' for salvation, but to this very world so loved by God ... At the end of the ages God will reveal His presence and will fill all creation with Himself ... all things will be made new. This world will again be that paradise for which it was originally created ... For those who love Him it will be paradise. For those who hate Him it will be hell." [45.]

In response to 2 Peter 3:10, which states that the earth will be destroyed by fire, the Orthodox Church teaches that the Bible never speaks of a "second creation" but rather consistently speaks of God's love of the world in which we live; therefore, "Orthodox Tradition never interprets such scriptural texts as teaching the actual annihilation of the creation by God. It understands such texts as speaking metaphorically of the great catastrophe which creation must endure." They do teach of an "eternal fire" for the ungodly, but this fire that destroys the ungodly in no way is understood as affecting the creation. Creation is not doomed to destruction; it cannot be, as God is a loving God and called His creation "very good" (Genesis 1:31). [45.]

The relationship among the Personages of the Godhead is a topic of controversy for several of the denominations, particularly the Jehovah's Witnesses, who deny the very existence of a Godhead, or Trinity, of Father, Son, and Holy Spirit. For purposes here, the Orthodox view of separate Personages, yet equality among Father, Son, and Holy Spirit, is supported by Scripture; the view of a supposed hierarchy between the three, however, is not.

The Godhead reveals one Divine Nature comprising three distinct Personalities. The one nature can be seen in passages such as Colossians 2:9: "For in Him (Jesus)[8] dwells all the fullness of the Godhead bodily." Whereas the separate Personages can be found, for instance, in passages such as these - God the Father: in 1 Peter 1:2, Peter refers to the saints as the "elect according to the foreknowledge of God the Father;" God the Son - In John 20:28, Thomas said "My Lord and my God;" And God the Holy Spirit - Acts 5:3–4 states, "Why has Satan filled your heart to lie to the Holy Spirit ... You have not lied to men but to God."

Passages of Scripture that seemingly promote a hierarchy among the Personages of the Son to the Father include the following:

> I am going to the Father, for the Father is greater than I. (John 14:28)
>
> But of that day and hour no one knows, not even the angels of heaven, but My Father only. (Matthew 24:36)

And He went a little farther and fell on His face, and prayed, saying, "O My Father, if it is possible, let this cup pass from Me; nevertheless not as I will, but as You will." (Matthew 26:39)

These must be taken in the context that Jesus, in His incarnated human condition, was temporarily "made for a little while lower than the angels" (Hebrews 2:9) to accomplish His work here on earth. In a similar fashion, the Holy Spirit seemingly subject to the Father in passages such as John 14:26 ("But the Helper, the Holy Spirit, whom the Father will send in My name, He will teach you all things, and bring to your remembrance all things that I said to you") must be taken within the context of His tasks on this earth as well.

Concerning the concept of theosis, the Scriptures attest that mankind does not unite with the Divine. God said,

> I Am. (Exodus 3:14)
> I am God, your God. (Psalm 50:7)
> Be still and know that I am God. (Psalm 46:10).
> I will be their God, and they shall be My people. (Hebrews 8:10)
> For as the heavens are higher than the earth, so are My ways higher than your ways, and My thoughts than your thoughts. (Isaiah 55:9).

God is God; mankind is not, nor will mankind ever become "as God"! Trying to justify theosis via Psalm 82:6 (and Jesus's subsequent quote found in John 10:34–36) is negated, as this passage refers to the unjust decisions made by the rulers and judges of Israel who represented God. The psalmist here is chastising these judges who were given the "authority of God" to rule "in place of God"; in this sense, acting as "gods" (Elohim) to men (and failing to do a good job). He is not equating them to God; if so, verse 7 makes no sense: "But you shall die like men!" In John 10:34–36, the Jewish leaders are about to stone Jesus for blasphemy when

He references this verse, making the argument, as J. W. McGarvey (1956) summarized, "If it was not blasphemy to call those gods who so remotely represented the Deity, how much less did Christ blaspheme in taking unto himself the title to which he had a better right than they?" [46.]

The concept of theosis (mankind slowly becoming deified), as defined by the Orthodox Church, violates Scripture, and incorporates several conflicting statements:

> God is forever unknowable and incomprehensible to creatures ... men will never know the essence of God. [40.]
>
> All other attributes of divinity must become ours ... men can share the life, the love, the truth, the freedom, the goodness, the holiness, the wisdom, the knowledge of God Himself. [43.]

According to these statements, God is unknowable, and humans will never know the essence of God, yet, they will know God by becoming Divine, sharing in all of God's attributes, and possessing His wisdom, His knowledge (omniscience), His love, and His holiness. This contradiction alone discredits the concept.

One final point concerning this theology needs to be addressed. As "we walk toward the Light of Christ and liberate ourselves from sin," according to Orthodoxy, "we thank God for the gift of deification by cooperating as best we are able with the process of our salvation." Let's be clear; we are not being deified, and we are not cooperating in the process of our salvation (other than our initial obedience to the gospel to accept God's offer of salvation). Paul tells us in Ephesians 2:8–9, "For by grace you have been saved through faith, and that not of yourselves (not your cooperation), it is the gift of God, not of works, lest anyone should boast." This process of deification lends itself to the idea that, somehow, we are "earning" our salvation. By becoming like God, our salvation is riding along on the coattails of this process—which could not be further from the truth. There is a clear separation here. God is giving us salvation. We are the sinners who, by faith in Christ, accept this free gift and rely on His blood to save us in the end. We in no way are helping in any process of salvation, certainly not in thinking we are becoming as God for our own benefit here.

The view that eternity for God's faithful children will be spent on a purified earth also violates Scripture. To suggest that Peter in 2 Peter 3:10 is speaking metaphorically in his pronouncement that the heavens and earth will be destroyed by fire is to suggest that the flood (referenced in verse 6), as a first destruction of the earth, was also a metaphorical statement and never really occurred.[1] In addition, if these verses are only symbolic or metaphoric, what meaning can we derive from verse 11—"Since all these things are to be destroyed in this way, what sort of people ought you to be in holy conduct and godliness"? Is Peter, as guided by the Spirit, suggesting we are to conduct ourselves in anticipation of something that will not actually happen?

A second creation that is somehow needed to accommodate humans, in the end, is indeed not spoken of, as it will not be needed. Scripture attests that a new heaven and new earth will be provided (2 Peter 3:13), with a new Jerusalem coming down out of heaven from God and "having the glory of God" (Revelation 21:10)—a residence with a stunning description as God's future city for His people to live with Him for all eternity (Revelation 21:11–27).

Salvation

The Orthodox Church teaches a faith-only / works-justified salvation: that "belief in Jesus must be combined with putting that belief into action—feeding the hungry, ministering to others, etc." This, then, is the plan of salvation for the Orthodox—a belief in Jesus, considered a believing faith, coupled with putting that faith into action with acetic works. Both are essential, as "faith without works is dead." [47.]

In an article by "Father [sic]" [13] John Breck, "Salvation Is Indeed by Grace," he describes salvation as being a product of grace, not by works, which seems to contradict "faith without works is dead." Immediately following this statement, however, Breck makes this comment:

---

1 Should you have doubts concerning the occurrence of the Genesis flood, references such as Apologetics Press (www.apologeticspress.org) provides extensive evidence in support of this occurrence.

> Orthodoxy does recognize, however, the importance of our "cooperation" with God, what we term "synergy." "Salvation", as we usually understand the word, is only the beginning of a pilgrimage that leads us through this life, through our physical death, and into life beyond.[48.]

This, then, ties into our discussion, where salvation is viewed as a process aligned with our deification to be like God. Here "Father [sic]" [13] Breck envisions our "small efforts" of such things as fasting, participation in long liturgical services, almsgiving, and other acts of love as essential in participating in this cooperation with—this tapping into the synergy of—God. He points out that these things are not the means of our salvation, but they are essential, along with a firm belief in Christ.

Even with belief in Jesus as our Savior and actions on our part (including adherence to proper worship activities as Christians, along with ascetic works—feeding the hungry, visiting the sick, almsgiving, and the like—salvation is taught as something we can never really be sure of; we can only live our lives with repentance and hope. As "Father [sic]" [13] Breck further explains in "On Preaching Judgment," the words of our Lord, as recorded in Matthew 25 concerning the "Last Judgment," indicate that though our words and actions may give us a sense of entitlement, in the end, God will judge the motivations of the heart, and that is something we cannot be absolutely sure of. "This is why an Orthodox Christian can never claim to 'be saved,' as though that were a once-for-all, established fact, an obligation on God's part to make sure that our will be done … We can long pray for salvation; but it is never guaranteed." [49.]

Scripture indicates that hearing, which produces faith by the Word (Romans 10:13–17), belief (Acts 16:31), repentance (Mark 1:15), confession (Romans 10:9–10), and baptism (Acts 2:38; 22:16) are the essentials to salvation. It's interesting that Orthodoxy doesn't include any of these steps of salvation in their description of faith, positing that simply a belief in Jesus would be sufficient for salvation, along with putting this belief only into action, through such actions as Jesus mentions in Matthew 26:31–46. These actions are certainly important, as Jesus indicates, but they fall more into the category of acts of love after one is a child of God, not acts to become a child of God.

Orthodoxy is correct in stating we are saved by God's grace, but faith is an integral part of this formula, and Paul confirms this in his epistle to the Ephesians: "For by grace you have been saved through faith, [10] and that not of yourselves; it is the gift of God not of works lest anyone should boast" (Ephesians 2:8–9). As grace includes all that God has done on our behalf, faith includes all humans are to do in response to God's grace (whatever actions God specifies as necessary) so that they can receive the offer of salvation in Christ.

These actions of faith, allowing mankind to receive God's grace and salvation, would include obedience to God's instructions concerning all of the above essentials, as mandated in Scripture. Again, these include belief or an assured mindset with no doubt that Jesus is the Savior—produced by hearing His Word; repentance, or a commitment to turn from sin; confession, or a verbal acknowledgment that Jesus is indeed the Son of God; and baptism, or immersion in water to gain access to the blood of Jesus and attain forgiveness for our sin. It's not just a belief in Jesus coupled with actions of loving our neighbor, assisting the needy, or participation in such things as fasting or worship services, as the Orthodox Church teaches is necessary for salvation (Scripture simply does not support this).

Once we have obeyed the gospel in this manner, we are immediately added to the Lord's church by God Himself (Acts 2:47) and put into a saved condition. Salvation is not a long pilgrimage, as envisioned by Orthodoxy, beginning in this life and extending through death and into the next life. Salvation is promised to be immediate. In addition, the Scriptures affirm to those who are obedient to God's instructions concerning His plan of salvation—if they remain steadfast and always strive to walk in the light—that they can have full confidence in their salvation (1 Corinthians 15:58; 1 John 5:13), not simply a life of repentance and hope, left with uncertainty.

Ephesians 1:13–14 tells us that those of us who have heard and believed the word of truth—and, by implication of other Scripture, have repented, confessed, and have been baptized (immersed) for the forgiveness of our sins—are then "sealed with the Holy Spirit of promise, who is the guarantee of our inheritance." Also, John gives a solid guarantee to his listeners in 1 John 5:10–13 that "God has given us eternal life" through His Son. He also states, "These things I have written to you who believe in the name of the

Son of God, that you may know [10] that you have eternal life" (1 John 5:13). This is the opposite of Orthodox teaching—from "I cannot know for sure. I must simply repent and hope" to "You may know you have eternal life."

Eschatology

The Last Judgment
Giotto di Bondone, 1306

The Orthodox Church teaches there are two judgments, a particular judgment (temporary) and a general judgment (final), much like that of Catholicism. OCA's "Outline of Orthodox Faith" tells us that after death, man's body returns to the earth, and his soul is immediately judged by God in an act referred to as the "Particular judgment." It goes on to claim that the final reward for men will take place at the general judgment and that in between the two, in the "intermediate state," men will experience a foretaste of either their blessing or punishment.

In addition, the state of one's soul following this Particular judgment, should it be found wanting, can be changed by prayers and petitions of the living offered on the person's behalf—this is the intermediate state, during which all souls will have a foretaste of blessings or punishment. This is similar to the Catholic doctrine of purgatory. Confirmation of this is directed to the Apocrypha as found in 2 Maccabees 12:43, where Judas Maccabaeus offers sacrifice for his men who have fallen. Also, St. Basil the Great, in his "Prayers for Pentecost," assures us of the following: "[The Lord] vouchsafes to receive from us propitiatory prayers and sacrifices for those that are kept in Hades, and allows us the hopes of obtaining for them peace, relief, and freedom." [50.]

"Father [sic]"[13] John Breck (OCA) answered the question of whether there are examples of praying to and for the departed in the New Testament. He wrote that indeed there were, as a "clear allusion to such a prayer can be found in 2 Timothy 1:18." Here Paul's brother Onesiphorus, who had helped Paul in the past in Ephesus, sought him out in Rome to comfort him. Paul first asks the Lord to grant mercy to Onesiphorus's household (2 Timothy 1:16), and then he asks, "May the Lord grant him (Onesiphorus)[8] to find mercy from the Lord on that day (meaning the day of judgment)[8]" (2 Timothy 1:18). This leads to the conclusion that Onesiphorus was no longer alive, yet Paul prays for him as he looks toward that final judgment. [51.]

Concerning the general, or final, judgment, Orthodoxy teaches that God will join our physical bodies to our spiritual souls and that those who have been assigned to heaven will be perfected, forever progressing toward a deeper and fuller communion with God to the point of deification, which equates with eternal happiness. Those souls assigned to hell will not experience punishment except as the soul's inability to participate in God's infinite love, which is given freely to everyone else. The fire that will consume sinners at the coming of the kingdom of God is actually a shine, or "splendor," emanating from the saints, reflecting God's love. Therefore, God does not torture the wicked in some material fire, causing physical pain and torment; rather, God simply reveals Himself in Jesus, and "the presence of God's splendid glory and love is the scourge of those who reject its radiant power and light." [52.]

Nowhere in Scripture can one find an account of more than one judgment where every knee shall bow.

> But the heavens and earth which are now preserved by the same word, are reserved for fire until the day (singular) of judgment and perdition of ungodly men. (2 Peter 3:7)

> And as it is appointed for men to die once, and after this judgment, (singular) so Christ, was offered once to bear the sins of many. To those who eagerly wait for Him He will appear a second time, apart from sin, for salvation. (Hebrews 9:27–28)

The addition of this second judgment is both a violation of Scripture (Revelation 22:18–19: "Do not add to His words …") and an accommodation to another Orthodox misconception, offering prayers for the dead, with an anticipation of changing the outcome for a particular soul. As with the Catholic belief in purgatory, if this is true, then Luke 16 (the account of the rich man and Lazarus, where a "great gulf" is fixed between the two that neither can pass over) must be rejected. Justification for this practice and, in turn, this secondary judgment is an appeal to an Apocryphal book (Maccabees) in which praying to the dead takes place, along with the pronouncements of church fathers, such as St. Basil the Great, cannot be reconciled with Scripture, as *neither is authoritative.* Pronouncements of the "church fathers" along with those of the early "ecumenical councils" are not authoritative – God neither sanctioned nor inspired either. And concerning the Apocryphal books, they as well have no divine authority – they are the words of men, not of God. One reason backing up this statement – it can be shown to contain error. An extensive rebuttal to this is included in my first Volume. [53.]

Second Timothy 1:18, where Paul prays on behalf of Onesiphorus, who is claimed to have passed away, is a poor example to use as a precedent for praying on behalf of the departed. That Paul hopes mercy will be extended is proof that Onesiphorus was still alive when Paul made this statement; as there can be no change from 'no mercy to mercy' after death, according to Luke 16:26. [54.]

Concerning eternal punishment for the ungodly, according to Scripture, souls going to hell will indeed experience punishment and torment. The fire spoken of in Scripture is not simply a splendor or shine from saints; nor is it the fire of God's love, which alone becomes a "scourge to those who reject it." Luke 16 gives an account of the rich man in Hades crying out to Abraham to have mercy on him: "Send Lazarus that he may dip the tip of his finger in water to cool my tongue; for I am tormented in this flame." Does this sound like a fire of "splendor" or a "shine"? If this is the environment of Hades for the unrighteous, one can only imagine what the second death, the lake of fire, or hell will be like for them in the end (Revelation 20:13–15).

The Holy Mysteries (Sacraments)

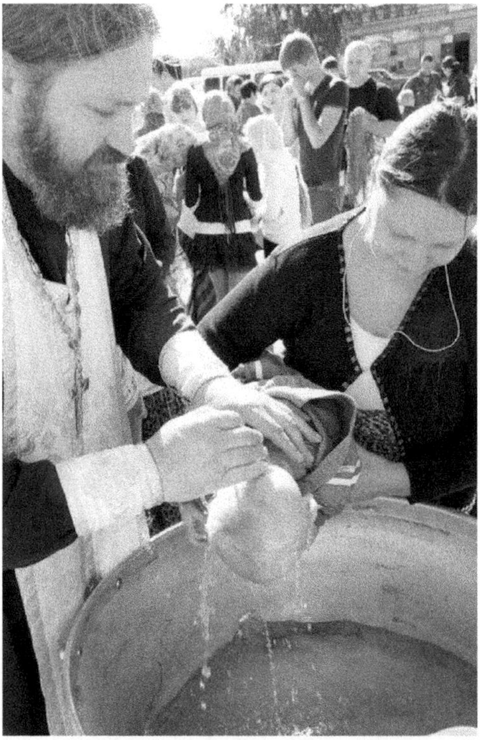

Orthodox Infant Baptism

The Orthodox Church recognizes seven sacraments or holy mysteries, relational to the spiritual life of the church and mankind. These include baptism, chrismation, the Holy Eucharist, penance, holy matrimony, holy unction, and holy orders. These sacraments are similar to those of the Roman Catholic Church, with some variation in doctrine, which is understandable—remember that the Catholic and Orthodox Communions were one and the same until the split in A.D. 1054; therefore, they share much the same doctrine. The view that Deity is involved within each of these sacraments, even to the extent of an unexplained physical/spiritual presence in their administration, certainly adds to this mystery.

Following are the basic teaching points from the Orthodox Church on each of these seven sacraments, followed by Scriptural considerations:

1. Baptism

According to Orthodox teaching, baptism is the mystery of transforming the old sinful man through rebirth into a new man, a new creation. The emphasis is to identify with the death and Resurrection of Christ and to start on a new path—along with the sacraments of chrismation, penance, and the Eucharist—to become a member of the Orthodox Church as well as a journey toward deification. (It is not, however, associated with or taught as essential to salvation.) The OCA describes baptism this way:

> "In the "new creation" of baptism the catechumen descends into the waters to "die" and be "co-buried" with Christ. Yet this gesture is only fulfilled by chrismation, anointing as the "seal of the gift of the Holy Spirit" ... baptism sets us on the pathway toward "deification." It creates the conditions – ecclesial and eucharistic – by which those who allow themselves to be led by the Spirit can pass through the ascetic stages of purification and illumination, to arrive at last at union and communion in the God of love." [55.]

Orthodox baptisms follow a particular procedure. Prior to baptism, the person being baptized must exhibit repentance and faith and proclaim the creed of the Christian faith, and if the person is a child or infant, the godparent or sponsor must recite the creed for them. The water is then prayed over and blessed, as is the person being baptized, who is anointed with sanctified oil and then immersed three times in the name of the Father, the Son, and the Holy Spirit. This person is then said to have "died to this world and is born again in the resurrection of Christ into eternal life." [56.]

Children of Orthodox families are normally baptized shortly following birth, though the reason for this practice may have been initiated centuries earlier as a means of addressing original sin. The Catholic Church has always justified infant baptism by this rationale, and Orthodoxy finds its roots in Catholicism. This appears not to be the case today, as the OCA denies original sin: "that committed by Adam and Eve ... while everyone bears the consequences of the first sin, the foremost which is death, only Adam and Eve are guilty of that sin." [56.]

Why, then, does the Orthodox Church continue to advocate this practice today? According to *The Longer Catechism of the Orthodox, Catholic, Eastern Church*, we should baptize infants because the Scriptures advocate it. "In the Old Testament, infants were circumcised at eight days old; in the New Testament, baptism takes the place of circumcision." [57.] We know this from passages such as Colossians 2:11–12, where Paul says, "You were also circumcised with the circumcision made without hands, by putting off the body of the sins of the flesh, by the circumcision of Christ, buried with him in Baptism."

The reasons for the use of sponsors in the case of infants and children too small to respond are twofold, according to this catechism. First, the godparents' or sponsors' faith is bolstered by this commitment, binding them to teach the faith to the young people they sponsor, and second, they stand as a surety before the church that they will indeed see this through—to confirm these individuals into the faith. [57.]

Orthodox apologists, such as "Father [sic]" [13] John Hainsworth give even more detailed explanations for their belief concerning the validity of infant baptism. In his work *Infant Baptism: What the Church Believes*, he dogmatically replies to the question, "Is infant baptism biblical?": "Yes, it is." Then he proceeds to give several Biblical references to support this answer. The first is to assert that the Bible describes no fewer than five household baptisms, all of which involve "families," with the comment, "It is hard to imagine that at least one of these households did not include children." He cites the households of Cornelius (Acts 11:13–14), Lydia (Acts 16:15), the Philippian jailor (Acts 16:33), Crispus (Acts 18:8), and the household of Stephanas (1 Corinthians 1:16). "Father [sic]" [13.] Hainsworth also brings up the circumcision of children at eight days old in the Old Testament versus New Testament baptism; his argument centers on the "inclusion" of children into the covenant, then and now, stating, "Nowhere in the Bible is it hinted that while absorbing the rite of circumcision, baptism would suddenly and without precedent exclude children … Jesus is in fact including children in His Kingdom." [58.]

In addressing the subject of a child's ability to understand or comprehend faith, the approach here is to question faith as a product of reason and to question individual faith versus group faith, where a reference is made to a quote from one of the church fathers: "Tertullian said famously that 'one Christian is no Christian … Our relationship with God is valid only if it is realized in communion with the whole Church.'" Children thus have a sense of belonging long before they can understand or believe anything resembling an individual faith. Their baptism is as significant to them (and to God) as any other; even if they don't fully understand what's going on, they "intuitively understand it." [58.]

Finally, as to whether children will be lost should they be unbaptized, Hainsworth agrees with the most recent Orthodox sentiment denying original sin in saying no to this, as he does believe sins are "washed away at baptism," and it would be "senseless to baptize a child if they have no inherited sin." That said, they still need to be baptized, as Christ's death not only washed away sins but also destroyed death itself, and it brings one into a union with the life of Christ." [58.] The child or infant, through baptism, though not needing remission of sin, gains an initiation into this union with Christ.

According to Orthodox teaching, baptism, along with the observance of other sacraments, including chrismation, penance, and the Eucharist, together with a statement of faith (their creed), allows one entry into the Christian church. Baptism is further described as a beginning or pathway toward deification and though not guaranteed, possibly our ultimate salvation within the church. Scripture, however, attests that baptism is not a beginning pathway but rather a culminating act of obedience. Having previously heard (Romans 10:13–17), believed (Acts 16:31), repented (Acts 2:37–38), and confessed Jesus as Lord (Romans 10:9–10), we are then immersed in the name of Jesus Christ for the forgiveness of our sins (Acts 2:38). At this point, we come in contact with Jesus's blood (spiritually), and we are given the gift of the Holy Spirit (Acts 2:38).

We are not required (after the fact) to undergo a "chrismation" (to separately receive the Holy Spirit), or confess our sins to a priest, or partake of the Lord's Supper (in connection with baptism), although we are to observe the Lord's Supper by remembering our Lord's death weekly via partaking of the emblems of bread and fruit of the vine (Acts 20:7). We also are not to verbalize a man-made creed in order to complete or validate our baptism and thus be joined with the Orthodox Church for a possible future reward. Baptism is indeed essential for salvation. Following baptism, God Himself adds us to His church (Acts 2:47) without any further requirements or formalities. Question – if God adds us to His Son's church immediately following baptism, does this not indicate His approval that we are saved at this point? Then why do the Orthodox feel baptism joins one to the Orthodox church for a "possible" reward in the future? This doctrine denies both the authority over (God adds) and the Divine results (in a saved condition to His Son's church) of baptism.

Focusing on the proper clergy and ritual, as the Orthodox Church advocates, does not validate the baptism either. Once again, a believing, penitent person is simply to be immersed in water for the forgiveness of his or her sins (Acts 8:38; 22:16), at which point he or she is saved by being automatically placed in Christ and becoming part of Christ's church. Nowhere in Scripture is there an example of the procedure used in Orthodox baptism, and certainly no mention is made of the use of a stand-in sponsor or godparent for infant baptism.

Though Orthodox teaching has, for the most part, recognized original sin to mean consequences of sin (death) and not actual guilt of sin (Adam's sin passed down, as a reason for infant baptism), they interestingly continue to baptize infants and children. The reasons cited, include whole households mentioned in Scripture that were baptized must have included children, that baptism in the New Testament is synonymous with circumcision in the Old Testament, that Jesus's including children in His kingdom is a sign He approves of such baptism, that faith is not necessarily a product of reason, and that an intuitive sense of belonging on the child's part is all that is necessary - are all indefensible when held up to God's Word.

The first reason can be dismissed on its premise alone—we don't know whether any of the households cited in Scripture included infants or small children, and even if they did, baptism cannot be assumed as a necessary inference. Second, though Colossians 2:11–12 beautifully connects circumcision under the First Covenant to baptism in the New Testament as a circumcision made without hands, the focus is on Jesus and what He has done for those who have submitted to Him in baptism: "Buried with Him in baptism, in which you also were raised with Him through faith in the working of God, who raised Him from the dead. And you, being dead in your transgressions and the uncircumcision of your flesh, He has made alive together with Him, having forgiven you all transgressions." (Colossians 2:12–13)

This was not a focus on infant circumcision then as justification for infant baptism now. In fact, these passages speak clearly for adult, not infant, baptism. Verse 12 states, "You also were raised with Him through faith." Faith requires cognitive understanding and assent—things an infant is incapable of. In addition, verse 13 connects the narrative of verses 11 and 12, claiming that those to be baptized were "dead in [their] trespasses," by which Christ made them "alive together with Him." Infants and small children, who have no understanding of sin, are not guilty of sin; thus, they certainly are not "dead in their transgressions."

Finally, the purpose for circumcision of male babies on the eighth day of life had more to do with God's wisdom (medically) than inclusion into Jewish life at an early age (see the appendix of Volume 1).[59] In addition, to argue similarity here is to argue against female infant baptism. The Scriptures indicating Jesus included children in His kingdom (e.g., Luke 18:16: "But Jesus called them to Him and said, 'Let the little children come to Me, and do not forbid them, for of such is the kingdom of God'") say nothing about a requirement of baptism. It is unwarranted to make this connection. Jesus was simply indicating that those sinless little children had no need of baptism, and their current state was one of innocence and security in His kingdom.

The excuse cited—that faith and reason are somehow not connected, and an infant can intuitively understand the purpose of baptism (even at a few weeks of age), seems a desperate grabbing at straws to rationally justify this position. The bottom line here is that infants and small children are not capable of (or expected to) cognitively hear (with understanding), believe, repent, or confess Jesus (all requirements, according to Scripture, prior to baptism).

Using sponsors to perform these stages will not work. Scripture gives us no such example and therefore does not allow it. In an attempt to validate "group think," the reference to a quote by Tertullian has no merit here either and stands as blatantly false. In our context here, if "one Christian is no Christian" and if "our relationship with God is only valid if realized in communion with the whole Church," does that mean "your baptism will suffice for me"? Does God hold Christians individually responsible for anything? What if Noah's relationship with God had been valid only if he was in communion with the whole church? We wouldn't be here! What a ridiculous statement!

One final point in association with "Father [sic]" [13.] Hainsworth's affirmation that infants are not in jeopardy of hell and need not be baptized; he believes that sins are "washed away at baptism" and that it would be "senseless to baptize a child if they have no inherited sin." Why, then, is the baptism of all those of accountable age not absolutely necessary to be saved? Do they not have sin needing to be "washed away"? And where or how else will this be accomplished?

2. Chrismation

According to Orthodox teaching, chrismation is a separate ceremony associated with and usually performed immediately following the baptism of an individual (except for infants), whereby the priest anoints said individual with a special oil, or "holy chrism," conferring upon him or her the Holy Spirit. This is the same sacrament we looked at under the Roman Catholic Church as "confirmation." Orthodoxy references passages such as Romans 8, 1 Corinthians 6, and 2 Corinthians 1:21 in support of this doctrine. Baptism is said to have no meaning without chrismation. The application is identical to that of the Catholics in that a special oil, or "holy chrism," is applied to the body of the baptized person by the bishop. This transference of the Holy Spirit is considered one of the mysteries of the church, and the bishops who perform the ceremony are sanctioned to do so, as they are "successors to the apostles" and have been given the gift of the Spirit themselves. [60.]

According to the Scriptures, the Holy Spirit enters individuals upon baptism, not during a separate ceremony conducted afterward—this is according to passages such as 1 Corinthians 12:13 and Acts 2:38.

The Orthodox ritual and liturgy associated with both these sacraments (baptism and chrismation) are not found in the Scriptures. We do see, however, examples of penitent believers confessing Jesus as their Lord and submitting to His command to be baptized for the forgiveness of their sins (e.g., the Ethiopian eunuch in Acts 8). The gift of the Holy Spirit is a natural (or supernatural) result of baptism, not a separate event demanding clergy with special oils.

Once again, we see apostolic succession being invoked to justify a human imagination—this time, chrismation. As stated previously, Acts 8:14–17 does indicate Peter and John gave the Holy Spirit to these Samaritans, but in this instance, since verse 16 states that the Gentiles were previously baptized "in the name of Jesus," it would indicate they already had the Holy Spirit as a result of their baptism. Therefore, when Peter and John "laid hands on them" (verse 17), this most likely represented an extra or supernatural portion of the Spirit, which is understandable, as this was a unique time when the Lord's church was just beginning. These Gentiles in particular were likely in need of encouragement, as well as the apostles, who may not have been fully convinced that the Spirit was for all people—that is, Gentile inclusion into the kingdom—since Peter's experience with Cornelius had not yet occurred. This additional measure of the Spirit, which most assuredly helped these Samaritans grow the kingdom, ceased, as did all miracles, following the first century. The passing along of any of these abilities—in this case, to the bishops of the Orthodox Church through apostolic succession—has been rebutted previously.

3. Holy Eucharist

The Holy Eucharist, considered by most Orthodox today as the most important of all sacraments, encompasses much more than a Communion memorial meal (a remembrance of Jesus's death through the partaking of bread and wine). The Eucharist is a "holy ritual meal," specifically connected to the Passover meal of the Old Testament, in which the original meaning of liberation from Egyptian bondage of the Jewish people is connected to Christ's freeing mankind from the slavery of sin as the New Testament Passover Lamb.

Thus, the Passover was changed by Christ, inviting the actual consumption of His body and blood (recall that Orthodox believe the elements of bread and wine actually become the body and blood of Jesus with the help of the Holy Spirit). That allows not so much a remembrance of our Lord as it does access to commune and experience the presence of God, a prime objective of participation. The Orthodox Church, though not calling this transubstantiation (the Catholic doctrine), has never formally affirmed, or denied it, preferring to state simply that it remains a mystery. Believing that Jesus's body and blood actually come to life is exactly what the Catholic Church believes, as do the Orthodox, whether the Orthodox Church wishes to call it transubstantiation or not.

Orthodox Holy Eucharist

Communion is given only to baptized and confirmed Orthodox Christians (including young children, and infants via their sponsors) who have fasted from the previous midnight. It is observed every Sunday in the church, as well as on feast days and in monasteries - some of whom observe it on a daily basis. The Orthodox Church denies that the elements of the body and blood are merely "intellectual or psychological symbols of Christ's body and blood," reasoning that if this were true, the congregation would simply be asked to "think about Jesus and commune with him in their hearts," thus "reducing the Eucharist to a simple memorial meal of the Lord's Last Supper." There could be no union with God as Orthodoxy has envisioned, only a recollection of the event in thought. [61.]

When Jesus instituted the Lord's Supper at the Passover meal, the focus was not on this Old Testament observance but on the establishment of a New Covenant in His blood, a means of remembering what was shortly to be His death—an atonement for mankind's sin. The Orthodox Church has taken this commanded remembrance, an act of New Testament worship, and added a tie-in with the Old Testament—a focus on the Passover as a holy ritual meal. As important as it may have been to the Israelites in the Old Testament, this Passover meal holds no special significance to New Testament Christians today. In fact, all feasts, meals, sacrifices, and observances of the Old Testament have been discarded; they have been "nailed to the cross," according to the Scriptures. (See Colossians 2:13–16 and Galatians 5:1–4.)

In addition, the Orthodox Communion portion of the Eucharist suggests direct contact with the presence of Christ through this activity. Though Orthodoxy does not call this mystery transubstantiation, it requires the same belief on the parishioner's part—that they are actually joining with the Lord's physical body and blood in this liturgy. Scripture does not support this understanding. In the first place, the Lord Himself called these elements bread and fruit of the vine (see Matthew 26:26–29).

Second, it falls under the same condemnation as with the Catholics. If the elements actually become Jesus's body and blood, this would mean Christ would be sacrificed over and over again with each occasion, falsifying Hebrews 9:28, where we learn that Christ was sacrificed only once.

A third reason to reject this idea focuses on two Scriptures. The first is Matthew 26:29, "But I say to you, I will not drink of this fruit of the vine from now on ***until*** that day when I drink it new with you in My Father's kingdom." And the second Scripture is 1 Corinthians 11:23–26: "He took bread … He broke it and said, 'Take, eat, this is My body which is broken for you; do this in ***remembrance of Me.'*** In the same manner He also took the cup … saying, 'This cup is the new covenant in My blood. This do, as often as you drink it, in ***remembrance of Me.***' For as often as you eat this bread and drink this cup, you ***proclaim the Lord's death till*** He comes." [8, 10.]

Notice the following. First, Matthew 26:29 says Jesus will not "drink of the fruit of the vine" (He will not be present) with His disciples (or us) **until**—a word denoting a later time—He drinks it anew in heaven with us. Second, Jesus tells us two times to partake of the emblem "in remembrance of Him." We don't have to "remember" Someone who is with us now (within the elements), do we? Third, in 1 Corinthians 11:26, Paul tells the Corinthians (and us) that whenever they eat or drink of this Communion, they "proclaim the Lord's death." Are the Orthodox proclaiming His death, thinking about His sacrifice and death, if they're celebrating His being with them in the elements? And fourth, we are to proclaim that death—think about that death—"till" He comes (another reference to time). Jesus is coming back, but **till** then, He is not here!

Serbian Orthodox Divine Liturgy
Holy Trinity Cathedral
Vranje, Serbia

Interestingly, Orthodoxy denies the doctrine of viewing the Communion elements as intellectual or psychological symbols, calling the people to merely think about Jesus and to commune with Him in their hearts as they partake of the bread and fruit of the vine, as this "reduces the eucharist meal to a simple memorial meal of the Lord's Last Supper, a 'recollection of the event in thought.'" But isn't this exactly what Jesus commanded us to do—to do this in remembrance of Him? (1 Corinthians 11:24-25).

Scripture also affirms that young children are innocent of sin and in no need of baptism or partaking of the Lord's Supper; they have no sins to wash away, and they are incapable of properly remembering or proclaiming Jesus's death (Matthew 18:3; 19:14; 1 Corinthians 11:24–29). As will be discussed further below, under "Church Building and Services," all who partake of this Divine liturgy must acknowledge their belief and affirm their baptism and chrismation prior to partaking "for themselves" (mandating further that no one can acknowledge for them—which would exclude sponsors), otherwise the service cannot continue. This is totally contradicted by allowing infants and young children to participate! And finally, the frequency of observance in addition to every Sunday - in the case of Orthodoxy, adding special feast days and daily observance in monasteries - violates the Scriptural pattern (Acts 20:7).

4. Penance

Orthodox Christians who have committed grave sins or who have not partaken of Holy Communion for an extended period of time are required to undergo formal or sacramental penance before a priest, in order to reunite with the church. Repentance and confession must be made to the pastor of the church, following which a prayer of absolution is offered, and the pastor bestows the forgiveness of God upon the penitent sinner, through Christ, who is said to be present within His church. Unlike Catholicism, the pastor does not purport to have the authority to forgive sin, but only to be a spokesman for Christ. The Catholic priest, in auricular confession, presupposes this authority via the Holy Spirit within himself; this is a slight yet important difference.

Communion and church fellowship can be withheld until this sacramental penance is fulfilled; this is true for any Orthodox member, including children. As with the Catholic Church, the Orthodox Church separates sin for purposes of dealing with it in their sacrament of Penance. This separation involves what they call grave sin and, for lack of another term, nongrave, or incidental, sin—the sin that "Christians are never completely without." [62.] If it is determined to be a grave sin, and this is determined by the priest, Orthodox Christians must deal with it through the sacramental ritual. This ritual must also be endured if parishioners have refrained from partaking of the Holy Eucharist for an extended time. In either of these instances, they must undergo a three-step process: first, an expression of sincere sorrow for their action; second, offering a heartfelt confession of sins (usually in private before the priest); and third, penance—the prayer of absolution, whereby forgiveness of sin is pronounced upon the sinner. Holy Communion is usually withheld until this ritual is completed. As a sign of absolution and the fulfillment of penance, Holy Communion is given.

The New Testament teaches we are to confess our faults, first and foremost, to God directly (1 John 1:9). We are also admonished to confess our sins to one another and to forgive one another (James 5:16). There is no mention that confession must be given exclusively before a pastor who acts on behalf of God. In fact, according to 1 Peter 2:9, Christians are all priests (as part of a royal priesthood) with direct access to God. We are no longer under a covenant whereby we need a priest to intervene for us, as was the case in the Old Testament.

Orthodox Confessional – Woman Making Confession

In addition, the idea that an Orthodox pastor or priest has the authority to determine a grave sin and thereby dole out discretionary punishment (withholding of the Lord's Supper and Christian fellowship) based on this sin unless penance is offered, is not supported by Scripture. Paul does speak to the Corinthian church concerning misuse of the Lord's Supper (treating the Communion as a common meal and condemning those who would partake of this Supper in an unworthy manner), but this has more to do with personal responsibility and focus than outside sanctions (1 Corinthians 11:27).

Paul also mentions that a man must "examine himself" before partaking of the Supper, lest he bring judgment upon himself (1 Corinthians 11:28). This may involve personal unresolved sin, particularly if this sin bothers us to the point of not being able to focus on Christ's death at this time. In this situation, perhaps we would be wise to refrain from partaking in the Lord's Supper and resolve things first. This might involve a personal confession to God, a reconciliation with a brother or sister, or, if the offense is against the church, perhaps a more public confession. In any case, the decision to participate in the Lord's Supper is ours individually; it is not to be forced upon us by a priest. Tying the Lord's Supper as a confirmation of this sacrament is also not found in Scripture.

The Orthodox Church claims that a priest does not have the authority to forgive sin, that only God has this authority., but in practice, personal private confession to a priest, who assures people through a prayer of absolution that their sins are forgiven and cites Christ's presence as that assurance, comes very close to the Catholic position of full inherent clergy authority for this forgiveness. Once again, no man stands between a sinner and Christ, who alone has the authority to remit sin (Luke 7:48). In addition, according to Scripture, there is no such thing as a grave sin. All sin is equally condemned by God (James 5:16; 1 John 1:9; Acts 19:18–19).

5. Holy Matrimony

The Orthodox Church allows marriage for priests and deacons, provided it takes place before ordination, and they marry only once. Also, their wives must not be widows or divorcees. Bishops, however, are to remain celibate. A man is not permitted to be a priest if he or his wife has ever been divorced. Concerning individual Orthodox Christians, the church teaches that marriage is the joining of one man and one woman into one flesh for eternity. As part of this union, the Holy Spirit is given to the couple by the priest to ensure the union will continue into the kingdom of God after death. It is taught that though Jesus stated in Matthew 22:23–33 that there would be no marriages in heaven, He was speaking of the "earthly purposes of marriage"—to suppress man's licentiousness and to procreate—which are irrelevant in heaven. The main aspect of marriage that continues is eternal love, since "Love never ends" (1 Corinthians 13:8). [63.]

No public vows are exchanged—for instance, "till death do us part"—in light of the above (since the marriage will extend into heaven), but personal vows made in private between the couple are encouraged and expected to be kept. Also, marriage is closely tied to the church, requiring the couple to be members of the Orthodox faith or have the blessings of the priest and church at large and to remain or strive to be within the Orthodox body. As with any sacrament, confirmation of the marriage must be accompanied by participation in Holy Communion.

Marriage within the Orthodox Church must be between members of this communion, but there are exceptions in which an Orthodox member may marry a baptized nonmember on the condition that both "sincerely work and pray for unity in Christ." [64.] They must also have the blessing of the Orthodox Church as a whole in order to remain members of the church and to continue to partake of Holy Communion.

Divorce is rare in the Orthodox Church. The church does recognize that there are occasions when it is better for the couple to separate, but there is no official recognition of civil divorce. Remarriage (or second marriage) of a separated couple, as well as widows and divorced individuals, is allowed but requires the permission of the priest and a commitment to remain faithful to the Orthodox Church; it also requires offering formal penance. Remarriage is discouraged, particularly in light of their doctrine of continuing or reuniting as marriage partners in heaven. The Orthodox Church forbids remarriage of widowed clergy, as a way of upholding this ideal. Members of second marriages are not excluded from Eucharistic fellowship if they so desire and if they fulfill all other conditions as members in good standing with the church.

The Scriptures are clear concerning marriage and divorce. When the Pharisees asked Jesus whether it was lawful for a man to divorce his wife for any reason, He responded as follows: "He who made *them* at the beginning *made them male and female*, and said, '*For this reason a man shall leave his father and mother and be joined to his wife, and the two shall become one flesh*'? 'So then, they are no longer two but one flesh. Therefore what God has joined together, let no man separate.'" (Matthew 19:3–6)

These Pharisees then used Moses's actions as an excuse to ask, "Why then did Moses command to give a certificate of divorce and to put her away?" Jesus replied as follows: "Moses, because of your hardness of hearts permitted you to divorce your wives, but from the beginning it was not so. And I say to you, whoever divorces his wife, except for sexual immorality, and marries another, commits adultery; and whoever marries her who is divorced commits adultery" (Matthew 19:7–9).

The Scriptures certainly allow marriage between a man and a woman—Peter, for instance, was married (Matthew 8:14)—but forced celibacy is not sanctioned (1 Timothy 4:1–3). Divorce, except for immorality or unfaithfulness, is also not sanctioned, and the bishop cannot impose a penance to sidestep this command. In addition, the idea that a priest or bishop has the authority to allow or not allow marriage, as well as the issuance of forced celibacy adhered to by the Orthodox Church, puts them at odds with Scripture. As previously noted, Scriptures actually require clergy (elders and deacons of Christ's church) to be married, with children—not celibate, as Orthodoxy also teaches. Again, if the clergy cannot show they can take care of their own household, why should they be selected to look after the household of God (1 Timothy 3:2–5)?

The concept that our earthly marriages will continue into eternity is also not supported by Scripture. Jesus indicates in Matthew 22:23–30 that there will be no marriages in heaven, and since all will be spiritual (non-human souls) in heaven, that would mean no spiritual marriages. This refutes the Orthodox idea that somehow a spiritual marriage will continue. Certainly, the idea that a priest can impart the Holy Spirit to a couple to ensure this has no merit, according to Scripture. The Holy Spirit is given by God as a promise to new Christians as a result of their obedience in baptism (Acts 2: 38). Man cannot control the actions of Deity.

6. Holy Unction

Anointing the sick with oil, or holy unction, is another sacrament of the Orthodox Church, this one traditionally reserved for the dying or terminally ill (often called "Extreme Unction"). It has evolved to a much more common usage, administered today to "all who are sick in body, mind, or spirit".[65.] The Orthodox Church offers it annually on Holy Wednesday to all believers. It is also offered on major feast days or any time the clergy feels it necessary (e.g. if they feel the congregation needs a spiritual lift).

Tamasos Bishop Russian Church - Cyprus

The Orthodox Church teaches that a particular procedure is required for administering this sacrament, involving the pronouncement of seven epistle lessons and seven gospel lessons, and offering seven prayers devoted to healing. The priest or bishop, as Christ's representative, claims the power to heal as Christ Himself remains in the church and works through the clergy. The laying on of hands is also part of this ceremony, with this being claimed to be a method of transferring healing power from the bishop to the afflicted person, with such power emanating directly from the Holy Spirit. The oil is considered the tangible portion of this sacrament, and the transference of the Spirit through the laying on of hands and the ensuing grace received is considered the spiritual mystery this sacrament holds. Orthodoxy claims, "Anointing with oil is quite common throughout the Scriptures, and so even today, we can obtain the same grace and healing dispensed by the Apostles by being anointed by an Apostolically ordained, Priest or Bishop." [66.] Justification for this sacrament comes from James 5:14–15, where James says that if anyone is sick, he or she should summon the elders (priests or bishops, according to Orthodoxy) to pray over them and anoint them with oil, and the prayer of faith will save them, and the Lord will "raise them up." If they have committed sins, they will be forgiven.

The traditional usage comes much closer to Scriptural intent than does the Orthodox usage today. In James 5:14–15, James is instructing one who is "sick" (presumably one who is incapacitated physically) to call upon the elders of his church family to pray for him and anoint him with oil for relief. The oil could have been a medicinal healer of the day (see Luke 10:34), and it would be reasonable to assume, according to this passage, that in some instances, God may have waited for the prayers of faithful elders to intervene.

Many biblical scholars, however, are confident that the application of oil, as mentioned in James 5:14–15, was symbolic in nature and that, in fact, these early church elders were empowered especially by the Spirit with supernatural healing capabilities. The New Testament associates anointing with oil and miraculous healing elsewhere in Scripture—Mark 6:13, for instance. The possibility that we're talking about elders with this power is borne out by passages such as Ephesians 4:8–11, where pastors (elders) are bestowed with these spiritual gifts.

The laying on of hands, as noted, was part of this sacrament, but the miracles associated with this action ceased toward the end of the first century, as confirmation of Jesus as the Christ had been established, along with His church, and the Word of God came to its perfection or completion. The abilities of these early church elders—if indeed they were a result of spiritual gifts—would have disappeared following the first century. The prayers of elders today (along with the prayers of any faithful

Christian) "avail much" (James 5:16) but are not miraculous in nature—at least not in the sense they were in the first century.

The Orthodox Church, however, has taken this passage—as with much of their doctrine, through the vehicle of apostolic succession—and applied first-century gifts and miraculous powers to current-day clergy, indicating, in this instance, that the priests can use specially formulated oils and prayer to effect miraculous healing, along with the forgiveness of sin associated with this sacrament.

They also have taken this passage in James, meant for one who is very ill physically, and applied it to the congregation as a whole for a completely different and unsanctioned reason—that of lifting up all people spiritually (who presumably are in good health physically) at the whim of the clergy. What was meant as a healing avenue for the sick, resulting in honor and glory to God, seems to have been altered by the Orthodox Church (and the Catholics, for that matter) to focus more on the oil and traditional procedure, as if these have some mysterious power to provide spiritual welfare.

7. ***Holy Orders***

The sacrament of "holy orders" in the broadest sense of the term, is the Orthodox teaching that the clergy of the church (bishops, priests, and deacons) have been chosen to guarantee the perpetual presence of Christ with his people.[67.] These clergies are able to minister the teachings of Christ and even to manifest Christ Himself to all men (the laity of the congregation) within themselves, since they have received the gift of the Holy Spirit for this purpose.

The roles of each clergy position were discussed previously under 'organization' - mainly concerning hierarchy; in this sacrament, the separation of powers is made much more evident between the stations. For instance, the OCA describes the function of a priest in relation to a bishop as follows: "The priests in the Church are assigned by the bishop and belong to the specific congregations which they serve … Apart from his bishop and his own particular parish community, the priest has no "powers" and, indeed, no services to perform. Thus, on the altar table of each Christian community headed by the priest as pastor, there is the cloth called the antimension signed by the bishop which is the permission to the community to gather and to act as the Church of God. Without the antimension, the priest and his people cannot function legitimately, and the actions of the assembly cannot be considered as being authentically "of the Church." [67.] A similar separation of power and responsibility seems to hold true between the balance of the Orthodox hierarchy (i.e., archbishop to bishop; priest to deacon, and so forth).

These internal separations in clergy positions, however, in no way deter the overall message to the laity – that Christ is working almost exclusively through all the clergy. The OCA describes the clergy's function as not acting on behalf of, instead of, as vicars of, as substitutes for, or as representatives of Christ. They are to function as manifestations of Christ Himself to the people (as if they were Christ). Of course, this presents one of the greatest of the mysteries of the sacraments. [67.]

It is claimed that Christ, through His ministers, exercising as priest, perpetually offers Himself as the perfect sacrifice to the Father on behalf of the people. Also, as teacher, He proclaims the Word to men. As the Good Shepherd, the one pastor, He guides the flock. He also acts as forgiver and healer, remitting sin and curing the sick. As deacon, He aligns with His ministers as the suffering servant, who is not to be served but who serves others. This sacrament of holy orders takes its name from the ministers who give order and unity to the church, as the doctrine of apostolic succession guarantees this continuity of the church from age to age, from the apostolic age until the establishment of God's kingdom in eternity. As the apostles received the special gifts of God to "go forth and make Christ present to men," so the clergy of the church receive the gifts of God to do likewise. "It is the doctrine of the Church that the clergy must strive to fulfill the grace given to them with the gift of the 'laying on of hands' in the most perfect way possible." [67.]

The only organization found in Christ's church is in the local churches, where Scripture sanctions oversight by a plurality of elders within each local congregation, assisted by appointed deacons. Each congregation is seen as being autonomous, independent from, and not accountable to any other church body, group, or individual, but accountable only to Christ and His teachings (see Acts 14:21–23, Titus 1:5). The job description of an Orthodox bishop as "overseeing a community of congregations" is not seen anywhere in Scripture, nor is this idea that the bishop has such overwhelming power over a priest, that the later cannot even call an assembly of the church without his 'permission.' This is so erroneous on several fronts – not only are "bishops" and "priests" not mentioned in Scripture as two separate positions of clergy (only elders of a local church), but Christ's church will meet - notwithstanding any dictate of a man! Many churches operated in the New Testament without "clergy" (elders), as they did not have qualified men at the time – this is why Paul traveled to "appoint elders" as he did, to better this situation (Acts 14:23). A church or congregation without elders is not the ideal situation, but it can be tolerated until or unless qualified men are appointed to lead – they don't just "not meet!"

The idea that individuals within the clergy can receive the Holy Spirit in a special way, enabling them to minister Christ's truth to others, and that they can also receive Divine gifts through apostolic succession by the laying on of hands is not supported by Scripture either. This elevation of the clergy goes well beyond simply acting on Christ's behalf; they claim to "manifest the presence and action of Christ to his people," and this presence is infused within all of their sacraments, which is both presumptuous and unscriptural.

The individual Christian is not without knowledge and thus totally dependent upon the clergy, as assumed and promoted within the Orthodox Church, nor does the child of God need an Orthodox priest to "manifest the presence and action of Christ" to them; for you see the Christian already has Christ living within them! (2 Corinthians 13:5) In fact, Christians have the entire Godhead living within them if they have truly obeyed the gospel and remain faithful to Christ.

Scriptures teach that as one believes, repents, confesses, and is baptized into Jesus, one receives the gift of the Holy Spirit. (Acts 2:38). This is confirmed as well in 2 Timothy 1:14, Ephesians 2:22, and again in Ephesians 4:30. As mentioned, Jesus Christ also dwells within each Christian. In fact, this truth is confirmed in no less than ten other passages in the New Testament: Romans 8:10 ("Christ is in you"); 2 Corinthians 4:6-7 (Christ is that treasure within the earthen vessel – the Christian);

Galatians 1:15-16 (God's "Son in me"); Galatians 2:20 ("Christ lives in me"); Galatians 4:19 ("Christ is formed in you"); Ephesians 3:17 (Christ dwells in our hearts through faith); Colossians 1:27 ("the mystery among the Gentiles: which is Christ in you"); 2 Thessalonians 1:10 (His glory will be revealed from within His saints - Christians); Hebrews 3:6 ("But Christ as a Son over His own house, whose house we are"); and John 14:23 ("Jesus answered and said to him, 'If anyone loves Me, he will keep My word; and My Father will love him, and We will come to him and make Our home with him."). Notice in this last verse both the Father and the Son will come and make their home *in* us, which completes the Godhead – all living within each and every faithful Christian). The fact that Deity dwells within the Christian as shown above is understandable when one considers further that according to 1 Peter 2:9, all Christians are priests (a royal priesthood) with direct access to God. We are no longer under a covenant whereby we need an outside priest to intervene for us, to make sacrifices for our sins, one of the main functions of a priest, as was the case in the Old Testament.

The topic of sin and the forgiveness thereof by an Orthodox bishop or priest deserves a bit more attention. The Scriptures have given Christians several ways to deal with sin and none involves clergy in the way the Orthodox suggest, they rather specify that as Christians, as "priests" ourselves, we are first and foremost to go directly to our Father in heaven with all of our prayers, including requests for forgiveness of sin; and to do so through our Lord Jesus Christ (John 14:6). When Jesus tore the curtain between the Holy and Most Holy place in the Temple at His death, He created that direct access to the Father for His people, His church, in prayer.

One way to approach God with our forgiveness requests was explained by Jesus, who instructed us how to pray, not through another priest, but directly to the Father, in Matthew 6: 9-13, "Our Father in heaven, Hallowed be Your name. Your kingdom come, Your will be done On earth as it is in heaven." First, we are to praise our most Holy Father in heaven, acknowledging His Holiness and our desire to be subject to His will in all things. "Give us this day our daily bread. And forgive us our debts, As we forgive our debtors." [Jesus would later clarify this last point, that we ask forgiveness on the condition we also forgive those who sin against us (verses 14 and 15)]. "And do not lead us into temptation, But deliver us from the evil one." The praises offered in verses 9 and 10 are followed by our petitions, including our supplication (or begging) for forgiveness of our sins. "For Yours is the kingdom and the power and the glory forever. Amen." Additional praise acknowledging His omnipotence follows our petitions to conclude this suggested or model prayer of Jesus.

Another avenue Christians have to deal with sin, according to Scripture, involves going to our brother or sister to both confess our trespasses and to pray for one another. This doesn't guarantee forgiveness without God's intervention; however, it does lead to "healing" and "availing us much." James confirms this, "Confess your trespasses to one another, and pray for one another, that you may be healed. The effective, fervent prayer of a righteous man avails much." (James 5:16). That would not only include an elder of the church (verse 14), but the faithful Christian as well. Jesus also stated a similar idea to those of His body in Matthew 18:15–20; here our Lord tells us that if a brother sins against another brother, the one sinned against is to go to the sinner alone—just the two of them—to talk it out, and "if he hears you, you have gained your brother." (Verse 15). If this doesn't work, the next step is to take one or two brothers with you to the sinner as witnesses to discuss the situation further. And if all else fails, we are to bring the matter before the entire church, which, if he refuses even to listen to the church, we must disfellowship him. (Matthew 18:17).

If the Orthodox clergy alone have Christ's sanction, as not only His ambassador but as the exclusive embodiment or manifestation of Christ Himself, to hear and deal with sin effectively on behalf of His people, the church (e.g., sacrament of penance), why doesn't this passage mention clergy? The taking of two or three witnesses (ordinary Christians) to verify the situation and, as a last step, communicating to the church at large (the communion of saints or Christians, also no mention of clergy, although elders may be included here as part of the church) speaks volumes as to each Christian's worth before God—and at the same time to the inconsistency of this Orthodox sacrament of Holy Orders.

The Orthodox Church's belief in apostolic succession (the root cause of all above contentions) to continue "until the establishment of God's kingdom in eternity" violates Scripture on two levels. The first we've already addressed, as false due to apostolic gifts being ended shortly following the first century; the second, concerning the establishment of God's kingdom in the future – this is discounted by such passages as Luke 9:27, where Jesus states there are some standing with Him "who shall not taste death till they see the kingdom of God." In Luke 17:21, Jesus tells the Pharisees, "The kingdom of God is within you." In Acts 28:23 and 31, Paul testifies and preaches about the kingdom. Revelation 1:6 reveals, "He (Jesus) has made us (Christians), to be a kingdom, priests to His God and Father" (NASB), and 1 Corinthians 15:24 says, "Then comes the end, when He (Jesus) delivers the kingdom to God the Father." All these passages confirm that Christ's church—His people—are, in fact, the kingdom of God, which was established in the first century on Pentecost, around AD 33 (not a "kingdom to come" at the end of time, something we would look forward to in heaven), emphasizing the importance of all Christians, not just a special few.

Once the main tenet of a denomination—in this case, apostolic succession—can be dismissed, the entire structure of that denomination falls. It bears repeating here that if we understand that this tenet of apostolic succession is false and nonapplicable, it erases the foundation upon which many of their sacraments are based—especially this one. As mentioned, the sacrament itself, holy orders, specifically presents the idea that bishops maintain this special standing. It also puts into perspective the overall relationship of clergy and laity, at least as the Roman Catholic and the Orthodox Churches have structured it, with an un-Scriptural separation of those who see themselves as supernaturally empowered to lead and those who are not.

Monasticism

Meteora Greek Monastery
Orthodox Mountain, Greece

Most Orthodox Christians are expected to participate in at least some ascetic works in response to Matthew 16:24 (and elsewhere): "If anyone desires to come after Me, let him deny himself, and take up his cross, and follow Me." Fasting; helping the needy, either through sacrificial giving of one's finances or time; and perhaps periodic missionary work are examples that come to mind. Though laypeople are not expected to live in extreme asceticism, those who choose to do so separate themselves from the world as monastics (monks or nuns), usually residing in remote areas within monasteries.

Monasticism started back in the third and fourth centuries. Most individuals who made this decision committed themselves to lives that were completely devoted to God in a state of "permanent prayer." [68.] They remain unmarried, so as not to be distracted, and they either lived in monasteries under common rule as hermits (Eremitic monks), or they elected to live a more communal (cenobitic) monastic lifestyle, in which two or more monks shared group living arrangements under their own rules with a bit less structure but with liturgical and corporate worship as part of their communal life.

Though Christians are not to conform to this world (Romans 12:1–2), we are not to be completely excluded from it; otherwise, how would others be saved through us? Consider the following from the Words of our Lord: "You are the light of the world. A city that is set on a hill cannot be hidden. Nor do they light a lamp and put it under a basket, but on a lampstand, and it gives light to all who are in the house. Let your light so shine before men, that they may see your good works and glorify your Father in heaven" (Matthew 5:14–16).

Also, Paul says to the Corinthians that while we are not to have fellowship with the world's sinful practices (Ephesians 5:11; 1 Peter 4:4), we cannot isolate ourselves from the world either. We are not to "go out of the world" (1 Corinthians 5:9–10).

The main point here is that Christians are not to isolate themselves from others. Jesus intermingled with sinners to turn them to God. By this example, we should do likewise.

Veneration of Saints and Icons

The Orthodox Church teaches that the congregation of the church is composed of both the living and the dead, and prayers for both are encouraged—even demanded. They claim that the Jews offered such prayers, as referenced in the Apocrypha (2 Maccabees 12), along with further references in the New Testament, such as, "Praying always with all prayer and supplication … for all the saints" (Ephesians 6:18). Paul said, speaking of Onesiphorus, "The Lord grant to him that he may find mercy from the Lord in that Day—and you know very well how many ways he ministered to me at Ephesus" (2 Timothy 1:18). It is asserted that since Paul was praying to the Lord for mercy on behalf of Onesiphorus at the time of "that day," assumed to be judgment day, he must have passed away prior to this petition. [69.]

All members of the Orthodox Church who have passed from this life and are claimed to be in heaven are considered saints, but there are also "Saints of Distinction," whom Orthodoxy claim are revered by God and must be recognized and venerated (shown respect and love but not necessarily worshipped, as God alone is to be worshipped). These saints, owing to their exemplary teachings or faithful lives, are officially recognized in celebrations of glorification by the church, whereby days are named in their honor, hymns usually are composed, and icons are created to commemorate the holiness of these individuals. As a result, many "saints" are celebrated by the church each and every day of the year.

In addition to prayers of the living offered on behalf of the dead, to better their outcome as they await the general, or final, judgment in what Orthodoxy calls the "intermediate state," prayers are also offered through saints as intercessory prayers. This is due to a belief that the holiness in the life of a saint may be accessed to assist in the salvation of others, as well as us. "Father [sic]" [13.] John Breck makes this comment: "We can and we must pray for them (those who have preceded us in death), for their salvation and for our own. We pray for them and request their intercession for the same reason the Church has always offered that prayer: because even now we are united with them in the eternal bond we know as "the communion of saints." [69.]

Of all the saints the Orthodox Church recognizes and reveres, the Virgin Mary and John the Baptist are considered the closest in perfection to Jesus Himself and therefore are the perfect intercessors on behalf of all humanity. Mary is recognized as not having committed sin, and many claim John the Baptist was exempt from sin as well.

Whereas John the Baptist is elevated to perfection as a result of the Lord's statement in Matthew 11:11, Mary, the mother of God—given the name Theotokos, meaning "birth-giver of God"—is said to have been given absolution from original sin by Gabriel. For the balance of her life, although she was a human being, she could have sinned but chose not to. The Orthodox Church also teaches that Mary remained forever a virgin and was assumed bodily into heaven. [70.]

"Father [sic]"[13.] Vladimir Berzonsky, OCA, in an article titled "Thoughts in Christ—Deesis," stated that high on the icon screen we find our Lord and Savior, Jesus Christ. On one side, we see the Virgin Mary, and on the other side we see St. John the Baptist, the "greatest who had been born of women." These two, who are nearer to perfection than any other people on earth, "passed through their times on earth without being affected by all the wiles of Satan." And though many insist it's impossible not to sin throughout life, these two are proof positive it is possible. Though we "lesser Christians" who have sinned and have been forgiven also pray for others, who but the prayers of the "perfect" could be counted "worthy as intercessors on behalf of all Christians and all humanity"? [71.]

Though icons are not to be considered idols or objects of worship, per the Seventh Ecumenical Council, the Orthodox Church teaches that once Christ became human, He was able to be depicted, and it is justified to hold in one's mind an image of God incarnate. This is one of Orthodoxy's strongest arguments in favor of remembering our Lord in this way. They call this the Christological argument, and any repudiation against this idea "is tantamount to a denial of the mystery of the incarnation." [72.] It's claimed that not only our Lord, but any revered individual (such as the Virgin Mary, John the Baptist, or Peter) may be depicted, and although wood or paint form the image, it's the "person it represents" we venerate. Icons are filled with symbolism, and Orthodoxy insists upon a prescribed method for how the person should be depicted (regarding body position, clothing, hairstyle, and the like). They claim that justification for this, in part, goes back to early Christian reverence for the dead, when Christians even offered the Eucharist on their graves. Icons often adorn the walls of churches, covering the inside structure completely, and most Orthodox homes have an area set aside for family prayer that includes many icons, usually along an east-facing wall.

Orthodox Prayer Wall

Iconoclasm, or the argument against the veneration of images or icons, is said to have been settled by the Seventh Ecumenical Council of 787. Iconoclasts suggested that such things as the divinity of Christ could not be depicted or represented in art of any kind without lapsing into idolatry, and veneration of the Lord's icon was nothing less than idolatrous worship of inanimate wood and paint, which is strictly forbidden in Scripture. The council disagreed in an article by the Greek Orthodox Archdiocese of America titled "The Iconoclastic Crises": "This seemingly cogent argument, however, did not convince the Fathers of the Seventh Council." [72.] This was discussed under a similar heading for Catholicism earlier; the argument is the same, with Orthodoxy claiming that the wood and paint of the icon constitute only a "symbol" of the entity depicted: "Icons are only 'relatively venerated' since the true object of veneration is ultimately the person imaged or depicted in the icon, not the image itself." This article then argues, "A clear distinction must indeed be drawn between veneration (proskynesis timelike) by which an icon should be honored, and worship (latria), which belongs alone to God." [72.]

Icon of The of Virgin Mary with Jesus
(The Theotokos of Vladimir)

Finally, one of Orthodoxy's strongest arguments in favor of this veneration is what they call the Christological argument, the supposed permission granted us, owing to the incarnation of our Lord, to depict Him pictorially or in any other art form we choose and the notion that any repudiation to doing so "is tantamount to a denial of the mystery of the incarnation." [72.]

The Orthodox Cross (as displayed within or as part of their building architecture, as well as iconic depictions of the cross) is usually ornamented with a single crossbar of either a budded, Jerusalem, or Celtic design. Some, however, carry special significance, such as the tri-bar cross, with a small and larger crossbar near the top and a slanted bar near the bottom of the cross. The smaller top crossbar represents the sign that Pilate nailed above Christ's head, reading "Jesus of Nazareth, King of the Jews"; the larger bar, just beneath, positioned the outstretched hands; and the slanted bottom bar represents the platform the crucified used to support their weight (until their legs were broken). The slant is said to depict Christ's extreme agony and suffering, as well as to signify the thief on Christ's right (as the bar is raised), who chose the correct path (unlike the thief on His left).

Three-Bar Cross

The justification for prayers to and through the dead focus most specifically on a reference in the Apocrypha; as discussed with regard to the

Roman Catholics, this is not inspired Scripture and cannot be used as such. The New Testament references, both Ephesians 6:18 and 2 Timothy 1:18, do not give license to interpret "the dead saints," as referenced here. Concerning 2 Timothy 1:18 – Paul's praying that the Lord have mercy on Onesiphorus in that Day – is simply stating a desire for forgiveness and mercy for the man, when that Day arrives – there is no justification to leap to the conclusion that Onesiphorus is already dead at this time, because of Paul's request.

Concerning their "Saints of Distinction," nowhere in Scripture are we admonished to revere others who have passed on in this way (celebrating special days, creating hymns and icons to venerate them, asking for intercessory help). Certainly, we are to learn from what Scripture reveals to us about the great heroes of faith in both the Old and New Testaments, recognizing that the Words we read are actually God's inspired Words, but we are not to hold certain individuals up as sinless and to pray for intercession through them. Instead, we are admonished to pray for the Holy Spirit's intercession, according to Scripture (see Romans 8:26–27), to help us find the right words to approach our God. We are not to depend on the righteous acts of other human beings for help.

In addition, Christians are all saints according to Scripture as we discussed earlier, and though we are not to think too highly of ourselves (see Luke 17:10), we are extremely valuable to God without these distinctions – all Christians. Passages such as 1 Corinthians 3:16 remind Christians that they are holy temples to God, and Ephesians 3:17–19 indicates that all saints may be "filled with all the fullness of God." And again, Matthew 18:12 emphasizes the importance to God of each individual. These passages do not align with the Orthodox teaching of "lesser Christians."

Though Mary, the mother of Jesus (she was never the "mother of God" [73]), and John the Baptist were great examples of faithful Christians in Scripture, they were not sinless. One cannot get around Romans 3:23 ("For all have sinned and fall short of the glory of God") and 1 John 1:8 ("If we say that we have no sin, we deceive ourselves, and the truth is not in us"). In addition, Mary states in Luke 1:46–47: "My soul magnifies the Lord, and my spirit has rejoiced in God my Savior." If Mary were sinless, why did she need a Savior? With regard to the claim that Mary remained forever a virgin and was assumed bodily into heaven, the Scriptures disagree again. As mentioned, Matthew 13:55–56 speaks clearly that Jesus had at least four brothers and more than one sister; in addition, there is no mention that Mary was assumed bodily into heaven.

Concerning icons, Christians are not to venerate idols (1 John 5:21; Acts 17:29). An argument is presented above, insisting that the image of the icon is what we should venerate, not the wood or paint it is displayed on, and the incarnation (where God became visible) gives us the license to create such images - Scriptures do not agree. In addition, recall that the word "venerate" actually means "to worship" and not just "to honor." Even if there were some distinction to the theologians, who tell themselves these are completely different connotations, God calls bowing down to an image a *sin*. In addition, who's to say the person, or someone else witnessing, is differentiating between the two?

The Veneration / Worship of Mary

Many activities in which we, as humans, engage may drift into idolatry if we're not careful. Paul warns of this in Colossians 3:5: "Therefore put to death your members which are on the earth: fornication, uncleanness, passion, evil desire, and covetousness, which is idolatry." Here even desires and emotions without form are called idolatrous. As for venerating Orthodox icons, who is to say that weaker or lesser Christians, as mentioned above, will always be able to make the distinction between an image and an object? Even inappropriate passion is dangerous here.

This doesn't mean we cannot picture people or events from the Scriptures in our minds. Aren't we to picture the event of our Lord's death on the cross each week during the Lord's Supper? Did Paul not warn us that to not focus on Jesus during Communion was essentially partaking of our Lord in an "unworthy manner" (1 Corinthians 11:27–29)? This, however, is not the same as venerating an object or image within an icon made by human hands.

Many icons of Jesus have been created, portraying Him in all manner of compassionate, attractive ways. This ignores the admonition given in Isaiah 53:2–3, which states, "He has no form or comeliness; and when we see Him, There is no beauty that we should desire Him." Our Lord obviously wanted us to remember Him by His words, His teachings, and certainly by His death for us, but not for His physical appearance, which these icons cannot help but to encourage.

Fasting

Fasting, as practiced by the devout Orthodox Christian, and as set by prescribed guidelines of the Orthodox calendar, can involve nearly a six-month process at certain levels of strictness. The Orthodox Church has institutionalized fasting in several doctrines, including the church's Typicon and the "divine books" of Menaia and Triodion. These sources outline fasting for the Orthodox Christian, to some degree, on every Wednesday and Friday throughout the year (except fast-free periods), the periods of Great Lent, the Nativity Fast, the Apostles' Fast, and the Dormition Fast, along with September 14 (the Exaltation of the Cross) and August 29 (the beheading of the forerunner).

The main benefits of fasting, according to Orthodox teaching, involve both personal gain in one's spiritual devoutness and preparation for major events during the church's liturgical year, such as the Lenten season and, more often, the Eucharist. According to Orthodoxy, fasting "purges toxins from the body, facilitates prayer, helps control various passions and temptations, and encourages solidarity with the poor … Its basic purpose, however, is to prepare us for the feast that follows (the Eucharist). We abstain from food before we receive Holy Communion, not simply to empty the belly, but to create a hunter for the true Eucharist, the Heavenly Banquet prepared for us from before the world's foundation." [74.]

Though Orthodox tradition maintains fasting should be balanced with moderation, particularly with regard to hardships among those with medical conditions, the elderly, and the like, dietary restrictions can be rigorous for those willing and able to participate. The Typicon, for instance, gives a full listing of what is and is not allowed to be consumed during certain fast days; for instance, fasting for Great Lent and the Dormition Fast allows wine and oil only on Saturdays and Sundays (except for a few feast days and vigils).

An individual's dedication in observing these fasts is said to be a personal communication between the Orthodox Christian and God, not to be judged by the community (Romans 14:1–4). Almsgiving and repentance, along with prayer and fasting, are considered pillars of the personal spiritual practices of the Orthodox Christian. Almsgiving, in particular, is important during fasting, at which time the individual is expected to share his or her monetary savings with those in need.

Fasting, as the Scriptures present it, generally means going without food in order to better spend time in prayer and devotion to God. Fasting was a requirement under the Jewish law as a Day of Atonement, once a year, per Leviticus 16:29–31 and 23:32. In addition, we see several instances of extended fasting done ahead of a special event; for instance, in the Old Testament, Moses fasted forty days and nights prior to receiving the engraving of the Ten Commandments (Exodus 34:28), and in the New Testament, Jesus fasted forty days prior to being tempted in the wilderness by Satan (Matthew 4:1ff).

We also see that the Pharisees practiced fasting twice a week (Luke 18:12), but in many cases, they did so "to be seen of men" and were thus condemned by Jesus accordingly (Matthew 6:16). That said, fasting was accepted and did have value, for Jesus went on to instruct His disciples as follows: "But you, when you fast, anoint your head and wash your face, so that you do not appear to men to be fasting, but to your Father who is in the secret place; and your Father who sees in secret will reward you openly" (Matthew 16:17–18).

In Matthew 9:14, when some who had been baptized by John asked Jesus why they and the Pharisees fasted often, and His disciples did not, Jesus, as He often did, answered a question with a question: "Can the friends of the bridegroom mourn as long as the bridegroom is with them? But the days will come when the bridegroom will be taken away from then, and then they will fast" (Matthew 9:15). This introduces another aspect of fasting—mourning. In this case, Jesus was answering them that at this time, they had no reason to fast (mourn), as He was with them, but a time was coming when He would not be with them, at which point fasting or mourning would be appropriate.

The Orthodox view—observing fast days on all Wednesdays and Fridays, along with additional days ahead of special events—aligns very closely to the Pharisaical practices of the first century. Fasting, in and of itself, is not wrong, but the extent to which the Orthodox Church has institutionalized this practice—setting special days to observe, along with withholding specific foods or drink—are human-made rules, not Scriptural guidelines.

In addition, the fasting requirement prior to partaking of the Lord's Supper is another Orthodox mandate not seen in Scripture. In fact, what we do see in the early church is a fellowship meal taking place just prior to or in close association with the observance of the Lord's Supper. Paul's condemnation of some of the Corinthians was made with regard to their not sharing food or drink in that common meal with others and then abusing the supper with an improper attitude, perhaps not separating the two or not truly focusing on Jesus's death during the Communion (1 Corinthians 11:17ff).

The comment above: "We abstain from food before we receive Holy Communion, not simply to empty the belly, but to create a hunter for the true Eucharist, the Heavenly Banquet prepared for us from before the world's foundation", is totally inappropriate. The Lord's Supper is not a source to satisfy 'hunger' – Jesus said "Take, eat, this is My body which is broken for you; do this (not to satisfy your hunger, but) in remembrance of Me." He also said: "This cup is the new covenant in My blood. This do, as often as you drink it, (not to satisfy your hunger or thirst, but) in remembrance of Me." (1 Corinthians 11:24-25). Jesus instituted a memorial, a symbolic action of partaking of a piece of bread and swallow of wine – to remember Him - to symbolize His upcoming suffering and death on the cross – totally separate from "fasting".

Though fasting does have some merit, it can be abused. This was one of the items Paul advised Timothy on with regard to the original departure from the Lord's church: "In … later times some will depart from the faith … forbidding to marry, and commanding to abstain from foods which God created" (1 Timothy 4:1–3).

These prophecies came to fruition with the Catholics in 1015, prior to the split from the Eastern Orthodox Church in 1054, when abstaining from eating meat on Fridays and especially during Lent and on Ash Wednesday was established, following the mandates of the Second Vatican Council.

Church Building and Services

Holy Trinity – St. Nicholas Greek Orthodox Church Cincinnati, Ohio – Eastern Wall - Iconostasis

Orthodox Church buildings are usually constructed in either a cross-shaped or rectangular design. The cross-shaped design symbolizes the crucifixion while facilitating larger choirs (positioned as "left and right choirs" within the worship area). The rectangular design is symbolic of Noah's ark, for which it is said, "The church brings us through the stormy sea of life to the calm haven of the Kingdom of Heaven." [75.]

The church interior is divided into three main parts:

1. The Narthex, or vestibule, where non-Orthodox visitors (catechumens) stand during services.
2. The Nave, the large central area, where the faithful of the congregation (those having been baptized and confirmed through chrismation into the Orthodox faith) gather for worship. Most of the buildings in the United States have pews, but some follow the old custom of having no seats, and the faithful stand only. On either side of the nave are often spaces for the choir, and on the left side of the nave is the bishop's throne, from which he presides as a living icon of Christ to his people.
3. The sanctuary is separated from the Nave at the eastern end by an icon-covered screen (iconostasis), raised several steps, and has a central entry called "the Royal Doors" or "The Beautiful Gate," which only the clergy may pass through. On either side of these doors is another set of doors within the screen, through which deacons may pass. Only clergy, deacons, and specially blessed faithful are allowed to enter the sanctuary.

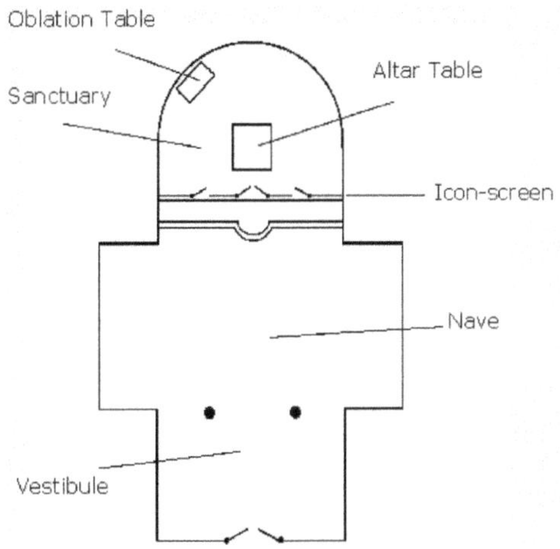

The raised area that extends several feet in front of the iconostasis screen into the nave is called the "Solea." The area immediately in front of the royal doors is considered a sacred space; it's called the

"Ambon," or "place of ascending." This space represents the Judgement Seat, where the faithful come to receive the Holy Mysteries (communion), and it is believed they must give an account for their reception of this communion at the Judgment. This is also the area where deacons intone the litanies and read the Gospels and where priests deliver sermons.

Orthodox Christians consider their church buildings to be holy places where the visitors (catechumen) cannot venture farther than the Narthex or vestibule area, and the members or laity stand (or sit on pews) within the Nave.

This general configuration is fashioned after the Jewish temple, with the focal point being the altar within the sanctuary. The altar, including all articles on or around this table, is considered sacred, and no one other than clergy are permitted to even touch these holy articles, which is reminiscent of the Holy of Holies within the Old Testament temple.

Serbian Orthodox Mass

Orthodox Church services are usually conducted daily in monasteries and cathedrals and on weekends and major feast days within parish or local churches, with Divine Liturgy (similar to the Catholic Mass) being their prominent service on Sundays. Their services follow a rigid protocol yet contain elements that change according to the day and time of year.

Daily services follow the liturgical day (from Jewish roots), which begin at sundown and adhere to The Daily Cycles of Prayer. Aspects of these services include the following:

- Vespers (in Greek, "*Hesperinos*," meaning "sundown"), the beginning of the liturgical day.
- Compline (in Greek, "*Apodeipon*," meaning "after supper"), after the evening meal, prior to bedtime.
- Matins (in Greek, "*Orthros*"), the first service of the morning, usually starting before sunrise.
- Midnight Office, or Nocturne, at midnight
- Hours: first, third, sixth, and ninth; sung either at their appropriate times or in aggregate at other customary times of convenience (If the latter, the first hour is sung immediately following orthros, the third and sixth prior to the divine liturgy, and the ninth prior to vespers.)
- Divine Liturgy, the Eucharist service (usually observed between the sixth and ninth hours), held by monasteries and all local parishes.

This daily cycle of services consists of readings from the Psalter, including prayers and hymns surrounding them. Orthodox services are sung nearly in their entirety, consisting of dialogue between the clergy and people (often represented by the choir), which is sung or chanted following a prescribed musical form.

Another aspect of Orthodox worship, revealing formality, is the elaborate "sacred vestments" and other attire required to be worn by the clergy (bishops, priests, deacons, subdeacons) during all services. These coverings are specially designed for each tier of clergy and must be "blessed" before they are put on. For instance, the priest must bless the vestments of the deacons and subdeacons, and he, himself, before vesting, must turn to the High Place and make three reverences before putting on his own vestments. Following are additional items worn exclusively by the bishop:

At all times, as part of his normal attire and for services, the bishop wears a *panagia* around his neck in addition to a cross. The panagia, which means 'all-holy' in Greek, is a small, round icon of the Saviour or the Theotokos, sometimes adorned with precious stones. When serving, the bishop wears a *miter* on his head, adorned with small icons and precious stones. Some say it signifies the crown of thorns which was placed on the head of the Saviour, others, that it represents the Gospel of Christ to which the bishop always remains subject ... During the Divine services, the bishops use a staff as a sign of ultimate pastoral authority." [76.]

Russian Orthodox Church Interior - Moscow

The Divine Liturgy, or Orthodox Mass, is conducted on the Lord's Day, Sunday, and on certain feast days, and daily in most monasteries. It is defined as "The common action of Orthodox Christians officially gathered to constitute the Orthodox Church. It is the action of the Church assembled by God in order to be together in one community to worship, to pray, to sing, to hear God's Word, to be instructed in God's commandments, to offer itself with thanksgiving in Christ to God the Father, and to have the living experience of God's eternal kingdom through communion with the same Christ Who is present in his people by the Holy Spirit." [77.]

Seventeen procedures, or protocols, are followed in Divine Liturgy and strictly held; these include Prothesis, Blessed is the Kingdom, Great Litany, Antiphons, Small Entrance, Epistle, Gospel, Fervent Supplication,

Offertory: Great Entrance, Love and Faith, Eucharistic Canon: Anaphora, Epiklesis, Remembrances, Our Father, Communion, Thanksgiving, and Benediction and Dismissal. These procedures all have reference to just one aspect of Orthodox worship—Divine Liturgy or Holy Mass (Communion). To give the reader a greater sense of what transpires at the heart of this liturgy, following is a brief description of nine of these acts. For explanations of what takes place within all seventeen, refer to the OCA online publication "The Orthodox Faith, Volume II—Worship: The Divine Liturgy." [78.]

The initial act of Divine Liturgy is called the Prothesis, which involves the preparation of the Eucharistic bread and wine that will be used in this liturgy. The priest cuts the specially prepared loaf of bread, called the prosphora, or "the Lamb," into four pieces, also piercing it with a knife or "spear" while reciting John 19:34–35, and places it on the *diskos*, or elevated platter. He then pours wine mixed with water into a chalice—symbolic of both Christ's spilling both water and blood at the cross from His side, and to refrain from "getting drunk" in obeyance to partaking in a worthy manner (1 Corinthians 11:27–32). Then specially cut pieces of the bread are placed on the diskos next to the Lamb—one for the Theotokos, or "mother of God," one in memory of John the Baptist, and others for prophets, apostles, hierarchs, famous saints, and the saint whose liturgy is being celebrated that day. Crumbs of bread are then taken and placed on the diskos in memory of special saints both living and dead as given to the priest for that liturgy. Finally, an aer, or cover, is placed over the chalice and bread for later use in the Communion. Special prayers are given, ending the service of prothesis.

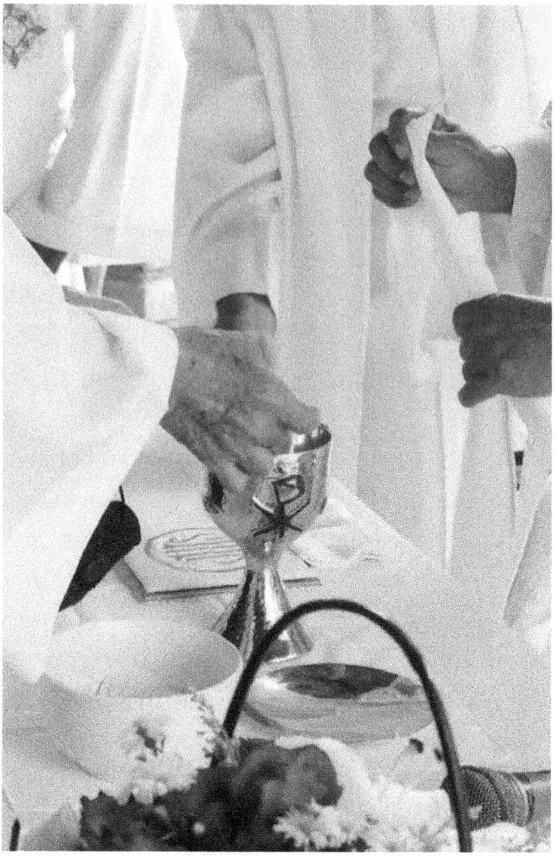

Preparing the "Gifts" for Communion
(Mixing of bread and wine)

After the prothesis and the next seven protocols encompassing the initial preparation and continued blessing of the elements of communion (bread and wine) by the clergy, the Offertory: Great Entrance takes place. Within this part of the Divine Liturgy, an offering (gifts of money for the work of the Church) is taken up, and communion participation by the faithful begins. The gifts of bread and wine are carried in solemn procession from the table of oblation into the middle of the church (Nave), and through the Royal Doors of the iconostasis, back to the altar table within the sanctuary. This procession is called the Great Entrance. In some churches, the Offertory procession of the Great Entrance is made around the entire Nave of the church building, before returning through the Royal Doors to the altar. During this portion of the service, a "censing" of the altar table, the icons, and all the people usually takes place, carried out by the priest.

Following the Great Entrance protocol, and before the Divine Liturgy can proceed further, there are two conditions that must be fulfilled by the faithful. These are the expressions of "Love and Faith." A proclamation is made from the altar for the Christians to "love one another." followed by a chanting of the symbol of Orthodox faith, their creed.

"The recitation of the Symbol of Faith at the Divine Liturgy stands as the official acknowledgment and formal acceptance by each individual member of the Church of his or her own baptism, chrismation and membership in the Body of Christ ... All through the liturgy the community prays in the plural we. Only here does each person confess for himself his own personal faith: I believe ... No person can believe for another. Each must believe for himself ... a person who affirms and accepts his baptismal membership in the Church, is competent to participate in the Divine Liturgy. A person who cannot do this, cannot participate. He simply is not able to since this specific faith is the specific requirement for membership in the Orthodox Church and for participation in its Divine Liturgy. Without this faith, the movement of the liturgy cannot proceed further. With it, and its official acknowledgment in the chanting of the Creed, the liturgical action goes on." [79.]

During the chanting of this creed, the clergy typically will fan the altar, thus venerating the book of the Gospels and the eucharistic gifts—a practice started in the Byzantine period as an act to venerate the earthly emperor, and later incorporated into the Church's liturgy as an act of veneration toward the "presence" of the Heavenly King.

Next the Eucharistic Canon: Anaphora, is given. Here the gifts of bread and wine, which have been offered on the altar, are lifted up from the altar to God the Father and receive Divine sanctification by the Holy Spirit, who comes to change them into the very body and blood of Christ. The celebrant (priest) then addresses the congregation with the Trinitarian blessing of the apostle Paul (2 Corinthians 13:14), followed by several prayers and responses by the people.

In association with the Anaphora and the "lifting of the Gifts" to the Father, a special prayer is offered by the priest in the next part of the service, called the Epiklesis.

The Anaphora (Lifting the Gifts to the Father)

"After the elevation of the eucharistic gifts to the Father, the celebrant of the Divine Liturgy prays for the Holy Spirit to come upon them, and upon all of the people, and to change (or as the Liturgy of Saint Basil says, to show) the bread and wine offered in remembrance of Christ to be the very Body and Blood of the Lord. The prayer for the coming of the Holy Spirit is considered by the Orthodox to be an essential part of Divine Liturgy. It is called the Epiklesis, which means literally the calling upon or the invocation. The Orthodox Church believes, as it prays, that the Holy Spirit is always "everywhere and fills all things" … He is the one who dwelt in Jesus making him the Christ. He is the one by whom Christ was incarnate of the Virgin Mary. He is the one who led Christ to the cross as the innocent Victim, the one who raised Him from the dead … He is the one who guarantees the indwelling of God with men in the Holy Communion of the Church and in the life of the Kingdom to come." [80.]

Following the Epiklesis, the protocol of Remembrances ensues, during which the remembrance of not only Christ but also the sacrifice of Mary and all the saints, as well as the entire church, is honored. Additional prayers are also offered, asking God to remember the city, the country, the travelers, the sick, the suffering, the captives, and the benefactors of the church, as well as remembering, by name, persons in need of special mercy from God. In addition, during this portion of the service, while the choir sings a hymn to the Theotokos (Mother of God), the celebrant censes the consecrated gifts once again while asking God to remember such saints as John the Baptist, the "saints of the day," the departed faithful, and the whole church and world in general.

Following Remembrances, Our Father is observed; here the people pray to God to allow them to worship "with one mouth and one heart." Remembering their baptism and chrismation, which allows them to approach God, they ask Him to send down His Divine grace and the gift of the Holy Spirit.

Serbian Army Col. Sasa Milutnovic Receives Communion from Bishop Irinej

Next is the observance of Communion, where the children of God come to the Ambon to receive the body and blood of Christ. Just prior to this, however, the clergy give themselves Holy Communion at the altar while the people sing. The clergy partake of the bread from the diskos and drink the consecrated wine separately and directly from the chalice. The celebrant then takes the bread, which was previously sliced during prothesis, putting a piece into the Chalice of wine and water, adding some additional hot water (symbolizing "the living character of the Risen Christ whose body and soul are reunited and filled with the Holy Spirit in the glorified life of the Kingdom of God")—this to be distributed to the people. A proclamation is then made: "Holy Things are for the holy!" All members who have been properly baptized and confirmed through chrismation are eligible, including infants, to participate in the Divine Liturgy. "Individuals approach the Holy Gifts and receive the Eucharistic bread and wine from the common chalice. The priest distributes the Holy Gifts by means of a communion spoon." [81.]

After all who desire have participated, Thanksgiving commences. Here the celebrant blesses the people with words and the chalice of the Communion, with songs and prayers of thanksgiving to follow. All parts of this service presuppose that the members of the church participate in the eucharistic mysteries and are receiving the gifts of Christ's body and blood. The Offertory: Great Entrance, the Anaphora, the Love and Faith, the Epiklesis, the Remembrances, the Our Father, the Communion, and the Benediction and Dismissal all affirm the active participation of the faithful.

Priest Censing Before Service

As mentioned, clergy often offer up incense to God during services to sanctify objects and to enhance the prayers of the faithful. As a carryover from Old Testament practice, censing shows respect for the altar and the icons within the sanctuary. When censing the laity while they are praying, it's asking God that their prayers "be heart-felt, truly reverent, and ascend to Heaven like the smoke of incense; and that the Grace of God might envelop them even as the smoke of the church." The people bow as this activity takes place.

The significance of these events to Orthodoxy cannot be overstated. Following are two comments, the first one from goarch.org:

"We knew not whether we were in heaven or on earth, for surely there is no such splendor or beauty anywhere on earth. We cannot describe it to you; we only know that God dwells there among men and that their Service surpasses the worship of all other places … These are the words the envoys uttered when they reported their presence at the celebration of the Eucharist in the Great Church of Holy Wisdom in Constantinople (latter part of the 10th century) … the profound experience … shared by many throughout the centuries who have witnessed for the first time the beautiful and inspiring Divine Liturgy of the Orthodox Church … The Orthodox Church recognizes the many facets of the Eucharist and wisely refuses to over-emphasize one element to the detriment of the others. In so doing, Orthodoxy has clearly avoided reducing the Eucharist to a simple memorial of the Last Supper which is only occasionally observed. Following the teachings of both Scripture and Tradition, the Orthodox Church believes that Christ is truly present with His people in the celebration of the Holy Eucharist. The Eucharistic gifts of bread and wine become for us His Body and His Blood." [82.]

And here is another from a San Francisco congregation:

"Once we have received Communion, we must remember that we have become one with Christ and with all those who received Communion with us. The same Christ now lives in all of us … After receiving Communion our bodies become holy chalices. God has come to live in us. His blood now flows through our veins … When we receive Communion, we become members of Christ's Body, the Church." [83.]

The New Testament does not specify church building design; in fact, it doesn't mention anything other than the instruction to God's children to be present whenever the church meets to encourage one another (Hebrews 10:24–25) and the mandate that Christians are to gather regularly on the first day of the week to worship our God (Acts 20:7), both of which suggest a building of some sort would be necessary to accommodate these gatherings. The concept that such a building is somehow holy or that God Himself resides within its walls, even without the presence of Christians—for according to Scripture, where two or three are gathered in Christ's name, He is present (Matthew 18:20)—and that this meeting place is something to be revered is also foreign to the New Testament.

The Old Testament, however, does specify much pertaining to temple worship procedures as well as furnishings. It appears the Orthodox Church (along with the Roman Catholic Church, Anglican or Episcopal Church, and others) have fashioned their worship activities and furnishings according to these Old Testament patterns.

The problem with this view, however, is that Old Testament laws, including worship procedure and articles of worship, were done away with by the coming of Christ. Paul told the Colossians, for instance, that in addition to forgiving them all their trespasses, Jesus "wiped out the handwriting of requirements (the Old Testament Law) that was against them … taken it out of the way, having nailed it to the cross" (Colossians 2:13–14). In addition, the Hebrew writer explained to those wavering Jewish Christians that the priesthood was being changed, which also necessitated a change in the law, and "Christ came as a high priest of the good things to come, with the greater and more perfect tabernacle, not made with hands." This is why He is the Mediator of a New and better Covenant, built on better promises, that by means of death, for the redemption of the sin committed under the First Covenant, those who are called may receive the promise of eternal life (Hebrews 7:12; 8:1, 6; 9:1, 11, 15).

The transfiguration account is another example of where God the Father expresses the change He desires from Old to New. While Jesus was still talking with Moses and Elijah, "suddenly a voice came out of the cloud, saying, 'This is My beloved Son, in whom I am well pleased. Hear Him!'" (Matthew 17:3–5). This indicated that Jesus was now to be followed. The age of the patriarchs and the law represented by Moses, and the age of the prophets, represented by Elijah, had passed. Finally, in Galatians 5:1–4, Paul vehemently attempted to persuade the Christians in that city not to return to the old law of Moses (including the worship laws and patterns commanded of the Jewish people under this law, warning that to do so would mean, "You have been severed from Christ, you who are seeking to be justified by law; you have fallen from grace" (Galatians 5:4 NASB). Therefore, to worship in this fashion, as Scripture indicates, puts one in jeopardy of being "severed from Christ" and "falling from grace"—in other words, losing one's soul.

"The woman said to Him, 'Sir, I perceive that You are a prophet. Our fathers worshipped on this mountain, and you Jews say that in Jerusalem is the place where one ought to worship.' Jesus said to her, 'Woman, believe Me, the hour is coming when you will neither on this mountain, nor in Jerusalem, worship the Father … the true worshippers will worship the Father in spirit and truth; for the Father is seeking such to worship Him. God is Spirit, and those who worship Him must worship in spirit and truth'" (John 4:19–24). In this passage, Jesus makes clear that the place of worship is not essential. Even I will suggest that the building is of no special significance either. Jesus is emphasizing what God the Father wants in the way of worship to Him: "spirit and truth."

In addition, the vestments and other attire as mandated be worn by Orthodox clergy indicate yet another link to Old Testament temple worship, which the Scriptures dismiss. Particularly disturbing are the panagia and the miter worn by bishops, signifying their alleged "all-holiness" status, with similarity to Christ's crown of thorns. Such outward expressions claiming near-Deity status (similar to the Roman Catholic pope), are presumptuous indeed! Passages of Scripture that seem appropriate to dismiss this include God's exclusivity to Deity (or, in this case, any confusion caused by man's claim of near-Deity), as stated in Isaiah 45:5 ("I am the Lord, and there is no other. There is no God besides Me") and in several of Jesus's woes given to the scribes and Pharisees as found in Matthew 23 ("But their works they do to be seen by men. They make their phylacteries broad and enlarge the borders of their garments. They love … to be called by men, 'Rabbi, Rabbi.' But you, do not be called 'Rabbi'; for One is your Teacher, the Christ, and you are all brethren. Do not call anyone on earth your father; for One is your Father, He who is in heaven" [verses 5–10]).

These words of Jesus admonish His followers—all His followers, including leaders and members of the church alike—to look only to Him as Teacher and to the God of heaven as Father and to view each other as simply brethren. Do you suppose a bishop and one of the laity of the Orthodox Church view themselves as spiritually equal and as "brethren," as Jesus describes above? As Jesus commands above? Do you suppose that bishop expects to be called "teacher" or "father"? There is nothing in the New Testament specifying what leaders or members are to wear when worshipping God, other than that they are to do things "decently and in order" (1 Corinthians 14:40), which suggests no inappropriate dress, among other things. Special buildings and special clothing tend to separate the clergy from the members or laity of only the Orthodox church; this goes against the above and many other passages in the New Testament.

Concerning the nine protocols of Divine Liturgy, as discussed in more detail above, most of these practices cannot be seen as having occurred within the early church, from what we read in the New Testament, and as they add to the Scriptures, they are condemned as such (Deuteronomy 12:32; Proverbs 30:6; Revelation 22:18–19). Though certain aspects of some of these protocols touch upon bona fide Scriptural acts of worship, most infuse Old Testament procedure and mankind's ideas to enhance the service, which is unwarranted.

The Prothesis, as a preparation exercise for the elements of communion, is also without merit according to Scripture. Do we see any of these detailed preparations of either the bread or the fruit of the vine in Scripture? Absolutely not. "Jesus took bread"—what bread? The unleavened bread from the table He and His disciples were at to celebrate the Passover. He simply "blessed and broke it and gave it to His disciples" (Matthew 26:26). He didn't cut a piece out for Mary or John the Baptist; He didn't memorialize any living or dead saints with it; nor did He drop pieces of bread into the cup of the fruit of the vine to "spoon" to His disciples. No, He simply broke the bread that was there and used it as a symbol, commanding them to eat it, so they would later "remember Him, remember His broken body."

In preparing for the drink, what did Jesus do? Did He mix the fruit of the vine with more water to perhaps keep the disciples from getting drunk or to symbolize His later side wound at the cross? Again, absolutely not! Jesus picked up a cup from the table, gave thanks, and gave it to them – asking simply that they drink from it. Why? That they would later "remember Him, remember His shed blood." Adding/changing these things to what Jesus commanded is just plain wrong; they amount to nothing more than man's ideas—ideas that render their worship "vain" (Matthew 15:9).

The Offertory: Great Entrance, though correctly observing the Scriptural act of giving for the work of the church, adds a second part of parading the elements of communion within the building and back through sacred doors to an altar—an activity both not seen and done away with (i.e., Old Testament sanctuary) in Scripture.

The chanting of a creed, as part of the ensuing Love and Faith protocol, is also not sanctioned by Scripture. Creeds are not authorized doctrine; they are not God's Word and should not be so honored! In addition, the mandate that each member personally acknowledge his or her belief, confessing his or her baptism, chrismation, and membership in the Orthodox body by reciting this creed, is faced with several other major problems. First and foremost, none of this has anything to do with the Lord's Supper as described in Scripture. It's adding to what God requires in worship, and during this act, it becomes a distraction to what our Lord has commanded: "Do this in remembrance of Me." The veneration of this creed by the clergy as the congregation chants, adds insult to injury. Again, show me the Scripture!

In addition, the Orthodox Church allows infants to participate in this Divine Liturgy. How, pray tell, can an infant "chant an acknowledgment of belief?" Finally concerning this protocol, the clarification is made that "No person can believe for another. Each must believe for himself … a person who affirms his baptismal membership in the Church is competent to participate in Divine Liturgy … without this specific faith, the movement of the liturgy cannot proceed further." [84.] According to these statements, an adult "sponsor" cannot be substituted here for an infant, as is usually done to accomplish cognitive requirements; and since the Divine Liturgy cannot move forward without all participants accomplishing this mandate, the service, by their own words, needs to end here if there is an infant present.

The next two protocols, the Eucharistic Canon: Anaphora, and the Epiklesis, constitute the focal point of Divine Liturgy, as they effect the supposed changing of the elements of bread and wine into the actual body and blood of Jesus. During the Anaphora, the elements are "lifted from the altar to receive the Holy Spirit," and within the Epiklesis prayer, they are supposedly transformed. Prayers and pronouncements are offered back and forth from the celebrant (clergy), with responses from the faithful during these protocols, centering around this unique experience in which contact with God is about to be made. The faithful acknowledge Jesus as their "perfect peace offering and sacrifice of praise to the Father, and their thanksgiving for sins forgiven and reception of the love and grace of God. According to this liturgy, "Through Christ and the Holy Spirit, the man of faith is transported in spirit to be with his Lord. The limitations of this age are left behind through grateful remembrance of Christ and his accomplishment of salvation."[85.] Again, this statement is false - we are to remember our Lord's death on the cross here, no more, no less.

The statement quoted from the OCA website as a further description of the Holy Spirit's role in this process, immediately following the above protocol, deserves closer scrutiny, as it contains a mixture of truth and fabrication, making it difficult, if not impossible for most to discern the difference. For instance, "He (the Holy Spirit) is the one who dwelt in Jesus making him the Christ." [86.] This statement can be argued several ways. In one sense, Jesus, as the incarnated human He had to be (Hebrews 2:17–18), was filled with the Spirit "without measure" to be able to recall the Father's Words (John 3:31). However, Jesus was also fully Divine Himself, part of the Godhead according to passages such as Colossians 2:9 ("For in Him dwells all the fullness of the Godhead bodily") and Philippians 2:6 ("Christ Jesus, who being in the form of God, did not consider it robbery to be equal with God"). These passages tell us Jesus was fully Divine, fully "Christ" in and of Himself. (The personage of Holy Spirit alone did not therefore necessarily "make" Him so.) God the Son, God the Holy Spirit, and God the Father were and have always been one.

The next statement is "He (the Holy Spirit) is the only one by whom Christ was incarnate of the Virgin Mary." [86.] No argument here; this is confirmed in Matthew 1:20. Next, "He is the one who led Christ to the cross as the innocent Victim, the one who raised Him from the dead as the triumphant Victor." [86.] This statement is too broad to categorically deny or confirm, but to dogmatically claim the Spirit was exclusively involved in both the leading and particularly the raising is denied in Scripture.

Whether the Spirit encouraged Jesus the incarnate man is certainly possible; that Jesus knew Himself, as a member of the Godhead the task set before Him, is undeniable (see Matthew 26:54–56, Mark 8:31–33). And whether the Spirit "raised Jesus from the dead," (exclusively) at least on the surface, is denied by Acts 26:8, where Paul, speaking to King Agrippa, says, "Why should it be thought incredible by you that God (*Theos*) raises the dead?" The Holy Spirit, who inspired this verse could have used "*Pneuma*" (the Greek word for Himself), however He used "*Theos*" (the Greek word for God); and though the Spirit is part of the Trinity, (God the Holy Spirit), this choice of words would indicate that the Trinity, all three within the Godhead, were involved in the resurrection of Jesus. This becomes the more probable answer, with further confirmation from the Scriptures that all Three were in fact involved. God the Father is said to have raised Jesus in Galatians 1:1-2; Jesus claims to have raised Himself in John 2:19, 21 and again in John 10:17-18; while the Holy Spirit is said to have raised Him in 1 Peter 3:18 and Romans 1:4.

It appears all these statements from Orthodoxy are being made to elevate the Spirit's role in the Godhead (i.e., the Spirit alone dwelt in Jesus, making Him the Christ, the Spirit led Jesus to the cross, the Spirit raised Him from the dead, etc.) in an attempt to justify their claim that in this Epiklesis, the Spirit's role expands again – this time to miraculously change the elements of bread and wine within the Eucharist into the actual body and blood of Jesus. The more plausible answer as to "who raised Jesus" however, is the Godhead – all three personages per the above.

The crux, at least concerning the protocol of Epiklesis, comes in the final statement describing the role of the Spirit: "He is the one who guarantees the indwelling of God with men in the Holy Communion of the Church and in the life of the Kingdom to come." [86.] This statement is incorrect concerning both claims. First, the holy mystery, or transubstantiation—the idea that the elements of bread and wine actually turn into the body and blood of Christ—has already been disproved. And secondly, the "kingdom of God" is not "to come" - the kingdom of God **has** come. The kingdom of God is Christ's church, as Jesus Himself said "But I tell you truly, there are some standing here (around A.D. 30-33)[8] who will not taste death till they see the kingdom of God." (Luke 9:27). (The kingdom of God, Christ's church, was established at Pentecost, shortly following Jesus's crucifixion, and ascension into heaven.) Other passages confirming the kingdom has come include Acts 28:23, 31; 1 Corinthians 15:24; Revelation 1:5–6; and Matthew 16:28.

The Orthodox protocols of Remembrances and Our Father are next. These are essentially prayers of remembrance, offered to God by the faithful not only on behalf of Christ but also for the sacrifice of the Virgin Mary, John the Baptist, the saints of the day, and the departed faithful, as well as what one would normally pray for: one's community, those traveling, the sick, and so on. The Our Father adds personal prayers for one's baptism and chrismation into the mix. None of these protocols (Remembrances or Our Father) belong within this act of worship, observance of the Lord's Supper, what should be a remembrance of our Lord, period! I would go so far as to say it falls under the condemnation of Paul's warning in 1 Corinthians 11:27 and following, where the Corinthians were taking the Supper in an unworthy manner—here, one's focus on Christ is being compromised by numerous additional "remembrances" by Orthodoxy.

The time for Communion has finally arrived; here the faithful come to the Ambon, or the space in front of the "Beautiful Gate," to be served by the clergy. As described, before the clergy offer Communion to the people, they serve themselves at the altar within the sanctuary. They partake of the consecrated bread first, directly from the diskos plate, then drink the consecrated wine, unmixed, from the chalice. Afterward, they bring the Communion elements, or "gifts," out to the people—but before serving them, they dilute the wine and water with additional hot water and mix the bread pieces into the chalice as well, to offer a single element—the body and blood together—to the masses, usually on a spoon.

There is nothing about this portion of their liturgy that can be sanctioned, when compared with God's Word. We've discussed many times the incorrect separation of clergy and laity brought about by "apostolic succession," and here again, it becomes abundantly clear. Nothing in Scripture allows the clergy to serve themselves first with elements different from those offered the people. In addition, nothing about the elements themselves is according to God's Word: the extensive preparation, the consecration—nothing. In addition, I discussed earlier the inconsistencies with "prothesis"; here, the mixing of the elements becomes an additional problem.

Recall the discussion with the Roman Catholic Church in Chapter 3 of Volume 1 in this series, concerning this issue. The Catholic Church approves of partaking of the elements in three ways: separately, dipping the bread into the wine and taking it (intinction), or taking only one element or species (bread or wine) to suffice for both. The Orthodox have two sets of standards: one for the clergy, where separation is observed, and one for the laity, where a mixture of bread, water, and wine is offered as a single element. The clergy are doing a disservice to their people! This is not what Jesus commanded; this is man's idea, not God's. Here's why (as if we need a reason other than Jesus's example): each element has a separate meaning, as Jesus pointed out. The bread represents His body; it needs to be consumed separately. Jesus didn't say it was fine to mix His blood (the wine) with the bread and consume them together as "His body and blood," did He? And the fruit of the vine needs to be taken alone; it represents His blood. We can't mix it with anything; otherwise, it loses the impact Jesus was trying to impart to us! Also, Jesus commanded we "take, eat the bread" and "drink from the cup"; how can the Orthodox Christian properly "eat" off that spoon? How can they properly "drink" off that spoon? The eating and drinking evoke specific emotions, and specific thoughts, that differ as we consume each individually in order to properly contemplate the cross and Jesus's sacrifice on that cross as He intended. Again, how can one do honor to these emotions, these thoughts if we short-circuit the process by combining bread and fruit of the vine? When combined, are we to "eat" by drinking and "drink" by chewing?

Jesus offered these elements to His disciples separately, did He not? Are we not to follow His example? There's a difference when one consumes bread alone. To remember Jesus's broken body on the cross, we consume the bread, thinking of that broken body, undefiled by any other substance. Likewise, there's a difference when we consume the fruit of the vine alone; we remember the blood issuing from Jesus's hands, feet, head, and side on the cross, undefiled by anything else. I've discussed this before; all of our five senses come into play when we put those elements into our mouths separately. They all help us "remember Him." We lose this when we mix them. Do you suppose God, in His wisdom, knew this would be an effective way for us to remember Him? Do you suppose changing God's plan for a perfect remembrance like this is a good idea?

Perhaps the reason the Orthodox (and others) have invented other practices for observing the Lord's Supper, than what our Lord commanded, can be found in the statement above by the Greek Orthodox Archdiocese of America: "The Orthodox Church recognizes the many facets of the Eucharist and wisely refuses to over-emphasize one element to the detriment of the others. In so doing, Orthodoxy has clearly avoided reducing the Eucharist to a simple memorial of the Last Supper which is only occasionally observed." [82.] Is not the example of the Last Supper where Jesus showed us, even commanded us concerning what He expected and how He wanted us to observe the Communion? And the "occasionally observed" comment, is man's weakness and error – Scripture clearly tells us we are to observe the Supper on the "first day of every week" (Acts 20:7), not 'occasionally', as unfortunately, many denominations have done and continue to do even to this day.

One other thing to consider here is that the Orthodox (and others we've looked at) have so elevated these elements of communion, the bread and fruit of the vine, as to "sanctify" or "consecrate" them—set them apart as holy articles—not even allowing one to "touch" them. They absolutely are not, nor were they ever meant to be, set apart! The Orthodox, along with the Catholics, have missed the whole point here. The elements are nothing more than symbols Jesus commanded us to use to remember Him in a special way. This of course ties in with Orthodox belief in transubstantiation, which we've previously refuted; Jesus is coming back, but not by way of man's calling. By changing this command of our Lord and making the elements themselves a focus of holiness, drawing people's admiration and awe to the means of remembrance, rather than the remembrance itself, they've added man's doctrine and they've changed the worship God desires to a worship of man's design—in direct violation of His Word—making such worship vain (Matthew 15:8–9).

Following Communion, a special period of Thanksgiving takes place, during which the priest blesses the people, and prayers and songs ensue.

In summary, Orthodox worship services follow a template of Old Testament temple worship, honoring their buildings as holy ground and their clergy as all-holy priests, following age-old practices—most having been done away with by New Testament teaching. The focal point of their service is the Eucharist meal, and even this has been altered from a simple memorial of remembering Jesus's death on the cross, as He commanded be observed weekly on Sunday, to a supposed "union with God" through elements "changed by the Spirit" at the bequest of a priest—a false doctrine that seems to have totally enthralled both clergy and parishioner alike. It's not where or through whom we worship our God that matters, it's how we worship Him. Do we "hear Him" (Matthew 17:5)? Jesus told the woman at the well (and us) that God desires we worship Him in "spirit and truth." Apparently, the Orthodox Church has abandoned both imperatives by ignoring Christ's instructions as recorded in the New Testament.

Questions to Consider

With regard to the Orthodox Church, the three questions posed at the end of our discussion of the Roman Catholic Church apply here as well: Can we have confidence in the accuracy of the sixty-six books of scripture? Can these books be understood by all men and women today? And what do these Scriptures have to say concerning the doctrines taught by this denomination?

Though many Scriptures have been highlighted throughout each Chapter to refute denominational error on a point-by-point basis, there seems to exist within each a main point or two of departure from God's Word specific to that denomination. Addressing these points convincingly will go a long way in revealing truth. In many cases, if openness of heart and mind is present, even the staunchest of denominationalists will either accept the evidence presented as credible or, at the very least, will become curious enough to investigate further, as perhaps a seed of doubt will be planted concerning previous convictions.

One of the major points of departure from God's Word in the Orthodox Church is their addition of sources of authority other than the Bible, particularly what they term "Holy Tradition." This term encompasses both the authority assumed by Orthodox clergy through apostolic succession and other authorities, including decisions and doctrines of church fathers, ecumenical councils, formulated creeds, and the like, so questions on this subject are in order. The first question to pull in apostolic succession and the authority add-ons to the Bible might be:

1). Does the Bible indicate that Jesus wanted His church today to be led by Orthodox bishops, archbishops, and patriarchs, or current-day apostles, with gifts or powers similar to the ones He imparted to His apostles in the first century? And how can Orthodoxy add authoritative documents encompassed within 'Holy Tradition' to the Bible while considering passages like 2 Timothy 3:16-17, Acts 20:27, and Jude 3?

In answering part one of this question correctly in the negative, one can reference Scriptural passages, such as Acts 14:21–23 and Titus 1:5, where we see elders appointed to each individual congregation as the leaders, without any oversight position mentioned. It follows that Jesus would not permit a contradiction to His Word (and indeed no Scripture supports one) to institute this third position for one of these elders to have additional authority over many elder-led congregations (i.e., the bishop).

The idea that apostolic gifts persisted beyond the first century via the laying on of hands from one generation to the next has been soundly refuted. As mentioned, Moises Pinedo lays out an extensive argument refuting Peter's statement in Matthew 16:18 as the basis for the Catholic papacy.[87.] The idea that authority from 'other apostles' can be handed down is debunked, at least in part, by Acts 8:14–17, where Peter and John are called from Jerusalem to travel to Samaria to bestow the Holy Spirit on those who had received the Word there, as Philip (who was with them) could not do so. Philip was given the Spirit via the laying on of hands earlier.

In Matthew 28:18–20, Jesus states, "All authority has been given to Me in heaven and on earth, Go therefore and make disciples of all nations, baptizing them in the name of the Father and of the Son and of the Holy Spirit, teaching them to observe all things that I have commanded you." Jesus's emphasis was not on passing on authority to more and more select apostles to keep His elders in line. His emphasis was on assuring His disciples that they were under His authority to go and make other disciples of all nations of people by baptizing and teaching them. They would, in turn, make other disciples by baptizing and teaching them—all with a comforting admonition that He would be with them.

In answer to part 2 of this question, when the Scriptures say, "All Scripture is given by inspiration of God, and is profitable for doctrine, for reproof … that the man of God may be complete, thoroughly equipped for every good work." (2 Timothy 3:16-17) "Contend earnestly for the faith which was once for all handed down to the saints" (Jude 3) and "I did not shrink from declaring to you the whole purpose of God" (Acts 20:27), how can human words, either from fathers, councils, or creeds, be considered valid additional revelation?

They can't. The Scriptures lock out any further revelation—period. Many centuries of arguing and disputing over subtleties to aspects of God's Word, such as the topics decided upon by the ecumenical councils (e.g., the nature and will of Jesus) could have been avoided had these men simply honored and obeyed Scripture. For instance, most of these arguments could have been avoided if churches were set up individually and led by elders who could address them as God designed and Scripture affirms. Also, to claim these council words or canons were inspired by the Holy Spirit lacks any credibility. No reference is made within Scripture of any future verifications or decisions needing to be made like this; quite the opposite was stated – "the man of God is "complete" and "thoroughly equipped" at that time; the faith was "once for all handed down to the saints" not later on; and Jude did not shrink from declaring the "whole purpose of God" not some then and some later, as spoken by a "church father or council or man-made creed."

One other aspect of unwarranted additional revelation should be considered here—that of the Apocryphal writings. The Orthodox observe all these books as inspired, and much of their theology is influenced by them, such as praying for the dead, where references are found exclusively in these books, but these books have no credibility to be considered inspired, as there is much contradiction and error exhibited within them.

Concerning Salvation, the Orthodox Church believes in a faith-only / works-justified salvation. They claim that Scriptures such as Matthew 7:21–23 ("Not everyone who says to me, 'Lord, Lord,' shall enter the Kingdom of heaven, but he who does the will of my Father in heaven …")

clearly indicate that individuals are not entitled to God's reward. No matter what we do, one cannot be sure of salvation, as "God judges not words and actions, but motivations of the heart ... we can long and pray for salvation; but it is never guaranteed ... there can only be ongoing repentance and hope." [49.]

Although direct confrontation of their faith-only salvation, with the Bible's plan of salvation via hearing and belief (Romans 10:13–17; Acts 16:31), repentance (Mark 1:15), confession (Romans 10:9–10), and water baptism (Acts 2:38) could be discussed, perhaps starting at the end might be a more effective way to open a door. A good question to create discussion considering the above would be:

2). "Do the Scriptures teach an uncertain or a guaranteed salvation?"

Two Scriptures clearly give us that guarantee: Ephesians 1:13–14 and 1 John 5:10–13. These guarantees are comforting, but they require obedience to God's plan of salvation as outlined in Scripture, not simply salvation by faith only or belief only, with associated good works, as the Orthodox teach. Once we have obeyed the gospel in this manner, we are immediately added to the Lord's church by God Himself (Acts 2:47) and put into a saved condition. Salvation is not a long pilgrimage, as envisioned by the Orthodox, beginning in this life and extending through death and into the next life. Salvation is promised to be immediate.

In addition, the Scriptures also affirm to those who are obedient to God's instructions concerning His plan of salvation that if they remain steadfast and always strive to walk in the light, they can have full confidence in their salvation (1 Corinthians 15:58), not simply living lives of "repentance and hope", left with uncertainty: "Therefore, my beloved brethren, be steadfast, immovable, always abounding in the work of the Lord, knowing that your labor is not in vain in the Lord."

Another point of departure from God's Word is their adherence to a Jewish form of worship. The Scriptures make it clear that Christians today are to be under the authority of the New Testament, the New Covenant of Christ, not Old Testament Law, so a third question one might pose could be:

3). Given the fact that the Scriptures make clear Christians today are to be under the New Testament, the New Covenant of Christ, how can the Orthodox justify adherence to Jewish Law and Old Testament Traditions in their worship service to God?

The similarity of Orthodox worship to Old Testament worship is profound. The church interior design with outsider separation from the main worship area, member separation from the altar and areas only the high clergy may enter, and the burning of incense, including the censing/blessing of items of worship, all can be traced to early Jewish temple worship. Even the practice of fasting, associated with and observed as an integral part of Orthodox life and worship, is laced with requirements to abstain from certain meats and dairy products, reminiscent of Old Testament restrictions (though Old Testament restrictions were more of an overall ban than a fasting ban).

Again, we are no longer under these guidelines. In Galatians 5:1–4, the Holy Spirit, speaking through Paul, makes several strong statements concerning a push by some to impose the Jewish requirement of circumcision on new Christians at that time. He warned that to do so would sever them from Christ and cause a fall from God's grace. If this strong warning was issued against the return to a single commandment, how much more would be the condemnation for a return to Old Testament worship procedures to the extent the Orthodox have implemented?

According to the New Testament, one's attitude has as much to do with proper worship of God as one's acts of worship. We see Christians meeting together in the New Testament simply to worship and glorify God while at the same time edifying one another. With the Orthodox, it seems more about procedure and formality, where blessings, pronouncements, chants, and choir singing by a select few take precedence and where the laity participate very little (in attitude or action); particularly the non-Orthodox visitors, who are restricted to stand in the Narthex or vestibule area – far from the worship area, barely able to see what's going on, let alone have any meaningful worship experience or be pleasing to God.

Many today give less priority to how God is to be worshipped (as long as He is worshipped), but the account of Aaron's sons, who offered "strange fire" (not commanded by God) during worship, should stand as a sobering reminder of how God views such things (Leviticus 10:1–2). Though this example is pulled from the Old Testament, it has more to do with God's character and expectations than it does an invalid or replaced Old Law. God's character, His insistence on worshipping Him as He desires, does not change.

One final question could be posed for discussion concerning Orthodoxy's view of the Trinity:

4.) **Orthodox teachings concerning the Trinity involve several conflicting statements:**

> **God is always and forever unknowable and incomprehensible to creatures ... even in heaven, men will never know the essence of God, that is, what God really is in Himself.** [40.]
>
> **AND:**
>
> **By the Holy Spirit given through Christ, men can share the life, the love, the truth, the freedom, the goodness, the holiness, the wisdom, the *knowledge of God Himself* ... the affirmation of the fact that the essence of Christianity is "the acquisition of the Holy Spirit" and the "deification" of man by the grace of God ... Christian life is the participation in the life of the Blessed Trinity ... it is the life of men becoming divine.** [43.]

How can this be? It cannot! According to these two statements, God is both knowable and unknowable. In addition, if mankind is to become Divine, man will become **omniscient**, which completely contradicts and negates this whole idea – since omniscience or "all-knowing" will allow man to know everything, including the "essence of God." (Claimed to be unknowable in the first quote).

Conclusion

The Orthodox churches were part of the original apostasy of the Lord's church following the first century. Indistinguishable from Catholicism for over two centuries (Roman Catholicism was developing in the West, and Orthodox Catholicism was developing in the East), differences began to surface around 325 as a result of the First Ecumenical Council. These eastern and western factions of Catholicism and Orthodoxy continued to grow farther and farther apart until a final break, termed the Great Schism, occurred in 1054.

Orthodox churches have maintained an institutional structure, much like the Roman Catholics, imposing a hierarchy of bishops and priests to rule over local parishes, and they have added to the Bible's authority by following uninspired books (the Apocrypha), as well as what they call "Holy Tradition" (doctrines proclaimed in the first seven ecumenical councils and teachings of the early church fathers). The Holy Tradition also precludes individual Orthodox Christians from accessing the Scriptures on their own, as Orthodoxy claims that the Holy Scriptures cannot be understood without this institutional aid (proclaimed by qualified and ordained clergy).

These changes in church organization and authority, along with Orthodox belief in the "Great Mysteries," including transubstantiation for Holy Communion, baptism as a mere formality or entrance requirement into the Orthodox Church, and a separate infusion (from baptism) allowing indwelling of the Holy Spirit, termed "chrismation," are all departures and perversions of New Testament teaching.

Orthodox rituals found in their worship services and the symbolism found in their church buildings, which tie to Jewish law, are specifically denounced in the New Testament with the coming of Jesus Christ and a New Covenant.

The Orthodox Church therefore cannot be the church of Christ established on Pentecost, as recorded in Acts 2.

CHAPTER 2

THE EPISCOPAL CHURCH

Introduction

The Episcopal Church, being the American version of the Church of England or Anglican Church, originated in England during the first half of the sixteenth century and was headed by King Henry VIII. It was and remains very similar in teaching and practice to the Roman Catholic Church.

Just how the seeds of Christianity came to be sown in England is uncertain. One tradition is that the apostle Paul, after his first imprisonment in Rome, traveled to the British Isles and established the church in what is now Cornwall. Another tradition is that Joseph of Arimathea came to Britain some thirty years after the Resurrection of Christ, bringing with him the cup that Jesus used at the Last Supper—the Holy Grail. Neither of these traditions is given serious consideration, however, as it seems more likely that the first Christians were probably Roman soldiers who had been converted to Christianity. But the invasions of the barbarians almost destroyed this early Christian community.

When England began to colonize America, they brought Anglicanism along with them. After the American Revolution, however, the Anglican Church in the United States felt it was better to be known as the Episcopalian Church (from the Greek word "*episcopes*" (bishop), since the church in America was headed by bishops). In 1785, the American Episcopalian Church reorganized as the Protestant Episcopal Church, and since 1967 this church has simply been known as the Episcopal Church.

Between 1783 and 1790, five men were consecrated as bishops in Pennsylvania, New York, and Virginia, marking complete independence from Great Britain. In addition, in 1789 a convention was held in Philadelphia to unify all Episcopalians into a single national U.S. church. A constitution was adopted, along with a set of canon laws, and the English *Book of Common Prayer* was revised into the American *Book of Common Prayer*.

The Anglican Church, as a collective, is known as the Anglican Communion (an association of churches in full communion with the Archbishop of Canterbury) and is composed of thirty-nine provinces of different national churches or dioceses, each headed by its own archbishop. Besides England, there are Anglican churches in Australia, Canada, New Zealand, South Africa, and many countries in Africa and Asia. The Episcopal Church in the United States of America is part of a province divided into nine dioceses; others in this province include Honduras, Taiwan, Colombia, Ecuador, Haiti, the Dominican Republic, Venezuela, the British Virgin Islands, and parts of Europe.

In keeping with Anglican tradition and theology, the Episcopal Church considers itself midway between Roman Catholicism and Protestantism. Several splits have occurred over the years from the Episcopal Church, including the Reformed Episcopal Church in America (which is more Protestant-minded), the Episcopal Orthodox Christian Archdiocese of America (which is more conservative), and the Anglican Catholic Church (which is more concurrent with Roman Catholicism).

The Episcopal Church in the United States of America has opposed the death penalty, supported the civil rights movement and affirmative action (some of its leaders and priests having marched with civil rights demonstrators), and called for full civil equality for gay and lesbian individuals (and has ordained openly gay men and women), and has ordained women to both the priesthood and the episcopate.

With over eighty million members, the Anglican Communion is the third largest Christian communion in the world, after the Roman Catholic and Eastern Orthodox Churches, representing roughly 3 percent of Christian denominations worldwide. There are approximately 2.3 million Anglicans (Episcopalians) in the United States, representing roughly 1.5 percent of all denominations there.

The English Reformation and Origin of the Anglican Church

Catholicism comes to the British Isles.

King Henry VIII – 1540
Portrait By Hans Holbein

In AD 597, Pope Gregory I sent a group of Roman missionaries to the British Isles under the leadership of Augustine, a Roman monk. One of their goals was "to bring a more disciplined apostolic succession to the Celtic Christians." [1.] They succeeded in converting many of the Celts to Roman Catholicism, including the king, Ethelbert, and many of his subjects. Augustine was the first English archbishop and ruled the church from Canterbury for ten years; the British were devoted to the pope until the Reformation.

During the fourteenth century, the first signs of a reaction against papal authority came from an Oxford professor, John Wycliffe, often called the Morning Star of the Reformation. Wycliffe spoke out against many of the practices of the Catholic Church, the vast land holdings of the bishops, and the political power of the pope. The pope denounced Wycliffe, but Wycliffe's personal popularity saved him from certain martyrdom.

One of Wycliffe's teachings was that the Scriptures should be the only law for the church, and this led him to translate the New Testament from the Latin Vulgate into the English language. Bibles were costly, and to facilitate the spreading of his message to the people, Wycliffe sent out "poor saints," called Lollards. Many of them were arrested, but Wycliffe suffered no harm. He later died in 1384 due to a stroke.

A century and a half later, Henry VIII (1491–1547) was on the throne. Remnants of the Wycliffe movement were still present in England, but a new factor to be reckoned with was the German Reformation under Martin Luther.

During the first part of his reign, Henry VIII was faithful to Rome, and because of his suppression of Luther's writings in England, Henry was declared Defender of the Faith by the pope. This was short-lived, however, as Henry soon faced a political problem. His wife, Catherine of Aragon, had borne six children, but only one of these, a girl, survived infancy. Henry's fear was that at his death, civil war would break out unless he produced a male heir. In addition, he had fallen in love with Anne Boleyn, one of the women in his court, and wanted to marry her. He didn't ask the pope for permission to divorce Catherine, but instead for an annulment of his marriage to her.

Here was the problem: Catherine had been married to Henry's older brother, and although she was a widow when Henry married her, the king wanted an annulment on the grounds that his marriage to Catherine had never been recognized by God, according to Catholic teaching. His proof was the fact that she had borne him no male heir. Ordinarily, the pope would have obliged the king, but Catherine's uncle, Charles V of Spain, had gained tremendous political power in Europe, and the pope didn't want to offend him. Henry took matters into his own hands, declared the Church of England free from any ties to Rome, and declared himself the protector and supreme head of the Church and Clergy of England in 1535. This marked the origin of the Anglican Church in England—and he married Anne Boleyn.

Shortly thereafter, Henry fell in love with Jane Seymour. Anne Boleyn was accused of adultery and treason and sentenced to death. Henry was "kind" to Anne Boleyn and spared her from being burned at the stake; he allowed her a quick execution via decapitation instead.

Henry forbade the sending of revenues to Rome, and English clergy were required to take an oath of allegiance to the king and to repudiate loyalty to the pope. Various Roman doctrines were also repudiated, including purgatory, indulgences, and the use or veneration of images. Priests were allowed to marry, and members were allowed to make a congregational confession of their sins, rather than confession solely to a priest.

Henry had no intentions of founding another church, but the movement gained strength, and the procedures of worship were revised and translated into English. This newly separated Anglican church was given further structure, particularly during the reign of Elizabeth I, starting in 1558.

The Six Wives of King Henry VIII
(R. Burchett; 1854-1860, Parliamentary Art Collection)

One of the results of this structure was the introduction of the *Book of Common Prayer*, first produced in 1549. It has been revised numerous times, but the 1662 English *Book of Common Prayer* remains to this day the basis for most Anglican liturgy around the world.

Origin of the Episcopal Church in America

It was only natural that the Church of England would be prominent in the early development of religion in America, as the colonies were governed by England. In seven states, the Church of England became the established religion, supported by public taxation.

During the Revolutionary War, the loyalty of the clergy was divided. Consequently, many priests left the country, fearing persecution. Not all members of the Church of England were sympathetic to the king's cause; for instance, two-thirds of the signers of the Declaration of Independence and the Constitution were members of that church, including Washington, Jefferson, Madison, Patrick Henry, John Jay, and John Marshall.

During the 1789 General Convention, the church was reorganized and essentially founded in America. The *Book of Common Prayer* was rewritten so that objectionable parts were removed, such as prayers for the king and queen. A separate constitution was adopted, and the name was changed to "Protestant Episcopal Church." This name remained until 1967, when the Protestant Episcopal Church was changed once again to simply the Episcopal Church.

Arms of the See of Canterbury

The Episcopal shield, adopted in 1940, is based on St. George's Cross, a symbol of England, with a saltire reminiscent of the Cross of St. Andrew in the canton, in reference to the historical origins of the American episcopate in the Scottish Episcopal Church.

The Compass Rose (Symbol of Anglican Communion)

The Archbishop of Canterbury has a place of honor and primacy over other archbishops of the Anglican Communion. For a province to be considered a part of the communion is for said province to be in full communion with the see of Canterbury. The archbishop is recognized as *primus inter pares*, or first among equals, though he does not exercise any direct authority in any province outside England. The current archbishop of Canterbury, the 105th holder of the chair of St. Augustine of Canterbury, is the "Most Reverend [sic]" [2] Justin Welby.

Several splits have occurred within the United States.

The Reformed Episcopal Church (which is more Protestant-minded) split in 1873 over transubstantiation and baptism as being not essential for salvation.

The Episcopal Orthodox Christian Archdiocese of America and the Anglican or Anglo-Catholic Church (which are more conservative-minded) saw themselves as an extension of Roman Catholicism.

As mentioned, the founding of the Anglican Church occurred when King Henry VIII broke away from Roman Catholicism in 1535 and established England's version of Catholicism. The establishment of the Episcopal Church in America occurred after the Revolutionary War, in 1789. The chart below graphs this denomination as a split from Roman Catholicism.

Founding of the Anglican Church (1535)
Founding of the Episcopal Church (America), 1789

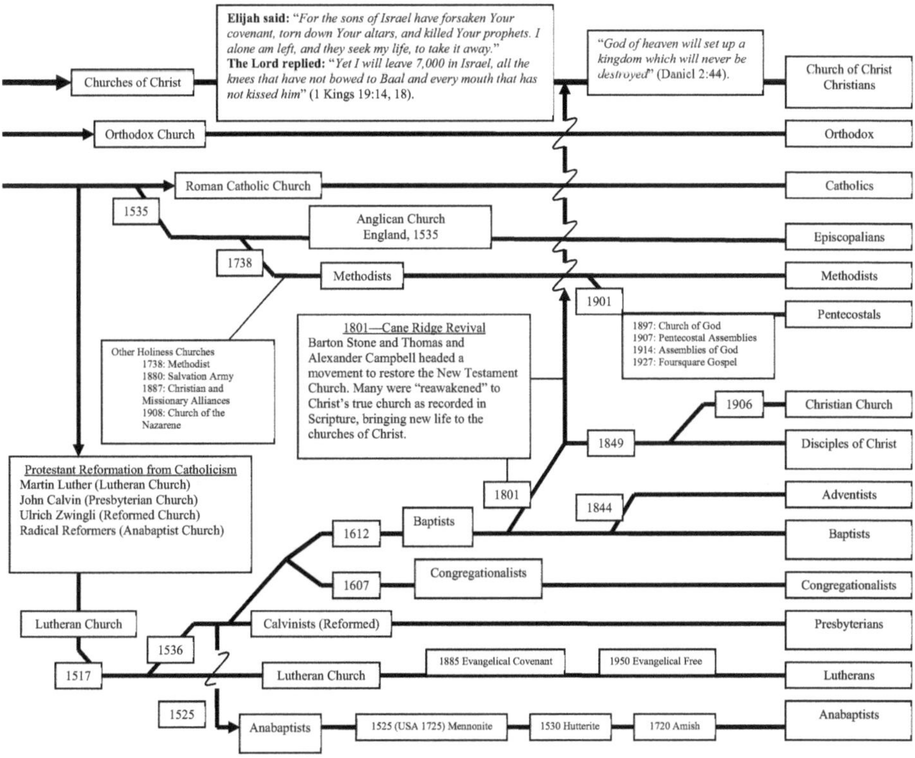
Elijah said: "For the sons of Israel have forsaken Your covenant, torn down Your altars, and killed Your prophets. I alone am left, and they seek my life, to take it away."
The Lord replied: "Yet I will leave 7,000 in Israel, all the knees that have not bowed to Baal and every mouth that has not kissed him" (1 Kings 19:14, 18).
"God of heaven will set up a kingdom which will never be destroyed" (Daniel 2:44).
Churches of Christ
Church of Christ Christians
Orthodox Church
Orthodox
Roman Catholic Church
Catholics
1535
Anglican Church England, 1535
Episcopalians
1738
Methodists
Methodists
1901
Pentecostals
1897: Church of God
1907: Pentecostal Assemblies
1914: Assemblies of God
1927: Foursquare Gospel
Other Holiness Churches
1738: Methodist
1880: Salvation Army
1887: Christian and Missionary Alliances
1908: Church of the Nazarene
1801—Cane Ridge Revival
Barton Stone and Thomas and Alexander Campbell headed a movement to restore the New Testament Church. Many were "reawakened" to Christ's true church as recorded in Scripture, bringing new life to the churches of Christ.
1906
Christian Church
1849
Disciples of Christ
Protestant Reformation from Catholicism
Martin Luther (Lutheran Church)
John Calvin (Presbyterian Church)
Ulrich Zwingli (Reformed Church)
Radical Reformers (Anabaptist Church)
1801
1844
Adventists
1612
Baptists
Baptists
1607
Congregationalists
Congregationalists
Lutheran Church
Calvinists (Reformed)
Presbyterians
1536
1517
Lutheran Church
1885 Evangelical Covenant
1950 Evangelical Free
Lutherans
1525
Anabaptists
1525 (USA 1725) Mennonite
1530 Hutterite
1720 Amish
Anabaptists

Organization of the Anglican (Episcopal) Church

The Anglican Communion, as stated previously, of which the Episcopal Church in America is a part, is a worldwide association of churches in full communion with the Archbishop of Canterbury (the focus of unity within the association).

Though the Archbishop of Canterbury does not exercise any direct authority in any province outside of England, he is considered the spiritual head of the communion worldwide, maintaining a certain moral authority with the right to determine which churches will be in communion with his see. He also exercises influence over the communion by hosting, chairing, and inviting representative bishops and archbishops from all thirty-nine provinces to the periodic conferences and primates' meetings, where overall church policy is discussed.

Westminster Abbey
London, England

Other than the influence exercised by the English archbishop, each of the thirty-nine provinces is independent, with its own primate and governing structure. The provinces either take the form of a national church (such as Canada and Japan), a collection of nations (such as the West Indies and Central and South Africa), or a geographical region (such as the Solomon Islands). Within communion provinces, there are frequently ecclesiastical provinces, each headed by a metropolitan archbishop. All Anglican provinces consist of dioceses under the jurisdiction of a bishop, who must be consecrated according to the strictures of apostolic succession, thus becoming part of what is called the "episcopate."

The governance of the Episcopal Church is essentially the same as other Anglican churches, but it does not share the same structure as the Church of England; it has its own system and canon law. The Episcopal Church is composed of 110 dioceses in the United States, Columbia, the Dominican Republic, Ecuador, Haiti, Honduras, Puerto Rico, Taiwan, Venezuela, and the Virgin Islands. It also includes a convocation of American churches in Europe and the Navajoland Area Mission. These dioceses are organized into nine provinces, each with its own synod. Unlike the Church of England, in which bishops are governmental appointees, the bishops in the Episcopal Church of America are elected at diocesan conventions and confirmed by a house of bishops.

Today there are some seven thousand congregations within the United States, each of which elects a vestry, or bishop's committee, subject to the approval of the presiding diocese bishop. The vestry of each parish elects a priest, called a rector, who has spiritual jurisdiction in the parish and who in turn selects assistant clergy, both deacons and priests. Diocesan conventions are usually held annually, where future bishops are elected.

Nationally, the Episcopal Church is governed by a general convention meeting that takes place every three years to set church policy. The General Convention is the highest legislative body of the church in the United States, made up of the House of Deputies and the House of Bishops. Roughly three hundred members are elected to the House of Bishops and eight hundred to the House of Deputies, their main purpose being the enactment of legislation governing the church, setting rules as contained in the constitution, and canons or broader guidelines on church policy called resolutions.

The General Convention also appoints interim bodies to carry out and oversee policy decisions, including standing commissions that usually consist of three bishops, three priests or deacons, and six laypersons, all appointed by the presiding bishop and president of the House of Deputies.

The presiding bishop of the Episcopal Church, elected by the House of Bishops and confirmed by the House of Deputies, is the chief pastor of the church in America (not unlike the archbishop of Canterbury, except without a territorial see). Elected for a nine-year term, the presiding bishop enjoys overall authority to visit and preside over dioceses, consult other bishops, and speak on behalf of the church as a whole. He also chairs the House of Bishops and the Executive Council of the General Convention (the most powerful of the interim bodies), as well as directing the affairs of the Episcopal Church Center (the national administrative headquarters), located in New York City. Currently, (as of August 2023) the presiding bishop and primate for the Episcopal Church is "Reverend [sic]" [2.] Michael Bruce Curry.

The hierarchical breakdown looks something like this:

- The Archbishop of Canterbury is the spiritual head of the Anglican Communion, with thirty-nine provinces worldwide. He has limited influence outside England and controls the General Convention, which meets every three years, as the final authority of the Anglican / Episcopal Church.
- Each province is independent, with at least one archbishop per province as head.
- The United States is part of a nine-province group known as the Episcopal Church, each with an archbishop and synod. The Church is headed by a General Convention consisting of two legislative bodies (the House of Bishops and the House of Deputies) and further overseen by a primate or presiding bishop.
- This nine-province group is divided into 110 dioceses, each with a presiding bishop.
- A diocese controls individual local churches or parishes. Each diocese must include at least six parishes.
- The local church or parish is controlled by a group of men elected by the congregation, known as a vestry. The vestry selects a preacher or rector (sometimes called a vicar), with the bishop's consent. The rector then has control of all spiritual affairs of the local church except financial affairs, which are in the hands of the vestry.

As with the Roman Catholic and Eastern Orthodox Churches (and many other denominations having a hierarchical structure), the organizational structure of the Anglican or Episcopal Church departs from what we see in Scripture. In the New Testament, each congregation was to be independent and autonomous; each was to be under the oversight of a plurality of elders, also called bishops, or pastors, according to Acts 11:30; 14:21–23; 20:28; Titus 1:5–7; and 1 Peter 5:1–5. Accountability to outside agents—in this case, a diocese, a synod, a province, and a General Convention—is not seen in Scripture.

The structure of the local congregation is also different from what we see in Scripture. A lone preacher or rector is not sanctioned to lead Christ's body alone. Scripture specifies Christ as head of His church, both universal and local, with a plurality of elders (a preacher may be one) as shepherds of the local congregation under Christ's head. In addition, the splitting of spiritual and financial affairs is a human idea, not God's.

Authority of the Episcopal Church

The official position of the Anglican Communion is that, like the Roman Catholic and Orthodox Communions, it is a full and distinct branch of the one, holy, Catholic and Apostolic Church, created by Christ. This "one church" has been handed down in what is called the "episcopate," where bishops who possess the fullness of the Christian priesthood are considered the successors of the apostles.

Primates, archbishops, and metropolitans are all bishops and members of this historical episcopate; they derive their authority through apostolic succession—an unbroken line of bishops, which can supposedly be traced back to the apostles of Jesus, through a process of "laying on of hands."

Believing this, the Anglican Church teaches that a priest or bishop has the authority from God to remit sins, and they allow their members to give confession to the priest to that end. Confession is not required as a condition to continue within the church, however, as it is in Roman Catholicism.

The Episcopal Church accepts the standard Protestant canon of sixty-six books (thirty-nine from the Old Testament and twenty-seven from the New Testament), but much like the Eastern Orthodox Church, they accept the entire Apocrypha (less 3 Maccabees and 4 Maccabees), though the Apocrypha is placed on a lower level of emphasis than the New or Old Testament. [3.]

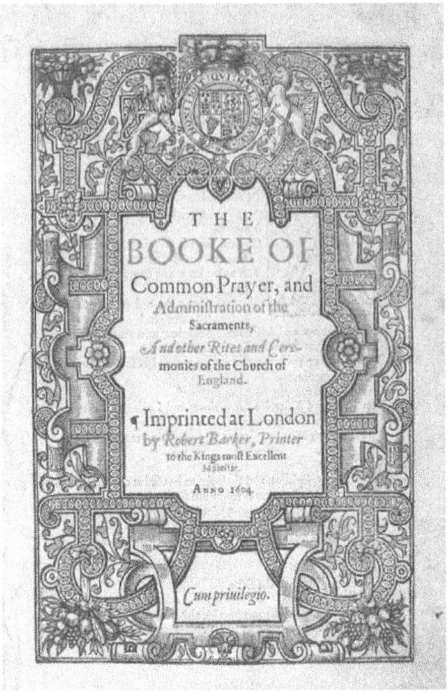
THE
BOOKE OF
Common Prayer, and
Adminiſtration of the
Sacraments,
And other Rites and Cere-
monies of the Church of
England.
¶ Imprinted at London
by Robert Barker, Printer
to the Kings moſt Excellent
Maieſtie.
Anno 1604.
Cum priuilegio.

Book of Common Prayer - 1604

In addition to the Bible, the *Book of Common Prayer* is added. Having guided the spiritual life of the church since 1549, this handbook contains instructions for order and manner of worship, prayers, and meditations (called "collects"), to be used at specific times during the year, and liturgies for the various observances and ceremonies, such as baptism, the Lord's Supper, confirmation, and consecration of bishops, priests, and deacons. "Many believe that while a Bible may be considered helpful to have at an Anglican or Episcopalian service, the *Book of Common Prayer* is indispensable." [4.]

The faith of Anglicans (Episcopalians) is founded in the Scriptures, the traditions of the apostolic church, the apostolic succession (historic episcopate), the first four ecumenical councils, and the early church fathers. This faith includes the Catholic creeds, which are interpreted in light of Christian tradition, scholarship, and reason. They accept the Apostles' and Nicene Creeds, in particular, as authoritative, believing the Apostles' Creed to be a baptismal doctrine and the Nicene Creed, a sufficient statement of the Christian faith, used predominately during the Eucharist service.

Most Episcopalians believe Scripture contains the truth that is necessary for salvation and is the primary norm for faith but must be interpreted considering tradition and reason. They are taught this from doctrine such as the "Sources of Authority" section of the "Episcopal Dictionary of the Church." Here it is stated that "The threefold sources of authority in Anglicanism are scripture, tradition, and reason. These three sources uphold and critique each other in a dynamic way. Scripture is the normative source for God's revelation and the source for all Christian teaching and reflection. Tradition passes down from generation to generation the church's ongoing experience of God's presence and activity. Reason is understood to include the human capacity to discern the truth in both rational and intuitive ways. It is not limited to logic as such. It takes into account and includes experience. Each of the three sources of authority must be perceived and interpreted in light of the other two ... This balanced understanding of authority is based in the theology of Richard Hooker (c. 1554-1600). It may be further traced to the teaching of Thomas Aquinas (1225-1274). Urban T. Holmes III (1930-1981) provided a thorough and helpful discussion of the sources of authority in his book What is Anglicanism? (1982)" [5.]

Though Thomas Aquinas may have introduced the idea of multiple sources of authority, it was Richard Hooker who solidified this thought into Anglican/Episcopal doctrine. By using his name in the Episcopal Dictionary, more insight can be gleaned on this subject. Following is some of that insight: "Hooker's major contribution was his monumental Of the Lawes of Ecclesiastical Polity ... In the Lawes he created both a distinctive philosophy of constitutional government and an Anglican theology that remains congenial to modern thought ... Hooker affirmed the threefold Anglican sources of authority-scripture, tradition, and reason. He countered the Roman Catholic argument which treated the Bible and tradition as equally authoritative for belief. He also countered the Puritans whose literal obedience to scripture was so absolute that they considered unlawful whatever scripture did not command. ... Reason was to be used in reading scripture. If scripture were silent or ambiguous, wisdom would consult the tradition of the church ... Hooker saw the church not as a static but as an organic institution whose methods of government change according to circumstances … He is commemorated in the Episcopal calendar of the church year on Nov. 3." [6.]

Digging a little deeper into how the Episcopal Church views Scripture, considering the above statements, the following is stated under a definition of the word "Scripture": "This word comes from the Latin for "writings" and refers to a collection of the most important documents in a given religious community. Many different religions have scriptures. The term "canon," which means a rule or listing, refers to the list of items included in a scripture. The word "Bible" is used by Christians to refer to the OT and NT, the two parts of scripture. Other books called the Apocrypha, are often included in the bible (BCP, p. 853). In the Jewish tradition, the OT is called Hebrew Scripture. When early Christians began to select writings for their scripture, they wanted to keep the Hebrew scripture and therefore chose to use the titles Old Testament (or covenant) for the Jewish writings and New Testament for the normative Christian writings. … After a long period of time, the currently accepted canon of scripture was determined on the basis of apostolic authorship or attribution and widespread acceptance of the texts included in the canon. … Scripture, along with tradition and reason, is one of the sources of authority in Anglicanism. Selections from scripture for the Episcopal Church's services of Holy Eucharist and Daily Offices are provided by the lectionaries of the BCP (pp. 889-1001)." [7.]

Not all Episcopalians self-identify with this image of a threefold source of authority, however, especially those whose convictions lean toward either evangelicalism or Anglo-Catholicism. Much like the Presbyterian Church (which we'll look at in the next volume), there are many different theologies within the Episcopal Church. Some hold to the authority of Scripture over all else; some do not. Once again, the Episcopal Church's glossary defines the sources of authority as a "balance between Scripture, tradition, and reason," further noting, "The Anglican balancing of the sources of authority has been criticized as clumsy or "muddy." It has been associated with the Anglican affinity for seeking the mean between extremes and living the via media. It has also been associated with the Anglican willingness to tolerate and comprehend opposing viewpoints instead of imposing tests of orthodoxy or resorting to heresy trials" [5.]

Some members of the church are concerned that the Episcopal

Church may not be able to continue its relationship within the Anglican Communion, who hold Scripture a little higher as authoritative, and downplays tolerance for such things as homosexual individuals being included in the episcopate, (to be discussed further below), which seems to be at least one of the reasons "tradition and reason" have been introduced as two additional legs of authority (in this author's opinion), while others see this as an asset that will allow a balance between Anglican and Episcopal relations.

The Episcopal Church holds several sources as authoritative doctrine to guide their belief, work, and worship to God. The episcopate, or those clergy claiming special authority due to apostolic succession, is certainly one of these sources. This will be discussed in more detail later. The Scriptures are mentioned as one of their sources; however, viewed by many Episcopalians as important, their Book of Common Prayer is "indispensable" and the go-to source for direction, particularly for a step-by-step worship protocol. As mentioned above, "Selections from scripture for the Episcopal Church's services of Holy Eucharist and Daily Offices are provided by the lectionaries of the BCP (pp. 889-1001)." [7.] Revised numerous times from the original 1549 Anglican version to its current 1979 Episcopal counterpart revision, this BCP, along with prayers and directions, including readings from the Bible that are generally taken from standardized lectionaries, which in turn are taken from the Bible (with some passages from the Apocrypha) to be read out loud in the church over a one-to-three-year cycle. In what is called "high church or Anglo-Catholic churches there are generally prayers for the dead included in many of these readings.

Similar to the Roman Catholics and Orthodox, they hold the decisions and writings of the Ecumenical Councils, especially the first four; along with the writings of the "Church Fathers," as important sources of authority for their work and worship. In addition, the creeds – the Apostles and Nicene Creeds in particular – are elevated to authoritative status, as Baptism and Holy Communion Rites respectively – to be repeated at each of these events.

As mentioned previously, the Bible claims its own authority, which is all sufficient and able to instruct humans to be "complete and thoroughly equipped for every good work" (2 Timothy 3:16–17). It is the "faith which was once for all delivered to the saints" (Jude 3). It has been given to Christians, containing "all things that pertain to life and godliness" (2 Peter 1:3). Paul did not shrink from proclaiming the "whole counsel of God" to the Ephesians (Acts 20:27).

These additional doctrines used to supplement God's Word—including the Holy Tradition of the Orthodox, the Divine Tradition of the Catholics, and here, the Episcopalian Book of Common Prayer, which again, references such things as Council decisions and creeds—are not sanctioned in Scripture (2 John 9–10; Galatians 1:6–9; Proverbs 30:6; Revelation 22:18–19).

In addition, "human tradition and reason" have nothing to do with God's authoritative Word, particularly in trying to combine them as somehow equal partners in that authority – that one must use tradition and reason to properly interpret Scripture, that "these three sources uphold and critique each other in a dynamic way." That "each of the three sources of authority must be perceived and interpreted in light of the other two" is false doctrine – this is man's idea, not God's.

The view of God's Word, the Scriptures, needs a bit more exploration, since not only the Anglican/Episcopal Church, but many denominations we'll be looking at moving forward, hold similar views concerning Scripture; and as I mentioned earlier, this author believes one reason for this is to allow them to do what they wish, despite what Scripture has to say. For instance, to allow such things as women and/or homosexual ordination into their ministries, by suggesting Paul's words in Scripture are archaic, that the Bible is instead "dynamic" and "living" (not static and unchangeable with the times), the Scriptures must, by necessity, be interpreted by such things as tradition and reason, opening the door to such acceptance.

These ideas didn't come out of the blue – as mentioned above, they began many years ago, most likely through the works of Thomas Aquinas (1225-1274) – but were solidified and carried to this day through the thoughts of individuals like Richard Hooker (c. 1554-1600) – with statements like these: "Reason was to be used in reading Scripture. If scripture were silent or ambiguous, wisdom would consult the tradition of the church …

Hooker saw the church not as a static but as an organic institution whose methods of government change according to circumstances." [6.] When denominations like the Episcopal Church hear words like these, they become music to the ear in supporting what they already believe; and so, they have been adopted into authoritative doctrine.

Not only these ideas of how the Scriptures need to be interpreted, but their idea of how the Scriptures Themselves came about, the determiners for Their inclusion in our current Bibles, and the Episcopal understanding of "canon" needs further attention. As claimed in their Episcopal Dictionary, under "Scripture" (above), many religions have scriptures, the Bible is not unique in this regard. Also, the term "canon" means a set of rules or listings included within any scripture. The word "Bible" is used by Christians to refer to the OT, also called the Hebrew Scripture, Apocrypha books, and the NT (BCP. p. 853). It also states, "When early Christians began to select writings for their scripture, they wanted to keep the Hebrew scripture and therefore chose to use the titles Old Testament … for the Jewish writings and New Testament for … Christian writings. … The selection of writings to be included in the NT was not final until about 360 A.D. … After a long period of time, the currently accepted canon of scripture was determined on the basis of apostolic authorship or attribution and widespread acceptance of the texts included in the canon." [7.]

In critiquing the above statements, I first want to refer the reader to a full explanation under the topic "Defending the Inspiration of Scripture," sub-topic, "The Canon of the Scriptures," found in my first volume's Appendix (pgs. 337-345). [8.]

One thing you'll notice is that the Apocrypha books can be discounted immediately from consideration as Holy Writ, for many reasons. One comes from Episcopal doctrine itself, when it states that "the currently accepted canon of scripture was determined on the basis of apostolic authorship or attribution and widespread acceptance of the texts included in the canon." [7.] In fact, the Apocryphal books were compiled in the fourth century or later, they do not reflect any apostolic attitude or influence as to which, if any, belong in the Bible. Therefore, this statement of determination by Episcopal doctrine is false. In addition, not only did no NT writer ever quote from an Apocryphal book, though almost all other thirty-nine books of the OT are quoted, but the quality of these books is also not befitting divine integrity – since several contain deception, error, and falsehoods. [8.]

In addition to the inclusion of Apocrypha books, which never did belong, the Episcopal understanding of how the canon of Scripture was assembled and finalized into our Old and New Testaments is amiss. The Old Testament Scriptures were sealed by the time of Jesus – evidence of their credibility is confirmed by statements coming from both the apostles and Jesus Himself in the New Testament (John 7:38, 5:39, 7:38; 5:46-47), and comprehensively, Jesus validated the Old Testament in Luke 24:44, confirmed by Luke in the next verse, 24:45. The statement above that the early Christians "wanted to keep the Hebrew scripture and therefore chose to use the titles Old Testament (or covenant) for the Jewish writings" [7.] – leaves one with the idea that they had a choice to include them or not – they didn't have a choice!

Also, the New Testament Scriptures were not "selected" by early Christians! More accurately, the Scriptures selected the early Christians – the first-century Christians knew most of the authors of the New Testament gospels and epistles, the apostles themselves, and their writings. They simply accepted these perfect, errorless, authoritative writings and rightfully included them into a collection now known as our "Bible." As stated in the appendix of my first volume on page 340, under "The Canon of the Scriptures," I refer to Neil Lightfoot's book "How We Got the Bible;" here I quote Lightfoot saying, "A book's canonicity depends on its authority." In other words, the book or writing must possess and exhibit inherent authority to be considered divinely inspired. Lightfoot then uses the example of Paul's words to the Corinthians: "If anyone thinks himself to be a prophet or spiritual, let him acknowledge that the things which I write to you are the commandments of the Lord" (1 Corinthians 14:37), where the letter possessed authority the moment that Paul, with the help of the Holy Spirit, wrote it; it was later "canonized," accepted because of its inherent authority. He then adds, "No church council (which would include "early Christians") by its "selection" or decrees can make the books of the Bible authoritative. The books of the Bible possess their own authority and, indeed, had this authority long before there were any councils of the church." [8.]

Back on the subject of adding doctrine as authoritative, to somehow understand Scripture better, another aspect - one must take note that Scripture's own Words self- proclaim truths that no other writings may be added, that no thoughts of man can be introduced to "filter" God's Words. Critiquing these statements, particularly seeing the need to add "tradition" and "reason" to "Scripture," consider the following verses from God's Word:

- There is a way that seems right to a man, but its end is the way of death. (Proverbs 14:12)
- But the Lord said to Samuel, "Do not look at his appearance or at or at his physical stature, because I have refused him. For the Lord does not see as man sees; for man looks at the outward appearance, but the Lord looks at the heart." (1 Samuel 16:7)
- "For My thoughts are not your thoughts, Nor are your ways My ways," says the Lord. For as the heavens are higher than the earth, so are My ways higher than your ways and My thoughts than your thoughts. (Isaiah 55:8–9)

On this last passage of Scripture, I wanted to comment a bit further. A good friend of mine in Ohio sends me past devotions from another devout Christian lady, now deceased, who commented on this verse from Isaiah – I thought it worth repeating here, as I believe it adds greatly to what I'm thinking - she writes,

"Earthly wisdom is rooted in the belief that all life can be understood, rationalized, and proved scientifically. But God moves in ways that are still a mystery to man. Science can never prove what causes a person to fall in love. It can never prove what happens to a person after death. It can never measure the breadth or depth of God's love and mercy … None of the world's information we have acquired or the tangible skills we have developed in order to acquire, maintain, and advance our lives on this earth will be useful in eternity. The wisdom of this world has no capability to carry a person from this life into the next." [9.]

Adding to these thoughts, concerning what today's scientific community can "prove," consider this – near the end of the book of Job, where Job makes the mistake of demanding God give an answer for his sufferings, God sits him down and asks him a series of questions - demonstrating His

Omnipotence as Creator of this Universe. In the course of this questioning, stretching from chapters 38 through 41, Job gets an earful, none of which he could answer. What's interesting, however, is the fact that we, today, with all of our scientific knowledge and intellect, cannot answer many of these same questions either!

Most of the sourcing for this evidence can be verified by visiting Apologetic's Press, and/or checking the references I provided in the Appendix of my first volume under this topic on page 353. [8.] Right out of the gate, God asked Job, "Where were you when I laid the foundations of the earth? Tell Me, if you have understanding (38:4). (I'll come back to this one). Starting in verse 16, we read, "Have you entered the springs of the sea? Or have you walked in search of the depths? Until very recently, science did not discover the freshwater springs that arise in many of our seas – have we found them all? We know there are deep recesses in the various oceans, such as the Mariana Trench, one of the deepest oceanic trenches on Earth, at over six and a half miles under the surface, located in the western Pacific Ocean – again, have we found all these trenches? Next verse (17), which aligns with the devotional quote above, "Have the gates of death been revealed to you? Or have you seen the doors of the shadow of death? Verse 19, "Where is the way to the dwelling of light? And darkness, where is its place? Light travels in a "way," a "path"; we didn't understand this until recently. Also, "darkness" does not travel – it can be described as residing in a "place." (I use some of this information as "Scientific Foreknowledge" to show evidence of God's Inspiration of Scripture in my first volume, in the Appendix, pg. 353, under "Astronomy." [8.]

Next are verses 25, "Who has divided a channel for the overflowing water, Or a path for the thunderbolt – coupled with 34 and 35, "Can you lift up your voice to the clouds, That an abundance of water will cover you? Can you send out lightnings, that they may go, and say to you, 'Here we are!'? God is asking Job if he can control the weather, can he predict a 'path for lightning'? Or exactly when a cloud will drop rain? – think of the lives we could save, of the betterments we could derive with knowledge of how to control the weather today – the problem is – we still cannot. Another question Job, nor we today, can answer is found in verse 36, "Who has put wisdom in the mind? Or who has given understanding to the heart? No explanation is needed here. And probably one of the most profound questions comes in verse 33, which Job could not have even understood, let alone answer; nor can we today fully appreciate, "Do you know the ordinances ("laws" – NIV) of the heavens? Can you set their dominion ("rule" – ESV) over the earth? For instance, one of these "laws" to which He set as "dominion" on this earth, is the creation of a complex genome making up the human body. Scientists have been trying to understand this for years and only recently have been able to begin mapping this genome, but to date, they are still far from understanding all God has designed – how all the "chemical communications" between our genes work to keep our bodies healthy. If we did understand, we could cure cancer, and many other diseases, we could prevent all maladies from even entering our bodies – we can't, why? Because today's science lacks the knowledge to even understand, let alone prove, all these marvelous systems - this chemical language that directs these many complex interconnections God has designed into us.

Finally, getting back to verse 38:4, this is one of those verses that espouse the claim that God created this earth (along with everything else in the universe) – which is vehemently denied by the scientific community, and particularly the evolutionally camp. This topic (the theory of evolution) deserves much more attention than I have here to give justice. However, for our purposes, it does fall into the category of subjects many scientists feel they have proven true, and though this may raise the eyebrows of many who read this – evolution cannot be proven true! To be fair, "creation" cannot be proven true either – since both cannot be "tested" or "witnessed/observed" as having taken place (no one was here in the very beginning, nor can one wait "millions of years" to observe/test evolutions' proposed validity). Observing, testing, and documenting are all criteria established by the scientific community to move proposed truths from a "Scientific Theory," to "Hypothesis," to "Law," to "Scientific Fact." [10.] Evolution remains a "theory," despite those who call it a "fact," Why? Because it cannot be proven to be anything other than what they themselves have defined as a theory!

So, how does one determine whether evolution or creation is the correct origin? This is accomplished by building "Scientific Models" – an "Evolution Model," stating the principle points this theory espouses, and a "Creation Model," doing likewise. Then collecting data or evidence, scientific evidence observable today, one can then compare the two. Whichever model we find the predominance of evidence agreeing with – this Model becomes the more plausible.[11.] (Not absolutely proven, but enough so that one should feel confident this model is favored over the other). For me to just tell you that the evidence in support of the Creation Model, far and above exceeds the scientific evidence supporting the Evolution Model doesn't mean much without presenting such evidence. I intend to do just that, by devoting my entire appendix in the fifth volume of this series to this topic – as I feel it has become that important, and that much of a stumbling block for so many, in reconciling God's Word with what many of today's scientists think they've proven, and what many within the general public, think is 'fact'. Why is this such a big deal? Why is the subject of evolution vs creation so important? Evolution teaches there is no God! If what I say is true concerning the evidence, why have so many people bought in? I'll give you two reasons – Dr. Henry Morris in his book, "The Twilight of Evolution," makes this statement,

"The main reason most educated people believe in evolution is simply because they have been told that most educated people believe in evolution." [12.]

In other words, evolution has been taught for so long as fact, precluding even the opportunity to present evidence of another view, that most people look no further and simply accept it so as not to appear 'uneducated.' Along with this, in their book, "Why Scientists Accept Evolution," Drs. James D. Bales and R.T. Clark make this statement:

"Evolution is taken for granted today and thus it is uncritically accepted by scientists as well as by laymen. It is accepted by them today because it was already accepted by others who went before them and under whose direction they obtained their education. So widely accepted is the doctrine of evolution that it is received by each oncoming generation for the simple reason that each generation finds that evolution is a part of the scientific world outlook in which it is reared." [13.]

A second reason so many accept evolution, though the scientific evidence does not appear to be there, can be summarized by the eminent evolutionist, D.M.S. Watson of the University of London when he stated,

"Evolution itself is accepted by zoologists, not because it has been observed to occur … or can be proved by logically coherent evidence, but because the only alternative, special creation, is clearly incredible." [14.]

This reason ignores any evidence whatsoever (even acknowledging proof to be out of reach), basing belief on a non-belief – the impossibility of a miracle. In other words, people believe in evolution because they refuse to believe otherwise; they choose not to believe in the "incredible," and they choose not to believe in God.

Let me ask the reader one question, which you may not have given serious thought to – How did evolution begin? How did the first "matter" or "material" it had to work upon arrive here, to supposedly change, progress, and mutate forward? In other words, how do you get "something" from "nothing?" Can you answer this? No one has been able to give me or anyone else I know a satisfactory answer to this question. Current scientific theory on "origins" of "the Big Bang" doesn't work – What blew up? Does it not have to be "something" that blew up and evolved into everything you see around you today? You can theorize as small a material as you wish for this "bang," – but in the end, it's irrelevant because it had to be "something," and you cannot get "something from absolutely nothing." Only an eternal God, existing outside of, preceding, and being of a "more adequate" status than our Universe, can make sense of origins and can fulfill one of science's most unshakable and revered Laws - "The Law of Cause and Effect" (a Law God allowed us to discover) – God being the Cause, the Universe being the grand Effect.

Speaking of Scientific *Laws*, as one of the terms used by the scientific community, we would do well to understand just how scientists define these terms for their own use, compared to how we non-scientists understand these same terms, particularly the top two, as put forth to us, the general public – a "Law," and a "Fact." A Law is defined (by scientists) as follows: "Laws in science are typically descriptions of how the physical world behaves under certain circumstances … these laws can be very useful in supporting hypotheses and theories." [10.] I might add here that all Scientific Laws have NEVER been disproved, not once, otherwise, they would be dropped down to a lower category or term – this is admitted by the NAS (National Academy of Sciences) by saying, "These laws can be very useful … but like all elements of science they can be altered with new information and observations." [10.] (Keep in mind that neither evolution nor creation can be observed.)

What's amazing to this author is their term for "Scientific Fact" as they understand, and many outsiders seem to understand. Here's their definition, "The word "fact" has a different meaning in science than it does in common usage. A scientific fact is an observation that has been confirmed over and over. However, observations are gathered by our senses, which can never be trusted entirely … Observations can change with better technologies or with better ways of looking at data … Ironically, facts in science often are more susceptible to change than theories – which is one reason why the word "fact" is not much used in science." [10.] According to this statement, a scientific "fact" is not as much use to a scientist as we've been led to believe – and what do we constantly hear – "evolution is an established scientific fact?"

I'm citing these definitions from a book that was put out by the National Academy of Sciences (NAS) in 1998 titled "Teaching Evolution and the Nature of Science" – a book to instruct public and university teachers exactly how to teach the "truth" concerning the theory of evolution. In light of this, the definition of a Scientific Theory has been elevated, though it is the lowest on the official scientific "term" scale. Here's their definition of "theory," "In science, a well-substantiated explanation of some aspect of the natural world that can incorporate facts, laws, inferences, and tested hypothesis." They go on to say, "Sometimes scientists themselves use the word "theory" loosely and apply it to tentative explanations that lack well-established evidence. But it is important to distinguish these casual uses of the word "theory" with its use to describe concepts such as evolution that are supported by overwhelming evidence … ideas are not referred to as "theories" in science unless they are supported by bodies of evidence that make their subsequent abandonment very unlikely. When a theory is supported by as much evidence as evolution, it is held with a very high degree of confidence." [10.] There you have it, the theory of evolution is atop this terminology food chain – it "incorporates all the other terms – facts, laws, and tested hypotheses – downplaying its vulnerability to be altered (as they suggest for all other terms.)

Since a "theory" is so elevated here, could we not apply all these accolades to the theory of creation as well? Evolutionists would likely say,

"No, we cannot - where's the overwhelming evidence?" To which I would reply, open your eyes - there is much more scientific evidence favoring the theory of creation than for that of evolution! One must simply be willing to consider such evidence (which most secular publications and particularly school textbooks have purposely left out, thus, not revealing to our students.)

One last thing on this topic concerning Scientific Laws - these laws have never been broken or disproved. They are more akin to what the NAS describes as a "theory," however, it's interesting that evolutionists rarely discuss them in textbooks (they've even been omitted from this teacher's guide published by the NAS to aid in indoctrinating our children). Why? They cannot easily be reconciled with their theory – here are just a few of these Scientific Laws and their official descriptions (the parenthesized comments, and reasons they're difficult to defend in favor of evolution, are from this author):

- **The Law of Biogenesis**: Life comes only from preceding life of its own kind or type. [15.] (Never been proven otherwise, God created life and locked out change of "kinds" from one entire species to another. (Genesis 1:21).
- **The First Law of Thermodynamics**: Matter/Energy can be neither created nor destroyed *in nature.* [16.] (Creation is the only logical solution to this. As stated above.)
- **The Second Law of Thermodynamics:** In any change, the Universe becomes a slightly more disorderly place; the entropy goes up, and the information content goes down. [17.] (In other words, every system left to its own devices tends to move from order to disorder. (We have *NEVER* documented a *SINGLE* case of a "good mutation" advancing evolution forward, let alone a series of "good mutations," which according to our next Law, is impossible!)
- **The Law of Probability**: The occurrence of any event, where the chances are beyond one in one, followed by 50 zeros, is an event we (scientists) can state with certainty will never happen, no matter how much time is allotted and no matter how many conceivable opportunities could exist for the event to take place. (This Law

applies to every other Law you see listed here! The probability of life evolving from non-life, according to the renowned evolutionist, Carl Sagan, is one chance in 1 x $10^{2,000,000,000}$ [that's one chance out of 1 followed by 2 billion zeros – a size so staggering, and so impossible, especially since it has been calculated that this entire Universe contains no more than 10^{80} electrons! [18.]

- **The Law of Cause and Effect**: Every Material effect must have an adequate antecedent cause. [19.] (Again, foundational, universal, and totally unquestioned by the scientific community to this day)
- **Law of Genetics** (Technically this is not a scientific "Law" per se – however, it is a relatively new discipline, discovered by George Mendel in 1857, later described as "Mendel's Laws." His discovery revealed that DNA and the genetic code's chemical instructions are reproduced faithfully time after time. As a good "Anti-Law" description or "Law in Reverse" this can be said, "There is no known law, no known process, and no known sequence of events which can cause information to originate by itself in matter." [20.] (As stated in the 2nd Law – no "good mutation," or a positive change to the chemical communication between organic cells, have ever been observed.)
- **The Law of Logic**: (Again, not a scientific "Law" per se, however, "logic" can be defined as, "The science of correct reasoning … describing relationships among propositions in terms of implication, contradiction, contrariety, conversion, etc. … correct reasoning … a necessary connection or outcome, as through the working of cause and effect.") [21.] – The creationist's contention that "*Design in nature demands a designer*" fulfills this definition – for instance, you don't see supposed 600-million-year-old "trilobite eyes" with lenses more complex and more sophisticated than anything we've ever seen in nature up to current day, without this being true. Let me expound on this last one if I may, since it's easy to make a claim, with what may appear to be just that, with no backing.

This creature, a trilobite, comes into view in the "fossil record" in what is identified by scientists as the Cambrian and Ordovician periods (supposedly 500 to 600 million years ago), where life suddenly "exploded" into view (another piece of evidence scientists have yet to explain) – one rock "layer" up from the "Pre-Cambrian Era" (the Pre-Cambrian consisting of either fossil-free or simple, mostly single-celled organisms. [22] A trilobite is an extinct primitive marine invertebrate – whose eyes, unlike a human eye, composed of living tissue only, are composed of *inorganic* calcite atop a layer of chitin – materials with precisely the right refractive indices to refract light from any distance – and a wavy boundary between them of a precise mathematical shape.

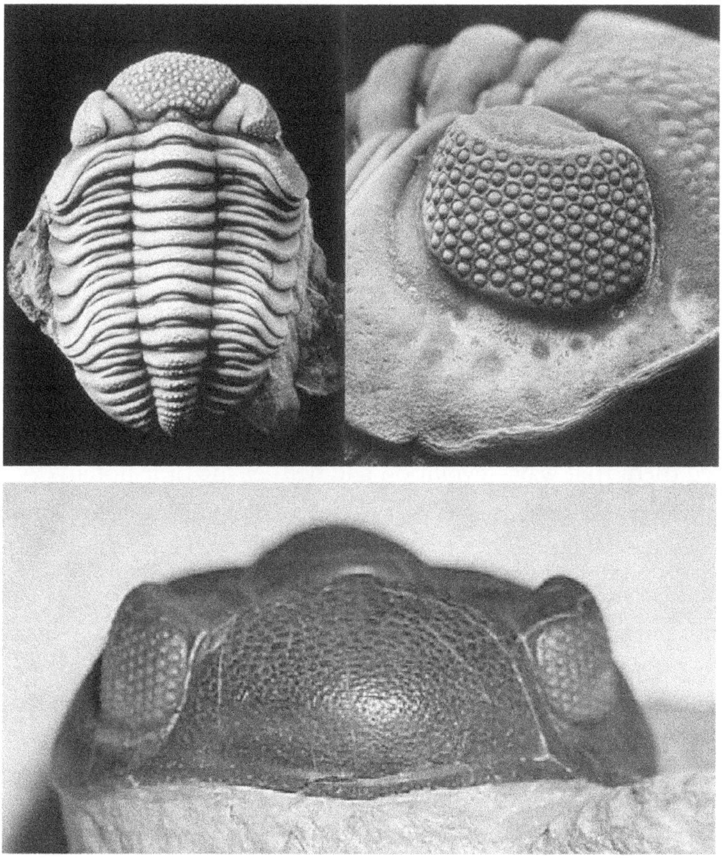

The Trilobite Eye

Some trilobites had a special double lens design with anywhere from 100 to 15,000 lenses within each eye – allowing them to see perfectly underwater (their natural habitat) as well as to focus on objects in the world above. The Designer here applied what we now know as the physical laws of Fermat's principle of least time, Snell's law of refraction, Abbe's sine law, and Birefringent optics. [23.] [24.] Listen to a few evolutionists describe this, and I'll let you decide:

Lisa Shawver, Science News, 1974, said that trilobites possessed, "the most sophisticated eye lenses ever produced by nature." [25.] (Keep in mind, we find this creature in Cambrian rock, right above "Pre-Cambrian – a predecessor to all supposed evolved life moving forward according to evolutionists - no time here to supposedly "evolve" these lenses).

Acknowledged worldwide authority on trilobites, Riccardo Levi-Setti, University of Chicago, in his book "Trilobites," made this statement, "That the interface between the two lens elements in a trilobite's eye was designed (his words not mine) in accordance with optical constructs worked out by Descartes and Huygens in the mid-17th century – borders on science fiction." [26.]

And finally, Niles Eldridge, paleontologist at the American Museum of Natural History stated, "These lenses (trilobite) [31] – technically termed aspherical, aplanatic lenses – optimized both light collecting and image formation better than any lens ever conceived ... these trilobites hit upon the best possible lens design that optical physics has ever been able to produce." [27.] (Let me add – trilobites did not "hit" upon these lenses – God designed them that way – evolution had neither the time nor any evidence of a supposed ancestral predecessor in the fossil record to move forward in producing these lenses.)

The bias presented in this book the NAS put out in '98 is over the top – not only to indoctrinate students, but also the teachers who instruct them, as exhibited in this comment, on page 4, "Those who oppose the teaching of evolution in public schools sometimes ask that teachers present the evidence against evolution. However, there is no debate within the scientific community over whether evolution occurred, and there is no evidence that evolution has not occurred." [28.] This statement is both false and misleading. The first claim, that there is "no debate within the scientific community over whether evolution has occurred, is just flat out false. Many reputable scientists do question this theory, and not just on a few small points, but on the validity of the theory as a whole. (This we will develop further in my fifth volume appendix.) The second statement is also highly misleading since it is only true with respect to direct empirical (observable) evidence (which is impossible to obtain). What's left out, however, is that no evidence of this type exists to show organic evolution *has* occurred either.

Here's another – on page 56 of "Teaching about Evolution" under the "Frequently Asked Questions" section (given to help teachers field difficult questions from parents and others who object to evolution being taught), the following is stated under the sub-heading "Is evolution a fact or a theory?":

"Theory does not mean 'guess' or 'hunch' as it does in everyday usage. Scientific theories are explanations of natural phenomena built up *logically* from *testable observations*" ('logically' is subjective, and 'testable observations' are not relevant in this case) "... Scientists most often use the word 'fact' to describe an observation" (this cannot be used for evolution – it's never been observed). "But scientists can also use fact to mean something that has been tested or observed so many times that there is no longer a compelling reason to keep testing or looking for examples. The occurrence of evolution in this sense is a fact." [29. 30.] (When one is biased in one direction, and that bias is *naturalism,* where creation is discarded out of hand, any testing will be skewed to that end, and the results, no matter how many times one tests, will either be discarded if they don't agree with the bias, or they will be rationalized away to favor or support the outcome desired – such is the case with "testing" evolution).

Just below this response, we see on the same page the question, "Why isn't evolution called a law?" Here's their answer, "Laws are generalizations that describe phenomena, whereas theories explain phenomena. Laws, like facts and theories, can change with better data. But theories do not develop into laws with an accumulation of data" (yes, they most certainly do, according to true scientific terminology – that's the criteria to establish a Law! – accumulate enough evidence to qualify at this level) "Rather, Theories are the goal of science." [29. 30.] [What a misleading statement! If this were true, why is the term 'theory' the lowest on the scientific term scale – lower than a hypothesis, and even lower than a 'law' or a 'fact', no my friends, the goal of science is not 'theories,' but is instead 'facts' and 'laws' – for facts and laws have never been proven untrue (for instance the Law of Causality or Cause and Effect which states that **every material**

effect must have an adequate antecedent cause), [30] otherwise they move out of that category!]. [31.]

On a personal note, and as you might already have suspected, this topic (evolution vs creation), along with "Christian Evidences" in general, are other passions of mine. When this book was published by the NAS in 1998, my son, Kyle, was concurrently being introduced and indoctrinated to the validity of evolution at his local high school. I decided as his father, I owed it to him to debunk this theory as best I was able – so I did some extensive research and wrote a book to him, not necessarily for public consumption, but to give to him - so that he could ascertain the truth for himself. I took this NAS book and refuted every point they made – using works, including the book written by a brilliant creation scientist, Jonathan Sarfati, Ph.D., E.M., titled "Refuting Evolution." [32.] (If you are on the fence at all on this issue – please do yourself a favor and get this book, (or one of his sequels) – in my opinion, you'll walk away with a different perspective). Much effort went into the book I put together for my son; he told me, and I truly believe, it helped him gain a better understanding of the subject - to be able to make an informed decision for himself – not one forced from one side. I also gained a wealth of knowledge during my study, which I will attempt to briefly develop the most irrefutable evidence in my fifth-volume appendix. No, I'm not a scientist, however, I can see the evidence put forth by creation scientists, and that of evolutionists, compared to the 'models' both have set up and acknowledged, which are the only way we can truly come close to ascertaining which was more likely to have occurred, and I can tell you, there is much more plausible evidence in favor of creation, evidence being withheld, misstated, or falsified by the evolutionary folks, so that you, the general public cannot see, let alone evaluate for yourselves.

Returning to the subject at hand – "authority" as perceived by the Episcopal Church - it's no wonder the apostle John stated that to teach any doctrine other than Christ's teaching is to go too far and thus not have God (2 John 9). Paul, speaking to the churches in Galatia, admonished them for deserting Christ and distorting His gospel for a different gospel—that "even if we, or an angel from heaven, preach any other gospel to you than what we have preached to you, let him be accursed!" (Galatians 1:8).

The addition of the Book of Common Prayer and the creeds (summary statements of belief considered authoritative by Episcopalians and so many other denominations) are examples of "this other gospel" and can be considered departures from Scripture and, according to Paul, are to be "accursed." Though some try to justify these additions by stating that most of the text within each consists of direct quotations from Scripture and summary statements of faith, and therefore are essentially the same, the question becomes this: If anything is added or subtracted from Scripture (or, in this case, pulled from Scripture and highlighted, summarized, or altered), does it not violate Scripture? (Proverbs 30:5–6; Revelation 22:18–19). And further, if the text is exactly the same as Scripture, why is it needed? Why not just quote Scripture and give credit to same?

Another danger exists in introducing these worship guides for repetitive use during services. When your worship service is confined to the pages of a book other than the Bible, it could easily lead to the type of worship condemned by Jesus in Matthew 6:7–8. Not only do "vain repetitions" become possible, but the emphasis commanded again by Jesus in John 4:24 (to worship "in Spirit and in truth") would seem less likely to occur when simply reciting words from a page.

To illustrate, consider the two creeds, as cited from Episcopal literature verbatim:

The Apostles' Creed
(Book of Common Prayer, 1662)

I BELIEVE in God the Father Almighty, Maker of heaven and earth:
And in Jesus Christ his only Son our Lord:
Who was conceived by the Holy Ghost, Born of the Virgin Mary:
Suffered under Pontius Pilate,
Was crucified, dead, and buried, He descended into hell [33.]; the third day he rose again from the dead:
He ascended into heaven, And sitteth on the right hand of God the Father Almighty:
From thence he shall come to judge the quick and the dead.
I believe in the Holy Ghost:

The holy Catholic Church; The Communion of Saints:
The Forgiveness of sins:
The Resurrection of the body,
And the Life everlasting.
Amen. [33. 34.]

The Nicene Creed:
(Book of Common Prayer, 1979)

We believe in one God, the Father, the Almighty, maker of heaven and earth, of all that is, seen and unseen.
We believe in one Lord, Jesus Christ, the only Son of God, eternally begotten of the Father, God from God, Light from Light, true God from true God, begotten, not made, of one Being with the Father.
Through him all things were made.
For us and for our salvation he came down from heaven: by the power of the Holy Spirit he became incarnate from the Virgin Mary, and was made man.
For our sake he was crucified under Pontius Pilate; he suffered death and was buried.
On the third day he rose again in accordance with the Scriptures; he ascended into heaven and is seated at the right hand of the Father.
He will come again in glory to judge the living and the dead, and his kingdom will have no end.
We believe in the Holy Spirit, the Lord, the giver of life, who proceeds from the Father and the Son.
With the Father and the Son he is worshiped and glorified.
He has spoken through the Prophets.
We believe in one holy catholic and apostolic Church.
We acknowledge one baptism for the forgiveness of sins.
We look for the resurrection of the dead, and the life of the world to come.
Amen [34.]

These creeds, though mostly true statements of faith, are not Scripture. They are human statements of belief, and these statements are not inspired by God. The harm in declaring them as such is that we are adding something God did not sanction. To illustrate further, consider a human error placed in the Apostles' Creed. The Anglican translation of the Apostles' Creed states that Christ "descended into hell and on the third day He rose again from the dead." Anglicans translate Hades, Sheol, and Hell as identical concepts (as is rooted in the King James Version). This is incorrect, as Christ did not descend into hell. He descended into Hades or Sheol, according to the Scriptures—there is a distinction.

The above translation of the Apostles' Creed was revised in their 2000 *Book of Common Worship* to read, "He descended to the dead." Though their understanding of this phrase "to the dead" is similar to that of "hell," it appears to have been altered to address this very argument. It remains in their *Book of Common Worship*, however, as authoritative. This same translation— "descended into hell"—is used by other denominations as well, including Roman Catholic, Lutheran, and others.

As an argument against the terminology of Hell, Hades, and Sheol being identical, consider the following:

> For David says concerning Him, "I foresaw the Lord always before my face, for He is at my right hand, that I may not be shaken. Therefore my heart rejoiced, and my tongue was glad; moreover my flesh also will rest in hope. For You will not leave my soul in Hades, nor will you allow Your Holy One to see corruption' … he, foreseeing this spoke concerning the resurrection of the Christ, that His soul was not left in Hades, nor did His flesh see corruption." (Acts 2:25–27, 31; ref. Psalm 116: 8–11)

> Therefore He says, "When He ascended on high, He led captivity captive, and gave gifts to men." (Now this, "He ascended," what does it mean but that He also first descended into the lower parts of the earth? He who descended is also the One who ascended far above all the

heavens, that He might fill all things.) (Ephesians 4:8–10; ref. Psalm 68:18)

So it was that the beggar died, and was carried by angels to Abraham's bosom. The rich man also died and was buried. And being in torment in Hades, he lifted up his eyes and saw Abraham afar off, and Lazarus in his bosom. Then he cried and said, 'Father Abraham, have mercy on me, and send Lazarus that he may dip the tip of his finger in water and cool off my tongue; for I am tormented in this flame. But Abraham said, 'Son, remember that in your lifetime you received your good things, and likewise Lazarus evil things; but now he is comforted, and you are tormented. And besides all this, between us and you there is a great gulf fixed, so that those who want to pass from here to you cannot, nor can those from there pass to us. (Luke 16:22–26)

For as Jonah was three days and three nights in the belly of a great fish, so will the Son of Man be three days and three nights in the heart of the earth. (Matthew 12:40)

And I saw the dead, small and great, standing before God, and books were opened. And another book was opened, which is the Book of Life. And the dead were judged according to their works, by the things which were written in the books. The sea gave up the dead which were in it, and Death and Hades delivered up the dead who were in them. And they were judged, each one according to his works. Then Death and Hades were cast into the lake of fire. This is the second death. And anyone not found written in the Book of Life was cast into the lake of fire. (Revelation 20:12–15)

> O Lord, You brought my soul up from the grave (Sheol in NASB); You have kept me alive, that I should not go down to the pit. (Psalm 30:3)
>
> But God will redeem my soul from the power of the grave (Sheol in NASB), for He shall receive me. (Psalm 49:15)
>
> For great is Your mercy toward me, and You have delivered my soul from the depths of Sheol. (Psalm 86:13)
>
> For you have delivered my soul from death. (Psalm 116:8)

By combining these Scriptures, we learn that the terms Hades, or Sheol (also referred to as "the grave" in NKJV), are used interchangeably, as a place where an individuals' soul goes upon death (temporarily) until God's judgment. Luke 16 reveals that the souls of both the righteous and unrighteous are present there. The righteous are in a place described as "with the Lord" (Ecclesiastes 12:7; 2 Corinthians 5:8; Philippians 1:23), and their condition is described as "comforted" (Acts 2:27; Luke 23:43; 16:22–25). The wicked, however, are in a condition described as being "tormented" and "in this flame" (Luke 16:22–24). The righteous are separated from the wicked by a great chasm, which is fixed (Luke 16:26).

At the end of time, God will judge all mankind according to their deeds (Revelation 20), at which time "death and Hades will give up the dead which are in them" for this judgment. Death and Hades itself, as a temporary abode, will then be cast into the lake of fire, or hell (along with anyone whose name is not written in the Book of Life), and those judged righteous, who were temporarily in Hades, awaiting this judgment, will be with the Lord.

Concerning our Lord and the statement in the Apostles' Creed as to His descending into hell, the Scriptures indicate Jesus descended into Hades (not hell) for three days and three nights. James 2:26 tells us that upon death, the body will separate from the soul, and our Lord was no different. Matthew 27:50 states Jesus "yielded up His spirit." The Scriptures reveal He was not abandoned to Hades (therefore, He went there but was not *left* there), and His flesh saw no decay. His body was left in the tomb for only three days, this attesting to the fact that Jesus was indeed resurrected from the tomb. His spirit left Hades after three days and was reunited with His body. Hell is what is called the "second death," the "Lake of Fire"—an eternal abode reserved for the devil and his angels, which was a place where Jesus did not go! Though this might seem a minor discrepancy, it nevertheless is a discrepancy not worthy to be considered God's inerrant Word.

There is another problem concerning these creeds unbefitting the status to which these denominations have given them – that is both begin with a statement confirming belief in "God the Father, Maker of heaven and earth …". [34.] The Apostles Creed continues with the next statement, confirming belief in "Jesus Christ his only Son our Lord"; while the Nicene Creed follows with a second statement: "We believe in one Lord, Jesus Christ, the only Son of God, eternally begotten of the Father …". The problem with this – God the Father was not technically the *only* "Creator or Maker" of heaven and earth – according to Scripture, the Godhead - Father, Son, and Holy Spirit, all Three, were involved. Genesis 1:1 says, "In the beginning, God (the Triune God, not God the Father alone) created the heavens and the earth."

How do we know this? Consider several additional Scriptures. John 1:2-3 says, "He (Jesus) was in the beginning with God. All things were made through Him (Jesus), and without Him (Jesus) nothing was made that was made." This passage tells us God the Father was with Jesus, but Jesus was the agent through whom creation was accomplished. Also 1 Cor. 8:6: "… yet for us there is one God, the Father, *of whom are* all things, and we for Him; and one Lord Jesus Christ, *through whom are* all things, and through whom we live." In discussing this passage, Wayne Jackson comments that "the one God" and "the one Lord" refers to the united nature of the biblical deity. That "God the Father" is the **source** of all created things in the divine plan of operation – we owe our origin to Him. There is also Jesus Christ, the agent of creation, **through whom** we have our existence (v.6; cf. Jn. 1:3; Col 1:16; Heb. 1:2). Thus, these two Persons (other texts supplement with references to the Spirit), each possessing the divine nature, operate in absolute harmony." [35.] In addition, one only needs to read a few verses further to Genesis 1:26, to confirm other members of the Godhead were involved: "Then God said, 'Let *Us* make man in *Our* image ..." – actually, this verse can be argued to involve all Three Persons of the Godhead.

The Holy Spirit was also involved in creation; He is mentioned in verse two of Genesis 1: "And the Spirit of God was hovering over the face of the waters." This is later referred to in Psalm 33:7, "He gathers the waters of the sea together as a heap; He lays up the deep in storehouses." The Spirit is often translated as "wind" or "breath" in the Old Testament; Psalm 33:6 picks up on this word – indicating the Spirit's help in creation; actually, this 6th verse establishes the Word of the Lord (Jesus) as having made the heavens, and "all the host of them by the *breath* of His mouth (the Holy Spirit) – indicating Jesus made the heavens, however, the Spirit added the final touches to those heavens, by addressing "all the host of them." This ties perfectly with Job 26:13, "By His Spirit He adorned the heavens."

In Dan Winkler's teaching series "Something Happened When I Prayed" – within the course of addressing how the Holy Spirit helps us to pray when we are weak and do not know what or how to pray as we ought (Romans 8:26-27), he introduces a special role the Spirit played in creation as a tie-in, referencing Job 26:13. Here are his words, "He (the Spirit) 'makes intercession' for us ... He takes the inexpressible thoughts of our hearts to God. We're talking about the one who had his own special role in the creation of everything. God, the Father, *crafted* the universe. God the Son *created* the universe. But God, the Holy Spirit, is the one that *colored* and made the universe a place of beauty. He "adorned the heavens" [i.e., he "garnished," or "made them fair"] (Job 26:13, cf. NKJV, ASV). His creative prowess has given us:

1. The soft shades of blue that coat a morning sky and accentuate the pillow of clouds gracefully skating across the horizon;
2. The lacy needles of a Douglas fir, the drooping branches of a weeping willow, and the majestic spire of a redwood;
3. The unmistakable scent of a rose bush, the undeniable presence of a honeysuckle vine, or the sweet perfume of a lilac blossom; and
4. The golden-brown breast of a robin, the yellow-feathered overcoat of a goldfinch, or the painted black mask of a male cardinal.

The Holy Spirit knows how to accessorize, He knows how to put things together and make them beautiful. And – this is awesome – he's the one that puts together the words I don't know how to speak when I struggle to pray."[36.] These are but a few of the passages indicating the Spirits' involvement in creation.

The bottom line to this – both of these creeds have flaws and are misleading, and neither one deserves to be honored as anything other than man's thoughts – certainly not to be held up as Holy Writ to be repeated at worship services! Many may view this as trivial – to criticize these creeds, these summary statements of faith, for a few flaws or inconsistencies. But consider this – when a congregation is asked to repeat these creeds week after week during worship, what do you suppose the people are thinking? What is God thinking? I can say from experience, that, many years ago, when I was involved in the Lutheran denomination, I can remember sitting in the pew, and, almost every week, being asked to recite the Apostle's Creed, either immediately before or immediately after a Scripture reading. At the time, I didn't give it much thought - Scripture - the words of the creed – they were repeated so frequently together, I didn't question that they were both being held up as God's Word.

This is the problem – the clergy have so separated themselves from the people that acts like this (reciting creeds) during worship, become commonplace and accepted as a good thing, and something God desires, when in fact, it's wrong, and God does not desire it, particularly during worship to Him. The only "confession of faith" found in Scripture, is a personal confession of our Lord prior to baptism, to allow us admission into His kingdom, not a summary confession of faith as in a man-made creed.

Apostolic Succession

Apostolic Succession

As we wrap up our discussion on authority, an important differentiation between this denomination, and others, including the Roman Catholic and Orthodox Churches, to the Scriptures concerns this idea of apostolic succession (also referred to with this denomination as "historic episcopate")—the claim that current-day clergy, and particularly the top clerics from these denominations, are able to inherit the authority and miraculous gifts of Jesus's apostles through a consecration process or laying on of hands, beginning with the apostle Peter and others and continuing forward.

These three denominations have elevated one individual in particular to a position atop their respective hierarchies. The Catholic Church asserts absolute authority to their pope as the vicar, or substitute for Christ, on earth. The Orthodox Church recognizes the Patriarch of Constantinople as their "first among equals," a less authoritative yet still spiritual icon. The Anglican/Episcopal Church looks to the archbishop of Canterbury as their first among equals, or *primus inter pares*, again more of a figurehead (particularly outside the borders of England) but still having some influence as a spiritual head over the thirty-nine provinces that make up this denomination worldwide.

The claim for apostolic authority rests not only with the top three in these groups but also with the various upper echelon of the clergy, including primates, archbishops, and bishops, who have been consecrated for purposes of such things as the receipt of confessions, pronouncement of forgiveness of sin, and, in the case of the Catholic pope, the proclamation of God's revelation itself.

Apostolic succession is a false doctrine. Moises Pinedo offered a most effective refutation of the idea of papal infallibility in his article "The Pope, the Papacy, and the Bible." [37.] To discredit a major tenet of these denominations' doctrine is to essentially collapse their entire structure. As mentioned previously, without a papacy and without the hierarchical structure upon which the Roman Catholic Church depends, its validity comes into question. With regard to the Orthodox and Anglican/Episcopal Churches, without the consecrated archbishops and bishops, a major tenet of their authority base disappears, all but unraveling the core ideology of these groups.

In addition to the apostle Peter, upon whom the Catholic Church, in particular, has based the authority of their papacy, these three denominations claim that several of Jesus's apostles have instituted a succession of authority to their present-day bishops and elders via a laying on of hands within their respective churches.

Ethan Longhenry, in two of his works— "A Study of Denominations—Roman Catholicism I: Authority, Apostolic Succession" and "Positions of Authority, A Hierarchy of Bishops," refutes this idea. Following are a few of his points on the matter:

Longhenry begins by establishing the error of hierarchies in general:

> There is no example in the New Testament of any positions of authority existing over more than one church. Furthermore, as far as we are able to see from the Scriptures, each church had a plurality of elders, not just one over many, as seen in Philippians 1:1: "Paul and

> Timothy, servants of Christ Jesus, to all the saints in Christ Jesus that are at Philippi, with the bishops and deacons." Beyond the elders in the local congregation, the only presently living authority is the head of the Body, Christ Jesus: "… and Christ also is the head of the church, being himself the saviour of the body, (Ephesians 5:23)." [38.]

He then focuses on the subject at hand: "There is no indication from the Scriptures that any gift of the Holy Spirit concerning knowledge or interpretation was given to them alone." (To the elders of the church, then or now, by the apostles) Furthermore, the role of the evangelist was delineated from a position of authority in Romans 12:7." [39.] The account, as recorded in Acts 8:14–17, also negates this idea. Peter and John had to come to Samaria from Jerusalem to bestow the gift of the Spirit to the Samarians, as Philip could not do so meaning the apostles could give this gift, but there is no indication others had this ability. When the apostolic age ended, so ended the miracles and so ended the gifts—all of them.

One of the main reasons apostolic succession developed and became popular was to justify current denominational doctrine by asserting that their leaders have ties, via an unbroken chain, with all leaders back to the apostles. It supposedly validates their teachings as true. As Longhenry points out, however, this is never a guideline in the Scriptures for legitimacy, as many churches even in the first century, though founded by apostles, developed false beliefs (cf. 1 Corinthians 1:1–16:24; 2 Corinthians 1:1–13:14; Galatians 1:1–6:18): "Thus, we can see that the Scriptures do not teach that there is an "apostolic succession" from Peter and the Apostles through a system of a pope and bishops through the ages. The Scriptures do show us a pattern of shepherds, a plurality of elders for each local congregation … Therefore, the system of authority promulgated by the Roman Catholic church (and others) is without Scriptural validity." [39.]

Refuting this doctrine is significant, as it involves the three largest Christian denominations in the world: the Roman Catholic Church, having over 1 billion members worldwide, or 50 percent of all denominations; the Orthodox Church, with up to 350 million members, or 14 percent; and the Anglican/Episcopal Communion, with over 80 million, or 3 percent worldwide. In the United States, these communions, as a collective, represent over 600 million individuals, or roughly 40 percent of all denominations.

Primary Beliefs and Doctrines

The Sacraments

Washington National Cathedral

All Episcopalians recognize baptism and the Lord's Supper as necessary (baptism to join the church and, through that union, to gain salvation, and the Lord's Supper to remember Jesus's death). They hold five additional sacraments, similar to that of the Roman Catholic Church, which they call "sacramentals," good to do but not as necessary as baptism and the Lord's Supper, since the latter are considered "dominical" sacraments because the Lord Jesus Christ commanded them;" unlike the other five, which are considered "means of grace" sacraments and not necessary for all people." [40.] As described in their online Glossary, under "What We Believe – The Sacraments," the following is stated: "Sacraments are outward and visible signs of inward and spiritual grace" (Book of Common Prayer, pg. 857). [41.] "Besides baptism and the Eucharist (Holy Communion), the church recognizes these other sacraments or spiritual markers in our journey of faith. Found in the Book of Common Prayer, these include:

- Confirmation (the adult affirmation of our baptismal vows), pp. 413-419
- Reconciliation of a Penitent (private confession), pp. 447-452
- Matrimony (Christian marriage), pp. 422-438
- Orders (ordination to deacon, priest, or bishop), pp.510-555
- Unction (anointing with oil those who are sick or dying), pp. 453-467" [41.]

Baptism

Baptism is one of the two pivotal sacraments of the Episcopal Church, which is interlaced heavily by instructions from their Book of Common Prayer. A basic description or definition of baptism is summarized on the site (https://www.episcopalchurch.org/what -we-believe/baptism/), where it states: "In the waters of baptism, we are lovingly adopted by God into God's family, which we call the Church ... and reminded that nothing can separate us from the love of Christ. Holy Baptism, which can be performed through pouring of water or immersion in it, marks a formal entrance to the congregation and wider Church; and candidates for the sacrament make a series of vows, including an affirmation of the Baptismal Covenant, and are baptized in the Name of the Father, Son, and Holy Spirit. They are marked as Christ's own for ever, having "clothed [themselves] with Christ" (Galatians 3:27). All people of any age are welcome to (*be*) [42.] baptized; we believe in one baptism for the forgiveness of sins, as the "bond which God establishes in Baptism is indissoluble" (Book of Common Prayer, p. 298)." [43.]

Adding to this definition, are these words from the Episcopal Dictionary of the Church, under Baptism: "... God adopts us, making us members of the church and inheritors of the kingdom of God (BCP, pp. 298, 858). In baptism we are made sharers in the new life of the Holy Spirit and the forgiveness of sins ... Each candidate for baptism in the Episcopal Church is to be sponsored by one or more baptized persons. Sponsors (godparents) speak on behalf of candidates for baptism who are infants or younger children and cannot speak for themselves at the Presentation and Examination of the Candidates. During the baptismal rite the members of the congregation promise to do all they can to support the candidates ... They join with the candidates by renewing the baptismal covenant. Candidates are baptized "in the Name of the Father, and of the Son, and of the Holy Spirit," and then marked on the forehead with the sign of the cross. Chrism may be used for this marking. The newly baptized is "sealed by the Holy Spirit in Baptism and marked as Christ's own for ever." [44.]

A reason is then given for infant baptism: "The Catechism notes that "Infants are baptized so that they can share citizenship in the Covenant, membership in Christ, and redemption by God." The baptismal promises are made for infants by their parents or sponsors, "who guarantee that the infants will be brought up within the Church, to know Christ and be able to follow him" (BCP, pp. 858-859)." [44.]

Baptism within the Episcopal Church also includes several additional components, one of which as mentioned above, is the "Baptismal Covenant." This involves a series of vows, made not only by the candidate for baptism (or their sponsor), but all present (BCP, pp. 304-305). After the candidates have renounced evil and committed themselves to Christ, the presider asks the congregation to join them and "renew our own baptismal covenant." Responding to a series of questions, the people affirm belief in the triune God (through the Apostles' Creed - BCP, pp. 96, 304) and promise to continue in the Christian fellowship ..." [45.]

"Baptismal Regeneration" is another doctrine taught, "that at baptism the candidates are not only initiated into the Christian community but are also "born again." That is, the Holy Spirit pours upon them the gift of new life. "The doctrine is rooted in the NT. The Fourth Gospel states that no one can enter the kingdom of God without being born of water and the Spirit ... You must be born from above (or born again)" (Jn 3:5-7). [46.] According to the BCP, candidates for Holy Baptism "receive the Sacrament of new birth" (p. 305) and are declared to have been "raised ... to the new life of grace" (p. 308). [46.] "Like the transformation of bread into the body of Christ at the eucharist, baptismal new life is "spiritually" discerned. The transformation of the baptized persons into participants in the risen life of Christ is not seen with ordinary vision. This transformation is seen with eyes opened by the Spirit." [46.]

"Renewal of Baptismal Vows" is another component associated with Episcopalian baptism. As mentioned under the Baptismal Covenant, these vows involve a repeating/confirming by the entire congregation of their baptism vows (in unison) at various times throughout the year, coinciding with the dedicated days set aside for new baptisms. The Episcopal Dictionary defines this doctrine by stating, "When there are no candidates for baptism or Confirmation at the Easter Vigil, the celebrant (priest) leads the people in the Renewal of Baptismal Vows (BCP, pp. 292-294). ... The address notes that the Lenten observance is ended and invites the people to renew the solemn promises and vows of (their own) baptism (BCP, p. 292). The Renewal of Baptismal Vows included nine questions by the celebrant with responses by the people (BCP, pp. 302-305) ... The affirmations of the Apostles' Creed (the Baptismal Creed) are made by the people ... (BCP, p. 96) ... This form for the Renewal of Baptismal Vows may also be used at the other baptismal feasts ... when there is no candidate for baptism. The Renewal of Baptismal Vows takes the place of the Nicene Creed at the Easter Vigil and the other baptismal feasts (BCP, pp. 295, 312)." (The Nicene Creed is used in the observance of the Lord's Supper, in contrast to the Apostles' Creed, used at baptisms.) [47.]

Finally, the topic of "when to baptize." As mentioned directly above under 'vows,' there are certain days throughout the year that have been set aside for purposes of new baptisms. According to the Book of Common Prayer, proper time is defined under their doctrine of "Baptismal Feasts": "Baptism is especially appropriate at the Easter Vigil, the Day of Pentecost, All Saints' Day or the Sunday after All Saints' Day, and the Feast of Baptism of our Lord (the First Sunday after the Epiphany). These feasts of the church year may be referred to as baptismal feasts. The BCP recommends that, as far as possible, baptism should be reserved for these feasts or occasions or when a bishop is present (p. 312)." [48.]

As previously discussed, the Scriptures dismiss infant baptism on many levels. One must "hear and understand" (Romans 10:14), "believe" (Romans 10:10–11; John 3:16), "repent" (Luke 13:3; 24:46–47), and verbally "confess" (Romans 10:9) prior to baptism. Upon completion of these 'cognitive' acts, they must then be immersed in water, defined as baptism into Christ's blood (Romans 6:3), for the forgiveness of that individual's sin. (Acts 2:39; 8:38; 22:16). An infant is incapable of accomplishing any of those prior acts, as just listed, leading up to baptism (the final act of salvation), not to mention the fact that baptism is not a necessity for them in the first place, it has no meaning at this point for them – God considers them innocent and sinless until they are old enough to know the difference between right and wrong, and therefore no forgiveness need be offered, via Jesus' blood, in the waters of baptism to erase sin that does not exist, at least not until that child is old enough to warrant it.

Again, the state of an infant is not in jeopardy, according to Scripture. Jesus attested to this fact, the innocence of infants: "Assuredly, I say to you, unless you are converted and become as little children, you will by no means enter the kingdom of heaven" (Matthew 18:3). How do we enter the kingdom of heaven? Answer – at the point of conversion – baptism (Jn. 3:5), where our sins have been washed away (Acts 2:38; 22:16). In this verse, Jesus compares the sinless condition following conversion with that of little children. In essence, what Jesus is saying here is this, "Assuredly, I say to you, unless you are converted (baptized, where My blood will cleanse you of all sin) and become as little children, (direct implication – little children are also sinless; otherwise, this comparison makes no sense. In addition, Jesus said, "and *become* as little children." Conversion/baptism is the conclusion of a process (preceded by belief, repentance, and confession) where sinners *become* sinless; little children do not become sinless, they *are* sinless, otherwise, Jesus wouldn't point to them as the 'end goal,' possessing this ideal condition of sinlessness, which completes and gives proper meaning to this verse) you will by no means enter the kingdom of heaven (sinlessness is a condition to enter the kingdom, Christ's church, and salvation).

Here's another example from Luke 18:15–17, "Then they also brought infants to Him that He might touch them; but when the disciples saw it, they rebuked them. But Jesus called them to Him and said, "Let the little children come to Me, and do not forbid them; for of such is the kingdom of God. Assuredly, I say to you, whoever does not receive the kingdom of God as a little child will by no means enter it." This verse, like the previous one in Matthew 18, claims innocence as a prerequisite for entry into the kingdom of God by making little children the personification of that innocence, the goal we are to shoot for, with the kingdom being the resulting reward. I believe another element is suggested in this verse supporting the innocence of little children – that being Jesus' statement in verse 16, "But Jesus called them to Him and said, "Let the little children come to Me, and do not forbid them; *for of such is the kingdom of God."* This phrase, "for of such is the kingdom of God" can and does, I believe, have two meanings – both involving "innocence." One we've discussed is innocence - a condition of kingdom entry, whether it be an adult who converted or repented to put themselves into a sinless/innocent condition or the child, who knew no evil. But there's another meaning Jesus is leaving for us here – "for *of such* is the kingdom of God" also means the kingdom contains these little children - infants and children who have died before ever knowing sin or understanding the concepts of 'right' and 'wrong.' Their innocence is inherent, and nothing has or will preclude them from entry into God's kingdom.

The practice of conducting special services for thanksgiving and dedication of children is also not seen in Scripture as a part of worship or as a precursor to baptism. Hannah's promise to God to dedicate her child to serve the Lord if He would grant her a son (1 Samuel 1:11) is an Old Testament example that comes to mind, but the Episcopal dedications today are not of this nature. Parents don't make a vow to dedicate a child's career or vocation to serving the Lord as, say, a minister or missionary, as much as they are simply asking for a general blessing or prayer on behalf of the child.

The view that one needs to be baptized as a requirement for membership into the Episcopal Church first and subsequently gain salvation through that association is simply not supported by Scripture. Baptism is *essential* - many Scriptures so indicate, including Acts 2:38 and John 3:5, not as an initiation into a denomination but to receive forgiveness for one's sins and the promise of salvation. In addition, immersion is the only form sanctioned in God's Word, not pouring, as the first choice, employed in most Episcopal baptisms (Acts 8:38).

The Episcopal Church not only sanctions infant baptism, they encourage it and have included additional doctrine in support of it, involving not only the candidate for baptism but the congregation at large. In their official doctrine "What We Believe," sub-heading "Holy Baptism – Celebrating Baptism," they state that candidates for baptism must "make a series of vows, including affirmation of the 'Baptismal Covenant.'" [43.] Then they go on to state that "All people of any age are welcome to (*be*) [42] baptized." [43.] They also state in a separate doctrine, "An Episcopal Dictionary of the Church", as a definition for the word "Baptism," "... Each candidate for baptism in the Episcopal Church is to be sponsored by one or more baptized persons. Sponsors (godparents) speak on behalf of candidates for baptism who are infants or younger children and cannot speak for themselves ... During the baptismal rite the members of the congregation promise to do all they can to support the candidates for baptism in their life in Christ. They join with the candidates by renewing the baptismal covenant." [44.]

Aside from infant baptism being unnecessary and not according to God's Word to start with, the doctrines Episcopalians have added here to enhance this sacrament, only compound the error. Where in Scripture do we see a "sponsor"? We don't. In every instance of conversion that we see involving baptism in the New Testament – we see adult individuals expressing their own belief in Christ, their own repentance for past wrongs, their own confession that Jesus is God's Son – never do we see, or does God allow, someone else as a proxy. And secondly, yes, when one of proper age and state of mind follows God's plan of salvation, finalized in baptism, we, as fellow Christians rejoice, and we do encourage that individual (as also we are to encourage one another – 1 Thess. 5:11). But to impose a promise or obligation upon the entire congregation, involving man-made "vows" and "covenants", and in addition to mandate all to repeat their own, personal confession of faith, their 'baptismal vows' – is not following Scripture, it's making up one's own rules.

The extraneous doctrines the Episcopal Church has added, to augment infant baptism in particular, include the "Baptismal Covenant" – where the framework for "renewing" of personal baptismal vows by the congregation is set. These "vows" are further defined in a doctrine titled "Renewal of Baptismal Vows," as a back and forth (Q & A between priest and congregation), at baptismal events – which in turn, brings in a reciting by the congregation of their personal confession of faith, the "Apostles Creed." The "Renewal of Baptismal Vows" doctrine additionally mandates certain times during the year when baptisms are encouraged to take place, in other words, be deferred, in order to accommodate yet another of their doctrines "Baptismal Feasts." (Which specifies exact times of the year when baptisms are to take place). Interestingly, at these times, for instance, "Easter Vigil", or "Day of Pentecost," if there are no candidates to be baptized, worship protocol (specified in their Book of Common Prayer) mandates that congregational confession of personal baptismal vows by all continue, regardless. [45, 47, 48.]

If we investigate God's Word, searching for any of these ideas, we simply cannot find them. We've mentioned this previously, and I'm sure we will again; God frowns on adding to His Word (Deut. 12:32; Prov. 30:6; Rev. 22:18-19). This goes well beyond simply adding to an otherwise God-given doctrine by perhaps changing/adding or removing words to fit a narrative (which is still condemned); this is adding to a false doctrine to begin with (infant baptism), which as stated earlier, compounds the error, the condemnation. From encouraging infant baptism by proxy to mandating congregational confessing of a personal vow they each took at their own baptisms, while in the process, confessing a man-made creed, to obligating that same congregation by making them responsible for bringing that child 'up in the Lord,' to even having to wait until a "Feast Day" for this baptism, only to have to wait until that infant comes of age to personally confess Jesus (Episcopalians call 'Conformation') to finalize the salvation process – is all not in accordance to God's Holy Word. On that last one, where do you see in Scripture (anywhere in Scripture) an occasion where an individual makes the decision to be baptized, then delays doing so to accommodate a church schedule? You don't – in almost, if not all instances we see in the New Testament, the word "immediately" is the time description from decision to action.

One other Episcopal doctrine is mentioned that we've not touched upon as yet, "Baptismal Regeneration." This is not so much an "add" to Scripture as it is a misunderstanding. Yes, it is added into their overall 'baptism package' in support of infant baptism, and their 'faith-only' salvation theology (to be discussed later), but this doctrine wants to interpret "born again" as meaning into the Episcopal Church, not into a saved condition, which, in fact, the term really means. This doctrine states, "At baptism the candidates are not only initiated into the Christian community but are also "born again." That is, the Holy Spirit pours upon them the gift of new life." This 'new life' is then further described as a "new life of grace," which can only be discerned and seen through the eyes of the Holy Spirit. [46.]

Additionally, this doctrine brings into focus John 3:5, where Jesus states, "Most assuredly, I say to you, unless one is born of water and the Spirit, he cannot enter the kingdom of God." One misunderstanding, I believe, lies here. Episcopalians do not see "the kingdom of God" as what it truly is – Christ's church, the church belonging to Christ, the church that He built, the church that He died and shed His blood for (just as He shed His blood for us sinners), the church that was purposed by God the Father before the world began (Ephesians 3:8-11) - just as the Father purposed His Son Jesus before the world began, to be sent to this earth to save mankind from their sins, for those who would believe in Him (John 3:16-17; Ephesians 3:11).

Again, the kingdom of God equals the church belonging to Christ – He gets to set the rules of engagement for entry or exit, and for entry, these He has set – one must be baptized (immersed) in water working in full accord with the Spirit, for the forgiveness of the penitent individual's sins (John 3:3)!

The kingdom of God also equals salvation; it's that simple; this kingdom is here now and can be accessed when one is baptized. Their doctrine interprets "born again" in every way possible, it seems, except the way it was meant – to indicate salvation. Ironically, John 3:5-7 has consistently been used as a proof text by many, including this author, to support the necessity for water baptism in order to enter God's kingdom and be saved. When one ties these words together – "born again" (not into the Episcopal Church, but into God's family, His church); "water and the Spirit" (the answer Jesus gave to Nicodemus in response to his question on this - one must be born of water and the Spirit, clearly indicating water baptism through or involving the Holy Spirit, making this a salvation issue); and "the kingdom of God" (the goal, the end result, of being born again - submitting to "water and the Spirit" or baptism) –– it screams baptism as the final act, the culminating vehicle required for our salvation and nothing else. These are beautiful words tying baptism to salvation, it's sad this denomination, and so many others, cannot see them as such.

This subject (Christ's singular church) deserves just a little more ink here, as it has and remains an "uncomfortable" topic, even among my own brethren within the Lord's church. Those who believe in Christ are admonished in 1 Peter 3:15 to always be ready to give a defense to anyone who asks and to be able to cite a reason or reasons for the hope we have in Christ. And to do so with "meekness and fear" (NKJV). The NIV translates this as "with gentleness and respect." I fear over the past number of years, many, particularly within the Lord's body, have focused on the latter part of this verse (the meekness, fear, gentleness, and respect) and have forgotten or at least downplayed the crux of Peter's (the Spirit's) statement – we must defend our hope, our truth in Christ. There is a hope we have here that needs to be defended – in this case – there is a church here that needs defending, Christ's church, which equals His body, which equals salvation. And yes, we are to infuse our defense of this hope, this truth, with love and with "gentleness and respect" when in conversation with others who have either confronted us or simply voiced an opposite opinion on topics like this.

As I understand, being "ready" is first, knowing the truth ourselves, which we obtain through the study of God's Word ("Your word is truth" John 17:17); and secondly, knowing how best to impart that truth wisely/respectfully, again relying on His Word. Focusing on imparting truth using the Scriptures, consider the following two sets of passages – both addressing our subject at hand (readiness to give account) with slightly different applications. First, Acts 17:16-33. Here, Paul was confronted by the various philosophers in Athens, who had constructed numerous statues of "gods" to worship, including a statue of an "unknown god," to cover their bases. Not knowing the existence of their Creator, Paul, very tactfully and with respect, introduced the true God and Father to them as that "unknown god" statue. Much more could be said here, but the point for our discussion – were Paul to have preached the hard truth, preached their need to abort all other false idols (statues), (including the unknown god statue Paul was using) and insist they confess Jesus alone - without understanding the degree of their unbelief (in essence, to give them the reason for his (Paul's) hope in a "take it or leave it" attitude with no compassion, no respect for where they were theologically), he likely would not have reached anyone (as it was, only a few followed him, due to the extreme set-in bias).

The application for us – listen/know where the person you are conversing with really is religiously – do they believe God is real? The Scriptures are true? It does no good to argue church affiliation when separation on basic belief exists. Paul recognized this and reacted accordingly with his appeals in Athens; we would be wise to do likewise.

The second passage, actually a set of related passages of Scripture, addresses our topic head-on. It begins with Ephesians 4:4, "**There is one body.**" Next, Ephesians 5:23, "Christ is the head of the church, and **He is the Savior of the body.**" And finally, Ephesians 1:22-23, "And He put all things under His feet, and gave Him to be head over all things to **the church, which is His body,** the fullness of Him who fills all in all." Also, "Colossians 1:18, "And **He is the head of the body, the church**." The Greek word the Spirit inspired Paul to use in Ephesians 4:4 for "one" *(heis)* is singular, not plural. I believe He did this for a reason, the very reason we're discussing here. When one combines these passages, the inescapable conclusion one must draw is that **Christ is the Head and Savior of one singular church – His church.** I go into more detail on this topic in my first volume, should the reader have interest." [49.]

The application of these passages seems obvious – here is where the line is drawn, the truth is stated, and for those confronted, the 'readiness' is tested. Many, even within my own brotherhood, I believe, feel the best way to impart this truth (the singularity of Christ's church) is not to address it at all since it might lead to that uncomfortable discussion of exclusivity - but rather to focus on more positive concepts, like the reward of heaven and how one may access that reward. To share and encourage obedience to God's plan of salvation – to truly hear, believe, repent of one's past sin, confess Jesus as God's Son, and submit to baptism. After one becomes a part of God's family, part of His church, then if someone inquires, either from within or without, most say, would be the time to discuss this topic – but only if asked. If one wishes to be a bit more proactive on this, limiting ourselves to a "by the way …" or "what's your thoughts …" seems the most harmless approach, some would say, without inviting confrontation or that "uncomfortable" conversation.

First, I see nothing unscriptural in this, pushing a difficult topic for another day, allowing time perhaps for additional study from God's Word, is not a bad thing. However, it's my opinion that putting off, or even worse, staying away from this subject (or any like it) entirely until or unless approached, in many instances, can be dangerous, it can result in complete pushing away. Being 'ready', however, means being ready to defend all of Scripture, not just the 'comfortable' sections. If a confrontation ensues and escalates to a point where, say, the question is posed, "Is your church the only one God approves? The only one I must become a member of in order to be saved?" – then being 'ready' must step up a notch as well; otherwise, our credibility concerning this issue, and by default, any issue moving forward, will be suspect and may result in rejection of God's truth. An excellent response to these questions is addressed below within the "Bogard-Hardemant Debate."

To me, this topic is no different than any other of God's truths. Its importance cannot be overstated. The blood of our Lord is what has saved those who have confessed Jesus and obeyed His plan of salvation, this blood has redeemed these individuals from their sins (1 Cor. 6:19-20; 1 Peter 1:18-19). One could say Jesus' blood of atonement is one, if not *the* most important and meaningful gift ever to be offered to mankind, for to access this blood grants eternal life. Many have not stopped to consider, that this same blood of Jesus we hold so dear, which was shed for us, was also shed for His church! In exhorting the Ephesian elders, the Spirit, through Luke says this, "For I have not shunned to declare to you the whole counsel of God. Therefore take heed to yourselves and to all the flock, among which the Holy Spirit has made you overseers, to shepherd the church of God which He purchased with His own blood" (Acts 20:27-28). Let that sink in. That makes Christ's church, His one and only church, just as important, just as valuable, as the sin He redeemed for the benefit of those who believe. To belittle the church of our Lord by avoiding discussions concerning it, or taking a non-committal position when asked, is to belittle the very same blood of the cross which bought it, and you. We are encouraged to share our story of conversion with others, why not share our church, His church, as well? As a Christian, I'm not ashamed to proclaim Christ as my Lord and Savior, or His church as the one and only receptacle able to save lost souls. Both are equally important. Both need to be proclaimed to a lost world.

God's Word is all we need to prepare or to be 'ready' to give reason for our hope – our responses coming both directly and indirectly from the Scriptures. Directly, meaning precise commands, examples, and necessary inferences from God's Word; and indirectly, for purposes here, focusing further on some of the 'examples.' Examples of individuals we see in Scripture exhibiting that characteristic of 'readiness,' so we may learn, better understand, and in turn, be able to emulate – examples like Timothy, whom Paul commanded, "… set an example for the believers in speech, in life, in love, in faith and in purity" (1 Tim. 4:12 - NIV). Looking at Timothy's life, and particularly his "speech," what he said, and how he responded to others, we gain knowledge on being ready ourselves. And again, Hebrews, the entire 11th Chapter, concluding in 12:1, "Therefore we also since we are surrounded by so great a cloud of witnesses, let us lay aside every weight, and the sin which so easily ensnares us, and let us run with endurance the race that is set before us …" We are to look at the lives of these great heroes of faith and the hardships they overcame, to better understand how they developed and exhibited a readiness to defend their hope – then do likewise, as we run and endure the challenges in our own races.

The testimony, and the responses of other godly individuals, even in our day and age, who have crossed these bridges before, I believe, have value to add here as well. And the possibility that some of these individuals just might turn out to be instruments through whom God is using to assist us in being prepared, being ready, makes this worth the mention.

An example of the testimony of another which might help us in this regard, was cited in the first volume of this series. [50.] A landmark debate was held on April 21, 1938, in Little Rock, Arkansas between N. B. Hardeman, then president of Freed-Hardeman College, Henderson, Tenn., also a prominent evangelist of the churches of Christ; and Ben M. Bogard, dean of the Missionary Baptist Institute, Little Rock, AR. and pastor of the Antioch Missionary Baptist Church, of the same city. One of the topics under discussion during that four-day debate was titled "Establishment of the Church." Dr. Bogard, whose position was that Christ's church was established during the ministry of Jesus (allowing, in his mind, for the Baptist Church to be that first church started by Christ; whereas Mr. Hardeman's position, aligning more with Scripture, suggested that Christ's church began instead at Pentecost, after Jesus' death, burial, and resurrection, precluding a Baptist (or any other) foreign connection. This date of establishment becomes important, as it ties into our discussion here.

In Dr. Bogard's fourth debate speech on this topic he made this comment, "All other churches started way down this side of Christ, and there are only two churches between whom there is any controversy – the Catholics and the Baptists, they both claim to go back to Christ ... All of the rest by consent acknowledge they can't. Hardeman says you can't neither, his church nor any other church ... Baptists say you can ... then the Baptist Church is the church of our Lord." [50. (Pg.47).]

Mr. Hardeman's response that evening was profound. It left his audience, even his opponent Dr. Bogart, speechless. Hardeman didn't try to correct Dr. Bogard's claims with dates and facts (which he could have done). [As an aside, I address this subject (the origin of the Baptist Church) in the fourth volume of this series; here I show conclusively that the Baptist Church was in fact established by John Smyth in 1611 in England. It started as a movement in opposition to the Church of England and had roots to the Calvinist reformed churches of 1541. In the U.S., the establishment of the Baptist Church is credited to Roger Williams – with the first one being built in Providence, R.I., in 1639.] Hardeman's response which went unanswered, was this, "The kingdom, friends, has always existed ... It existed in Purpose, in the mind of God; it existed next in Promise, as delivered unto the patriarchs, and it existed in Prophecy; and then it existed in Preparation; and last of all, when the New Testament went into effect, it existed in Perfection." (1938, p. 178, italics in orig.). [50. (Pg.32)]

Dr. Miller, in his article "The Unique Church" adds, "More than sixty years have come and gone since that insightful observation. But it remains an accurate expression of biblical truth. Before Adam and Eve inhabited the Garden of Eden together; before the skies, seas, and land were populated by birds, fish, and animals; before the Sun, Moon, and stars were situated in the Universe; and before our planet Earth was but a dark, watery, formless mass – God purposed to bring into being the church of Christ." [50. (Pg.32)]

The takeaway for us – sometimes getting bogged down in a fact-chasing, finger-pointing argument leads to no avail for anyone. In context, Mr. Hardeman simply stepped back to reveal the Scriptures' sweeping description, not only of the eternal nature of Christ's church, but its purpose, its promise, and its perfection – taking this far away from a discussion of "who was the first church" to concepts much more valuable – concepts with eternal implications to those who would consider aligning or not aligning with Christ's church. I developed these concepts in greater detail in my first volume under the heading, "The Establishment of the Church of Christ." [50.] The application for us, perhaps would be to avoid a 'dogfight,' when possible; even if the facts are on your side, even if you're knowledgeable of those facts – and instead, choose to search for a more comprehensive response, one which introduces other passages; not unrelated, but perhaps unexpected, making the point(s) a little differently, and sometimes as above, more impactful, or more meaningful, yet without being overly confrontational.

One last example from this same debate, and this one focusing directly on the subject at hand. Just an hour or so earlier that night, in his third speech, Dr. Bogard confronted Mr. Hardeman, even to the point of ridiculing him concerning his church affiliation with these words, "Nobody will be saved unless he belongs to the church that Brother Hardeman belongs to ... which cuts out ... all Baptists, Methodists, Presbyterians, and others, who happen not to belong to his church." [50. (Pg.48)] This confrontation and ensuing accusation has not changed from that 1938 debate, to the present day; if anything, considering our current societal leanings towards tolerance, it's ramped up. Truth will not change; however, it's the way that truth is presented in many cases, that will determine if it has any hope of being recognized as such. Mr. Hardeman's response, once again, is well worth our attention:

"Dr. Bogard suggests that I announced this afternoon that everybody that wasn't in my church couldn't be saved. Well, he just missed that. I never claimed to have a church. I did say, however, that there is salvation only in the church of the Lord, and nowhere else ...

That doesn't spell that the church does the saving, but Jesus Christ is the Savior of the body ... there are but two kingdoms in which men can be ... either in the kingdom of God, or in the kingdom of the devil ... all of God's children, by virtue of the fact that that they are born again, are born into his family. And the very minute that a man becomes a child of God, he is right then and there a member of the body of Christ, the church of our Lord, the family of God, the kingdom of high heaven ... That's not saying that anybody's lost. I'm not sitting in judgment; nor is it saying that any particular person is saved. There is no need for an appeal to prejudice, but it is saying that if you and I are ever saved, it will be by virtue of the fact that we have been translated out of darkness into the kingdom of God's dear Son, which is the church of the living God. In that there is salvation and nowhere else." [50. (Pg.48)]

We can learn much from this response. Hardeman defused this attack by first removing the "personal" and toning down the anger – he used Bogard's words against him – it wasn't "his church" it was "the church of the Lord." Next, similar to his other response, he appealed to Scripture in a broader, more comprehensive way – capturing truths and concepts that could not easily be denied – such as, "There are only two kingdoms – one of God (he had already established the kingdom of God to be the church) and one of darkness or the devil." And "the very minute a man becomes a child of God, he becomes a member of the church of our Lord." Notice how church affiliation (Baptist vs Methodist vs church of Christ) is missing here. What is in focus now, however - "The Lord's church," "the kingdom of God vs the kingdom of darkness," and "salvation" – found only in the church of the living God. Dr. Bogard could not argue with these concepts, these truths. To do so would be to argue directly against God's Word. Notice also that Hardeman took any perceived personal feelings out of the equation – showing no prejudice or bias by saying he was not sitting in judgment, not considering anyone lost or saved. He simply let the Scriptures speak, and with his last statement dealing with what I believe to be the final blow, letting God win the argument.

In summary, baptism is important, not a theological marker to be embellished and expanded as the Episcopal Church has done here, by adding special 'vows' (including those of the congregation), 'creeds,' 'covenants,' 'feast days,' and the like. No, from what I read in my Bible, baptism, very simply, is described as the last stage of God's perfect plan of salvation, offered to us. It's an essential element or stage to be sure for accessing the kingdom of our dear Lord, but no less essential than any of the other four stages preceding baptism in that salvation plan (which this group, nor any other denomination hardly, if ever mentions). For example, "hearing" is required to be saved (Romans 10, 17; Acts 2:36-37); as is "belief" (Acts 16:31); so is "repentance" (Luke 13:3); and before the final, obedient act of baptism, "confession" is required – not suggested, but essential for salvation (Romans 10:9-10).

I'll end this section with this thought, baptism is a re-enactment – a re-enactment of the Gospel, the Good News. Just as our Lord, before His death, gave instructions on how to remember Him that involved physical acts of weekly partaking of bread and wine, not relying on simply reading or hearing words about His death – so it is with baptism. When a penitent believer submits to baptism, he first 'dies to sin' (repents of past sin, which is more than just acknowledging 'I'm sorry.') Biblical repentance is a commitment to change one's life, to turn 180 degrees, not that slip-ups won't occur ever again, but committed to trying – this is 'dying to sin'. Dying to sin re-enacts Christ's death on the cross. The next one is 'buried' (immersed – Acts 8:38-39) in the waters of baptism, which emulates or re-enacts the burial of our Lord in the tomb (sprinkling and/or pouring as modes of baptism will not work, they are expedients God never intended). And finally, one is resurrected or rises from those waters as a new man or new woman, a new life, 'born again' – just as Christ was resurrected and arose from the grave. (1 Corinthians 15:3-4). This re-enactment is a beautiful illustration of the results of our salvation process – if any additional thoughts or ideas need to be added to 'baptism' it should be these.

The Lord's Supper

On the official website of the Episcopal Church, under "What We Believe," sub-heading "The Eucharist, Holy Communion," the following is stated:

"It goes by several names: Holy Communion, the Eucharist (which means "thanksgiving"), the Lord's Supper, the Mass. But whatever its formal name, this is the family meal for Christians and a foretaste of the heavenly banquet. As such, all persons who have been baptized, and are therefore part of the extended family that is the Church, are welcome to receive the bread and wine, and be in communion with God and each other. Before we come to take Communion together, "we should examine our lives, repent of our sins, and be in love and charity with all people" (Book of Common Prayer, p. 859)." [51.]

Episcopalians generally accept the doctrine that in the Lord's Supper, Christ is truly present, but they accept this doctrine without attempting to explain or define this holy mystery (other than it is accomplished through the Holy Spirit). This view is similar to the Lutheran position that after consecration, and during the distribution of the sacrament, the substance of the actual body and blood of Jesus Christ co-exists with the substance of the emblems of bread and wine—a doctrine commonly known as "consubstantiation."

The following two descriptions/definitions sourced from the "Episcopal Dictionary of the Church," verify this. Under "Eucharist" it states, "Christ's sacrifice is made present by the eucharist, and in it we are united to his one self-offering (BCP, p. 859)." [56.] The second definition from the same source, this time under "Eucharistic Elements," reads, "Bread and wine that are consecrated in the eucharist. The bread recalls the work of human hands required to harvest the wheat and make the bread and the companionship of sharing. The wine recalls festivity and celebration, along with sacrifice ... The body and blood of Christ are understood to be really present in the eucharistic elements after consecration. They represent the inward and spiritual grace of Christ's Body and Blood that is given to his people and received by faith (BCP, p. 859)." [57.]

It should be noted that this view is not universal among all Episcopalians or Anglicans. A segment of both groups, known as the "High Church" or "Anglo-Catholic," hold a view very similar to that of the Roman Catholics regarding the elements of bread and wine. They believe Jesus' body and blood not merely co-exist with the substances of these elements, but the elements actually *become* the body and blood of Jesus; this transformation is known as "transubstantiation." (A complete refutation of this doctrine is covered in my first volume.) [52.]

One small division occurred in 1873 when a group of men withdrew from the Episcopal Church and created the Reformed Episcopal Church. Basically, over this very issue – they rejected the idea that the bread and wine become the literal body and blood of Jesus. (They also rejected the doctrine that baptism into the church is essential for salvation.)

One other aspect of Anglican/Episcopal observance of the Supper needs attention – the use of the Nicene Creed. Within the Episcopal online Dictionary, under this creed, the following is stated, "The use of the Nicene

Creed in the eucharist (right after the gospel), in contrast to the use of the Apostles' Creed in baptism, began in the fifth century in Antioch and became the universal practice in the church. The Nicene Creed is expressed in its original form of "We believe" in the Rite 2 eucharistic liturgy of the 1979 BCP, and this communal expression of faith is also presented as the first option in the Rite 1 eucharistic liturgy. The Rite 1 eucharistic liturgy also offers the "I believe" form as a second option (see BCP, pp. 326-327, 358)." [53.]

The doctrine of transubstantiation was discussed at length in my first volume (pp. 212-224), [52.] however, consubstantiation, the doctrine as adopted by the Episcopal (as well as the Lutheran) Church is an attempt to reduce the pushback from members resisting or not accepting transubstantiation (the complete transformation of the elements of the Supper into Jesus' body and blood), to, in their minds, a more palatable idea, that the elements only transform into the "essence" of Jesus; they "mix" with the substances of the elements, not turning into Jesus' actual body and blood, but instead, allowing His "essence," or His "presence" to exist within those elements. As an overall rebuttal to this, let me start by saying – if either scenario were true, then Jesus did not recognize it, for He still called the cup "*the fruit of the vine*" (Matthew 26:29; Mark 14:25), nor did Paul, for he called the body "*bread*" (1 Corinthians 11:26–27). Though many point to the Last Supper, where Jesus did refer to the bread as His body and the wine as His blood, one must understand He was using metaphors, and symbolic language, as is frequently done in Scripture, to make powerful statements like this. (Other symbolic statements include John 10:7-10 – Jesus as the "door of life"; 11 – Jesus as the "good shepherd'; and 15:5 – Jesus as the "true vine.")

The account of the Last Supper was one instance of this partaking of Jesus' body and blood, however, John records another where similar verbiage was used, though with a different connotation, earlier in Jesus' ministry, through an argument recorded between the Jews and our Lord. This argument began with Jesus' statement, "I am the bread which came down from heaven" (John 6:41). The Jews then reasoned that Jesus had a mother and father here on earth, so this certainly could not be true.

Following Jesus' successful dismantling of this "reasoning," He made this statement in verses 48-51, "I am the bread of life. Your fathers ate the manna in the wilderness, and are dead. This is the bread which comes down from heaven. If anyone eats of this bread, he will live forever; and the bread that I shall give is My flesh, which I shall give for the life of the world." Of course, the Jews tried to rationalize this statement as well by quarreling among themselves over this question, "How can this Man give us His flesh to eat?" Jesus' response, "Most assuredly, I say to you, unless you eat the flesh of the Son of Man and drink His blood, you have no life in you. Whoever eats My flesh and drinks My blood has eternal life, and I will raise him up at the last day. For My flesh is food indeed, and My blood is drink indeed. He who eats My flesh and drinks My blood abides in Me, and I in him. As the living Father sent Me, and I live because of the Father, so he who feeds on Me will live because of Me. This is the bread which came down from heaven – not as your fathers ate the manna, and are dead. He who eats this bread will live forever" (John 6:53-58).

In this discourse, Jesus expounds upon His statement, for He certainly foreknew not only those he was addressing at that moment but also those in the future who would misunderstand this. Jesus moved these thoughts from the physical to the spiritual in these verses – consider these words again, "If anyone eats of this bread, he will live forever;" "My flesh is food indeed, and My blood is drink indeed;" "He who eats My flesh and drinks My blood abides in Me, and I in him." These are spiritual words, and spiritual thoughts, more specifically, they are salvational words and thoughts. The phrase, "My flesh is food *indeed*, and My blood is drink *indeed*, (NKJV) goes well beyond the physical; the NIV translates this, "For My flesh is *real* food and My blood is *real* drink." These words, "indeed" and "real" signal an elevated meaning here, a spiritual meaning the Jews back then, and for purposes here, Episcopalians have not recognized.

Jackson's commentary on these verses is 'spot on' and worth our consideration:

"Jesus continues his discussion about spiritual bread. Several points are emphasized. (a) The one who practices the divinely prescribed faith is promised eternal life (v 47). (b) The manna in the wilderness sustained life only when voluntarily consumed, and even then temporarily; the true bread of life was Jesus. If one "eats" of this bread (not literally, but in terms of ingesting the Savior's teaching), he will not die (spiritually). (c) The bread which Christ gave involved the sacrifice of his life for the remission of sins (v. 51). …

… The Jews misunderstood the nature of Christ's symbolic language (as many today do). Surely, they thought, he cannot give his flesh for food (v. 52). Jesus spoke of "eating" his flesh and "drinking" his blood. This is not to be pressed literally, as evidenced by the fact that: (a) the law of Moses forbade drinking blood (Lev. 17:10); (b) he spoke of those who already were "eating" and "drinking" (verbs revealing contemporary activity) his flesh and blood (v.54). …

… This eating and drinking are said to produce: (a) eternal life and (b) a relationship in which "you abide in me, and I in you." Elsewhere, these blessings are attributed to (a) believing in Christ (v. 40) and (b) keeping his commandments (1 Jn. 3:24). "Eating" and "drinking" are **figurative** expressions; "believing" and "keeping commandments" are **literal**. The abuse of this text, in an attempt to support the Catholic dogma of transubstantiation, is void of any justification. (As is the doctrine of consubstantiation).[54.] Nor does this text have reference to the Lord's Supper, though many well-meaning souls have misapplied it in this fashion." [55.]

Jackson's last statement needs further clarification. I mentioned earlier, the words referencing the partaking of Jesus' body and blood, as used at the Lord's Supper, have a different connotation than similar verbiage used in John 6. And though Jackson does not elaborate on this, I feel we need to do so here. There are some things in common between the two sets of passages, the most glaring commonality is the symbolic nature of "eating" and "drinking" Jesus' body and blood. This may be the only common element, [though I noticed Jackson did reference the Supper in his explanation of spiritual bread, first paragraph, point (c)]. That said, the differences as I see between them are these:

In the John 6 passages, Jesus focuses on spiritual matters, having eternal consequences. He speaks of eating His flesh and drinking His blood in the sense of 'abiding in Him', and 'He, as abiding in the one consuming Him'; also, as one consumes this spiritual bread and wine, they will 'live forever'. And finally, His flesh (food), His blood (drink) are *real* food and *real* drink – indicating they have much more significance than surface meaning, they have spiritual meaning. And I agree with Jackson, that one may interpret these John 6 passages of eating of this special bread in terms of ingesting the Savior's teaching. Jackson expands this thought later, to include "believing in Christ" and "keeping His commandments."

Switching to the Lord's Supper, Jesus also referred to the bread as His body, and the wine as His blood, even personalizing it by saying, "Take, eat; this is *My body*," and "Drink from it, all of you. For this is *My blood* of the new covenant, which is shed for many for the remission of sins" (Matthew 26:26-28). The focus here, however, is not on the spiritual aspects of accessing Jesus to gain eternal life; to 'consume' His teachings, His commandments, as a means to this end. The focus here is "remembrance." The focus here is "the cross." When we eat of the bread, Jesus wants us to "consume Him in thought, in remembrance of His body," not literally of course, but consume Him in the sense of shutting out all other thoughts and picture in our minds His tortured, beaten, and broken body, which He offered up as a sacrifice for our sins. Consuming this bread adds so much to our remembrance; unlike simply reading about or even hearing from the pulpit, we engage all five senses weekly to remember Jesus' death. This is powerful and exactly what God intended in His wisdom, that we never forget the sacrifice of His Son on our behalf.

The same goes for the cup, the wine, and Jesus' blood. When we partake of this element in the Supper, we are to shed, as best we can, all extraneous thoughts, thoughts of work, of school, of where we're contemplating to go for lunch after services, even other worship activities, if they hinder our focus at this time. Again, God wants our total attention, consume Jesus in our thoughts entirely – and here – thoughts of His blood that He shed on the cross; picturing that blood flowing from His hands, feet, head, and side, and remembering – this was for me, this was for my sin.

Continuing on the subject of the "elements," there are several other beliefs held by Episcopalians, which do not align with God's Word. The first comes from their definition of "Eucharist", where they say, "Christ's sacrifice is made present by the eucharist, *and in it we are united to his one self-offering* (BCP, p.859)." [56.] First, our directions do not come from the BCP – they come from the Bible! Second, the italicized section above indicates we unite, we join with Christ in this sacrifice. Really? Where does one read this in Scripture? No, we do not unite with our Lord in this sacrifice – we remember HIS sacrifice, His one and only sacrifice. Woe to those who think we humans had any part in Jesus' suffering and death, His sacrifice, and His offering Himself on the cross as an atonement for our sins!

Another false belief held by this denomination is revealed in their definition of "Eucharistic Elements," where they say, "The bread recalls the work of human hands required to harvest the wheat and make the bread, and the companionship of sharing. The wine recalls festivity and celebration, along with sacrifice." [57.] The bread does not recall how the bread was made – it "recalls" our Lord's body. And the wine certainly does not recall "festivity and celebration" – it recalls Jesus' blood on the cross. A sad moment to be sure, which should bring one to tears – not tears of joy but of sadness. The only joy, the only reason for celebration that comes to mind, would be the thought of our sin being atoned for, as a result of Jesus' commitment to come to this earth to save mankind, which was completed on that cross. But this joy was not meant to be manifested at this moment of remembrance, as we read Paul's words in 1 Corinthians, "For as often as you eat this bread and drink this cup, you proclaim the Lord's death till He comes (1 Cor. 11:26)." Our joy, our celebration over our redemption can be expressed at other times – this time is reserved to focus on Jesus' death – to "proclaim His death." Their attempt to include Jesus' sacrifice as a secondary connection to this "recall" of wine, with the words "along with sacrifice," is more of an insult than anything else since their first thought was 'celebration,' as the object to recall by partaking of wine. By putting Jesus' sacrifice as a trailer, and not recognizing it as the sole purpose of this exercise, which it is, they show this to be only an afterthought to them.

In addition to the elements, the Episcopal Church has errored on several other points concerning the Lord's Supper, as compared to Scripture. Their official doctrine, "What We Believe – Holy Communion" [51.] suggests three components associated with this event, and all three, to one degree or another, introduce variants to God's Word. The first is a statement that the Supper is a "family meal for Christians and a foretaste of the heavenly banquet." First, this is not a 'meal' in the sense of satisfying our physical needs of nourishment to the body, as normal meals accomplish – this is partaking of a small piece of bread to represent, to remember our Lord's body and drinking a small cup of wine or grape juice, reminiscent of His blood. Second, it is by no means a "foretaste of the heavenly banquet." In heaven, we will rejoice and celebrate to be sure; we will also unite in a 'heavenly banquet;' however, it will have nothing to do with this Supper. In this Supper, we remember Jesus; in heaven, we'll be with Jesus – there will be no need to remember Him any longer.

The second component of this doctrine is perhaps less offensive but still borders on being inconsistent with God's perfect Word and unworthy of inclusion as a directive for worship. This involves the second statement in their doctrine, "As such, all who have been baptized, and are therefore part of the extended family that is the Church, are welcome to receive the bread and wine, and be in communion with God and each other." Two thoughts again come to mind with this statement – first, "all who have been baptized … are welcome to receive the bread and wine." On the surface, this sounds fine, that is, until one factors in infant baptism. This sets up a situation where little children, (i.e., 3-year, 4-year, or 5-year old's), who are just learning, "Jesus loves me, this I know, for the Bible tells me so," in Bible class, are now encouraged and expected to understand the deeper meanings associated with the Lord's Supper. I can see two possibilities here, both negative: (a) the child grows up consistently taking the Supper and being unable to participate cognitively, they consider this a "treat time." As they mature, particularly within the Episcopal framework of putting the remembrance of Jesus' sacrifice as an "afterthought" to other equal if not more important aspects of the Supper, this person may never really transition from treat time to a proper understanding of the meaning and purpose of this Supper. And (b) small children can, at times, be a distraction; small children offered food can ramp this up a notch. Let me stop here for a moment. Children of all ages belong in the worship assembly; if they become disorderly, it behooves the parent to step out for a moment for the benefit of the congregation. That's not what I'm saying here; small children are prone to be disruptive at times, and this is likely to occur throughout the service, including during the Supper. However, my point here is this - children need not be participating in this Supper in the first place; they are sinless and in no need of baptism for sin, which God does not recognize. By encouraging all children in the congregation to unnecessarily partake of the Supper, the possibility of interrupting the thought process of others, as our Lord commands, is elevated. Is there anything wrong with a child taking the Supper? No. But the occasional child eating and drinking the Supper and encouraging/mandating all children to do so are two different things.

The second part of this statement, "and be in communion with God and each other," does not describe the Supper correctly either. If one consults a dictionary to assign meaning to the word "communion," here's one dictionary's definition, "(1) the act of sharing; possession in common; participation [a communion of interest]; (2) the act of sharing one's thoughts and emotions with another or others; (3) an intimate relationship with deep understanding; (4) a group of Christians professing the same faith practicing the same rites; (5) [C] (a) a sharing in or celebrating of, the Eucharist, or Holy Communion (b) the consecrated bread or wine of the Eucharist; Holy Communion."[58.] By the way the word "communion" is phrased in this statement, with an uncapitalized "c" would indicate it refers to any of the definitions other than #5 above – forcing communion to mean "sharing" or "having a relationship with …" - neither of which pertain to the Lord's Supper. In addition, even if the "c" in communion were to be capitalized, it wouldn't matter, since the phrase itself conflicts. We are not in communion with God and each other at this time; we are not sharing our thoughts, or emphasizing our relationship, or professing our faith with God or others at this time – we are to be focusing on and remembering Jesus' death upon the cross – nothing more, nothing less.

The items referred to within the third component in this description of Holy Communion, under the Episcopal Churches' "What We Believe" section, (except for the first directive to "examine our lives") are also not to be found in Scripture, their directive is as follows: "Before we come to take Communion together, "we should examine our lives, repent of our sins, and be in love and charity with all people (Book of Common Prayer, p, 859)."[51.] Certainly, in 1 Corinthians 11:27-34, Paul gives a stern warning that we need to examine or "test" ourselves prior to partaking the Lord's Supper, that we might not be found doing so in an "unworthy" manner. In context, Paul was speaking of the abuse of the Supper the Corinthians were exhibiting as described in verses 17-22; the broader meaning, and the takeaway for us, can be discerned by combining verse 28 with passages like Hebrews 10:29, where "unworthy manner" takes on a whole new meaning. Here, mental disposition grabs our attention: if you cannot focus on Jesus' death at this moment, totally focus (not thinking about the person across the room, good or bad, or the sports event later that afternoon), it would be best not to take the Supper. To do so with this mental state risks bringing judgment or condemnation upon oneself (vs. 29).

The next directive in this statement, "repent of our sins," is a grey area in my view. In and of itself, to repent of sin as a requirement to partake of the Supper is not according to Scripture – this is man's idea. Where do you see this in God's Word – Did Jesus withhold the Supper from His disciples until they repented? Did Paul, with any of his listeners? That said, there may be a connection involving the first directive – if our state of mind is "unworthy" due to a sinful act that remains unrepented, then before we can truly clear our mind and focus on Jesus, repentance may be necessary. The last section of this statement, that we must "be in love and charity with all people" is a good virtue, but again, not a requirement to participate in the Supper, not according to Scripture.

One other practice/doctrine of the Episcopal Church needs attention, as it is yet another doctrine, out of touch with the authority of God's Word – that is, their use of the Nicene Creed. Within the definition of this creed in their 'Dictionary of the Church,' this is stated, "The use of the Nicene Creed in the eucharist (right after the gospel), in contrast to the use of the Apostles' Creed in baptism, began in the fifth century in Antioch and became the universal practice in the church." [53.] As with the Apostles' Creed, the Nicene Creed is disqualified as an authoritative doctrine – it lacks divine authorship or Scriptural sanction. These creeds are man-made statements of faith – no more. Their overuse (the Apostles Creed, cited at every baptism, and the Nicene Creed, at every observance of the Lord's Supper) causes members to equalize them with the authority of the Bible, something I believe the clergy of this church has already done. This is yet another example of "adding to" God's Word, which God condemns (Deut. 12:32; Prov. 30:6; Rev. 22:18, 19).

In summary, I dive a little deeper into this topic for a reason – its elevated importance as an act of worship. Not that all topics I cover here or in other volumes are less or unimportant, but the observance of the Lord's Supper, Holy Communion, the Eucharist, whatever one chooses to call it, seems to be the centerpiece, the focal point of so many of these denominations including this one; and when I see many, if not all groups taking liberties in their observance of the Supper, by adding to or changing what God has commanded on this, as outlined in Scripture, I get concerned, very concerned. We're talking about worshiping our God here – a subject God has warned mankind time and again not to mess with, not to circumvent His directives, especially with inventions/ideas of man's own choosing.

Why do we attend church services? Is it to check a box? Make us feel better? Do we forget about God during the week only to remember Him on Sunday? Or do we strive to always live a life reflective of a Christian, assembling to worship our God in a way He has asked of us, a way that pleases Him? Though perhaps slightly off-cue, I believe the following connects with our discussion here:

In a recent Wednesday evening Bible study at our congregation, conducted by Dr. Paul Spicer (whose day job is radiologist, and whose evening passions include teaching, weaving in his extensive knowledge of the Hebrew and the Aramaic languages, which his master's degree in Old Testament allows him to do), I learned something from our study of Hosea. One of the passages focused on that night was Hosea 6:6, a passage familiar to most Bible students, but Paul shed some new light on this passage, that I'd not considered before. Here's the passage, "For I desire mercy and not sacrifice, And the knowledge of God more than burnt offerings." This passage is also quoted by Jesus in Matthew 9:13 and 12:7. In context, Hosea is appealing to a Jewish population who, for the most part, had forgotten their God – they continued to sin by worshipping idols, such as Baal, during the week, then offered sacrifices of worship to the true God on the Sabbath, thinking this would be acceptable.

[In a way, the people can be seen as not entirely to blame here, being ignorant of God's Word and His Law due to a lack of access. There were no Bibles in the hands of the common Jew at that time, only reliance on hearing readings of the Law from their leaders, which, unfortunately, was lax or untruthful. Making the leaders the ones with greater sin, the ones with more blame. (This has application to denominational leaders today, particularly those leaders who discourage their parishioners from consulting their own Bibles – indicating they cannot fully understand the text, such things as the deeper Hebrew and Greek meanings/extrapolations, as they, the clergy, have knowledge of and can better convey to them.)]

There are two profound thoughts the Spirit has imparted to us in this passage from Hosea, that I feel have a connection/application to our discussion here, concerning the Episcopal Church and their observance of the Lord's Supper. The first is the word "not" in 6:6(a), "For I desire mercy and *not* sacrifice." As Dr. Spicer touched on in his class that evening and enumerated to me later in more detail, "There are two words in Hebrew that are translated into English as no/not or even stop. They both have multiple meanings, but when it comes to the idea of not doing something, they carry different weight. The Hebrew word *Lo* carries a stronger meaning. Some may suggest it is as strong as saying, "You better not ever do X." This is the word in Hosea 6:6 and in the 10 commandments. [("Thou shalt not ..." (KJV)]. [54.] *Al* carries a less forceful meaning. Some may suggest it as saying, "Stop doing what you are doing." This is seen in Hosea 4:4. Note – there are two words which, when transliterated into English, are spelled *Al,* but they are spelled differently in Hebrew." [59.]

When Hosea made this statement to the Jewish people of his day, he was saying, "Offering sacrifice to Baal during the week shows your heart is not with Me; if you do this, don't you ever bring a sacrifice to Me on the Sabbath and think I will accept it – I will not! Your worship will have been in vain. (There's a direct application for many today, which we won't address here, that being the tendency to leave God at the church door on Sunday, not to think about Him again until the following Sunday, or whenever we return). However, the application to our discussion here, if I may paraphrase Hosea's verse, is this, "Offering sacrifice to (allowing equal authority be given to) the "Book of Common Prayer," the "Nicene Creed," and all other doctrines you have invented, other than My Word, along with reducing the significance and meaning of My Son's sacrifice [i.e., misunderstanding His death on the cross – thinking you are in communion with Me, that you are somehow sharing in My Son's sacrifice (BCP, p. 859), or that My Son's "presence" is somehow within your elements of communion, when in fact, I've told you He's coming back, but only one more time, in the same manner in which He left (Acts 1:11)], shows your heart is not with Me; therefore, do *not* (*Lo*) think I'll accept your sacrifice (your worship) you offer to Me."

Hosea 6:6(b) is no less a powerful statement, "And the knowledge of God more than burnt offerings." It has an application here as well. The burnt offerings and the correct worship of God are important, but what God values more is our heart in knowing Him. Again, in context, the people Hosea addressed did not know God – whether they were personally ignorant of Him, didn't know Him due to inept leadership (as discussed), or perhaps knew God (or remembered parts of His Law), but "they did not glorify Him as God, nor were thankful, but became futile in their thoughts, and their foolish hearts were darkened (Romans 1:21)." In the end, Israel's split loyalty, to offer sacrifice to two deity's, resulted in total rejection.

For purposes here, the way in which the Episcopal Church 'worships' God through the partaking of the Lord's Supper, shows they really don't know God either. And like the people of Hosea's day – I suspect this is due to either a lack of knowledge of God, perhaps brought about by knowing something of God, but "not rightly dividing the word of truth" (2 Timothy 2:15), not knowing God due to following leadership who purposely add/change God's directives, or possibly knowing God, yet choosing to ignore those directives. The 'burnt offerings,' in this case, is properly remembering Jesus' death as an act of worship. Not unlike the other acts of worship God has commanded we observe when we assemble on the Lord's Day (singing, praying, giving of our means, and listening/absorbing His Word.) However, according to Hosea 6:6, God has a greater desire for our heart and "knowledge of Him," than simply to perform these acts of worship without such attributes. Concerning the Supper, knowing Jesus' commands on how we are to properly remember Him, and conditioning our hearts and minds to properly focus on Him at this time, are as important, if not more so, than the act itself - for without this knowledge and focus, the Supper not only loses its' intended meaning for us, but it also becomes unacceptable to God. 'Knowing God' is following Jesus' words in Matthew 26:26-29 (along with the other Gospels) and Paul's words in 1 Corinthians 11:17-34; not knowing Him is to follow the BCP, the Nicene Creed, and/or all other doctrines that foster man's thoughts, thus supplanting the pure Word of God.

The remembrance of Jesus' death on the cross is the whole purpose of the Lord's Supper (1 Cor. 11:26). The knowledge of how God wishes for us to accomplish this 'remembering' is paramount. If abused, God will not accept our worship; it's that simple and that profound.

Sacramentals

The Episcopal Dictionary defines the word "sacramentals" as follows, "The Prayer Book Catechism notes that the sacramental rites of Confirmation, Ordination, Holy Matrimony, Reconciliation of a Penitent, and Unction evolved in the church under the guidance of the Holy Spirit (BCP, pp. 860-861). These other sacramental rites, or sacramentals, are distinguished from Baptism and the Eucharist, the two great sacraments of the gospel. Baptism and Eucharist are known as "dominical" sacraments because they were commanded by the Lord Jesus Christ. The five other sacramental rites are means of grace. However, unlike Baptism and Eucharist, they are not necessary for all persons." [60.]

Having discussed what the Episcopal Church considers their "dominical" or necessary sacraments of baptism and the Lord's Supper, we turn our attention now to the five remaining sacraments. Each of these have been addressed and refuted previously, both earlier in this volume with the Orthodox Church, and in my first volume with the Roman Catholic denomination in Chapter Two. Sourcing to the latter, citing these sacraments as termed by the Roman Catholic Church, can be found within the Endnote section of this volume. [61.]

With all five, we'll cite the official doctrine of each sacrament as defined in their online Dictionary, with Scriptural responses to follow.

Confirmation

The sacrament of Confirmation is defined by the Episcopal Church Dictionary as follows:

"The sacramental rite in which the candidates 'express a mature commitment to Christ, and receive strength from the Holy Spirit through prayer and the laying on of hands by a bishop' (BCP, p.860) ... Those who were baptized at an early age and those baptized adults without laying on of hands by a bishop are expected to make a mature public affirmation of their faith, recommit themselves to the responsibilities of their baptism, and receive laying on of hands by a bishop (BCP, p. 412) ... Confirmation/Reception/Reaffirmation may be done at the service of Holy Baptism or at the Easter Vigil when a bishop is present (BCP, pp. 292, 309-310) ... The candidates reaffirm their renunciation of evil, and renew their commitment to Jesus Christ. They reaffirm the promises made by them or for them at the time of baptism … The bishop leads the congregation in renewing the baptismal covenant … The bishop lays hands on each candidate for Confirmation. The BCP provides prayers to be said by the bishop for Confirmation, for Reception, and for Reaffirmation … The Episcopal Church's theology of Confirmation has continued to evolve along with its understanding of baptism … Confirmation has been increasingly understood in terms of a mature, public reaffirmation of the Christian faith and the baptismal promises. Some dioceses require that candidates for Confirmation be at least sixteen years old to ensure that the candidates are making a mature and independent affirmation of their faith." [62.]

As with Catholic *confirmation* and Orthodox *chrismation*, the Episcopal Church also claims a distinction between baptism and the bestowing of the Holy Spirit, calling this distinction Confirmation. The main reasoning behind this is their insistence on sanctioning infant baptism. Since infants cannot confirm their relationship with Christ, time must elapse until that individual matures, and so complete the baptism process by making a personal confirmation of their vows (their sponsor made for them years earlier). In simple terms, the Scripture teaches we receive the Holy Spirit from God at the point of baptism (Acts 2:37-38). Nowhere in Scripture will you find this separation. God is the giver of His Spirit, and the Spirit dwells in those who obey Him and are His children (Acts 5:32; Galatians 4:6), not any human who acts on His behalf, choosing a day and announcing they have control to give God's Spirit at their discretion!

Several additional points to what was said previously concerning other denominations and, more specifically, this one, include this Church's incessant reliance on the authority of their Book of Common Prayer for everything they do in lieu of the Bible. We discussed this at length under the 'authority' sub-head, so I'll refrain from repeating it here – just know it's not according to Scripture. It adds to God's Word. Also, such things as involving the congregation in 'renewing their baptismal vows, requiring a 'reaffirming of each individual's Christian faith,' or dictating an age requirement for this supposed confirmation/reaffirmation" – all these teachings are so far removed from truth. Where do we see any of this in Scripture? You don't!

Reconciliation of a Penitent (Confession)

Under "Reconciliation of a Penitent" within the Episcopal Dictionary, is written,

"Sacramental rite in which those who repent may confess their sins to God in the presence of a priest and receive the assurance of pardon and grace of absolution (BCP, p. 861). It is also called penance and confession. The church's ministry of reconciliation is from God, "who reconciled us to himself through Christ, and has given us the ministry of reconciliation" (2 Cor 5:18). The ministry of reconciliation has been committed by Christ to the church. It is exercised through the care each Christian has for others, through the common prayer of Christians assembled for public worship, and through the priesthood of the church and its ministers declaring absolution (BCP, p. 446) ... Only a bishop or priest may pronounce absolution ... After the penitent has confessed all serious sins troubling the conscience and giving evidence of contrition, the priest offers counsel and encouragement before pronouncing absolution." [63.]

Another definition is given for this sacrament under the phrase, "Confession of Sin," here we find, "Confessions of sin during the liturgy are general, made by all people. The church also provides for confessions of sin by individual penitents and for their absolution, pronounced by a bishop or priest. A declaration of forgiveness may be stated by a deacon or lay person who hears a confession." [64.]

There are at least five points of conflict between the above statements (including one from a claim in their "sacramentals" definition on this topic) and Scripture.

First, a distinction is made within their definition of "sacramentals" between what they term as the 'lesser' five sacraments, including Confession, and the other 'greater' two – Baptism and the Lord's Supper – apparently noting the 'lesser sacraments' as such for two reasons. (1) "They are not necessary for all people" and (2) as baptism and the Lord's Supper are singled out as sacraments having been "commanded by the Lord Jesus Christ," these other five, being 'lesser' are inferred not to have been so.

Both reasons are erroneous, and both can be dispatched with one verse of Scripture: "If you confess with your mouth the Lord Jesus Christ and believe in your heart that God raised Him from the dead, you will be saved. For with the heart one believes unto righteousness, and with the mouth confession is made unto salvation" (Romans 10:9-10). In this verse, God the Spirit (inescapably connected as part of the Godhead and One with the Son and the Father), speaking through Paul, tells us confession is both commanded of deity and necessary unto salvation.

The second point I emphasized in the Catholic rebuttal in Volume One of this series, that being, only God has the authority to forgive sin – not the priests of the Catholic Church, and not the priests here with the Episcopal Church. Quoting my words from volume one, "The New Testament teaches that Christians are to confess their sins to God directly (1 John 1:9), and we are to confess our faults to one another and to forgive one another. We don't have to confess private sin(s) to others; those are between the sinner and the Lord (James 5:16). No Scripture authorizes a secret question-and-answer session with a priest. Regarding penance (absolution of sin) in the New Testament, no man stands between a sinner and Christ, who alone has authority to remit sin (Luke 7:48)." [65.]

Third, under "Reconciliation of a Penitent," the "ministry of reconciliation" of 2 Corinthians 5:18, is suggested to have been committed by Christ to the church and exercised (or enacted) in three ways: "through the care each Christian has for others, through the common prayer of Christians assembled for public worship, and through the priesthood of the church and its ministers declaring absolution (BCP, p. 446)." [63.] The first two seem to have a connection to this verse; the last one does not. To gain the full impact of what Paul is saying here, one must consider verses 17-21. Paul begins by saying, "Therefore, if anyone is in Christ, he is a new creation …". He's a new convert, a new Christion; in verse 18, from this individual example, a generalization is then made that "all things are of God, who has reconciled us (brought us back together again) to Himself (to God) through Jesus Christ." [We all were once together, but sin separated us; when we heard and obeyed the gospel (the ministry of reconciliation), as a result, we were reconciled/brought back]. Verse 18(b) tells us, "Jesus Christ ... has given us that ministry of reconciliation." How are we to impart this ministry? Verse 19: "Christ ... has committed to us the word of reconciliation" (Through His Word, the Gospel). What, then, does God expect of us (His people, the church)? Verse 20: "Now then, we are ambassadors for Christ, as though God were pleading through us: we implore you on Christ's behalf, be reconciled to God." (Christ is commissioning us, members of His body, the church, to become ambassadors for Him and to bring this ministry of reconciliation to those who are still separated from Him by sin).

Thus, with a more complete understanding of this verse, the first two ways to enact this ministry of reconciliation, according to Episcopalians, as the "care each Christian has for others," connects since we as Christians are admonished to be ambassadors for Christ's Word to others. The second suggestion, to enact this ministry through public prayer, connects as well, since prayer is always a good idea (Mk. 11:24), however, this passage is encouraging action; action for us, who have been the recipients of reconciliation to in turn, actively spread this word of reconciliation. The third enactment, as suggested by this Definition, that the ministry of reconciliation is "exercised through the priesthood of the church and its ministers declaring absolution" is misleading at best and flat-out false at worst. Paul, in this set of passages, first takes the reconciliation (the bringing back to God) of one individual as a new creation, then expands it, moving it beautifully into the kind of reconciliation God desires for all Christians to be engaged in, calling it a ministry of reconciliation. Christ is then introduced as instrumental in reconciling the world to Himself through the Word (the Gospel), encouraging us to do likewise. Closing this section with a plea for Christians, as ambassadors for Christ, to individually take this ministry of reconciliation to the world on His behalf.

Enactment of this ministry through the "priesthood of the church and its ministers declaring absolution" is not what these verses are saying! Can the ministers of a church be involved in this ministry, along with other Christians? Certainly. However, this statement seems to focus more on the ability of the clergy of the Episcopal Church to forgive sin, making this the "reconciliation" referred to in these verses, rather than what it truly is - the "ministry of reconciliation" Christ commissioned His body to plead on His behalf, as His ambassadors, to those still in sin and needing reconciliation. Sin must be forgiven here to allow for reconciliation; however, it appears the ministers of the Episcopal Church not only wish to take credit for this [a violation of Scripture (only God can forgive sin Luke 5:20-21)], but they also confuse the gospel call given to all Christians to reconcile the lost to Christ and focus instead on taking pride in a power they do not poses.

The fourth point of conflict concerns a statement made in the second paragraph of the definition of "Reconciliation of a Penitent": "After the penitent has confessed all serious sins troubling the conscience and given evidence of contrition, the priest offers counsel and encouragement before pronouncing absolution." [63.] This concept of separating "serious" from what can only be inferred here as "non-serious" sin is man's idea – not God's. We've discussed this previously with both the Roman Catholic and Orthodox Churches. The Catholics consider "mortal sin" as those more serious sins leading to eternal punishment, where considerable remedy is involved, versus "venial sins" or "lesser sins" – considered as "unhealthy attachments to humankind." The latter does not necessitate formal confession and absolution.[66.] The Orthodox (discussed above under Penance) likewise separate sin, calling it "grave" versus "incidental" sin. In both denominations, the priests assume roles approaching that of deity by first determining which sins are major, then doling out punishment (particularly the Catholics, i.e., withholding Eucharist for certain mortal sins), and finally absolving or forgiving same – all without Scriptural support. The Episcopal Church, by making this statement, can only be assumed as following suit here with the Catholics.

The fifth and final point of conflict, in addition to being unscriptural, is a contradiction in terminology (or at least a point of confusion) made within their online Dictionary between definitions of "Reconciliation of a Penitent" and "Confession of Sin." This concerns who among the clergy of this denomination supposedly has the authority to forgive sin. Under "Confession of Sin" it states, "a bishop or priest may pronounce absolution" and "a declaration of forgiveness may be stated by a deacon or lay person who hears a confession." [64.] Under "Reconciliation of a Penitent" it states that "Only a bishop or priest may pronounce absolution." However, the very next sentence states, "A declaration of forgiveness may be used by a deacon or layperson who hears a confession." [63.] This would not be of any major significance (since we've established that any assumed authority to forgive sin other than God's authority, violates Scripture), were it not for the elevated status the Book of Common Prayer gives these words. For instance, under "Confession of Sin," it states, "The Reconciliation of a Penitent is one of the sacramental rites of the church (p. 861)." [64.] That makes this doctrine (since, in the minds of Episcopalians, the BCP is on a par with the Bible) significant – my point being that the BCP is not the Bible; it's man-made, and unlike Scripture, it contains errors such as this.

Marriage

The Episcopal Church defines 'marriage' as, "The sacramental rite of the church in which two persons '"enter into a life-long union, make their vows before God and the Church, and receive the grace and blessing of God to help them fulfill their vows' (BCP, p. 861). The union is understood to be intended by God for their mutual joy, for the help and comfort given one another in prosperity and adversity; and, when it is God's will, for the procreation of children and their nurture in the knowledge and love of the Lord (BCP, p.423) ... In the Episcopal Church it is required that at least one of the parties be a baptized Christian, that the ceremony be attested by at least two witnesses, and that the marriage conform to the laws of the state and the canons of the church." [67.] Marriage is further defined under the term "Celebration and Blessing of a Marriage," in the Dictionary with the words, "A priest or bishop normally presides at the marriage. If no priest or bishop is available, a deacon can preside if permitted by civil law." [68.]

At first glance, this appears to be a fair and accurate description of the institution of marriage and does not seem to disagree with God's Word, that is, until one digs a little deeper into the words of this text and a few things that are not mentioned, affecting those words. The modernization of the Episcopal Church since 1976 has included many controversial changes related to racism, pacifism, theology, worship, homosexuality, the ordination of women, a redefinition of the institution of marriage, and the adoption of their new prayer book. For purposes here, "redefinition of the institution of marriage" comes to the forefront.

This redefinition began with an affirmation at their 1976 General Convention that homosexuals are "children of God who deserve acceptance and pastoral care from the church" as well as "equal protection under church law." The 1994 General Convention then ruled that church membership would not be determined by marital status, sex, or sexual orientation. This '94 Convention also discouraged conversion therapy to "change" homosexuals into heterosexuals. Finally, as one of those 'unmentioned things' in the above definition, on June 29, 2015, at the Seventy-Eighth General Convention, a resolution was passed by the House of Bishops to remove the definition of marriage entirely from their doctrine, as being between one man and one woman. This is why you see verbiage in their Dictionary, and current Book of Common Prayer such as, "two persons enter into a life-long union" (instead of "one man and one woman for life"); and "when it is God's will, for the procreation of children." (Also, an accommodation for same-sex marriage).

The Episcopal Church is the first denomination we've seen thus far that has vacated a heretofore established doctrine and, in this author's opinion, succumbed to public pressure to be inclusive of certain minority factions and ideology, in this case, homosexual insistence on same-sex marriage. The Catholic and Orthodox Communes have erred on the celibacy aspect of marriage, but concerning "one man and one woman," for the most part, they've resisted this pressure and remained faithful to the Scriptures (That is until very recently (Nov. 2023), when pope Francis of the Catholic Church indicated he may soon sanction the "blessing" of same-sex unions, where previously he stated this was akin to "Asking God to bless sin"; this may be considered the first step in full sanctioning.) As for a "Scriptural" justification by the Episcopal Church to make this change, I'll defer to a more detailed explanation in the next chapter on this topic with the Lutheran Church, which has also sanctioned this practice.

Romans 1:18–32 states, in no uncertain terms, God's disapproval and condemnation of homosexuality. Have these bishops not read how Jesus responded to the Pharisees who asked Him about divorce in Matthew 19? (And in the process gave God's definition of marriage). "And He answered them and said to them, 'Have you not read that He who made them at the beginning made them male and female, and said For this reason a man shall leave his father and mother and be joined with his wife, and the two shall become one flesh? So then, they are no longer two but one flesh. Therefore what God has joined together, let not man separate" (Matthew 19:4–6). Though the topic was divorce, this also has application here, since Jesus referred back to the beginning (Genesis 2:24), where God's original intent for marriage to be between one man and one woman couldn't be clearer; becoming "one flesh," as God intended, as God created, is a physiological and spiritual unity that simply cannot be accomplished in a same-sex relationship. In fact, as stated, it's condemned by God if attempted between same-sex individuals.

There are several other points mentioned in the Episcopal definition of "Marriage" that are at odds with Scripture. Of the four requirements within the phrase, "In the Episcopal Church it is required that at least one of the parties be a baptized Christian, that the ceremony be attested by at least two witnesses, and that the marriage conform to the laws of the state and the canons of the church," only one is required by Scripture – the others are requirements of the Episcopal Church only. That one being "conformity to the laws of the state," which aligns with Romans 13 in that we are to submit to our governing authorities. The other three simply are not mandates of Scripture. Religion as an institution and marriage as an institution are two different things. Baptism for instance, is a requirement for those who believe, to be united with Christ, to marry Christ as it were, as His bride (Mark 2:19, Rev. 19:7) to fulfill God's plan of salvation, whereas baptism is not a requirement in mankind's institution of marriage.

Concerning witnesses that "the ceremony be attested," this may well be a requirement of the local or state governments, but in Scripture, witnesses are usually associated with verifying egregious acts. Peter and the apostles, for instance, responded to the Jewish leaders who had just murdered our Lord, "We are witnesses of this" (Acts 3:15; 5:32). Also, the familiar passage in Matthew dealing with a sinning brother, where after going directly to the brother who sins against you and he does not hear, then, "take with you one or two more, that 'by the mouth of two or three witnesses every word may be established.'" (Matthew 18:16). [69.]

The "cannons of the church" as further requirements for marriage is a general term, and would include a promise to adhere to all church doctrine, including sacraments such as observance of Confirmation, etc. Again, these are religious mandates set by the Episcopal Church, not requirements set by God.

Finally, a statement is made in the "Celebration and Blessing of a Marriage" definition, to what appears to be a mandate (although the word "normally" is used) that the marriage ceremony be conducted by a priest, bishop, or if neither is available, a deacon of the church. Presiding at a marriage ceremony is more a matter of expediency than anything else. The local municipality may have some requirements, and certainly, the couple must comply with such things as a marriage license, 'blood testing,' and the like to satisfy their requirements with the government, but other than this, nothing in Scripture precludes anyone from presiding over a wedding ceremony. If indeed the Episcopal Church strictly enforces this requirement of "priest, bishop, or deacon" presider – or no wedding until or unless – this sets up an interesting situation that could have negative ramifications, not the least being a delay giving the opportunity for the couple to change their minds and call off the wedding altogether. As serious as this possible delay may seem, particularly to the couple being married, "religious presiding delays" could be worse. We'll look at one with the Methodist Church in volume three of this series, for instance, where neither the Lord's Supper nor baptism is allowed to occur unless a "licensed and ordained minister and elder of the United Methodist Church is present to administer!"

Orders / Ordination

Ordination, as defined by the Episcopal Church is, "A sacramental rite of the church by which God gives authority and grace of the Holy Spirit through prayer and the laying on of hands by bishops to those being made bishops, priests, and deacons (BCP, pp. 860-861). The three distinct orders of bishops, priests, and deacons have been characteristic of Christ's holy catholic church. Bishops carry on the apostolic work of leading, supervising, and uniting the church. Presbyters (often known as priests) are associated with bishops in the ministry of church governance, along with the church's ministry of missionary and pastoral work, in preaching the Word of God, and in the administration of the sacraments. Deacons assist bishops in all of this work, and have a special responsibility to minister in Christ's name to the poor, the sick, the suffering, and the helpless (BCP, p. 510)." [70.]

The authorization and description of these three orders are said to originate with the ordination rites found in the Apostolic Tradition of Hippolytus (c. 215). "The Form and Manner of Making and Consecrating of Archbishops, Bishops, Priests, and Deacons" was then published in 1550, as an amendment a year after the publication of the original Book of Common Pray in England, in 1549. [70.] Though the BCP has undergone several revisions over the years, and some changes since the establishment of the Episcopal church here in the States, these three orders have not changed, nor is it the intent to ever change them, per the preface of the latest Episcopal BCP. [70. 71.] (Archbishop is grouped with "bishop" in these orders). No person is to exercise the office of bishop, priest, or deacon unless he or she has been ordained. [70.]

The process of ordination is specified as well in the BCP (pp. 510-555). This to include a "Declaration of Consent," by the ordinand, stating conformance to belief in the Scriptures and all doctrine of the Episcopal Church, along with acknowledgment by the people, consenting to his or her ordination; a public "Examination," [72.] the singing of special hymns ("Veni Creator Spiritus" or "Veni Sancte Spiritus"), several select prayers including a prayer of consecration, and the laying on of hands by the ordaining bishop or bishops. Immediately following, a "re-vesting" of the newly ordained bishop takes place, who then leads the congregation in a celebration of the Eucharist. Prior to ordination, "the canons call for theological instruction in the Holy Scriptures; church history, including the ecumenical movement; Christian theology; Christian ethics and moral theology; studies in contemporary society, including racial and minority groups; liturgics and church music; and theory and practice of ministry." [70.]

In the basic definition of Ordination, it simply states, "The three distinct orders of bishops, priests, and deacons have been characteristic of Christ's holy catholic church." [70.] The claimed authority for this "characteristic" originates with a belief in "Apostolic Succession" or "Historic Episcopate" which amounts to the same thing. Episcopalians don't give a reason, as the Catholics attempt to do for this belief (i.e., Jesus' statement in Matthew 16:18, confirming Peter's confession was the "rock" or foundation of the church, not that Peter himself was that rock of the church, as Catholics infer (making him their first pope); they simply claim succession and leave it at that. The definition of 'Apostolic Succession' in the Episcopal Dictionary states, "The belief that bishops are the successors to the apostles and that the episcopal authority is derived from the apostles by an unbroken succession in the ministry. This authority is specifically derived through the laying on of hands for the ordination of bishops in lineal sequence from the apostles, and through their succession in episcopal sees traced back to the apostles. The apostolic succession is continued in the bishops of the Episcopal Church, who seek to "carry on the apostolic work of leading, supervising, and uniting the Church" (BCP, p. 210)." [73.] The Historic Episcopate, though having an identical meaning as apostolic succession, does carry some additional significance to the Episcopal Church; and under this definition, an explanation is given as to how it officially became established here in the U.S. from England. [74.]

The Episcopal Church has also accepted women to serve in all positions within their leadership. Beginning with the 1967 General Convention's resolution to recognize women currently serving as "deaconesses" to be recognized as full members of the diaconate; the 1976 General Convention approved of women to the priesthood and the episcopate in the Episcopal Church and stated such ordinations might begin on Jan. 1, 1977. This issue escalated, and in 1997, the GC revised canons to prevent any diocese from denying access to the ordination process or refusing to license a member of the clergy to officiate, solely on the grounds of gender." [75.] After the ordination of "Reverend [sic]" [2.] Margaret Lee as priest of a Quincy, Illinois, church on October 16, 2010, all 110 dioceses of the Episcopal Church in the United States followed suit and ordained women as priests and bishops.

Ordination, as defined by the Episcopal Church is a man-made doctrine, just as with the Roman Catholic and Orthodox Communes. We've discussed this previously – there are two positions of leadership within the Lord's church according to Scripture, not three. And these two are not associated in any way with the powers or authority of Jesus' apostles in the first century. Apostolic succession and/or 'Historic Episcopate' are false doctrines that this church and the ones before them have attempted to use to elevate their clergy, causing separation between leadership and the people, which God never intended. (For a complete rebuttal, I refer to my first volume on this topic); and for another good analysis, I would also refer you to the Orthodox Church in this volume, under the "Organization" section.

The Scriptures speak only of elders (also called bishops), who are appointed to lead autonomous individual congregations with the help of deacons, who act as servant leaders, assisting the elders in carrying out the work of the church—not bishops, and under them, elders or priests, and under them, deacons. With the initial congregations of the Lord's church, the apostles did this appointing of elders; but subsequent to this, up to and including today, elders are appointed by the Christians within each congregation, according to a list of qualifications outlined in Scripture (1 Timothy 3:1–7; Titus 1:5–9). Also, deacons are to be appointed within each congregation; again, qualified men are submitted from among the Christians within each congregation of the Lord's church to meet a list of qualifications (1 Timothy 3:8–13). All of these rules and processes associated with ordination as described above, are merely thoughts devised from the mind of man – they are based on a Book of Common Prayer, which itself is a man-made, unauthorized addition to God's Word.

The New Testament also speaks very clearly concerning the issue of women leading in public worship. First Corinthians 14:34–35 and 1 Timothy 2:11–15 indicate women are not to "teach or exercise authority over a man" but rather to remain quiet, with respect to activities in the public assembly. As women have gained equal rights in society, these verses have not translated well, not only with this church but with most of the denominations moving forward. However, we're not talking about "Paul's day versus our day" here, and these verses are not "suggestions" – there are good reasons God wants men to lead. As I discuss this topic in detail in the next chapter with the Lutheran Church, under "Ordination of Women (Ministers, Elders, Deaconesses) – I'll defer to this discussion for further explanation.

Extreme Unction

The Episcopal Church defines the sacrament of Extreme Unction as the "Use of oil for the anointing of the sick at the time of death. [76.] This meaning has changed over time, however, as the definition continues, "After the seventh century, western Christianity associated the rites of anointing with penitence and death. This differed from the earlier practice of anointing for healing and recovery from illness. Unction became a rite reserved for situations in extremes, near death the various movements of liturgical renewal in the twentieth century have recovered the anointing of the sick in its ancient sense as a rite of healing. Anointing may also be done at the time of death." [76.]

A similar idea to Unction, "Ministration to the Sick," (considered a pastoral office), is also defined, here they say, "In its basic form the service is an abbreviated eucharist, including a rite for laying on of hands and anointing. The priest may suggest the making of a special confession if the sick person's conscience is troubled. The form for the Reconciliation of a Penitent is used. The BCP also includes various "Prayers for the Sick" (pp. 458-460) and "Prayers for use by a Sick Person" (p. 461) after the form for Ministration to the Sick. If one or more of the "Prayers of the Sick" are used in the service, they may follow the reading and precede the confession (p. 454). The service emphasizes the healing power of Christ and the connection between the worshiping community and the sick person." [77.]

The Episcopal Church's definition of 'Extreme Unction' as "Use of oil for the anointing of the sick at the time of death," was sufficient. Further verbiage in trying to define this sacrament only confused if not contradicted their initial statement. (i.e., Prior to the 7th century this sacrament was understood as being associated with healing and recovery from illness; after the 7th century however, the meaning changed to one of penitence and death; now, in the 20th century, it has reversed back to a meaning more in line with healing and recovery once again – although – anointing may still be done at the time of death, and extreme unction is "reserved for situations in extremes."

Ministration to the Sick only adds to the confusion since its description seems to better describe a situation where the death of the sick person is imminent (for which 'Extreme Unction' was meant). A description calling for "an abbreviated eucharist" (perhaps this person's last), a "laying on of hands and anointing" (to add comfort), and a suggestion by the priest for the person to make a "special (perhaps final) confession, if the sick person's conscience is troubled." For this last one, the confession, the form of "Reconciliation of a Penitent" is used. If you recall from our discussion on this earlier, this sacrament allows an individual who repents, to confess their sins to God in the presence of the priest and receive assurance of pardon (forgiveness) of those sins immediately from that priest (BCP, p. 861). To a dying person, this would be the ultimate comfort. Unfortunately, as was also discussed earlier, this could well be a false comfort, a false hope.

Let me pause for a moment to reflect on this. To me, this is perhaps one of, if not the worst abuses of a priest's assumed authority resulting from their belief in apostolic succession. A person who is about to leave this world is given assurance by their priest, a mere mortal, that they are 'right with God,' when in fact, they very well may not be. Apostolic succession is not only a misconception but also an evil conception. God never meant for His creation to assume the role of His Son here on this earth, following Jesus' completion of His task to die on the cross for our sins. This assumed separation and power, whether it be in the worship assembly where the priest supposedly changes the bread and wine into our Lord's actual body and blood (Catholic belief) or adds His "presence" (Episcopal belief), and thereby receives man's praise and honor for his perceived godly actions, or here, at the deathbed of one poor individual (where forgiveness of sin is pronounced, and comfort offered) – is wrong and not according to Scripture. Let me ask this – who are the members of denominations such as the Roman Catholic, Orthodox, or Episcopal Churches more likely to run to, with their confessions of sin? To Almighty God, who promises forgiveness to a contrite and repentant heart, though they must believe He will indeed forgive them, for only He alone has the power to do so (Luke 5:20-21; 7:48) – or – are they more likely to run to a priest, who promises he stands in the place of God, has God's blessing and authority to pardon sin, if they make confession to him, and he in return, can immediately offer forgiveness to put their minds at ease? Does this not encourage less dependence on God? Do you suppose God is pleased with this situation?

Moving forward with the definition stated for 'Ministration to the Sick' – the "Prayers for the Sick" and "Prayers for use by a Sick Person" [77] are then suggested, as written prayers cited in the BCP (pp. 458-461), to precede the confession. Being prayers read off a page of an unauthorized book (other than the Bible), does not qualify as the type of prayer James was speaking of when he said, "The effective, fervent prayer of a righteous man avails much" (James 5:16). Rote prayers are not from the heart, they usually consist of other's thoughts, and while there may be times such may be appropriate, they will not "avail much" here.

Finally, just when we think we've understood this definition of Ministration to the Sick as a

formula for dealing with a person close to death, we read the last statement, which seems to contradict the entire definition, "The service emphasizes the healing power of Christ and the connection between the worshiping community and the sick person." [77.] In other words, this ministration is really about healing and recovery after all!

Having discussed the sacraments and sacramentals of the Episcopal Church, a few more issues need our attention – we'll call these 'Faith Issues.' Following are four of these Faith Issues to round out our discussion of the Primary Beliefs and Doctrines of this denomination: Salvation, Veneration of Saints, Controversial Issues, and Ecumenism.

Salvation

Tied closely to their teaching the necessity for infant baptism is the Episcopal adherence to the doctrine of original sin and the Calvinistic belief of total depravity—that man has fallen short and can do nothing to come to God; that man cannot do any good work. This is born out in their definition of 'Original Sin' as well as Article IX of the Episcopal "Articles of Religion." The definition states in part, "The shared sinful condition of all humanity. This Christian doctrine is drawn from the Pauline writings, such as Rom. 5:12-19 and 1 Cor. 15:21-22, which suggest that humanity shares by nature in the fall of Adam described in Gn. 3. Paul likewise urges that the consequences for humanity of Adam's fall are to be reversed through saving participation in Christ's victory over sin and death. Original sin has been described as "hereditary sin" …

Luther's understanding of original sin led him to emphasize humanity's utter dependence on God's grace and the need for faith. Calvinism came to emphasize humanity's total depravity relative to original sin ... Article IX of the Articles of Religion, "Of Original or Birth-Sin," states that "man is very far gone from original righteousness, and is of his own nature inclined to evil" (BCP, p. 869) ... Original sin may be understood as humanity's innate self-centeredness. A consequence of this condition is human weakness and fallibility relative to sin. Another consequence is the influence of human sinfulness in our history and environment, to which we are subjected from birth. These influences all serve to restrict the actual freedom of moral choices, requiring us to look to God for hope and salvation." [78.]

This total dependence on God leads naturally to the idea that we are saved by faith alone (apart from any works we may do to assist in our salvation such as baptism); and that salvation is said to be a process – a process beginning with faith in Christ, to be completed when He returns, bringing the Kingdom of God, which is to come. This concept is expressed within three terms as defined in the Episcopal Dictionary – "Salvation," "Soteriology," and "Righteousness." Here are a few excerpts from each confirming this.

'Salvation' is defined as, "Eternal life in the fulness of God's love ... Salvation history is the ongoing story of God's activity and initiative for salvation. The OT records how God reached out to save the people of Israel through the law and the prophets ... Christians affirm the life, death, and resurrection of Jesus constitute the climax of salvation history ... Salvation in Christ is made available to us through the Spirit, especially in the life and sacraments of the church. By the water of baptism, we are buried with Christ in his death and share his resurrection (BCP, p. 306; see Rom 6:3-4). The consecrated elements of the eucharist are for God's people "the bread of life and the cup of salvation," by which we share the body and blood of Christ (BCP, pp.363, 375; see Jn 6:53-56; 1 Cor 10:16-17) ... We may participate in a saving process of salvation by which the saving life of Christ is increasingly the reality of our own lives ... Completed union with God is the end of this saving process ... This union with God is not yet completed, and the eschatological Kingdom of God is not yet fulfilled. But the coming of the Kingdom of God has been inaugurated by Christ. The

Kingdom of God was revealed in Jesus ... We are now in the "in between times." We can know the present reality of salvation in Christ, even though the Kingdom of God is not yet complete in our world, our church, or our hearts. The fulfillment of the Kingdom of God is associated with Jesus' second coming in power and glory." [79.]

'Soteriology' is termed "The theology of salvation" by this dictionary. Explaining further that - "In Christ, we are redeemed from sin and death and restored to a right relationship with God. We are made righteous and justified in Christ, despite the inadequacy of our works for salvation ... We may participate in a saving process of sanctification by which the saving life of Christ becomes increasingly our own reality. The process is completed and revealed in Christ, and it is begun in us through faith in him. Although this saving process is not yet completed, we look with hope for its fulfillment in the final coming of the kingdom of God." [80.]

Finally, 'Righteousness' can be tied into this discussion of "faith only salvation." The initial definition of "Living in a right relationship with God and others," is expanded, as it continues, "Paul states that 'all have sinned and fall short of the glory of God' (Rom 3:23). We share by nature in the tendency to turn away from God and the demands of righteousness (see Art. IX, Articles of Religion, BCP, p. 869). But human righteousness is made possible through faith in Christ and participation in Christ's life by the Holy Spirit (see Rom 1:17, 5:5, 9:30). The "many will be made righteous" by Christ's obedience (Rom 5:19), which enables us to "walk in newness of life" (Rom 6:4)." [81.]

The doctrine of original sin was discussed at length in connection with the Roman Catholic Church in volume one of this series (pages 193-198). [82.] It is a false doctrine that has misled many unnecessarily. The first passage referred to in this definition as support, if understood correctly, discredits this idea and one need go no further. Paul states in Romans 5:12, "Therefore, just as through one man sin entered the world, and death through sin, and thus death spread to all men, because all sinned ..." Stop right here. Why did death enter the world? Answer – Because of Adam's sin. Did we, as his offspring, "inherit" this sin? Answer – no! We inherited the penalty or consequence of Adam's sin – death, not the guilt of his sin. Look again at the last words of verse 12 – "because all sinned." We are not "inherently" sinful or "inclined" toward evil, as original sin advocates, including those of the Episcopal Church, insist. We choose to sin – and therefore we suffer death – it's that simple. The other passage in 1 Corinthians does not change this fact – "For since by man (Adam) came death, by Man (Christ) also came the resurrection of the dead. For as in Adam all die, even so in Christ all shall be made alive." (1 Cor 15:21-22). Adam sinned, and as a consequence this brought death - we also willfully sin and as a consequence, due to Adam's bringing death into this world, we too must suffer death – not his sin or propensity to sin or the guilt of his sin – the consequence or penalty his sin brought into this world – death.

The Episcopal Church has several misconceptions concerning 'salvation' according to the three terms defined above. None of the 'acts' of obedience commanded by God in order to obtain salvation, typically referred to as His plan of salvation recorded in Scripture, are expressed as requirements for salvation in any of these. Baptism is mentioned in the definition of salvation, even referencing a verse that is often used to confirm its requirement: "By the water of baptism, we are buried with Christ in his death and share his resurrection" (Rom. 6:3-4);" however, by coupling baptism with another sacrament (the eucharist) and emphasizing salvation even more so in it, "the bread of life and the cup of salvation," the significance of baptism is diluted, if not negated.

When we speak of salvation by "faith only" or "faith alone," one usually considers baptism (i.e., apart from baptism) as the only missing component; however, each of God's five mandates or "steps" must be considered. For instance, one must first "hear" the gospel – one cannot be saved without faith, and "faith comes by hearing, and hearing by the word of God" (Rom. 10:14, 17). Notice also here – "by the word of God" (not by the Book of Common Prayer, a man-made book). Next, one must "believe" Jesus is the Christ, the Son of God. "Believe on the Lord Jesus Christ, and you will be saved" (Acts 16:31). The reverse of this is also true, "He who does not believe will be condemned." (Mark 16:16). Belief is not just a state of mind, Jesus called it a "work of God!" When asked by the people "What shall we do, that we may work the works of God?" Jesus replied, "This is the work of God, that you believe in Him whom He sent." (John 6:28-29).

The third requirement of salvation – is "repentance." What was the first thing Peter said to the crowd in Acts 2:38, when they inquired, "What shall we do (to be saved)?" [83] Peter said, "Repent!" Also consider Luke 13:3, "Unless you repent you will all likewise perish." Repentance, then, is an absolute requirement of salvation. Fourth – is the mandate to "confess" – confess the Name of Jesus as Lord. "If you confess with your mouth that God raised Him from the dead, you will be saved. For with the heart one believes unto righteousness, and with the mouth confession is made unto salvation" (Romans 10:9-10). Again, can we leave this component out? Can we be saved by doing all except confessing? NO! Finally, one must be "baptized" (immersed) for the forgiveness of their sins in order to be saved. The rest of Peter's statement in Acts 2:38 and verse 39 confirms this, "Repent, and let every one of you be baptized in the name of Jesus Christ for the remission of sins; and you will receive the gift of the Holy Spirit [we are sealed with the Holy Spirit of promise, who is a guarantee of our inheritance (Eph. 1:13-14)]. For the promise (of salvation, of eternal life) is to you and to your children, and to all who are afar off (us), as many as the Lord our God will call" (if you are obedient to what I just said). [83.]

In my first volume of this series (pages 86-90), I discuss baptism as an entry requirement to Christ's church, [the one body (Eph. 4:4), which is His church (Eph. 1:22-23), of which He is Savior (Eph. 5:23)] and starting on page 87, I list several passages confirming baptism as a "dividing line between being lost and being saved." [84.] Each of these passages confirms that baptism is absolutely required in order for one to be saved. They include 1 Peter 3:21; Galatians 3:27; Acts 2:38; Hebrews 10:22; Romans 6:4; and Titus 3:3-5.

Many argue that one can be saved on the basis of faith only, citing Scriptures such as, "Believe on the Lord Jesus Christ and you will be saved" (Acts 16:31), and "For by grace you have been saved through faith; and that not of yourselves, it is the gift of God; not of works, lest anyone should boast (Eph. 2:8-9). The quote from Acts neglects to mention the next verse (32) this Philippian jailer 'heard' the Word, and the verse after that (33), we see this jailer being baptized (within the same hour). The other two acts of salvation (repentance and confession) though not mentioned here, had to have taken place, as the Scriptures elsewhere so mandate. The question here is this – if this jailer was saved upon belief alone, why did he submit to baptism? And why was it necessary to baptize him immediately like this??

Regarding this second reference to Ephesians 2, several points are worth quoting again from Dr. Dave Miller:

> Paul summarizes the twofold plan of salvation in Ephesians 2:8–9: "For by grace you have been saved through faith, and that not of yourselves; it is the gift of God, not of works, lest anyone should boast." Notice that "grace" sums up God's redemptive activity in making a way for people to be saved. "Faith" in this passage refers to the response which we human beings are to make without thinking we are earning our salvation or in some way matching God's contribution to the salvation process. "Grace" includes all God has done on our behalf and "faith" includes all man is to do in response to God's grace so that man can receive the offer of salvation in Christ.
>
> Anytime the New Testament speaks of being saved "by faith," it is referring to a faith that includes whatever actions God specifies as necessary. James makes this clear in James 2:22: "Do you see that faith was working together with his works, and by works faith was made perfect?" And notice his concluding remarks in James 2:24,26: "You see then that a man is justified by works, and not by faith only. For as the body without the spirit is dead, so faith without works is dead also. [85.]

Trinity Episcopal Cathedral
Cleveland, Ohio

Surprisingly, the Episcopal Church does not mention any of this, at least not within their doctrines (i.e., the definitions and BCP references I researched); instead, they seem to focus on the "process" of salvation and the "Kingdom of God" which they claim represents the completion of that process, not to arrive until Jesus' second coming. They do mention baptism under their definition of salvation, but only as a sacrament of future salvation, along with the eucharist. The process of salvation in which we supposedly participate, however, is mentioned several times; this process includes a connection to the kingdom of God. For instance, under "salvation" is stated, "We may participate in a saving process of sanctification by which the saving life of Christ is increasingly the reality of our own lives ... Completed union with God is the end of this saving process ... This union with God is not yet completed, and the eschatological Kingdom of God is not yet fulfilled ... We are now in the "in between times." We can know the present reality of salvation in Christ, even though the Kingdom of God is not yet complete in our world ... the fulfillment of the Kingdom of God is associated with Jesus' second coming in power and glory." [79.]

Under the definition of Soteriology, we read, "We may participate in a saving process of sanctification by which the saving life of Christ becomes increasingly our own reality. This process is completed and revealed in Christ, and it is begun in us through faith in him. Completed union with God is the end of this saving process ... Although this saving process is not yet completed, we look forward with hope for its fulfillment in the final coming of the kingdom of God." [80.]

Scripture tells us salvation is not a process (at least not as the Episcopal Church defines it). We do not "begin with faith in Christ now, synonymous with beginning our salvation process, then wait until Christ's return to complete or realize that salvation. All the stages or acts of salvation we read in Scripture save us, not in the future, but now. Baptism as the final stage is no different – it saves immediately. This is why we see *every* example of baptism in Scripture to be an example of immediacy – once an individual (not an infant) has been taught the truth, believed in Jesus, and decided to be baptized –baptism takes place shortly thereafter. Think back to the Philippian jailer (who, within the hour was baptized, Acts 16:33), or Lydia, following the hearing with an open heart of Paul's words (Acts 16:14-15), or the Ethiopian eunuch, who immediately after hearing of Christ from Philip said, "See, here is water. What hinders me from being baptized?" (Acts 8:36), or the crowd, after hearing Peter's sermon on the day of Pentecost who asked him, "Men and brethren, what shall we do? (to be saved);[83] Peter replied, "Repent, and let every one of you be baptized for the remission of sins ... and that day about three thousand souls were added to them" (Acts 2:37-38, 41). If salvation was a "process" not to be realized for an extended period of time, why the urgency for baptism? Reason – baptism is essential for salvation, and delay can only invite Satin to change our minds.

Elsewhere in the first letter of Peter, he compares the saving of Noah and his family "through water" on the ark with the waters of baptism, which also saves us. Peter says this, "... in the days of Noah, while the ark was being prepared, in which a few, that is, eight souls, were saved through water. There is also an antitype which now saves us – baptism (not the removal of the filth of the flesh, but the answer of a good conscience toward God), through the resurrection of Jesus Christ" (1 Peter 3:20-21). There is no getting around this passage – baptism saves us; and not later – NOW!

As we discussed earlier under "Baptism," Scripture also clearly tells us the "kingdom of God" has come and is here now, living in Christ's church – it is not "to come" later; it is not part of any "salvation process" that Christ will be bringing with Him at the time of His second coming to complete that saving process. There are several passages in Scripture that bear this out, I'll reference four. When Jesus was confronted by the Pharisees directly on this issue, the discussion went as follows, "Now when He was asked by the Pharisees when the kingdom of God would come, He answered them and said, "The kingdom of God does not come with observation; nor will they say, 'See here!' or 'See there!' For indeed, the kingdom of God is within you" (Luke 17:20-21). The NASB translates this, "Now having been questioned by the Pharisees as to when the kingdom of God was coming, He answered them and said, "The kingdom of God is not coming with signs to be observed; nor will they say, 'Look, here it is! or, 'There it is! For behold, the kingdom of God is in your midst."

There is considerable controversy among scholars over these verses, particularly focusing on the words "within you" (NKJV) or "in your midst" (NASB). Wayne Jackson has some good observations on this section of Scripture when he comments, "The Pharisees asked Jesus when the "kingdom of God" would come. They probably had in mind the establishment of a political regime similar to that of David and Solomon's era. Their inquiry may even have been sarcastic. Christ gave a brief answer – exactly what they deserved. The kingdom will come not with "observation." This, obviously, is a terse response to their question. "The kingdom will not come as you anticipate, with much fanfare, ostentation, prancing horses, and marching armies. The kingdom will be within [among] you." There is respectable disagreement among scholars on the meaning of "within you" (KJV, ASV), or "in the midst of you" (RSV, ESV). Whichever view one settles on, it must harmonize with Scripture generally. Possible meanings are (a) "The one who is responsible for the kingdom is in your midst already, but you have not recognized him." (b) "The kingdom will not come with a flamboyant conquest, but quietly, by means of the gospel operating on your hearts." [86.] I'd like to add another possible meaning to "behold, the kingdom of God is in your midst" – "Those who will soon be a part of the kingdom, who will be a part of My church, are currently among you, they are in your midst."

A second passage that confirms the kingdom of God to be here now and to be identified as Christ's church is found in Revelation 1:6, "To him who loves us and has freed us from our sins by his blood, and has made us to be a kingdom and priests to serve his God and Father – to him be glory and power for ever and ever! Amen." A similar third passage appears a few chapters later, "You are worthy to take the scroll and to open its seals, because you were slain, and with your blood you purchased men of God from every tribe and language and people and nation. You have made them to be a kingdom and priests to serve our God, and they will reign on the earth" (Rev. 5: 9-10). The verbiage in these verses describes Christians – "freed us from our sins by his blood" and "with your blood you purchased men of God from every tribe …." The tie-in to Christ's church comes from Luke's words to the Ephesian elders in Acts 20:28, "Therefore take heed to yourselves and to all the flock, among which the Holy Spirit has made you overseers, to shepherd the church of God which He purchased with His own blood." The same blood that saves us, that Christ purchased/redeemed our sins with is the blood He purchased the church of God with. Notice also in these verses, Christians are not only referred to as the "kingdom of God," they are called "saints," a term this denomination and others have typically reserved for men and women of "distinction" (Mary, John the Baptist, all the disciples, etc.).

Finally, a fourth passage confirming the "kingdom of God" is here today and not "coming" can be found in Mark 9:1, "And He said to them, "Assuredly, I say to you that there are some standing here who will not taste death till they see the kingdom of God present with power." (The NIV translates this as "… before they see the kingdom of God come with power.") This verse puts the kingdom of God at least initially to arrive no later than the lifespan of some of the individuals listening to Jesus at that time. Jesus' statement that this kingdom will come "with power" strongly suggests what Peter referred to in his sermon on the day of Pentecost – quoting the words of the prophet Joel, that "in the last days, says God, I will pour out My Spirit on all flesh." This is exactly what happened on that day, Christ's church began with power, with the "pouring out of God's Spirit" on the heads of the apostles. This power allowed them to speak in other languages, to proclaim the gospel to all peoples. (Acts 2:3-4; 17-21; Joel 2:28-32).

In explaining Mark 9:1, the writers of "Defending the Faith Study Bible" said, "First, the Bible teaches that the Kingdom exists now, and has existed since approximately A.D. 30. While Jesus was on Earth, He went to Galilee, "preaching the gospel of the kingdom of God, 'The time is fulfilled, and the kingdom of God is at hand: repent, and believe in the gospel' (Mark 1:14-15). He also stated 'Assuredly, I say to you that there are some standing here who will not taste death till they see the kingdom of God present with power' (Mark 9:1). In fact, Jesus 'has delivered us from the power of darkness, and translated us into the kingdom of the Son of His love' (1 Colossians 1:13). To insist that the kingdom is yet to be established is to fail to recognize that the Bible plainly declares that the Kingdom already exists on Earth ..."

"... Second, in the New Testament the words "Kingdom," "Israel," and "Church" refer to the same group of people – i.e., the saved, Christians, the body of Christ, or spiritual Israel. Jesus predicted that He would build His "Church," and give to Peter the keys of the "kingdom" (Matthew 16:18-19). Jesus did not build one institution and then give Peter the keys to a different institution. Paul told the Galatian Christians: "Therefore know that only those who are of faith are sons of Abraham ... and if you are Christ's, then you are Abraham's seed, and heirs according to the promise" (Galatians 3:7, 29; also 6:16). He told the Christians in Rome: "For he is not a Jew who is one outwardly, nor is that circumcision which is outward in the flesh; but he is a Jew who is one inwardly, and circumcision is that of the heart" (Romans 2:28-29). Spiritual Israel is the Church of Christ – that is, the Kingdom." [87.]

Veneration of Saints

There are four words or phrases defined by the Episcopal Church that center around this topic – "Veneration," "Veneration of Saints," "Mary the Virgin, Mother of Our Lord Jesus Christ, Saint," and "Hail Mary." Though this denomination accepts the existence of saints and holds them up as examples of devoted, faithful Christians, even honoring them by such things as erecting special "buildings" over their graves and celebrating the eucharist on the anniversaries of their deaths, they do not place as much emphasis on them as do others, including the Catholics. For instance, they do not believe in the process of canonization to sainthood of the recently departed, nor, as in the case of Roman Catholicism, do they elevate the Virgin Mary to the degree that she becomes their "co-redemptrix" and their "mediatrix" [positions where Mary is credited as being a "co-redeemer" and a "mediator or intercessor" with Christ (She, along with her Son are believed to have and continue to redeem us from our sin, and all prayers are said to go through Mary, as she intercedes for us)]. That said, there are some Anglicans, especially those inclined toward the Anglo-Catholic traditions, who may explicitly invoke saints, including Mary, as intercessors in prayer. For a more detailed examination of all this, I'll refer to my first volume, where I give considerable attention to this topic. [88.] Here, I simply intend to cite the above definitions and briefly address each according to Scripture.

The Episcopal Dictionary defines "Veneration" as, "The reverence of honor paid by Christians to saints, crosses, altars, images, etc. Veneration is distinguished from the absolute worship that is due to God alone. Various Puritans and iconoclasts have failed to make this distinction and wrongly accused others of idolatry." [89.] This definition is then applied to Saints, "Christians began to honor their departed heroes of the faith as early as the second century. After Polycarp, Bishop of Smyrna, was martyred in about 155, his ashes were gathered up by the faithful and laid in a suitable place. The cult concerning the relics of saints began at the same time. Memorial buildings came to be built over the graves of saints or martyrs, and the eucharist was celebrated on the anniversaries of their deaths. Christian teaching about the communion of the saints is the foundation for the custom of the veneration of the saints." [90.]

The Virgin Mary is then separated as one of the more notable of the saints to be venerated. The first definition, titled "Mary the Virgin, Mother of Our Lord Jesus Christ, Saint" states, "Mary the mother of Jesus has been an object of veneration in the church since the apostolic age ... Her humility and obedience to the message of God at the time of the Incarnation have made her an example for all ages of Christians ... Early in church history she was honored and esteemed. Irenaeus called her the New Eve, Athanasius taught her perpetual virginity, and the Council of Ephesus in 431 declared her Theotokos, Mother of God, because of the hypostatic union of divinity and humanity in the one person Jesus Christ. Anglicanism has not generally accepted beliefs concerning Mary's perpetual virginity or bodily assumption to heaven after her death, but some hold these views as pious opinions ... Mary the Virgin is commemorated in the Episcopal calendar of the church year on Aug. 15." [91.]

The last definition, the "Hail Mary," is a prayer made up of three parts as revealed in the definition – two are drawn from Scripture, and the third part is said to have been added in the fifteenth and sixteenth centuries as a concluding petition. The term "Hail Mary" is defined as, "Prayer addressed to the Blessed Virgin Mary. The first two of its three parts are drawn from the salutation of the Archangel Gabriel to Mary at the Annunciation, "Hail, O favored one, the Lord is with you!" (Lk 1:28, RSV); and Elizabeth's words to Mary at the Visitation, "Blessed are you among women, and blessed is the fruit of your womb!" (Lk 1:42, RSV). These verses have been used as a single formula in Christian liturgy since the sixth century ... The third part of the Hail Mary is the concluding petition, "Holy Mary, Mother of God, pray for us sinners now and at the hour of our death. Amen. Various concluding prayers for this devotion were added in the fifteenth century. The concluding petition in its present form has been dated from the sixteenth century." [92.]

Though the Episcopal Church does not seem to give as much attention to the veneration of images and objects as the Catholics, they still "give reverence of honor" to their saints, crosses, altars, and other images. By putting this phraseology under their definition of "veneration," it opens them up to what that word really means and infers. As I mentioned in my first volume, most dictionaries will list "to worship" as one of their first definitions for veneration (including Webster's New World Dictionary – the one I used). [88.] Claiming that veneration is distinguished from worship, and further stating "Puritans and iconoclasts have failed to make this distinction" doesn't make it so! Bowing to images or statues of saints, and even bringing wooden crosses into the worship assembly, bowing, and kissing same (as part of 'The Prayer Book Good Friday service') to give reverence and honor to this cross, [93, 94] communicate a different story, particularly to onlookers or visitors. The Catholic, Orthodox, and now the Episcopal

Church can dance around this all they want; they can say God's words in Exodus 20:4-6 (confirmed again in Acts 17:29) applied mostly to images of animals (such as the many gods fashioned after animals in Egypt at that time), or that the paint and wood are not what's being venerated (it's' what the image represents) – the fact remains – God said we are not to bow down or give honor to any image or object. We don't need to know His reasons, we don't need to make up excuses to do what we want, we simply need to do what He said – to do otherwise is to disobey God.

Under the definition of 'Veneration of Saints' a clearer picture of Episcopal belief emerges, as a particular saint, certain acts of veneration, and the Christian teaching said to be foundational to veneration of saints is identified. The definition states, "Christians began to honor their heroes of the faith … Polycarp, Bishop of Smyrna, was martyred in about 155 … Memorial buildings came to be built over the graves or martyrs, and the eucharist was celebrated on the anniversaries of their deaths. Christian teaching about the communion of the saints is the foundation for the custom of the veneration of the saints." [90.] Most of the things mentioned in this definition fall outside Scriptural boundaries.

Starting with Bishop Polycarp, who was their "hero of faith." Polycarp was supposedly a disciple of the Apostle John, living between A.D. 70 and 155 as an early 'Father of the Church,' and like many of these 'Fathers,' much authority has been attributed to their words, unnecessarily. Notice who their 'heroes of faith' are compared to the Bible; (i.e., Hebrews, Chapter 11) this gives one indication of their valuation of Scripture versus other sources of authority. There's nothing wrong with putting elaborate headstones, or in this case, erecting buildings over the graves of individuals; we do this even today. I do see a problem however with celebrating the Eucharist or Lord's Supper to align with the anniversaries of their saints. Scripture does not allow this (unless it would fall on the first day of the week); and just the idea of observing an act of worship to our God, a memorial of Jesus' death, to accommodate a memorial to a man, is anything but alright. Finally, this definition claims the practice of 'veneration of saints' is founded on the Christian teaching of the "communion" (or fellowship) of the saints. This is an incorrect understanding of 'Christian teaching,' or what Scripture says. Nowhere in Scripture do we find teaching like this, to venerate or honor the kind of 'saints' Episcopalians are thinking of; all mention of 'saints' related to communion or fellowship, speak of other Christians, other members of Christ's body, His church. Paul refers to his brothers and sisters in Christ as saints many times in the New Testament (Acts 9:32; Rom. 1:7; Rom. 8:27; Eph. 1:1). Christians are not only referred to as saints, they are called a "royal priesthood (1 Peter 2:9), and Jesus called His followers "a kingdom" and "priests to serve His God and Father" (Rev. 1:6); also see Rev. 5:10 (NIV).

Moving on to the Episcopal Dictionary definition of "Mary the Virgin, Mother of Our Lord Jesus Christ, Saint," we see Mary has been made an example to be honored and esteemed throughout church history, since the apostolic age. Early 'church Fathers' are again referenced to sing her praises – Irenaeus teaching she was the 'New Eve' and Athanasius teaching of her 'perpetual virginity.' These teachings are false, making these 'Fathers' false teachers, and not 'saints' to be memorialized. [91, 88.] The third claim, made by the Council of Ephesus in 431 (as we discussed with the Orthodox Church in Chapter One), declaring her "Theotokos" or "Mother of God" is also false. Mary was the mother of Jesus, the incarnated nature of Christ; not the "mother of God, His Divine nature." I reference several solid arguments made by Moises Pinedo from Apologetics Press in my first volume to validate this; [95.] I'll cite one of these arguments here.

This argument that Pinedo points out concerns Jesus's encounter with the Pharisees in Matthew 22:42-45. Here, Jesus asks them:

"What do you think about the Christ? Whose Son is He? They said to Him, 'The Son of David.' He said to them, 'How then does David in the Spirit call Him Lord,' saying: 'The Lord said to my Lord, sit at My right hand … 'If David calls Him 'Lord,' how is He his Son?"

The Pharisees could not answer this because they were thinking of the physical Messiah. Though the incarnated Christ was a descendent of David, physically (Matthew 1:1; Luke 1:32), He did not have a physical father, since He, His divine nature, is before all (John 8:58). Similarly, as David could not be the father of the divine Messiah, since David called Him "Lord," Mary cannot be the "mother of God," since she called Him "Lord" in Luke 1:38 and again in verses 46-47! [95.]

The end of this definition does attempt to diffuse some of this by saying, "Anglicanism has not generally accepted beliefs concerning Mary's perpetual virginity or bodily assumption to heaven after her death, but some hold these views as pious opinions." There are two problems with this statement. "Anglicanism" is the Church of England, not the Episcopal Church or the US version – there are differences; if the Episcopal Church were strongly in favor of this disclaimer, why not just own it? Couple this with "some hold these views," which indicates some do not, makes this a shallow denial at best. Of note also - the Anglo-Catholic sector of this denomination is even more likely to accept these views.

The "Hail Mary" definition – "Holy Mary, Mother of God," is addressed above, except for what is defined as a "third part" of this prayer – "Holy Mary, Mother of God, pray for us sinners now and at the hour of our death. Amen." This is akin to the Catholic doctrine, attributing Mary as a "mediatrix" or mediator/intercessor for all prayers destined for God. Again, as I discuss in volume one, nothing in Scripture supports this. [88, 92.]

The Scriptures do not support special honoring of past "saints," at least not to the extent Anglicans or Episcopalians do—particularly those closest to Catholicism. That said, the Scriptures do list examples for us of past faithful servants for our admonition. As mentioned above, Hebrews 11 encompasses one such listing of many Old Testament heroes of faith. At the completion of this chapter in Hebrews, the writer says, "And all these, having obtained a good testimony through faith, did not receive the promise, God having provided something better for us, that they should not be made perfect apart from us. Therefore we also, since we are surrounded by so great a cloud of witnesses, let us lay aside every weight, and the sin which so easily ensnares us, and let us run with endurance the race that is set before us, looking unto Jesus, the author and finisher of our faith" (Hebrews 11:39–12:2). Here the Hebrew writer focuses on what holding up faithful saints is all about—to encourage us to "lay aside the sin which so easily ensnares us" and run our own races with endurance, looking to Jesus, holding onto our own faith, to finish the race in order to receive "something better for us."

Controversial Issues

Though some of these issues have been discussed previously, for instance under "Ordination (of women)," it would be good for us to look at the changes the Episcopal Church has undergone and some of the contributing factors, including influential Conventions effecting these changes. The modernization of the Episcopal Church since 1976 has included many controversial changes related to racism, pacifism, theology, worship, homosexuality, the ordination of women, a redefinition of the institution of marriage, and the adoption of their new prayer book. The most contentious issues have been the ordination of women, the role of homosexuals in the church, the institution of marriage, and the liberalization of traditional theological concepts.

Archbishop Desmond Tutu

Following World War II, figures including Archbishops Desmond Tutu and Ted Scott were instrumental in mobilizing Anglicans worldwide against the apartheid policies of South Africa. Rapid social change in the industrialized world during the twentieth century compelled the church to examine issues of gender, sexuality, and marriage.

In 1976, the General Convention was pivotal in passing resolutions for change. For instance, this Convention passed a resolution calling for an end to apartheid in South Africa; later in 1985, it called for dioceses, institutions, and agencies to create opportunity employment and affirmative action policies to address any potential racial inequity in clergy placement. In 1991, the General Convention further declared the practice of racism a sin.

This 1976 General Convention also approved the ordination of women and a new prayer book, which greatly revised and modernized the previous 1928 edition. Full realization of this ordination would take another 30-plus years; however, it was realized – after the ordination of "Reverend [sic]" [2] Margaret Lee as priest of a Quincy, Illinois, church on October 16, 2010, all 110 dioceses of the Episcopal Church in the United States followed suit and ordained women as priests and bishops.

The Episcopal Church also affirmed at their 1976 General Convention that homosexuals are "children of God who deserve acceptance and pastoral care from the church." This led to a calling for homosexuals to have equal protection under church law, which in turn opened the door for ordination. The first openly gay woman ordained as a priest in the Episcopal Church was Ellen Barrett in 1977, and the first openly gay bishop, Gene Robinson, was elected in June 2003 at St. Paul's Church in Concord, New Hampshire.

Eighteen years after this landmark 1976 Convention, the 1994 General Convention ruled that church membership would not be determined by marital status, sex, or sexual orientation. This Convention also discouraged conversion therapy to "change" homosexuals into heterosexuals. On June 29, 2015, at the Seventy-Eighth General Convention, a resolution was passed by the House of Bishops to remove entirely the definition of marriage as being between one man and one woman.

As a result of this resolution, the current Archbishop of Canterbury, Justin Welby, expressed "deep concern" over the ruling. In 2016, Anglican leaders announced a temporary suspension of the U.S. Episcopal Church from key positions in their global fellowship because the church permitted its clergy to officiate at same-sex weddings. Though the Anglican Church has affirmed gay rights, they do not accept physical sexual expression in any relationship other than the monogamous, lifelong "union of husband and wife." The church may bless same-sex marriages, but they do not perform the actual marriage ceremonies of these couples. It is uncertain whether the more liberal U.S. Episcopal Church and the worldwide Anglican Communion will continue to experience friction over this issue or not.

Concerning Anglican efforts to correct apartheid issues in South Africa and the like - there are no Scriptures within the New Testament that teach Christians are to attempt to reform the social structures in which we live. Christians are to pray for those in the world, including kings (1 Timothy 2:1–4), and they can offer assistance to those in distress (James 1:27) and are certainly commissioned to preach the good news of Christ to all men (Matthew 28:18–20), but no mention is made of Christians changing society.

The New Testament also speaks very clearly concerning the issue of women leading in public worship and the acceptance of homosexuals. First Corinthians 14:34–35 and 1 Timothy 2:11–15 indicate women are not to "teach or exercise authority over a man" but rather to remain quiet, with respect to activities in the public assembly. Romans 1:18–32 states, in no uncertain terms, God's disapproval and condemnation of homosexuality.

The rift between the worldwide Anglican Communion and the more liberal U.S. Episcopal Church over these issues is noteworthy. Episcopalians, being strongly in favor of social conformity, seem to excel in tolerance and accommodation despite Scriptural warnings to the contrary. The 1994 General Assembly's decision to "discourage conversion therapy" for homosexuals and sanction full marriage ceremonies for them is but one example. The ideas of being "born this way" or having an unavoidable "gay gene" are lacking in (and in many respects go against) the evidence. [96.]

The Seventy-Eighth General Convention redefined marriage by removing entirely the definition of marriage as being between one man and one woman (which put the Anglican Communion over the edge). These actions, however, are refuted by Jesus Himself, as we see how He responded to the Pharisees who asked Him about divorce in Matthew 19: "And He answered and said to them, 'Have you not read that He who made them at the beginning made them male and female, and said For this reason a man shall leave his father and mother and be joined with his wife, and the two shall become one flesh?' So then, they are no longer two but one flesh. Therefore what God has joined together, let not man separate" (Matthew 19:4–6). Though the topic was divorce, it has application here, since Jesus referred to the beginning (Genesis 2:24), where God's intent for marriage to be between one man and one woman couldn't be clearer; becoming "one flesh," as God created, as He intended. This is a physiological and spiritual unity that simply cannot be accomplished and, in fact, is condemned (via Romans 1:18–32) if attempted between same-sex individuals.

The modernized theology of the Episcopal Church in some dioceses also has taken considerable heat on other subjects, for example:

- The late bishop James A. Pike referred to the biblical account of the Garden of Eden and the virgin birth of Christ as "myths." There have been some attempts to defend this - that suggested a "myth" is simply a sacred story of origins and not untrue, as laymen would define it. I'll let you decide the more likely scenario.
- Ernest Harrison, an Anglican clergyman from Canada, denied the Divinity of Christ, the inspiration of the Bible, and many other fundamental beliefs. This may be an exception to traditional Episcopal belief, but it nonetheless exemplifies where liberal theology can lead.

Ecumenism

The Episcopal Church is a strong supporter of the ecumenical movement, an effort to unite the various denominations, though they say that any unification must accept:

- The Holy Scriptures,
- The Apostles' Creed and the Nicene Creed,
- Baptism and the Eucharist (Lord's Supper), and
- The historic episcopate (governed by bishops).

Anglican efforts in ecumenical dialogue date back to the Reformation era of the sixteenth century, during which dialogues with both the Orthodox and Lutheran Churches were initiated. The Oxford Movement of the nineteenth century pushed for a union with the Catholic confession. The Episcopal Church, like many Anglican churches today, has entered into full communion with the following denominations:

- Old Catholic Churches of the Union of Utrecht
- Philippine Independent Church

- Mar Thoma Syrian Church of Malabar, India
- Union Churches of South Asia: The Church of Bangladesh, the Church of North India, the Church of Pakistan, and the Church of South India
- The Evangelical Lutheran Church in America (ELCA)

In addition, the Episcopal Church currently maintains ecumenical dialogues with the United Methodist Church, the Roman Catholic Church, the Moravian Church of America, the Oriental Orthodox Churches, United Methodist–Episcopal, Historical African Methodist Episcopal Churches, Anglican–Orthodox, Anglican Reformed, Presbyterian Church USA, Churches Uniting in Christ, Consultation on Church Union, Episcopal–Reformed Episcopal, and the Polish National Catholic–Episcopal Church.

The Episcopal Church is a founding member of the National Council of Churches, the World Council of Churches, and the new Christian Churches Together in the USA.

A more in-depth study of ecumenism among denominations will be included in the fifth volume of this series, in a Chapter titled "Ecumenical Movements." For purposes here, a brief Scriptural response will suffice.

The goal of Ecumenism is not the establishment of new or different churches, but rather the attainment of full communion amongst all constituent churches numbered within the movement. To attain this 'full communion,' member churches attempt to work with one another in shared events, including worship settings, collaborate in mission efforts, and conduct dialogue to bridge doctrinal differences. Organizations such as the World Council of Churches (WCC) and the National Council of Churches of Christ (NCCC) have facilitated such efforts. "Unity-in-diversity" has become the battle cry in the twenty-first century among churches within this movement, proclaiming all churches are essentially the same, thus pushing for a wider worldview of "the church."

While unity is certainly a desirable goal that God desires for His people as supported by Scripture (1 Corinthians 1:10, Philippians 2:2, John 17:21), unity not in accordance with God's will, is not pleasing to

God! Comparing some of the goals of ecumenism with the Scriptures, we can better evaluate this movement; we'll look at two of these goals here.

The first goal of ecumenism is to promote the idea (and inherent requirement of any member of this movement) that the universal "Church of Christ," encompassing many denominations, is more inclusive than one's own church or denomination – that the Holy Spirit has been working throughout history within each individual denomination and that each should learn from one another the various aspects of faith, found within all. This idea presupposes that all participants involved in ecumenism represent legitimate and divinely approved expressions of Christianity and that no one individual denomination truly manifests the entire truth found in the New Testament.

The Scriptures, however, do not support this idea. For this to be true, revelation would by necessity be a continuing process throughout history – to be infused into each denomination as they are formed (i.e., the Catholic Church established in 607 A.D., the Lutheran Church formed in 1517 A.D., etc.). This would also acknowledge revelation is ongoing even today (i.e., The Witnesses and Mormons – as more recent groups). A number of passages in Scripture attest to the fact that God's revelation and will for His people through His Word ended sometime at the close of the first century. Concerning His will regarding activities in His Church, consider 1 Timothy 3:15: "...but in case I am delayed, I write so that you will know how one ought to conduct himself in the household of God, which is the church of the living God, the pillar and support of truth." And again, consider Jude 1:3: "Beloved, while I was making every effort to write you about our common salvation, I felt the necessity to write to you appealing that you contend earnestly for the faith which was once for all handed down to the saints."

In both these passages, the audience is recognized as having (or receiving at that moment) the entire truth or revelation of God concerning His church. They are not told of any future revelation, which will be granted to denominations centuries from that point in time. Other confirmations of this truth can be found in Acts 20:27 (where **"all the counsel of God"** was declared and 2 Peter 1:2-4 (where Peter declares that God **"hath given us all things that pertain unto life and godliness"** – notice this verbiage "all things" (not some things now and some later).

Another goal of the ecumenical movement is the concept of "unity-in-diversity," where a plea to agree on "essential matters" (i.e.: the Trinitarian nature of God and the acceptance of Jesus Christ as Savior), while tolerating the "non-essential matters" (diversity of theological traditions seen as the "diverse gifts of the Spirit") is promoted. These "non-essential" matters are equated with the 'liberty' Christians are permitted, such as matters of "food and drink" as noted in Romans 14:17.

Though we should expect some level of diversity within each congregation, these would involve the cultural/ethnic differences mentioned in Galatians 3:28, Colossians 3:11, and Revelation 7:9 along with differences in terms of experiences and talents cited in 1 Corinthians 12:12-28. And yes, there is a degree of freedom described as matters of "food and drink" in Romans 14:17, however, these freedoms and differences are a far cry from the differences among the various denominations, which they wish us to believe are the same.

These 'non-essential' denominational differences espoused by Ecumenism include such doctrine as infant versus adult baptism; baptism as sprinkling or pouring versus immersion; the very purpose of baptism (i.e.: "for obedience" versus "for the remission of sin"); the nature of the elements of the Lord's Supper, a hierarchical organization versus autonomous local churches with elders overseeing and deacons serving within each; the validity of the papacy in Rome; Calvinist preordination versus free will, the status of homosexuals before God, and the elevation of women to the priesthood, to name a few.

When we compare Scriptural intolerances to the doctrinal differences cited above - such as pronouncing one "accursed" who would teach another they must follow the Old Law (i.e.: to be circumcised - Galatians 1:6-9), or that one who adhered to worldly philosophy and the traditions of man violated God's will (Colossians 2:8), or those who presented 'stumbling blocks' contrary to what was taught by the Apostles were to be marked and avoided (Romans 16:16-17, 2 Thessalonians 3:16-17) – how can this movement justify such vast disparity?

This then is the crux of ecumenism – the boundaries of *koinoinia* fellowship or association. Those of this movement would claim that any exclusive attitudes are sinful and divisive (save an out-and-out denial of

Jesus Christ as Lord or the very existence of God the Father, the Son, and the Holy Spirit).

According to the Scriptures, our association with one another is to be based on our shared walk with the Lord (1 John 1:5-7), and one can only walk with the Lord when one follows His commandments and walks in the ways that He walked (1 John 2:3-6). We are not to have association (spiritually) with those who fall short of this directive.

If God commands that those who are His obedient servants are to be immersed in water for the remission of their sins (Acts 2:38, Romans 6:3-7), assemble with other Christians in a local congregation, organized under the oversight of a plurality of elders (Hebrews 10:24-25, Philippians 1:1, Acts 14:23, 20:28, Titus 1:5-7) meeting to worship Him and observe the Lord's Supper on the first day of each week (Acts 20:7) along with preaching the one true Gospel (Romans 1:16-17, Galatians 1:6-9) - and there are those who profess Christ, who do not do some or all of these things –once again, how can there be association? Unfortunately, a chilling revelation awaits some, for not all those who profess Christ will be saved according to Matthew 7:21-23.

Christians are called to test the spirits and judge those who are within (1 Corinthians 5, 1 John 4:1); we will be held liable for the decisions we make with our associations – if too broad, we may give a false impression of a shared communion with our Lord thus violating divine commands (Romans 16:16-17), whereas if too limited, we will not be building up as we should (Hebrews 10:24-25). While there can be toleration of some forms of diversity, the New Testament makes it clear that the Gospel and righteousness, joy, and peace in the Holy Spirit are not to be compromised (Galatians 1:6-9, Romans 14:17).

The prayer of unity expressed by our Lord in John 17:20-21 is certainly a message of hope and inspiration to attain; however, though ecumenists use this very passage to essentially justify opening the gates of hope to everyone professing Jesus as Lord, this passage clearly states the unity God desires is "to be one as the Father and the Son are One."The vast diversities professed by denominations are certainly not something the Father and Son are in agreement with, nor by implication are we as Christians to be in agreement with.

Unity is a noble desire. However, the truth in Christ should never be sacrificed for the sake of superficial unity (Galatians 1:6-9).

Worship Service

Anglican worship is as diverse as its theology. A congregation or a particular service often will be referred to as either "High Church" or "Low Church." High Church, especially the very high Anglo-Catholic element, is ritually inclined toward embellishments, such as incense, formal hymns, and a higher degree of ceremony, with the clergy in full formal dress, vesting in albs, stoles, and chasubles. This formal liturgy is almost indistinguishable from a Roman Catholic Mass.

Low Church, by contrast, is simpler or less formal and may incorporate elements such as informal praise and contemporary worship music. These church services tend toward a more traditional Protestant or Evangelical service. Between these extremes are a variety of styles of worship, often involving a robed choir and the use of an organ to accompany the singing and to provide music both before and after the service.

"Broad Church" is a term commonly used to describe the in-between churches that have elements of both High and Low Church services. One element remains constant with all, however, and that is the central binding aspect of the 'Book of Common Prayer' as a guide for worship order and substance. The Episcopal Church publishes its own Book of Common Prayer (similar to other Anglican BCPs). The full name is "Book of Common Prayer and Administration of the Sacraments and Other Rites and Ceremonies of the Church Together with the Psalter or Psalms of David According to the Use of the Episcopal Church." The current edition, which is the official doctrine used today, dates from 1979.

Until the mid-twentieth century, the main Sunday service was typically a morning prayer service only, but the Eucharist has once again become the standard form of Sunday worship in many Anglican churches (similar to the Roman Catholic practice).

Emanuel African Methodist Episcopal Church Service
Charleston, South Carolina

As in the Roman Catholic Church, it is a canonical requirement to use fermented wine for the Eucharist, but those wishing to avoid alcohol are free to decline the cup. Typically, the Eucharist is served as part of an early Sunday morning service, this is an abbreviated serving following a service of morning prayer and a service of evening prayer; some have midweek or even daily celebration of the Eucharist. Many churches have two Sunday morning services, a 'traditional' service, which is more formal, and a 'contemporary' service, much less formal, usually to cater to the younger crowd. These services are typically offered as one early (i.e., 8:00 AM) and one mid-morning (i.e., 10:00 -11:00 AM). The Eucharist is served at both.

All Anglican prayer books contain offices (prayer services) for morning prayer (Matins) and evening prayer (Evensong). In addition, most prayer books include a section of prayers and devotions for family use. In England, the United States, Canada, Australia, New Zealand, and several other Anglican provinces, the modern prayer books contain four offices:

- Morning prayer, corresponding to matins and lauds.
- Prayer during the day, corresponding to the combination of terce, sext, and none (noonday prayer in the United States)
- Evening prayer, corresponding to evensong, or vespers

- Compline

A typical Episcopal Church worship service would include the following, as posted on the website of St. John's Episcopal Church, Jackson, WY [97.]; referencing their service bulletin dated September 24, 2023. [98.]

An opening hymn is sung, followed by "The Opening Acclamation" by the priest (responded to by the people – all statements/prayers offered by the Priest, Deacon, or Lector are given a response by the people in unison). This acclamation is followed by an opening "Collect' (ordered set of prayers), followed by another hymn and "The Collect of the Day." The Lessons are then recited by a Lector; first a reading from the Old Testament, then a reading from the Psalms (the Lector reciting the first part of a verse, and the people responding in unison with the second part of each verse). This is followed by a reading by the Lector of a passage from the New Testament. A "Sequence Hymn" ensues, and then the Deacon reads a section from one of the Gospels.

A sermon then is given – this day the sermon was presented by Mary Erickson. Since 1549, a sermon has been required at every Eucharist service. Following the sermon, the congregation confesses the Nicene Creed in unison. Next are the Prayers of the People. The prayer book offers several forms, but the Prayers of the People always involve offering prayer with intercession for:

- The Universal Church, its members, and its mission.
- The nation and all in authority.
- The welfare of the world.
- The concerns of the local community.
- Those who suffer and those in any trouble; and
- The departed (with the commemoration of a saint when appropriate).

St. Martins Episcopal Church, Houston, TX
Funeral Service of George H.W. Bush
December 6, 2018

Confession of sin follows these prayers. The congregation asks for God's forgiveness as a body. This is a written confession in the bulletin, which the people repeat verbatim. The priest, in giving absolution, assures [the people] that all who make a sincere confession are forgiven by God through our Lord Jesus Christ, by the power of the Holy Spirit.

As a prelude to the Eucharist, the "Celebrant" (the priest) offers "The Peace" to the people (a proclamation that, "The peace of the Lord be always with you".) Next is the Offertory. Here, we give back to God from the gifts God has given us (a hymn is usually sung – here, a soloist sang one song, followed by a hymn sung by the people). The Great Thanksgiving then occurs. The priest addresses the bread and wine. An incantation is offered back and forth between the people and the priest to a particular order, as prescribed in the liturgy. A hymn is sung, then the priest continues with an explanation of the Last Supper. At the conclusion of this explanation, the priest then prays that God will send His Holy Spirit upon the gifts (the elements of bread and wine) that they may be the Sacrament of the Body of Christ and His blood of the New Covenant, and that we may be united and sanctified by the Spirit (this is an inference to invoking the Spirit to assist in allowing the elements not to change into Jesus's actual body and blood but to allow the elements to be infused with the "Presence" of Jesus Christ.)

Following this prayer, the congregation, along with the Celebrant recites the Lord's Prayer, again in unison. Next is the Breaking of the Bread. The priest breaks the consecrated bread and invites the people to partake, all according to a set order and liturgy. Communion hymns are sung as the elements are distributed. A note is put in the bulletin, mostly for visitors, that reads in part, "All are welcome to receive communion in this parish. If it's your first time to receive communion or the first time in this church … you may kneel or stand as you approach the communion rail … You may eat the bread and receive communion as bread alone. You may dip the bread in the wine chalice (there's a fancy word for this – intinction) or you may drink from the chalice. In the act of receiving communion, we remember the life and teachings of Jesus, along with his death and resurrection. AND it's something we do TOGETHER in order to remember we are connected – communing with one another through this life and what's to come." [98.]

Following the distribution, a "Post Communion Prayer" is offered – the priest invites with, "Let us pray," and then the people pray in unison what's written in the bulletin. This is followed by a final blessing upon the people by the priest, a closing hymn, and "The Dismissal."

A close look at the worship service of the Episcopal Church reveals several practices that are not in accordance with Scripture. First and foremost is the liturgy used, specifically the adherence to a *Book of Common Prayer* from which to pattern all worship and content. Scripture tells us the Bible is the only guidebook we are to use for this purpose (2 Timothy 3:16–17; Acts 20:27; Jude 3).

Concerning their "High Church" or "Anglo-Catholic" element who worship much like the Roman Catholics in their formal Mass, Anglican/ Episcopal adherence to the Old Testament Jewish form of worship in the form of ceremonial dress, processions, incense burning to bless, and the like, is also against New Testament decree. In addition to passages such as Galatians 5:1–4, where Paul informs those who are pushing to return to the practices of the Old Law, "You have been severed from Christ, you who are seeking to be justified by law; you have fallen from grace" (NASB). Consider Matthew 17:1–5; in this familiar account of the transfiguration, Jesus is joined by Moses (who represents the Old Law) and Elijah (who represents the prophets of the Old Testament). Matthew 17:5 tells us, "A voice came out of the cloud saying, 'This is My beloved Son, with whom I am well-please. Hear Him!'" This is a clear indication that we are to follow the teachings of Christ, not the Old Law.

In the worship example above, there are several infringements to God's Word concerning how this Episcopal Church observes the Lord's Supper. First, it is to be observed on the 'first day of the week,' Sunday, every Sunday, not midweek, daily, or whenever is convenient (Acts 20:7). God has His reasons for this – to do otherwise is to disobey God. Second, the elements of bread and fruit of the vine are just that according to Scripture – they don't change into Jesus's actual body and blood (if that's what the Anglo-Catholic Episcopalians believe), and they don't allow for the "Presence of Jesus" to intermingle at the bequest of the Holy Spirit, as the rest of the Episcopal Church believes. Third, Jesus asked we take each element and pause in between to fully appreciate and focus on the different aspects of each – to take the bread and focus on His body, then, we are to drink of the cup to remember, focus on His blood that was shed on the cross. Allowing only the bread to be taken to suffice for both, or to dip the bread into the cup, or drink only of the cup, makes a mockery of the Supper! Doing any of these destroys one's focus as Jesus commanded.

And finally, a fourth infringement – the statement to visitors and the congregation at large, "In the act of receiving communion, we remember the life and teachings of Jesus, along with his death and resurrection. AND it's something we do TOGETHER in order to remember we are connected – communing with one another through this life and what's to come." No, it is not!! Paul said in 1 Corinthians 11:26, "For as often as you eat this bread and drink this cup, you proclaim the Lord's death till He comes." We eat and drink the symbols of the body and blood of our Lord in remembrance of <u>HIS DEATH</u>; not His life and teachings, not "along with his death and resurrection" (as if to say, "by the way, we should probably also remember His death and resurrection); His death only (even remembrance of His resurrection is not asked for in this 1 Corinthians passage). And this Supper is not "something we do together in order to remember we are connected – communing with one another through this life and what's to come." Yes, we observe this Supper together as Christians; however, to highlight "coming together" and "remembering we are connected" as seemingly the reason for partaking of the communion, and to suggest these reasons are just as important if not more important than remembering our Lord's death, falls very close to Paul's warning of taking this Supper in an "unworthy manner" (1 Corinthians 11:27)!

Music is to be vocal, not instrumental, and women are not to lead in public worship services [1 Corinthians 14:34–35; 1 Timothy 2:11–15; For a detailed analysis on this topic, see "Ordination of Women (Ministers, Elders, Deaconesses) in the next chapter – The Lutheran Church)].

Confession of a creed (an addition to Scripture) is not seen anywhere in Scripture, nor is the practice of confessing one's sins to a priest (either publicly or privately). We are to confess our faults to one another and forgive one another (James 5:16; 1 John 1:9; Acts 19:18–19). No one has the authority to remit sin except God alone.

To summarize this section, Episcopal worship does not appear to be in sync with what God desires, either in their formal, High Church or Anglo-Catholic worship service, with a more Jewish adherence, nor in their Low or Broad-Church services, which, as we've discussed, violate so many New Testament doctrines. It seems what is missing in their services is the Bible. I believe God desires His Word is to be used throughout all services to Him – in all five acts of worship as identified in Scripture.

In partaking of the Lord's Supper, we should read from His Word to focus our minds on Jesus's death on the cross (not focus on other aspects of Jesus's life and certainly not each other; and we are to observe this Supper on the first day of every week per Acts 20:7, not other days; and the elements are to be taken per His Word, not as we imagine). When we pray, we should remember His Word, how He wishes for us to pray, and then pray from our heart (not recite a rote prayer from a man-made book, along with following set guidelines as to who to pray for). Our singing needs to be acappella, not with instruments (more will be said on this in future volumes, but know this, for 600 years, until the Catholic Church introduced the organ, the Lord's church did not use instruments in public worship to God). All teaching, readings, sermons, etc. are to be taken from the Bible (no readings of man-made creeds, no confessions, and absolutions of sin, no order of service mandated from a "Book of Common Prayer"). And God desires our giving to involve personal thought and encouragement to give cheerfully as we have purposed in our heart (2 Cor. 9:7), following this and other examples from His Word (i.e., 2 Cor. 8:10-15, 9:6-10; Prov. 11:24-25, 22:9; Luke 21:1-4). (The 'Offertory' in this worship service had no prayer focusing on a Scriptural verse or otherwise (unless one was offered and not listed in their bulletin), but instead included a poem, sung by a soloist, followed by a hymn, leading into the Lord's Supper.

Questions to Consider

There are several questions one could pose if in conversation with, or consider, if a member of this denomination that stand out from our discussion. As with the Roman Catholic and Orthodox Churches, there seem to be many misunderstandings concerning the validity of the Scriptures as the singular source of authority for all things related to our work and worship to God. All three questions posed in my first volume concerning the Roman Catholic Church (Chapter 3, pages 310-315) have application here as well – Beginning with "Can we have confidence that the sixty-six books of the Bible are the complete revelation of God, which have been divinely inspired and handed down through the ages correctly? The second question builds on this by asking if there exists at least some confidence, can these same Scriptures be understood by men and women today without the need for an institution (such as the Catholic, or in this case, the Episcopal Church), to basically step in and "interpret" God's Word for them). The third asks that if understood properly [it is possible for the common person to fully understand and react to God's Word without outside help (Acts 17:10-12; Romans 10:17; John 4:39-42)], and knowing these Scriptures are from God (inspired by the Holy Spirit), then what do they say concerning the doctrines under discussion which conflict?

The Scriptures are under further scrutiny by this denomination, particularly concerning "understanding properly" (the second question to the Catholics) by introducing the idea that Scripture must be filtered through man's lens of "tradition and reason." In other words, it must make sense to us in the 21st century in order to be valid for us today. (I commented earlier that this was nothing more than a pathway to allow certain doctrinal changes to take place, such as women's leadership roles and same-sex marriage blessings – changes which otherwise the Scriptures do not allow.) Under "Sources of Authority" in the "Episcopal Dictionary of the Church," we read, "The threefold sources of authority in Anglicanism are scripture, tradition, and reason. These three sources uphold and critique each other in a dynamic way … each of the three sources of authority must be perceived and interpreted in light of the other two … this balanced understanding of authority is based on the theology of Richard Hooker (c. 1554-1600). [5] Looking further into Richard Hooker's philosophy, again under his name from the official Dictionary, "Hooker affirmed the threefold Anglican sources of authority – scripture, tradition, and reason. He countered the Roman Catholic argument which treated the Bible and tradition as equally authoritative for belief. He also countered the Puritans whose literal obedience to scripture was so absolute that they considered unlawful whatever scripture did not command … Reason was to be used in reading scripture. If scripture were silent or ambiguous, wisdom would consult the tradition of the church" [6].

The Episcopal Church has fully embraced this philosophy. Having said all this, a good first question might be:

1) **"Are you aware of the Episcopal Church's view concerning the authority of the Scriptures, as sharing this authority equally with tradition and reason? If so, do you agree with this view?"**

It might be the person you're conversing with may not be aware of the "scripture-tradition-reason" view at all, or if they are aware, they may not agree with it. If, however, a defense is put up for the view, this would indicate at least some uncertainty concerning a person's ability to simply read the Bible and come away with the truth, without having to consult man's wisdom of tradition and reason. At this point, a second question could be posed, such as:

2) **"If the Scriptures cannot be properly understood without applying such human traits as tradition and reason, which**

may alter the Scripture's meaning, then how were the Bereans able to confirm Paul's words without mentioning such added scrutiny in Acts 17:10-12? Or how could Paul so boldly state that "faith comes from hearing and hearing by the word of God," in Romans 10:17? (No mention here that God's Word cannot stand on its own to produce faith).

Granted, this is a response to defend Scripture with Scripture. However, these passages are so straightforward and easily understood that they're difficult to dismiss, particularly if the person you're conversing with has any respect for God's Word. Should this fail to make sense, I would refer to the Appendix of Volume One in my series titled "Defending the Inspiration of Scripture" to hopefully add credibility to God's Word for them. [99.]

Another response would be to cite several verses that extol God's wisdom and understanding as being far above our own – that though we may not understand something, even within Scripture at times, we need not immediately try to rationalize from our own human wisdom, particularly if it seems to alter the meaning of what we're reading – to do so is to put our thoughts on a par with the divine Word of God! These passages include Proverbs 14:12, "There is a way that seems right to a man, but its end is the way of death." And 1 Samuel 16:7, "For the Lord does not see as man sees; for man looks at the outward appearance, but the Lord looks at the heart." And finally, Isaiah 55:8-9, "For My thoughts are not your thoughts, Nor are your ways My ways, says the Lord. For as the heavens are higher than the earth, so are My ways higher than your ways and My thoughts than your thoughts."

The Scriptures themselves self-authenticate their singular authority and leave no room for additional revelation or "authoritative" doctrines with passages such as 2 Timothy 3:16-17, Jude 3, 2 Peter 1:3, and Acts 20:27. In addition to filtering down the authority of the Scriptures by adding tradition and reason as co-equals, the Episcopal Church has added several additional sources as authoritative doctrine, thus denying these passages, not uncommon to what the Catholics and Orthodox have done. Such additions as the Apocrypha (not supported by any other portion of Scripture, and containing deception and error), the "Creeds" (man-made summaries of faith, also containing error in some); and even the Episcopal Book of Common Prayer, which they hold in high esteem, (valued above Scripture in some cases), is but a man-made directory for church activities including worship, certainly not divinely inspired). These doctrines not only abridge the above Scriptures, which denounce additional authority sources, but they also "add to" the Word, a violation of yet other passages, including Proverbs 30:6, Revelation 22:18-19, and Galatians 1:6-9. In this last passage, for example, Paul is warning the Galatians that the gospel of Christ, the words of Christ, have been written down for their edification, and to "turn away" from those words (that could mean here, diluting or changing them, adding to them with other doctrines, or ignoring them altogether), is "to be accursed." And this could be said concerning *all* of Scripture (not just the first four books – the gospels).

Though other non-Scriptural practices could be cited concerning this denomination, including their adherence (in many of their churches) to a portion of Old Testament forms of worship (refer to Galatians 5:1–4 and Matthew 17:1–5, which cites strong evidence that we are not sanctioned to do so today; the Episcopal hierarchal church organization; infant baptism; their use of musical instruments, and so forth, the Episcopal belief in their "Historic Episcopate" stands out. This was focused on in a similar question from our previous chapter with the Orthodox concerning "apostolic succession;" however, it's worth another look here with the Episcopal Church, as it seems to affect both the clergy and members in such a profound way.

The Anglican/Episcopal Church believes in what they call the historic episcopate, or the succession of bishops, from the apostle Peter and the other apostles down to the bishops of the church today. Episcopalians do not openly suggest that their archbishops are infallible, but the concept of authority remains unquestioned.

Interestingly, the Archbishop of Canterbury has precedence of honor over the other primates of the Anglican Communion and is considered first among equals and the spiritual head of the Anglican Church worldwide, a position coming close to that of the Roman Catholic pope in honor, though his administrative authority outside England's borders is limited. In the United States, a presiding bishop has overriding authority as head of the General Convention, which sets policy over the nine provinces within this group in the U.S.

A question similar to the question the chief priests and elders asked of Jesus could be posed here:

3) "By what authority are You doing these things, and who gave You this authority?" (Matthew 21:23).

In Jesus's answer to this question, we find there are ultimately only two sources of authority: "from heaven or from men" (Matthew 21:25). Episcopalians and others, including the Catholics and Orthodox, attempt to tap into the heaven source by citing Matthew 16:18-19 and a supposed succession of authority from Jesus's disciple Peter, in particular. This false idea has been accepted by many people over the years. It elevates and separates the clergy from all others. One unfortunate outcome - it gives parishioners the false hope they maintain a right relationship with God – they are forgiven and absolved of sin by confessing to a priest rather than to God, when in fact, their sin may remain. A detailed refutation of this idea can be found in Volume One of my series (Chapter Three). [99.] Another source of refutation to this idea can be obtained from several works by Moises Pinedo – one a book he published in 2008, "What the Bible Says about the Catholic Church." [95.] The other is an article he published in 2005 titled "The Pope, the Papacy, and the Bible." (https://www.apologeticspress.org/article/626)

Yet another question that could be asked of a member of the Anglican/ Episcopal Church would simply be:

4) "How is a person saved?"

I suspect the response would be: "We are saved by the grace of God through faith, and not of works." (Eph. 2:8). Though some would not admit it, this can be translated as "by faith alone" or faith apart from baptism (as baptism is considered a work of mankind). In truth, faith encompasses more than just a mental acknowledgment of Jesus as the Son of God; it encompasses whatever actions God specifies as necessary under this term (see James 2:24, 26). Baptism is one of those actions specified.

Therefore, a person cannot be saved apart from baptism, according to Scripture.

Conclusion

The Church of England, or Anglican Church, originated as a result of King Henry VIII breaking all ties with Rome and the Catholic pope in 1535. The Episcopal Church in America originated in 1789 as a reformation of the Anglican Church after the Revolutionary War.

The Episcopal Church is organized under a hierarchy of priests, bishops, and archbishops who have control over numerous congregations within a diocese, all of whom are under the authority of their General Convention. The New Testament, on the other hand, teaches that each congregation is to be autonomous and under the oversight of their own elders.

The Episcopal Church teaches that the Bible contains truth but that it "must be interpreted in light of tradition and reason." In addition, they teach that other documents are authoritative, including the *Book of Common Prayer*, the creeds, and the Apocrypha. The New Testament teaches that only God's Word is authoritative—without additions or subtractions resulting in "man's traditions or reason."

The Episcopal Church teaches salvation by faith alone; baptism by pouring for infants or adults, as a vehicle for entrance into the church; and the Lord's Supper as being truly the body and blood of Jesus, or His "Presence;" and it has put women in authority over men, all of which are refuted by Scripture.

Many of the Episcopal clergy hold liberal views concerning doctrine and Scripture, attempting to take all supernatural events from the Bible and interpreting God's Word in "light of tradition and reason."

The Episcopal Church thus cannot be the church of Christ established on Pentecost, as recorded in Acts 2.

CHAPTER 3

THE LUTHERAN CHURCH

Introduction

The Lutheran Church was the first and oldest protestant denomination in existence, formed out of the protest against Catholicism during the Reformation Movement. "Protestants" simply meant "protestors."

Lutheranism is also one of the largest denominations, having over 66 million members worldwide. Of these, 36 million live in Europe, 13 million in Africa, 8.4 million in North America, 7.3 million in Asia, and 1.1 million in Latin America. In addition, Germany, Norway, Sweden, Denmark, and Iceland maintain Lutheranism as the "official state church." The Lutheran population worldwide is estimated to be approximately 3 percent, and here in the United States, 5 percent.

Within the United States, there are three main divisions: the Evangelical Lutheran Church in America (ELCA), based out of Minneapolis, Minnesota; the Lutheran Church–Missouri Synod (LCMS), based in St.

Louis, Missouri; and the third-largest division, the Wisconsin Evangelical Lutheran Synod (WELS), located in Milwaukee, Wisconsin.

Origin of the Lutheran Church

On October 31, 1517, Martin Luther, a Catholic monk, took his treatise of ninety-five theses and tacked them onto the door of the Castle Church in Wittenberg, Germany, in protest to several Catholic doctrines he recognized as not being supported by Scripture. These included the authority of the pope, the doctrine of transubstantiation, and, most importantly in his view, the doctrine of "indulgences."

The sacrament of indulgences was instituted in A.D. 1192 and referred to as "A remission of the temporal punishment due, in God's justice, to sin that had been forgiven." [1.] This remission could be either partial or complete. (The pope, through apostolic succession, is said to have been given the power to forgive sin, including the granting of indulgences or any temporal punishment for that sin otherwise due).

To obtain an indulgence, one generally had to perform some work of merit, such as reciting prayers, fasting, or giving alms. However, in 1506 it was announced that an indulgence would be given to anyone who contributed toward the construction of St. Peter's Cathedral in Rome. John Tetzel, a Dominican monk, was commissioned to announce this throughout Europe and to collect the money. Luther was confident the pope would not approve of this and would instead correct the abuses if he only knew about them. Luther was giving notice that he was willing to debate the question of indulgences. (No one accepted his challenge). One of his theses (Article 27) stated, "Those who assert that a soul straightway flies out (of purgatory) as a coin tinkles in the collection box are preaching an invention of man." [2.]

Martin Luther
By Friedrich Fleischman (1810)

Article 50 of the ninety-five theses read, “Christians must be taught that if the pope knew the exactions of indulgences, he would rather have St. Peter’s Basilica reduced to ashes than built with the skin, flesh, and bones of his sheep.” [2.] And Article 51 read, “Christians are to be taught that the pope (as is his duty) would desire to give of his own substance to those poor men from many of whom certain sellers of pardons are extracting money; that to this end he would even, if need be, sell the basilica of Saint Peter.” [2.]

However, Luther was wrong about the pope’s beliefs, as the pope issued a statement defending the sale of indulgences. It was later revealed that the pope (Leo X) had colluded with the German archbishop at the time, Prince Albert, to sell indulgences and split the profit between them (promising the people that such purchases would release loved ones from purgatory). The corruption associated with indulgences went even deeper, as it was promoted that a vast storehouse of “good works” accumulated through the works of Jesus and Mary (the Lord’s mother), along with others, was available for purchase—and if people were a little “short” on these good works, they could “buy” some and have them credited to their accounts!

Because of his teachings, Pope Leo X excommunicated Luther from the Roman Church in June of 1520. In protest, Luther publicly burned the papal bull of excommunication at Wittenberg in December of that same year, and though it was ordered that he be arrested, and his books burned, an ally, Frederick the Wise, who ruled Luther's home territory, gave him sanctuary. Luther was later taken to Wartburg Castle and lived in seclusion under an assumed name, during which time he translated the New Testament from Greek into the German dialect. Luther lived to see the reformation firmly established in other countries. Interestingly, he never intended to establish a church that would bear his name. Rather, he made this statement: "I beseech you, above all things, not to use my name; not to call yourselves Lutherans, but Christians. What is Luther? The doctrine is not mine; I have been crucified for no one. Paul would not suffer the Christians to say: I am of Paul; or I am of Peter; but, I am Christ's. How, then can the followers of Christ call themselves after the unsanctified name of a poor stinking mass of corruption … such as I am? Let us blot out all party-names, and call ourselves Christians, as we follow Christ's doctrine" [3.]

According to this statement, Luther didn't want any group to be called after his name, alluding to several passages in 1 Corinthians where Paul (denouncing division within the Corinthian church) spoke with similar language (1 Corinthians 1:12–13 and 3:4–5). As members were divided over whom they felt were influential leaders, Paul confronted and rebuked this idea. Luther, likewise, recognizing these Scriptures, used them to implore others not to follow suit (unfortunately to no avail).

God wants no other name for His followers than the name of, or that associated with, His Son, Jesus Christ. In Acts 11:26, followers of Christ are called "Christians"; in Romans 1:7 they are called "saints." In Acts 5:14 the term "believer" is used, and in other passages "disciple" and "brother" are used. Never do we see a person being called a "Pauline Christian" or an "Apollonian Christian"—nor, for purposes here, do we see anyone being called a "Lutheran Christian."

In addition, as discussed previously, the name of His church is spelled out in the New Testament, using such terms as "The church of the Lord" (Acts 20:28), "The house of God" (1 Timothy 3:15), "The kingdom of God" (Acts 28:23), "The temple of God" (1 Corinthians 3:16-17); "The bride of Christ" (Revelation 19:7), and, collectively, as "The churches of

Christ" (Romans 16:16). These are more akin to descriptions of Christ's church than formal monikers. The point is that nowhere do we find Christ's church referred to as "Lutheran." (Thus making association with Martin Luther rather than the true owner and head, Jesus Christ).

Martin Luther's break with the Catholic Church signaled the start of what is referred to as the "Reformation Movement." Though Luther correctly recognized a number of flaws inherent in Catholic doctrine, after studying the Scriptures, he sought to correct them within the Catholic Church, never meaning to establish a new church or denomination. Though Luther's work brought attention to several inconsistencies as compared to Scripture, he stopped short of correcting many others, as we shall see in the balance of this discussion, concerning the Lutheran Church. (Luther's unwillingness to let go of his Catholic background or doctrines completely may also have been the reason he could not recognize the Lord's true church as described in those Scriptures—the nondenominational church of Christ).

The chart below highlights the second break from Catholicism in 1517 (the first being the Orthodox Church in A.D. 1054) as the founding of the Lutheran denomination.

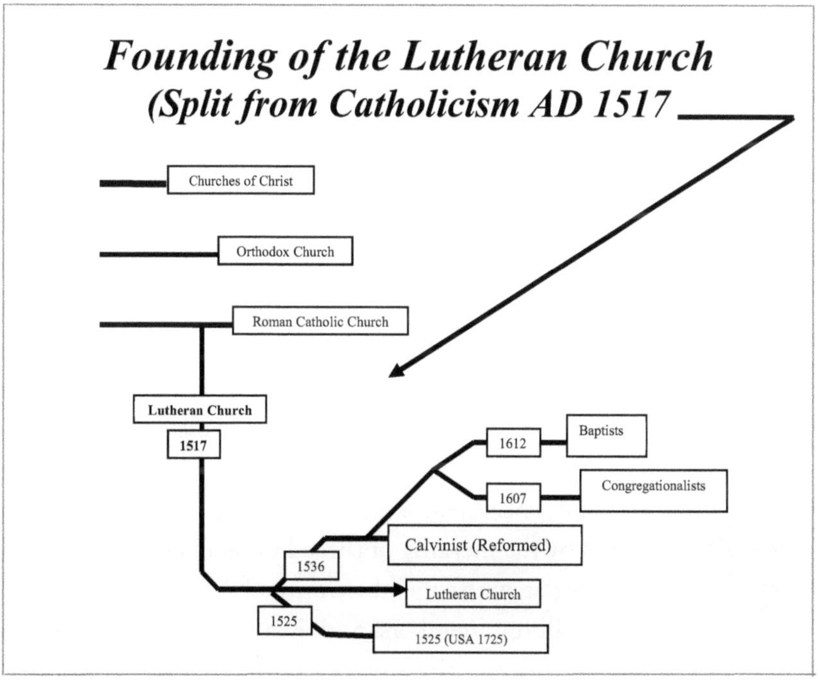

Organization of the Lutheran Church

Hallgrimskirkja Lutheran Church
Reykjavik, Iceland

The Lutheran Church within the United States is organized predominately into three "synods" or synod groups, which govern all church affairs in this country. A synod is defined as "an ecclesiastical council; a regional or international meeting of bishops; a high government body in certain Christian churches; a national or district organization of Lutheran or certain other Protestant churches; a district governed or represented by a Protestant synod." [4] Following are these synod groups:

The Evangelical Lutheran Church in America (ELCA), headquartered in Chicago, Illinois, formed in 1988 by the merging of three Lutheran church bodies, is the largest, with a membership as of 2019 of approximately 3.3 million members and just under nine thousand congregations. The ELCA is a nationwide organization comprising nine regions and sixty-five synods, with each synod overseeing between thirty and three hundred congregations. The synods are governed by a single bishop, and the ELCA as a whole is governed by a presiding bishop; currently that position is filled by Rev. Elizabeth Eaton.

Internationally, the ELCA associates with groups such as the Lutheran World Federation (LWF), which has over 148 member churches, representing some 77 million members in ninety-nine countries. Churches wishing to join the LWF must formally accept the federation's doctrinal statement as outlined in their constitution (Article 2), which basically commits agreement to the Old and New Testaments of the Scriptures along with the ecumenical creeds and the Lutheran Confessions.

The Lutheran Church–Missouri Synod (LCMS) is the second largest in the United States, with just under two million members and just under six thousand congregations nationwide; it is headquartered in St. Louis, Missouri. Nearly half of the membership is located in the Upper Midwest of the United States. The LCMS is structured as a single national synod headed by a "chief ecclesiastical officer" or president (as of 2020, this is Rev. [sic] [5] Dr. Matthew C. Harrison) and six vice presidents or presidium. Together they supervise all doctrines taught and practiced by the synod. The synod is further divided into thirty-five middle-level districts, each with a governing president, who in turn has supervision over the local congregations, all of which are governed by individual pastors. Internationally, the LCMS has thirty-nine partner churches around the world with whom they have full altar and pulpit fellowship. Many LCMS partner churches are also members of the International Lutheran Council, a worldwide association of confessional Lutheran church bodies.

The Wisconsin Evangelical Lutheran Synod (WELS) is the third largest group in the United States and by far the most conservative of the three. The Wisconsin Synod, as of 2020, had a membership of 349,014, making up 1,269 congregations located in forty-seven states and four provinces of Canada. They are headquartered in Waukesha, Wisconsin. Though the synod's government allows a bit more autonomy to the local congregations, each is led by an ordained pastor; the synod as a whole, similar to the LCMS, is led by a president and two leadership groups: "The Conference of Presidents" and "The Synodical Council." These groups assist the president in implementing the decisions of the "Convention," which meets every other year. The current president of WELS is Mark G. Schroeder. The synod is further divided into twelve districts (geographically), each having its own presidents and conventions (again meeting every other year), which representatives from member congregations, made up of pastors and male teachers, attend as "voting delegates" to decide on their own leadership as well as to formulate resolutions to send to the main synod convention (among other things). This group is also active internationally, with an outreach to forty countries and a direct presence in twenty-four countries.

The Organization of the Lutheran Church, per above, focuses on the synod. The following are common characteristics that apply to all the synods, the ELCA, the LCMS, and the WELS:

- Each synod has a bishop or president ruling over the affairs of that synod in general, with secondary synods or districts having their own bishops or leadership to in turn govern multiple local congregations.
- Individual "pastors" preside "over" individual congregations. The ELCA Constitutions, Bylaws, and Continuing Resolutions, section 7.31.12, for instance, discusses how "Every ordained minister shall: a) Preach the Word; administer the sacraments; conduct public worship; provide pastoral care; seek out and encourage qualified persons to prepare for the ministry of the Gospel. And b) offer instruction, confirm, marry, visit the sick and distressed, and bury the dead; supervise all schools and organizations of the congregation; impart knowledge of this church and its wider ministry through distribution of its periodicals and other publications; endeavor to increase the support given by the congregation to the work of the churchwide organization and synod of the ELCA; install regularly elected members of the Congregation Council; and with the council, administer discipline." [6.]
- Each member of the clergy of the Lutheran Church must have special training and formal education and must have been recommended

by a superior to attain his or her position. For instance, within the ELCA, candidates must complete the requirements for the Master of Divinity degree from an accredited theological school to qualify as a minister, along with other requirements.[6.]

The New Testament states that each congregation is to be an independent organization, with the members of that congregation under the oversight of a plurality of male elders, (this term is also referred to as bishops, overseers, shepherds, or pastors – they are used synonymously - Acts 11:30, 20:17, 28; Titus 1:5–9; 1 Peter 5:1–4; 1 Timothy 3:1–2; Ephesians 4:11). The Bible never mentions any level of authority superseding the local congregation (other than Jesus as head of His church universal) —not a "district level" or a "synod"—nor any individual clergy, such as a single bishop, leading a synod (which has oversight over multiple districts and in turn multiple local congregations). A lone pastor who is given authority over a local congregation was discussed at length under the "Sacrament of Holy Orders" section of the Roman Catholic Church previously in my first volume. [7.] In fact, the danger of interpreting the Greek word for "elder" or, more accurately, "overseer" ("*episkopos*"), as "bishop" and the word for "shepherd" ("*poimen*") as "pastor" has come to fruition here in the Lutheran hierarchy.

In addition, Biblical qualifications to be a leader of the Lord's local church (referred to in Scripture as "elder," "bishop," "overseer," "shepherd," or "pastor"), are listed in 1 Timothy 3:1–7 and Titus 1:5–9 in particular. The ELCA constitutional requirements, however, conflict with these passages, as detailed above and within the next section.

Authority of the Lutheran Church

Unlike the previous denominations we've looked at thus far, where authority is vested both within their clergy via the claim of apostolic succession and within external doctrine inclusive of the Scriptures, the Lutheran Church maintains an authority base and hierarchy via election through synods, (not their clergy) while also honoring external doctrine inclusive of the Scriptures. As mentioned above, the majority of Lutheran churches in the United States are under the umbrella of three main synods – the ELCA, the LCMS, and the WELS, and though each synod is structured similarly (concerning their hierarchy of authority within the synod itself, as well as a basic agreement on what they hold as authoritative documents), they differ on how these documents, including the Scriptures, should be interpreted and put into practice.

All three synods hold the Scriptures in high regard. The Missouri Synod, for instance, claims the Bible as their "Sole Authority" (sixty-six books: thirty-nine from the Old Testament and twenty-seven from the New Testament) and makes the following statement: "We teach that the Holy Scriptures ... are the Word of God because the holy men of God who wrote the Scriptures wrote only that which the Holy Ghost communicated to them by inspiration, 2 Tim. 3:16; 2 Pet. 1:21 ... Hence the Holy Scriptures are the sole source from which all doctrines proclaimed in the Christian Church must be taken and therefore, too, the sole rule and norm by which all teachers and doctrines must be examined and judged." [8.]

From this quote, it seems clear that the Bible should be the "sole source" and "sole rule" from which all doctrines of this synod of the Lutheran Church in general radiate. In truth however, this is not the case; the following is taken from another LCMS website (same synod) concerning "The Lutheran Confessions": "The Lutheran Church - Missouri Synod accepts the Scriptures as the inspired and inerrant Word of God, and the LCMS subscribes unconditionally to all the symbolical books of the Evangelical Lutheran Church as a true and unadulterated statement and exposition of the Word of God. We accept the Confessions because they are drawn from the Word of God and on that account regard their doctrinal content as a true and binding exposition of Holy Scripture and as authoritative for our work as ministers of Jesus Christ and servants of the Lutheran Church – Missouri Synod." [9, 30.]

Question: If the Bible is the complete Word of God and is able to thoroughly equip the man of God for every good work (2 Timothy 3:16–17), then why would these people who claim the Bible as their sole authority need several hundred pages of additional texts written by humans to "govern" their lives? This verse and others we've looked at previously preclude *any* additional doctrine as Divine revelation, be it "drawn from the Word" or not!

In the ELCA Constitution, Confession of Faith, section 2.07, it reads: "This church confesses the Gospel, recorded in the Holy Scripture **and** confessed in the ecumenical creeds **and** Lutheran confessional writings, as the power of God to create and sustain the Church of God's mission in the world." [10.] The introduction to "Constitutions, Bylaws, and Continuing Resolutions of the ELCA," written August 12, 2022, claims these documents "to be rooted in Scripture, the Lutheran Confessions, and the experiences of predecessor church bodies. Intentionally connected to this past, they also have been amended over the years to address the current context in which we have been called to serve. They incorporate important provisions that unite us as this church, yet provide organizational flexibility to congregations and synods. As such, they should facilitate ministry, not inhibit it. We, as members of this church, find ourselves consulting these documents frequently to guide, direct, and assist us in mission and ministry together." [11.]

The Wisconsin Evangelical Lutheran Synod (WELS) makes this statement: "As a synod ... we believe that the Bible is the final authority in all matters of doctrine, that it is fully inspired by God and without error. The three ecumenical creeds, the primary creedal statements of historic Christianity, summarize well our faith. In addition, we wholeheartedly subscribe to the Lutheran Confessions (contained in the Book of Concord of 1580) because they are correct expositions of biblical truth." [12, 30.]

In the "Constitutions and Bylaws" of all three synods—the ELCA, LCMS, and WELS—the claim to view several other documents as "true declarations of faith" is made as found in their common *Book of Concord,* which includes:

- The "Creeds" (Apostles, Nicene, and Athanasian).
- The "Unaltered Augsburg Confession" and "Apology of the Augsburg Confession"; and
- The "Smalcald Articles, the Small Catechism, the Large Catechism and the Formula of Concord"

As the LCMS and the WELS hold very similar views (WELS being slightly more conservative), the balance of this section on authority will focus on the two larger branches (the LCMS and the ELCA). Though even these two share similar views concerning what they hold to be authoritative (i.e., the Bible, along with The Book of Concord, the creeds, the confessions, and so forth), they differ as to the degree to which these "authoritative documents" hold sway over current practices within their respective synods – including the Bible itself. In an article written by Dr. A. L. Barry, past president of the LCMS, he made several observations concerning this issue, particularly regarding the differences between these two synods in accepting the authority of Scripture.

St. Peter's Lutheran Church
Columbus, Indiana

While both the LCMS and the ELCA profess the Scriptures to be the supreme authority for the church's doctrine and life, the LCMS claims they are the one who truly believes this and puts this into practice, citing the fact that they believe the Bible to be the Word of God, totally truthful and free from error. The ELCA, however, looks at Scripture with a different view; being more liberal in their theology, they "avoid making statements that confess the full truthfulness of the Bible," [13.] believing instead that "Scripture is not necessarily always accurate or trustworthy in all its details and parts." [13.] With this mindset, the ELCA ends up tolerating and encouraging ways of interpreting Scripture so as to allow for this preconceived error and unclarity they feel the Bible contains in promoting various doctrines.

Doctrinal differences being alluded to here include things like the ordination of women and homosexuals and abortion. The LCMS takes the high road in this article, claiming they do not ordain women to the pastoral office, while the ELCA does. The LCMS teaches that homosexual behavior is sinful, as it is contrary to God's Word, whereas the ELCA "cannot take a clear Biblical stand against this behavior." [13.] And concerning abortion, the LCMS condemns willful abortion, again as contrary to God's Word (similar to His condemnation of murder), while the ELCA cannot condemn the practice; in fact, they patronize it, as they include abortion as a "benefit" in their insurance plans they provide for in member health plans.

Within this same article, a comparison is also drawn on their differences concerning the authority of the "Lutheran Confessions." "The LCMS binds itself to the entire doctrinal content of these sixteenth-century Lutheran confessional writings as authoritative, stating, 'We agree with the confessions of our church not merely insofar as they agree with the Bible (a position which would allow individual members to reject certain doctrines – (the position taken by the ELCA) [15.], but because these confessional statements are in complete harmony with God's inspired and inerrant Word.'" [13.] The ELCA however, does not require their congregations to accept the full doctrinal content of *The Book of Concord* (inasmuch as it conforms precisely to Scripture), rather viewing these Lutheran confessions as "historical expressions of the faith held to be true at the time that they were written, but not necessarily as normative standards for teaching and practice today." [13.]

This topic has also been officially addressed by the LCMS. Under their Beliefs/Frequently Asked Questions – Denominations page, second question: "What are the main differences between The Lutheran Church – Missouri Synod and the Evangelical Lutheran Church in America (ELCA)?

Here is what is stated, "ANSWER: In terms of the official position of our two church bodies, the three main areas of difference between the LCMS and the ELCA are the following:

1. The doctrine and authority of Scripture. The LCMS believes that the Bible is without error in all that it says. The ELCA avoids making such statements, holding that Scripture is not necessarily always accurate on such matters as history and science. Differences between the LCMS and the ELCA on the authority of Scripture also help to explain why the ELCA ordains women to the pastoral office, while the LCMS does not (based on 1 Cor. 14:33-36 and 1 Tim. 2:11-14). Similarly, on the basis of what Scripture clearly teaches (Rom. 1:18-28; 1 Cor. 6:9), the LCMS position on homosexual behavior is unequivocal: homosexual behavior is contrary to God's will, while the ELCA has declared that it lacks a consensus regarding what Scripture teaches about homosexual activity. Consequently, those who disagree with one another in the ELCA have been called to respect the 'bound conscience' of others. The ELCA has also determined to allow the ordination of practicing homosexuals as long as they are in a life-long committed relationship.
2. The commitment to Lutheran confessional writings. The ELCA, while affirming its commitment to the Gospel of Jesus Christ as witnessed in the Lutheran Confessions, also tends to emphasize the historical character of these writings and to maintain the possibility of dissent to confessional positions that do not deal directly with the Gospel itself understood in a narrow sense. All LCMS pastors are required to affirm that the Lutheran Confessions are a correct explanation of the teachings of Scripture.
3. The level of agreement necessary to join together in one church body. While the LCMS believes the Bible requires agreement in all that the Bible teaches, the ELCA holds that disagreement in some matters of doctrine, such as the mode of Christ's presence in Holy Communion, do not prohibit church fellowship." [14.]

From the writings of all three major branches of the Lutheran Church in America, it's clear that the Bible, along with the writings found in *The Book of Concord* (not the Bible alone, as claimed), are the binding, authoritative rules for all members of the Lutheran Church. Though the WELS and LCMS synods may have a more conservative view of the Scriptures than the ELCA, they nonetheless have added other documents of authority to the Bible.

The statement above that "all LCMS pastors are required to affirm that the Lutheran Confessions are a correct explanation of the teachings of Scripture," makes no provision for dissent, or room for other ideas, due to empathy for the historical character of these writings, especially in dealing directly and narrowly with the Gospel – the position taken by the ELCA. This opens the door to speculation as to just what ideas within the confessions are outside or in addition to, the Scriptures. As will be seen below and elsewhere in this volume, these confessions and creeds not only add to Scriptural verbiage but in many cases also conflict with those same Scriptures. We've mentioned previously that it doesn't matter if man-made doctrines such as the Lutheran Confessions or Creeds "agree with the Bible," even closely affirming it – these additional documents are unnecessary. If they are that close to truth – why not just quote and give credit to Scripture?

Major Problems with Claiming "Other Sources" as Authority

First and foremost, the Bible gives stern warnings regarding "adding to" or "taking away from" God's Word (e.g., Deuteronomy 12:32, Proverbs 30:6, and Revelation 22:18–19); we are forbidden to go beyond the revealed will of Christ (2 John 9, 10); and we are not to teach anything other than the gospel revealed by the apostles in the New Testament or we will, by example, be "accursed" (Galatians 1:6–9).

In addition, the Bible does not agree with all declarations made in *The Book of Concord*, therefore forcing one to choose which to accept. In the New Testament, for instance, certain qualifications are given in order for a man to be appointed as a pastor (2 Timothy 3:1–7 and Titus 1:5–9). The terms "elder," "bishop," and "pastor" are used synonymously in Scripture to refer to the leaders who meet the qualifications mentioned by Paul.

According to God's Word, those men who meet these qualifications are eligible to be pastors.

The "Constitutions, Bylaws, and Continuing Resolutions of the ELCA" including the "Model Constitution for Congregations of the ELCA," however, have other criteria:

- "Only a member of the roster of Ministers of Word and Sacrament of the Evangelical Lutheran Church in America or a candidate for the roster of Ministers of Word and Sacrament who has been recommended for this congregation by the synod bishop may be called as a pastor of this congregation." (Model Constitution for Congregations of the ELCA, Chapter 9, Section C9.02.).[15.]
- "A candidate for the ministry of Word and Sacrament shall have satisfactorily completed the requirements for the Master of Divinity degree from an accredited theological school in North America." (ELCA Constitution – Nov. 2022, Section 7.31.03, paragraph c).[16.]
- "A candidate for the ministry of Word and Sacrament shall have completed the expectations and outcomes established for Lutheran learning and formation in a seminary of this church or of the Evangelical Lutheran Church in Canada, except when waived by the appropriate committee in consultation with the faculty of a seminary of this church or of the Evangelical Lutheran Church in Canada." (ELCA Constitution – Nov. 2022, Section 7.31.13, paragraph d).[16.]

If these additional qualifications are considered Scriptural and thus authoritative, that would mean those early Christians who were appointed pastors and elders would not be eligible in modern-day Lutheran churches. In truth, the apostle Peter would not be eligible for the pastoral office of the Lutheran Church, owing to his lack of formal education!

Yet another problem the Lutherans have with claiming other sources as authority is that several of the statements in the writings found in *The Book of Concord*, which the Lutheran Church accepts, are no longer followed by the church (contradicting the authority of their own official doctrine).

For instance, Luther believed and taught that infants and children were possessed by the devil and that they would go to hell unless otherwise saved from the devil through baptism. This is clearly recorded in Luther's "Small Catechism," within *The Book of Concord*, as "authoritative." Luther also taught that baptism was absolutely necessary for salvation (as recorded in Luther's *Large Catechism*), yet neither one of these positions is held by Lutherans today. (See "The Lutheran Church's Position on Baptism" and "Infant Baptism" below, under "Primary Beliefs and Doctrines.")

Other ideas put forth in these confessions and creeds, as will be discussed later, conflict with the Bible, including the doctrine of "Original Sin," "faith-only" salvation, and even erroneous verbiage within some of the creeds themselves.

The Bible, on the other hand, claims its own authority, which is *all-sufficient*:

- "All Scripture is given by inspiration of God, and is profitable for doctrine, for reproof, for correction, for instruction in righteousness, that the man of God may be complete, thoroughly equipped for every good work." (2 Timothy 3:16–17). "Thoroughly equipped for every good work" is not a time-sensitive statement; it applied in the first century, and it applies now.
- In Jude, we read an exhortation for Christians to "contend earnestly for the faith which was once for all delivered to the saints" (Jude 3). Within the "Constitutions, Bylaws, and Continuing Resolutions of the ELCA," under "Introduction," they claim that though the doctrines contained herein are rooted in Scripture, the Lutheran Confessions, and so forth, these resolutions are fluid, having been and continuing to be amended (including Scripture or the interpretation thereof) "to address the current context (culture) [17.] in which we have been called to serve. They incorporate important provisions that unite us as this church, yet provide organizational flexibility to congregations and synods. As such, they should facilitate ministry, not inhibit it." [11.]

This attitude, this doctrine of the ELCA, is far removed from what Jude 3 indicates. "*The faith*" (Eph. 4:5) refers to a unified body of Christian doctrine, the gospel (Gal.1:23, 1 Tim. 5:8). The gospel system was "once for all time" delivered to the church in the first century (anticipating the imminent suspension of divine revelation). With the completion of the sacred canon of Scripture, there was to be no ongoing revelation (cf. 1 Cor. 13:8ff; Eph. 4:8-16). All Christians today are under obligation to defend this faith. It was perfect in the first century, and it's perfect now; it needs no modifications to accommodate changing times. Truth is timeless (Acts 26:25).

- o In 2 Peter 1:3, we read that in Peter's day, God had given the Christians "all things that pertain to life and godliness." From the first century on, people were following God according to His will, without the writings found in The Book of Concord! Once again, "all things" do not leave room; nor does it necessitate future instruction of revelation.

Trinity Evangelical Lutheran Church
Milwaukee, Wisconsin

Primary Beliefs and Doctrines

Justification by Faith Alone

The central precept of Lutheran doctrine today is justification by "faith alone." Martin Luther's version of "faith only," however, has been largely misunderstood. Luther never taught that a person could be saved by believing in God on faith alone, without being baptized in water. He focused on the fact that meritorious works could not earn a person salvation, as the Catholic Church of his day taught. Because Catholics taught works (even the purchase of good works) would earn a person salvation, Luther ran in the opposite direction and taught the doctrine of faith alone, that is, faith apart from works.

When Luther translated the New Testament, he added the word "alone" to the text of Romans 3:28. The text states, "Therefore we conclude that a man is justified by faith apart from the deeds of the law." (not "Therefore we conclude that a man is justified by faith [**alone**], apart from the deeds of the law.") Confronted with this, Luther said he was fully aware that the word "alone" was not to be found in either the Latin or Greek texts, "But the word has to be added if the sense of the passage is to be expressed clearly."

When reminded that James stated, "faith without works is dead," Luther responded by saying that James was a "*right strawey epistle.*" (Essentially, he rejected the book of James). Lutherans today associate "faith only" or "faith alone" with salvation apart from baptism (rather than the "faith vs. works" issue Luther focused on). For instance, according to LCMS doctrine, "*Faith Alone*" (sola fide) is captured in these thoughts: "By His suffering and death as the substitute for all people of all time, Jesus purchased and won forgiveness and eternal life for them. **Those who hear this Good News and believe it have the eternal life that it offers.** God creates faith in Christ and gives people forgiveness through Him." [18.]

The ELCA has a similar view claiming *sola fide* or 'Faith Alone' salvation. On the ELCA website, under "What We Believe – What do Lutherans believe?" – the following is stated, "We believe that all people are imperfect and are saved (made right with God) by God's grace and God's grace alone, through Christ. There is no special prayer you need to pray, no special state of mind you need to achieve and no good deed you need to perform … We believe that we receive the gift of grace by faith alone on account of Christ." [19.]

One other document highlights their view on this 'faith only/grace only' idea – that being the "Joint Declaration on the Doctrine of Justification" by the Lutheran World Federation and the Catholic Church; an agreement made in 1994 in an effort to unit these two denominations, at least on some level. Under section 3. "The Common Understanding of Justification," sub-sections 15 & 16, we read, "Justification thus means that Christ himself is our righteousness, in which we share through the Holy Spirit in accord with the will of the Father. Together we confess: By grace alone, in faith in Christ's saving work and not because of any merit on our part, we are accepted by God and receive the Holy Spirit, who renews our hearts while equipping and calling us to good works … Through Christ alone are we justified, when we receive this salvation in faith. Faith is itself God's gift through the Holy Spirit who works through word and sacrament in the community of believers and who, at the same time, leads believers into that renewal of life which God will bring to completion in eternal life." [20.]

In the next section of this Joint Declaration on the Doctrine of Justification, 4.1 "Human Powerlessness and Sin in Relation to Justification," sub-section 21, it states, "According to Lutheran teaching, human beings are incapable of cooperating in their salvation, because as sinners they actively oppose God and his saving action." [20.]

This topic was discussed at length in the previous chapter. The New Testament does not teach we are saved by "faith alone" or by "grace alone." The statement made by the LCMS makes two claims, both of which are false. The first, "Those who hear this Good News and believe it, have the eternal life that it offers," [18] negates all passages that conjoin baptism with that belief (i.e., Mark 16:16; John 3:5; Acts 2:38). Indeed, "hearing" and "believing" are two of the five steps or acts of salvation as described in Scripture (the other three being "repentance," "confession of Jesus as Lord," and "baptism"). One cannot gain salvation without obeying all of these acts, however, the last one, baptism, is essential and cannot be ignored, for it is the dividing line from being lost or saved; it is where one contacts the blood of Christ (Romans 6:3) to wash away our sins and receive the Holy

Spirit (Acts 22:16; 2:38); it is the one act Jesus instructed His disciples as a last and "great commission" to "Go therefore and make disciples of all the nations, baptizing them in the name of the Father and of the Son and of the Holy Spirit … ." (Matthew 28:19). If hearing and believing were enough to make disciples, why did Jesus say baptizing was necessary?

The second claim made by the LCMS, "God creates faith in Christ and gives people forgiveness through Him," [18.] is also without merit. God does not "create faith in Christ" and then offer forgiveness based on that faith He has just given them, without any effort on man's part – that's not how it works! Faith must be developed by mankind – as we discussed in the previous chapter under 'salvation,' grace includes all God has done on our behalf, and faith includes all man is to do in response to God's grace so that man can receive the offer of salvation in Christ. "Faith" refers to whatever acts God specifies as necessary to qualify for His free gift of grace and salvation. James 2:22 and 24 says this, "Do you see that faith was working together with his works, and by works faith was made perfect" … You see then that a man is justified by works, and not by faith only."

The ELCA view on *sola fide* or faith-only salvation is similar and without Scriptural moorings:

"We believe that all people are imperfect and are saved (made right with God) by God's grace and God's grace alone, through Christ. There is no special prayer you need to pray, no special state of mind you need to achieve and no good deed you need to perform … We believe that we receive the gift of grace by faith alone on account of Christ." [19.] Let's dissect this statement of the ELCA. "We believe all people are imperfect" is to affirm the Calvinistic doctrine of "Total Depravity" and "Original Sin" – both are refuted as false doctrines in the first chapter of my next volume in this series (Volume Three) titled "Calvinism." "There is no special prayer (the so-called sinner's prayer), no state of mind you need to achieve (what about belief? repentance? forgiveness?), "and no good deed you need to perform" (what about confession? what about baptism?) Does the ELCA think mankind can develop faith without obedience to any of these actions on man's part? The last statement, "We believe that we receive the gift of grace by faith alone on account of Christ," seems to answer this question since, like the LCMS, believing that due to man's sinful nature and inability to come to God or even develop a faith, one's faith must be given from God "on Christ's account," along with His free grace, which offers forgiveness of sin and salvation (all without man having to lift a finger!).

These thoughts of "free grace" and "free faith" were carried into the agreement made between the Lutheran and Roman Catholic Communes. This "Joint Declaration of the Doctrine of Justification" is yet another compromise on the truth, this time to attain unity. The statement quoted above, "Together we confess: By grace alone, in faith in Christ's saving work and not because of any merit on our part, we are accepted by God and receive the Holy Spirit, who renews our hearts while equipping and calling us to good works ... Through Christ alone are we justified, when we receive this salvation in faith. Faith is itself God's gift through the Holy Spirit who works through word and sacrament in the community of believers and who, at the same time, leads believers into that renewal of life which God will bring to completion in eternal life,"[20] is simply not according to Scripture (which does not bode well for either the Catholic or the Lutheran Church). God's grace is the only "free gift" here. Grace is unmerited salvation offered to mankind, but with a caveat – grace is God's part, faith, being man's obedience to God's ordained acts of salvation (hear, believe, repent, confess, submit to baptism), is man's part. As we've discussed previously, faith involves the building up of certain "works" of man (James 2:14-25); verse 24 says, "You see then that a man is justified by works, and not by faith only." The above "Joint Declaration" statement makes grace, faith, and the Holy Spirit, all free gifts of God – this is simply not true.

The last statement of this Joint Declaration brings in the Calvinistic doctrine of Total Depravity and Original Sin with words like, "According to Lutheran teaching, human beings are incapable of cooperating in their salvation, because as sinners they actively oppose God and his saving action." [20.] This false doctrine will be examined fully in the first chapter of my next volume; however, as a quick response to "human beings are incapable of cooperating in their salvation," let me suggest this is true of God's grace, not of man's faith. With faith, we are commanded to "cooperate": "Jesus answered, Most assuredly, I say to you, unless one is born of water and the Spirit, he cannot enter the kingdom of God." (John 3:5). This is a reference to our submitting to water baptism as the last step in God's plan of salvation.

Baptism - Adult

The Lutheran Church's position on baptism is a story of change (both of necessity and form). First, we'll look at necessity. The historical view acknowledges Martin Luther's position; Luther was adamant about the necessity of baptism, stating in his Large Catechism, "Baptism is no human plaything but is instituted by God Himself. Moreover, it is solemnly and strictly commanded that we must be baptized, or we shall not be saved, so that we are not to regard it as an indifferent matter, like putting on a red coat." [21.]

The present-day Lutheran Church no longer acknowledges this statement as accurate. Both the ELCA and LCMS seem to be changing their beliefs about the necessity of baptism for the salvation of sinners. From the official website of the LCMS comes this statement: "The LCMS does not believe that baptism is **ABSOLUTELY** (emphasis added) necessary for salvation. The thief on the cross was saved (apparently without baptism), as were all true believers in the Old Testament era. Mark 16:16 implies that it is not the absence of baptism that condemns a person but the absence of faith" [22.]

Concerning "form," though Luther taught that baptism should be by immersion, the present-day Lutheran Church teaches that any type of water application, such as sprinkling, pouring, or immersion, is acceptable and valid. In addition, the ELCA claims in their published guideline "The Use of the Means of Grace" (principle 26), concerning the water used in baptism, that "Water is a sign of cleansing, dying, and new birth. It is used generously in Holy Baptism to signify God's power over sin and death." [23.] Application 26A of this text adds that the modes of immersion and pouring show God's power in baptism—immersion to signify dying and rising with Christ and pouring to suggest cleansing from sin. Martin Luther made full use of water when possible, "For baptism … signifies that the old man [self] and the sinful birth of flesh and blood are to be wholly drowned by the grace of God. We should therefore do justice to its meaning and make baptism a true and complete sign of the thing it signifies." [23.] To defend this point of view, the Lutheran Church claims it is impossible to know fr0m the biblical text whether the word "baptize" means "to dip," "to wash," "to pour," or "to immerse."

If the Lutheran Church claims to believe that in baptism God "cleanses us from sin" (as highlighted in application 26A above), how, then, can it claim that baptism is not "ABSOLUTELY" necessary for salvation? The Lutheran position on baptism is confused and stands in serious contradiction.

The Scriptures are very clear on this matter: "He who believes and is baptized will be saved" (Mark 16:16), and "Truly, truly, I say to you, unless one is born of water and the Spirit he cannot enter into the kingdom of God." (John 3:5 NASV). The statement above from the LCMS website claiming that Mark 16:16 implies faith is required, not baptism in this passage, ignores the conjunctive "and," which ties the two (belief and baptism), making them inseparable as prerequisites to salvation. The New Testament teaches we are not saved by "grace alone" or "faith alone"; we've discussed this previously; however, [an even more detailed discussion of this argument can be found in my next volume (Volume Three) under "The Presbyterian Church," in the subsection "Salvation / Baptism."]

The argument often used that water baptism is unnecessary since the thief on the cross was not baptized, [the thought being, since Jesus said he would join him in paradise (Luke 23:43) without having been baptized, it's not required of us today], is thoroughly dismissed in Appendix A of Kyle Butts's book *What the Bible Says about the Lutheran Church.*[24.] To summarize, first, it's entirely possible the thief was baptized prior to being placed on the cross (ref: Matthew 3:5–6, John 4:1–2, Mark. 1:4–5, Luke 3:21, 7:29–30), and second, the thief was not subject to the New Testament command to be baptized into Christ's death (Romans 6:3–4), just as Moses, Abraham, and David were not subject to it, having lived under different law codes and prior to the cross. They could not have been baptized into Christ's death since Christ had not yet died! In addition, Christ offered forgiveness to others during his time on earth, just as He offered it here (Matthew 9:1-8; Luke 7:48).

Concerning baptismal "form," the New Testament teaches it is to be by immersion only. (For a detailed refutation of "sprinkling" and "pouring," refer to the Catholic Church's *The Sacrament of Baptism / Salvation.* [25.] Note: This denomination and many others use similar arguments to discredit immersion only). The following conclusions cannot be denied:

- o The Greek word for "baptize" itself ("*baptidzo*") means to "dip, immerse" (Arndt, Gingrich, and Danker 1979, 131).
- o Paul defined the word "baptism" as a burial in both Romans 6:3–4 and Colossians 2:12 (To miss the fact that baptism is a burial in water is to miss a major significance; just as Christ died, was buried, and rose again, so the candidate for baptism dies to sin, is buried (immersed completely) in water, and rises from that water as a resurrected being to walk in new life.
- o When the Ethiopian treasurer wanted to be baptized, both he and Phillip "went down into the water" [30.] (Acts 8:38). (Immersion is so indicated.)
- o When Jesus was baptized by John in the Jordan, "And immediately, coming up from the water, [30.] He saw the heavens parting and the Spirit descending upon Him like a dove." (Mark 1:10 - Immersion is so indicated.)

The practices of sprinkling and pouring, therefore, do not find their authority in the New Testament.

Baptism - Infant

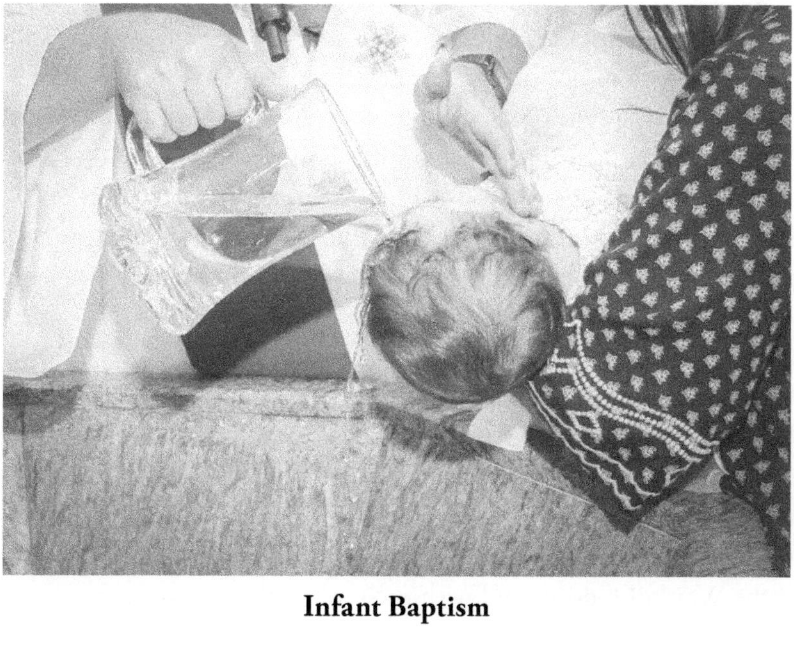

Infant Baptism

In spite of his insistence upon the necessity of faith, Luther approved of infant baptism. Believing in original sin, he believed infants are possessed by the devil and baptism drives the devil away from them. Luther further believed that infants are aided by the faith of others, namely, those who bring them to baptism (i.e., sponsors) and that the Word of God can change the heart of an infant, cleansing their inherent sin and "inpouring faith." (Notice how this conflicts with Luther's own condemnation of those who would transfer "good works" from one person to another (i.e., Catholic indulgences). [26.]

Luther also had this to say concerning infant baptism: "That the Baptism of infants is pleasing to Christ is sufficiently proved from His own work, namely, that God sanctifies (makes holy) [27] many of them who have been thus baptized, and has given them the Holy Ghost; and that there are yet many even today in whom we perceive that they have the Holy Ghost both because of their doctrine and life; as it is also given to us by the grace of God that we can explain the Scriptures and come to the knowledge of Christ, which is impossible without the Holy Ghost. But if God did not accept the baptism of infants, He would not give the Holy Ghost nor any of His gifts to any of them; in short, during this long time unto this day no man upon earth could have been a Christian." [28.]

What Luther is saying here is explained in a recent LCMS "Q and A," where the question, "How does faith play a role in infant Baptism? Is answered as follows, "When an infant is baptized, God "creates faith" in the heart of that infant "during baptism" – "Although we do not claim to understand how this happens or how it is possible, we believe (because of what the Bible says about Baptism) that when an infant is baptized God creates faith in the heart of that infant. This faith cannot yet, of course, be expressed or articulated, yet it is real and present all the same (see, e.g., 1 Peter 3:21; Acts 2:38-39; Titus 3:5-6; Matt. 18:6; Luke 1:15; 2 Tim. 3:15; Gal. 3:26-27; Rom. 6:4; Col. 2:11-12; 1 Cor. 12:13). [29.]

Luther continues, "Further, we say that we are not so much concerned to know whether the person baptized believes or not; for on that account Baptism does not become invalid; but everything depends upon the Word and command of God. This now is perhaps somewhat acute, but it rests entirely upon what I have said, that Baptism is nothing else than water and the Word of God in and with each other, that is, when the Word is added to the water, Baptism is valid, even though faith be wanting. For my faith does not make Baptism, but receives it. Now, Baptism does not become invalid even though it be wrongly received or employed; since it is not bound (as stated) to our faith, but to the Word." [28.]

The ELCA and LCMS, early founders of the denomination, stated another reason: "It is necessary to baptize little children in order that the promise of salvation might be applied to them according to Christ's mandate (Matthew 28:19), "Baptize all nations." Just as salvation is offered to all in that passage, so baptism is offered to all - men, women, children, and infants. Therefore, it clearly follows that infants are to be baptized because salvation is offered with baptism" (Kolb and Wenger 2000, 184).

The Lutheran Church today still maintains a position requiring the baptism of children and infants; however, their reasons for doing so have expanded. For example, on the official LCMS website, under "Frequently Asked Questions," the question "Why do Lutherans Baptize Infants?" three answers are given:

1. "**God's command to baptize** [30] (Matt. 28:18-20; Mark 16:16; Acts 2:38). There is not a single passage in Scripture which instructs us not to baptize for reasons of age, race, or gender. On the contrary, the divine commands to baptize in Scripture are all universal in nature. On the basis of these commands, the Christian church has baptized infants from the earliest days of its history." [31.]
2. "**Our need for Baptism** [30.] (Psalm 51:5; John 3:5-7; Acts 2:38; Rom. 3:23; Rom. 6:3-4). According to the Bible, all people–including infants–are sinful and fall short of the glory of God (Rom. 3:23) … Like adults, infants die - sure proof that they too are under the curse of sin and death. King David confesses, "I was brought forth in iniquity, and in sin did my mother conceive me" (Ps. 51:5). According to the Bible, Baptism (somewhat like Old Testament circumcision, administered to 8-day-old babies – see Col. 2:11-12) is God's gracious way of washing away our sins – even the sins of infants – without any help or cooperation on our part. It is a wonderful gift of a loving and gracious God." [31.]
3. "**God's promises and power** [30.] (Acts 2:38; Mark 16:16; Acts 22:16; 1 Peter 3:21; John 3:5-7; Titus 3:5-6; Gal. 3:26-27; Rom.

> 6:1-4; Col. 2;11-12; Eph. 5:25-26; 1 Cor. 12:13). Those churches which deny Baptism to infants usually do so because they have a wrong understanding of Baptism. They see Baptism as something we do (e.g., a public profession of faith, etc.) rather than seeing it as something that God does for us and in us. None of the passages listed above, nor any passage in Scripture, describes Baptism as "our work" or as "our public confession of faith." Instead, these passages describe Baptism as a gracious and powerful work of God through which He miraculously (though through very "ordinary" means) washes away our sins by applying to us the benefits of Christ's death and resurrection (Acts 2:38-39; Acts 22:16), gives us a new birth in which we "cooperate" just as little as we did in our first birth (John 3:5-7), clothes us in Christ's righteousness (Gal. 3:26-27), gives us the Holy Spirit (Titus 3:5-6), saves us (1 Peter 3:21), buries us and raises us up with Christ as new creatures (Rom. 6:4; Col. 2:11-12), makes us holy in God's sight (Eph. 5: 25-26) and incorporates us into the body of Christ (1 Cor. 12:13). All of this, according to the Bible, happens in Baptism, and all of it is God's doing, not ours. The promises and power of Baptism are extended to all in Scripture — including infants — and are available to all." [31.]

In addition to these reasons although Lutherans hold to their doctrine that infants must be baptized since, as mentioned above, baptism is the vehicle through which they initially receive "faith" via God creating this faith in the heart of that infant during baptism, they also conversely believe infants and small children have the ability to "believe" or to have "faith" on their own somehow, even without baptism! They reference three Scriptures in particular, as support. The first is found in Psalm 22, "Yet you are he who took me from the womb; you made me trust you at my mother's breasts. On you was I cast from my birth, and from my mother's womb you have been my God. (Psalm 22:9-10). In this Psalm, David discusses his faith and in doing so references the fact that he had faith at a time when he was still nursing. How is this possible? The answer is just as clear, "you made me trust you." [32.]

A second example can be found in Luke 18, where Jesus rebukes his disciples, stating, "Let the little children come to Me, and do not forbid them; **for of such is the kingdom of God** ..." [30.] (Luke 18:15–17). Though not addressing infant baptism directly, it is claimed that according to Jesus, these babies had what it took to be members of the kingdom of God, feeble intellect and all! Therefore, when He says about babies, 'for of such is the kingdom of God,' He is telling us that babies can believe (for how else could they enter the kingdom?!) Another Lutheran site, "Just and Sinner" had this to say concerning Luke 18:15-17, "This text is significant because it uses the term "βρέφη" which refers to infants rather than to children in general. Jesus plainly admits in this text that infants can obtain the kingdom of God. How does one obtain the kingdom of God? Through faith. Some might argue that this is an invalid argument because the point Jesus is making is not about infant faith and salvation, but about humility. He is using a child merely as an illustration. Even if this is the case, this does not negate the fact that the illustration is real. Even if he is primarily making the point that becoming like a child is necessary to enter the kingdom, this is only the case because children indeed do have faith. He says that "to such belongs the kingdom of God." This includes both infants and those who approach God with childlike faith." [32.]

Finally, a third reference is recorded in Matthew 18:1-6: "At that time the disciples came to Jesus, saying, "Who is the greatest in the kingdom of heaven?" And calling to him a child, he put him in the midst of them and said, "Truly, I say to you, unless you turn and become like children, you will never enter the kingdom of heaven. Whoever humbles himself like this child is the greatest in the kingdom of heaven. "Whoever receives one such child in my name receives me, but whoever causes one of these little ones **who believe in me** [30.] to sin, it would be better for him to have a great millstone fastened around his neck and to be drowned in the depth of the sea." This text demonstrates that children can and do believe at a young age. The Greek term used here "παιδία" usually has reference to an infant or young child." [32.]

A second posting on the LCMS website states: "Lutherans do not believe that only those baptized as infants receive faith. Faith can also be created in a person's heart (any person's heart) [27] by the power of the Holy Spirit working through God's (written or spoken) word. Baptism should then soon follow conversion ... Mark 16:16 implies that it is not the absence of baptism that condemns a person but the absence of faith, and there are clearly other ways of coming to faith by the power of the Holy Spirit (i.e., reading or hearing the Word of God)." [33.]

Let's summarize the above. Martin Luther in the Book of Concord, Large Catechism, claims that infants are "possessed by the devil" (born into sin) and must be baptized in order to be saved. He also claims that infant baptism is pleasing to Christ and that the Holy Ghost is given to mankind primarily through infant baptism. Though Luther condemned indulgences of the Catholic Church, he sanctioned the transference of the good works and faith of others, namely sponsors, to aid infants in their walk with Christ following baptism. Luther believed baptism was nothing more than water mixed with the Word of God – so it didn't matter who was being baptized or what they believed (even if they had no belief or faith going into baptism) – the baptism would still be valid since he believed faith does not make Baptism but receives it. In addition, the Large Catechism states that infants are included in Christ's mandate to "Baptize all nations" (Matthew 28:19) and claims that in baptism God "washes away sins." Though these are dated reasons used by Martin Luther and early reformers, which have been modified in recent times by other rationale, the Lutheran Church still defends them as valid reasons for baptizing infants today. The modern-day Lutheran Church claims to accept these teachings but then states there are other ways to be saved that do not include water baptism, such as the creation of faith in one's heart (infant or adult heart) by the Holy Spirit, whereby conversion occurs (in the case of an adult, by the willingness of a penitent heart, without baptism - (baptism to follow).

The current-day Lutheran also maintains Luther's basic belief that God 'sanctifies' the infant in baptism as well as imparts the Holy Ghost to them at that time. This has been further clarified that the heart of an infant is "changed by God" in the waters of baptism – adding the "faith and belief" that is missing and is necessary to fulfill Scripture (i.e., Mark 16:16, "He who believes and is baptized shall be saved"). At the same time, they believe an infant can "believe" or has the capacity to believe in Christ ahead of, or even despite baptism – since it is claimed the Scriptures confirm this in passages such as Psalm 22:9-10, Luke 18:15-17, and Matthew 18:1-6. [35.] As was mentioned under "Adult Baptism," there are other ways for people (infants to adults) to obtain faith other than in the waters of baptism – "faith can be created in a person's heart by the power of the Holy Spirit working through God's (written or spoken) Word." [23.] Therefore, "Baptism is not ABSOLUTELY necessary for salvation ... Still, Baptism dare not be despised or willfully neglected, since it is explicitly commanded by God and has His precious promises attached to it. It is not a mere "ritual" or "symbol," but a powerful means of grace by which God grants faith and the forgiveness of sins." [22.]

Other beliefs have been added as well - one was hinted at above—that baptism replaces circumcision in the Old Testament, citing Colossians 2:11–12, which states that baptism is the "circumcision made without hands." Since eight-day-old infants were circumcised and at that point became part of God's covenant people, it follows that newborn babies today can be baptized and become members of His kingdom (similar to the Orthodox Church's position).

Also, infants were "in all probability" included when "whole households" were baptized (referencing passages such as Acts 16:15 and 16:33 and citing as precedent the inclusion of infants in the word "household" in Old Testament passages such as 1 Samuel 22:16. [34.]

Finally, infants are to be baptized because this was the practice of the early church. "Polycarp (69–155 AD), a disciple of the Apostle John, was baptized as an infant ... (as was) Origen (185–254 AD) and Cyprian (215–258 AD), and the Council of Carthage in 254 where the 66 bishops stated: 'We ought not hinder any person from Baptism and the grace of God ... especially infants ... those newly born.'" [34.]

Infant baptism is rooted in the idea that infants and small children bear or inherit both the guilt and the consequences of Adam's sin, a doctrine known as "Original sin," and therefore need to be freed from this "sinful nature" as soon as possible after birth through baptism. This doctrine was discussed at length in our last volume with the Roman Catholic Church, [36.] and will be discussed again in my next Volume (3), Chapter One – Calvinism, "Total Depravity." For purposes here, suffice it to say this denomination, as well as many others who currently baptize infants, do so primarily for this underlying reason. The consequences of Adam's sin we all suffer – is death; however, the guilt of Adam's sin is not transferable; we do not share this aspect of Adam's sin. This is what Lutherans and others say is inherited or passed down. Adam was responsible for the guilt of his own sin and so are we! [Ezekiel stated, "The soul who sins shall die. The son shall not bear the guilt of the father, nor the father bear the guilt of the son. The righteousness of the righteous shall be upon himself, and the wickedness of the wicked shall be upon himself" (Ezekiel 18:20)]. Also, we read in Deuteronomy 24:16, "Fathers shall not be put to death for *their* children, nor shall children be put to death for *their* fathers: a person shall be put to death for his own sin."

As Moises Pinedo stated, "Infant baptism might be a necessity **if** original sin were passed down through the generations. However, children do not inherit the sins of their parents, so ultimately, no one can inherit the sin of Adam (cf. Exodus 32:32-33; Deuteronomy 24:16; 2 Kings 14:6; 2 Chronicles 25:4; Jeremiah 31:30; Ezekiel 18:20; Pinedo, 2009). Therefore, babies and little children do not have "sickly souls," nor do they need baptism for spiritual healing ... no one should subject a baby to a baptism that is designed to forgive sins which he or she **cannot** commit (cf. Mark 16:16; Acts 2:38; 22:16; 1 Peter 3:21) ... The Bible never gives a command, provides an example, or implies that infant baptism should be administered. There is not a single Bible verse that mentions it." [37.]

The Scriptures dismiss infant baptism on many levels. The most obvious being based on common sense - one must "hear and understand" (Romans 10:14), "believe" (Romans 10:10–11, John 3:16), "repent" (Luke 13:3; 24:46–47), and "confess" (Romans 10:9) prior to baptism. An infant is incapable, either cognitively or physically of accomplishing any of these. Knowing this and to purposely circumvent these obvious facts, Lutherans (and others) have misused/circumvented the sacred texts and employed what is called the "eisegesis interpretation of Scripture." Eisegesis is a process of seeking biblical support for pre-existing views or reading into the text one's own ideas, rather than allowing the biblical text to explain itself naturally. This method is wrong since it does not allow the text to teach us objectively. The correct form of biblical interpretation is called exegesis interpretation, which involves studying the text without preconceived views so that the truth of Scripture is allowed to be impressed upon our hearts without bias. The examples cited in Psalm 22:9-10, Luke 18:15-17, and Matthew 18:1-6 were all interpreted eisegetically to supposedly prove that infants are capable of developing "faith" or "belief" even at this stage of life. If studied correctly (via exegesis), however, we would find that none of these verses are teaching on the subject of infant baptism explicitly, nor do they imply the conclusions drawn.

Looking at these verses exegetically (without any bias), one finds the following:

Psalm 22:9-10. David wrote this Psalm in the 10th century B.C. It is unquestionably a Messianic psalm – citing many details that forecast the death of the Messiah. For example, "My God, My God, why have you forsaken Me?" (Psalm 22:1/Matthew 27:46); "But I am a worm, and no man; A reproach of men, and despised by the people. All those who see Me ridicule Me; They shoot out the lip, they shake the head, *saying*, He trusted in the Lord, let Him rescue Him; Let Him deliver Him!" (Psalm 22:6-8/Matthew 27:39-43); "They pierced My hands and My feet" (Psalm 22:16/Matthew 27:35); "They divided My garments among them, And for My clothing they cast lots." (Psalm 22:18/Matthew 27:35).

This is relevant to our discussion here since the Lutheran Church has referenced a portion of this 22nd Psalm (verses 9 and 10) to justify infant baptism by dogmatically applying these words to David as the subject when in fact, these verses are not conclusively speaking of David; they have been argued as well to be speaking of our Lord. Being a Messianic Psalm, all subject references lean toward Jesus throughout this Psalm. Taking Psalm 22:9-10 and defining the capitalized words as Deity (as the translators did in the NKJV), it would read as follows, "But You (God the Father) are He (God the Father) who took Me (God the Son, Jesus) out of the womb; You (God the Father) made Me (God the Son, Jesus) trust *while* on My (God the Son, Jesus) mother's breasts. I (God the Son, Jesus) was cast upon You (God the Father) from birth. From My (God the Son, Jesus) mother's womb, You (God the Father) *have been* My (God the Son, Jesus) God (God the Father)."

Lutherans assert that David is spoken of here (as the translators of many other Bible versions did not choose to capitalize those words as did the translators of the NKJV); they claim, "In this Psalm, David discusses his faith and in doing so references the fact that he had faith at a time when he was still nursing." [32.] Even if David is spoken of here, it doesn't necessarily mean he actually had faith from infancy forward; he could have just as easily been expressing his current faith and love for God *symbolically* to that earlier time to emphasize his current feelings.

To add clarity to this, I consulted a friend at Apologetics Press, Dr. Dave Miller, who thought this worthy enough to write an article on this subject for the benefit of all his readers. This article, titled "Psalm 22:9 and Infant Salvation" can be found both on the Apologetics Press website (www.apologeticspress.org) and within their monthly journal "Reason & Revelation" published February 2024 (Vol. 44. NO. 2). Dr. Miller leaves little doubt as to the Psalmist's intended meaning(s) concerning this verse; in fact, he offers several interpretations – neither of which support the Lutheran contention that infants obtain a miraculous 'soul-saving' faith. I would encourage the reader to access this article for a full explanation, with Scriptural support. For purposes here, the suggestions I make above are mentioned in Dr. Dave's article; all quotes that follow are cited from that article.

One interpretation of Psalm 22:9-10 focuses on the extensive Messianic message it contains – and the fact that the verses in question (9-10) are sandwiched in the midst of these Messianic anticipations which speak exclusively of Christ. The rationale used here by Dr. Miller is that if these verses are speaking of Christ and not David (as the translators of the NKJV so understood – since they capitalized both the "He" and "Me" throughout, including verses 9-10), "it pertains to the divine mission that Jesus fulfilled … this mission required Him to assume human form by being physically born as a baby via a human female. That infant body was specifically "prepared" (Hebrews 10:5) by God for Jesus – not David- to indwell. Consequently, verse 9 would refer to the submissive role that Jesus voluntarily assumed in order to accomplish the divine scheme of redemption … Accordingly, it makes perfect scriptural sense to speak of God taking Jesus in bodily form out of Mary's womb in a state of eternal trust/compliance with the divine will to save mankind."

A second interpretation is then offered for consideration – one that assumes Psalm 22:9 refers to David, however, **not** as Lutherans (and others) conclude. Dr. Miller states that though "several English translations render the verse in such a way that God is represented as making or causing the psalmist to **believe/trust** Him while still in infancy … such language may be nothing more than a figurative way for David to indicate that

God had been with him and cared for him throughout his entire life." As support for this, Dr. Miller introduces a number of translations describing those Hebrew words for "faith and trust" differently – such as "thou didst make me **hope**" (KJV, AMPC, KJ21, GVN, WYC); and "made me **feel secure**" (NET, HCSB, CSB); and "made me **feel safe** (ERV, CEB, GW, GNT, GW, ISV, RSV, NRSV); "you **protected me** when I was a baby at my mother's breast" (CEV); also, "**You took care of me** at my mother's breasts" (EASY). "Even the renderings of "trust" or "faith" are not referring to **religious faith** – as if the psalmist was suggesting David "accepted Jesus as his Savior" while in the womb or shortly thereafter. Rather, they are referring to the reliance on God that David realized he had enjoyed his entire life. As a baby learns to feel secure and trust his mother through the comfort of breast feeding, so David would have learned to trust God throughout his life, from beginning to end."

Either of these interpretations by Dr. Miller works well for our discussion here and is much more plausible than believing God miraculously imparts religious faith into an infant's heart! This author is leaning more towards the first interpretation – that being, the psalmist is speaking of Jesus here, not David. It seems more likely that with most all verses in this Psalm being Messianic, why would verses 9 and 10 (which are sandwiched between verses 8 and 11 – both Messianic) be isolated and divert to speak of David here and nowhere else - thus not carrying the overall theme of the Psalm? This is a difficult passage; however, I again refer the reader to Dr. Miller's article for a fuller explanation, that you may decide for yourself.

Luke 18:15-17. Lutherans interpret the words of Jesus in these verses, "Let the little children come to Me, and do not forbid them; *for of such is the kingdom of God* … whoever does not receive *the kingdom of God as a little child* will by no means enter it" as little children, (even infants) having faith or belief in Him. In this passage, Jesus is calling the little children as an example of what those who enter the kingdom are to be—**innocent and sinless!** (Just as children are innocent until they are old enough to know right from wrong, we as adults can return to an innocent and sinless state when we accept and acknowledge Jesus and come in contact with His blood in the waters of baptism, thus washing our sins away). To answer the question "How else could they enter the kingdom?" The proper answer - they are sinless! (Not because they have faith as suggested above).

They don't need to have their "sins" washed away, for they have none at this point. The contention is based on the false doctrine of original sin—a topic discussed briefly below and, in more detail, when we get to the first chapter of our next volume (3) on Calvinism.

Matthew 18:1–6. These verses are also used to support infant belief and the need for baptism, "At that time the disciples came to Jesus, saying, "Who then is the greatest in the kingdom of heaven?" Then Jesus called a little child to Him, set him in the midst of them, and said, "Assuredly, I say to you, unless you are converted and become as little children, (innocent/sinless) [27] you will by no means enter the kingdom of heaven. Therefore whoever humbles himself as this little child is the greatest in the kingdom of heaven. Whoever receives one little child like this in My name receives Me. Whoever causes one of these little ones **who believe in Me** [30] to sin, it would be better for him if a millstone were hung around his neck, and he were drowned in the depth of the sea." Adding to the Luke 18 passage where entering the 'kingdom of heaven' supposedly proves infants and little children must have faith and need baptism, Lutherans here focus on verse six – where they claim it is clear **infants do "believe"** in Christ. The problem with this is that the context does not support this conclusion. Even if the Greek word for "little children" means "occasionally infants" – in this verse, the reference is limited to little children only. Notice verse two, "Then Jesus called a little child to Him." Infants are not capable of responding to commands like this, much less "walking over to Jesus." Again, verse four, "Therefore, whoever humbles himself as this little child …" Infants do not humble themselves; they are totally dependent upon their parents or others – little children, however, are capable of "humbling themselves."

Wayne Jackson put it this way, "He called a little child and set him among the disciples, and said, "Unless you turn [change your ambitious disposition] and become **as** [30] little children, you will not enter the kingdom" (v. 3). The simile stresses a pure, child-like absence of self-aggrandizement. (The text has no reference to conversion or to receiving infants into the church, as commonly alleged by those who practice infant baptism.) The next verse transitions to taking care not to "offend" a "little one" who believes in Christ, i.e., those tender in faith. To carelessly treat harmfully such a young and sincere one is a spiritual crime of great magnitude. It would be better if such a senseless one were drowned in the sea with a millstone around his neck. This implies that eternal punishment will be worse than mere death (cf. Heb. 10:29). [38.]

In addition, R.C.H. Lenski had this to say concerning these verses, "The child in Jesus' arms looked up to him, depended on him, was content with what he did. This was its humility or lowliness. It claimed nothing, pointed to no merits, was proud of no achievements. This was the natural state of this child; Jesus uses this to illustrate what the spiritual state of greatness in the kingdom is." [39.] Concerning verse 6 Lenski said, "To believe means to trust. Even in adults the inner essential of their faith, let it be filled with ever so much discursive thought, intelligent knowledge, introspective consciousness, is childlike trust. In the matter of this trust the child is the model for the man, not the man for the child. Jesus uses the natural traits of a child to illustrate what he desires his disciples to become." [39.]

Finally, H. Leo Boles, in his Commentary of Matthew 18:6, said this, "Jesus speaks of little ones able to believe; the word translated "stumble" means to lead into sin, to cause to offend; the meaning of it is that it is better for him who causes one to stumble to have a millstone hanged about his neck and be cast into the depth of the sea. Jesus speaks here of children who believe, or of the simplest childlike persons who believe." [40.] H. Leo Boles places as much emphasis on this little child being led into sin (most likely for the first time) as to the capacity to believe. Both having a simple, child-like, trusting faith and being vulnerable to sin show this child is NOT an infant.

Evidence that infants are sinless can be seen in the account of David's son as recorded in 2 Samuel. Chapter 11 records the account of David and Bathsheba, where David committed sin with Bathsheba and had her husband Uriah killed in battle to avail her as his wife. Bathsheba bore David a son as a result of this illicit affair, but "The thing that David had done displeased the Lord." (2 Sam. 11:27). Soon after, the Lord struck the child that Uriah's wife bore to David, and he became ill and died (2 Sam. 12:15, 18). Although David pleaded with the Lord to reconsider beforehand, God would not relent; and after the child's death, David knew his child was in heaven – that it was he who committed sin, not his son. David then declared in 2 Sam. 12:22-23, "While the child was

alive, I fasted and wept; for I said, 'Who can tell *whether the* Lord will be gracious to me, that the child may live? But now he is dead; why should I fast? Can I bring him back again? I shall go to him (I shall go to be with him in heaven when I die),[27] but he shall not return to me (here on Earth)."
[27.] David's son was sinless, and he died in this condition – allowing him to enter the kingdom of God.

In addition to all that has been said concerning infant "belief and faith" being inherent in infants, the Lutheran Church also claims God "creates faith" in the heart of infants during baptism. This idea originated with Martin Luther, who not only believed God "inpoured faith," but he invented the idea of sponsors as surrogates to aid the child's faith growing up. Baptism to him was nothing more than water and the Word of God mixed – therefore it didn't matter if one believed or not – it was God who did all the work in the waters of baptism. Luther claimed, "Baptism is valid, even though faith is wanting. For my faith does not make Baptism, but receives it … since it is not bound to our faith, but to the Word." [28.] **All of these statements are without Scriptural support.**

Repeating what was stated earlier, one must "hear and understand" (Romans 10:14), "believe" (Romans 10:10–11, John 3:16), "repent" (Luke 13:3; 24:46–47), and "confess" (Romans 10:9) prior to baptism. An infant is incapable of accomplishing any of these. This statement has not been disproved by anything the Lutherans have claimed here. Imagining God creates faith in an infant's heart during baptism or that infants somehow develop their own faith remains unproved and unprovable. The problem seems to be a Lutheran misunderstanding of baptism altogether. They understand baptism as Martin Luther understood it – simply a mixture of water and the Word of God, whereby God does all the "work" and humans simply receive it – sometimes even without belief or faith! This is not what the Scriptures say. Baptism is the fifth and final stage or act of salvation as stipulated in Scripture; the other four are listed directly above – all require obedience and some effort on the part of the candidate to fulfill; even baptism requires effort. One must submit willingly to immersion. Baptism is where one comes in contact with Christ's blood – the vehicle required for sin forgiveness. Since infants have no sin, this forgiveness is unnecessary for them – Lutherans just don't understand or refuse to admit this – they would rather hold onto their "original sin" idea.

Consider the Ethiopian in Acts 8. The Ethiopian heard the Word – he was reading the Bible, a Messianic chapter in Isaiah (likely Isaiah 53), and Philip joined him to help explain Jesus in this reading (studying/comprehending Scripture is an action/work). He then believed and confessed Jesus as the Son of God (Acts 8:37); these are also actions or "work" on his part to obey the Gospel. The Ethiopian then asked Philip if he could be baptized (vs. 36) – verbally requesting baptism is another action/work. (Repentance is not mentioned here but is assumed (another action/work) – not all acts of salvation are recorded in every example). Philip then stopped the chariot and both he and the eunuch went down into the water - the Ethiopian obeyed this command of God; he exerted effort to do so; he had to "do" something - although he was passive during the actual baptism, he got out of the chariot, went into the water, and allowed Philip to baptized him. Both came up from the water following baptism, following contact with the blood of Christ (washing away the eunuch's sin), and he went away rejoicing.

Dave Miller said this concerning "faith and works" "Anytime the New Testament speaks of being saved "by faith," it is referring to a faith that includes whatever actions God specifies as necessary. James makes this clear in James 2:22: "Do you see that faith was working together with his works, and by works faith was made perfect?" And notice his concluding remarks in James 2:24,26: "You see then that a man is justified by works, and not by faith only. For as the body without the spirit is dead, so faith without works is dead also."[48.] To claim baptism is strictly a work of God that we receive at infancy (involuntarily), not even requiring faith or belief on the candidate's part to make valid, or that no effort is required even of adults in this process – is simply not what the Scriptures attest.

The Lutheran contention that infants are included as part of "all the nations" in Jesus's command recorded in Matthew 28:19 that we are to "Go therefore and make disciples **of all the nations**, [30] baptizing them in the name of the Father and of the Son and of the Holy Spirit" is taken out of context and it ignores other clear Scriptures defining candidates for baptism. Once again, not all examples we see in the Scriptures include all five acts of salvation as stipulated in God's plan; in this example, Jesus assumes we know the other four steps required, and He simply shortens His command to "make disciples … baptizing them …" (the final stage, that puts one into the kingdom). This passage further discounts the contention that infants are included in His command to make disciples and baptize them since if we are to make *disciples* of all nations, a disciple can be defined as a "follower" or "pupil" (i.e., a follower of Jesus—one capable of learning by emulating a teacher), then infants, just as they are not capable of "believing," "repenting," or "confessing," are not capable of becoming disciples, which negates this argument entirely!

Addressing the three answers given on the LCMS website in response to the question, "Why do Lutherans Baptize Infants?" - the following is a Scriptural response:

1. **"God's command to baptize."** (Matthew 28:18-20; Mark 16:16; Acts 2:38). The claim here is that "there is not a single passage in Scripture which instructs us **not** to baptize for reasons of age, race, or gender." That baptism is universal in nature per Scripture, and "the Christian church has baptized infants from the earliest days of its history." The first statement is both weak on its premise and tries to cash in on today's cultural drama by adding "age" to a familiar "race/gender" slogan. To say Scripture does not prohibit infant baptism is analogous to saying the Scriptures do not prohibit harmful drug use, jumping off a cliff, or you name it; what is important, however, is that the Scriptures do not have a single example authorizing infant baptism! We are to obey the commands, examples, and necessary inferences within Scripture because they are God's Word – we do not obey what the Scriptures do not say!

The examples we see in Scripture are not "universal in nature," meaning "all-inclusive" – which might include the "whole households" that were baptized (i.e., Acts 16:15 and 16:33) – this and the final contention that infants were baptized in the early church will be addressed below. The first two passages listed above have been addressed, but the last one has not – Acts 2:38 does not work well as a claim for infant baptism. "Peter said to them, "Repent, and let every one of you be baptized in the name of Jesus Christ for the remission of sins …" First – how can an infant "repent?" Second, baptism is purposed here for the "remission of sins" – we've discussed this previously – infants have no sins to be forgiven of.

2. **"Our Need for Baptism."** (Psalm 51:5; John 3:5-7; Acts 2:38; Rom. 3:23; Rom. 6: 3-4). This answer focuses on "Original Sin," which we've discussed as not having merit. Psalm 51:5 is a recurring passage when we're talking about this topic – it supposedly portrays man's sinful nature from birth. The Psalm reads, "Behold, I was brought forth in iniquity, And in sin my mother conceived me." This verse has been misunderstood by Lutherans and many others – the words "brought forth **in iniquity**" and "**in sin** my mother conceived me," refer to the environment, the world David was born into – it was and still is a sinful world, not that he (as an infant) was sinful from birth. The statement concerning the circumcision of 8-day-old babies will be addressed later. Acts 2:38 refutes infant baptism. John 3:5-7 (one must be born of water and Spirit to enter the kingdom of God) was discussed earlier – infants will enter the kingdom if they die, not by being born of water and the Spirit (being baptized), but because they are sinless. The same goes for Romans 3:23 – "all have sinned" – all, that is, except infants and those not capable of discerning right from wrong. Romans 6:3-4 also does not apply to infants – being buried into Christ's death (His blood) for the forgiveness of sin is meaningless to a sinless infant.
3. **"God's promises and power"** (Acts 2:38; Mark 16:16; Acts 22:26; 1 Peter 3:21; John 3:5-7; Titus 3:5-6; Gal. 3:26-27; Col. 2:11-12; Eph. 5:25-26; 1 Cor. 12:13). This answer as to why Lutherans baptize infants seems to blaspheme all those who do not agree with their way of thinking on this topic. The comment, "They (all others)[27] see Baptism as something we do (e.g., a public profession of faith, etc.)[27] rather than seeing it as something that God does for us and in us,"[31] shows a complete misunderstanding of baptism and God's overall plan of salvation. The fact is, our public confession of faith, conjoined with baptism accomplishes steps four and five of God's plan! Confession is usually step four – accomplished by the candidate standing in water about to be baptized. They make the good confession, and upon that confession are baptized (Acts 8 – Eunuch; Acts 9 – Paul).

Most of the passages listed above attest to the benefits of baptism if correctly understood. There is one verse, however, that Lutherans do not adhere to – 1 Corinthians 12:13, "For by one Spirit we were all baptized into one body – whether Jews or Greeks, whether slaves or free – and have all been made to drink into one Spirit." They make mention that baptism, "incorporates us into the body of Christ." If they knew what that meant, they would not call themselves "Lutherans." We talked about this in Volume One, Chapter Two, under the heading of "One Church." [41.] Lutherans admit that baptism incorporates us into the body of Christ (which it does), however, there is but one body (Eph. 4:4; Christ is the head of this one body (Eph. 5:23; Col. 1:18); and the body is the church – Christ's only church. This church was started by our Lord and belongs to Him – it is not to be confused with the Lutheran (or any other denominational church).

The circumcision in the Old Testament of eight-day-old male babies has nothing whatsoever to do with the justification of infant baptism under the New Testament. The passage referred to, Colossians 2:11–12 reads, "In Him you were also circumcised with the circumcision made without hands, by putting off the body of the sins of the flesh, by the circumcision of Christ, buried with Him in baptism, in which you also were raised with Him **through faith** [30] in the working of God, who raised Him from the dead." Though circumcision and baptism are connected by Paul here, the candidate under consideration is an adult or at least one who has sinned and has acquired a subsequent faith in the Lord. Once again, infants do not have sin needing "burial" to wash it away; nor do they have "faith" in the working of God! The hope is that faith will be developed if they are "trained up in the way they should go" (Proverbs 22:6), but in infants or small children, this faith has not yet been developed, nor can it be exhibited (faith encompasses all actions required of man to qualify as a recipient of God's grace, i.e., hear and understand, belief, repentance, confession, baptism. In addition, the eighth-day requirement for circumcision had more to do with a medical reason for this procedure than a mandate to bring infants into the Jewish covenant at this specific time (see appendix in Volume One). [41]

The contention that "in all probability ... whole households," including infants and children (in passages such as Acts 16:15 and 16:33), were baptized, ignores the context of these statements, particularly concerning the jailer, where verses 31 and 32 make it clear Paul and Silas are addressing the family unit in asking for "belief," by preaching the word of the Lord to the jailer and all within his house. A commitment to believe and accept God's word involves commitments beyond the capacity of infants and children. In addition, "in all probability" is not a certainty; there is a possibility these households were without infants – one cannot base doctrine on assumptions!

Both of the above arguments have been raised previously (under the infant baptism sections of both the Catholic and Orthodox Churches), and as we'll see, it will continue to be a common go-to for other denominations. Though they sound plausible on the surface to the unwary, the Scriptural rebuttals given in each case are solid and irrefutable.

Another claim that the early "Church Fathers" set a precedent for the baptizing of infants does not give Biblical authority to the practice. The teachings of the Catholic and Orthodox Churches (where we see this reference more often) were well on their way to distorting Christ's church by this time, and infant baptism was but one of those distortions.

Lutheran theology on infant baptism exhibits both misunderstanding and contradiction. The summary above reveals much of this. Martin Luther believed in infant baptism for all the wrong reasons, he promoted the idea of original sin as the main reason, and since infants cannot declare nor develop "faith" at the time of baptism, he invented things like God sanctifying infants and inpouring the Spirit during baptism, as well as introducing sponsors to nurture the faith of these infants as they mature - all being Luther's thoughts – all without Scriptural foundation. Current-day Lutherans accept Luther's doctrine but have added a few thoughts of their own. In an attempt to justify Scripture, they've added to God's creating faith within infants during baptism by contending certain passages support infants having or developing faith/belief without the need for God's help, i.e., Psalm 22:9-10; Luke 18:15-17; and Matthew 18:1-6. Contradicting all of this, Lutherans contend baptism is not "absolutely" necessary for salvation! In even further contradiction, they state this, which pertains to all baptisms (infant through adult), "Still, Baptism dare not be despised or willfully neglected, since it is explicitly commanded by God and has His precious promises attached to it. It is not a mere "ritual" or "symbol," but a powerful means of grace by which God grants faith and forgiveness of sins" [22.]

Just stop and think about this – if baptism is "explicitly commanded by God," do Lutherans really wish to make this optional, as not "absolutely" necessary? If baptism is attached to God's precious promises (i.e., eternal life) do Lutherans really think baptism is not necessary to receive those promises? If baptism is God's powerful means of grace, able to forgive our sins (no other way of forgiveness is mentioned in Scripture, one must come in contact with the blood of Christ, period), do Lutherans really want to remain in sin?

Old Law vs New Testament Teaching

Lutherans teach that the Ten Commandments are God's instructions for Christians today. In the LCMS Lutheran Confessions – Large Catechism, this is stated, "Thus we have the Ten Commandments, a compend of divine doctrine, as to what we are to do in order that our whole life may be pleasing to God, and the true fountain and channel from and in which everything must arise and flow that is to be a good work, so that outside of the Ten Commandments no work or thing can be good or pleasing to God, however great or precious it be in the eyes of the world … Therefore they should be taught above all others, and be esteemed precious and dear, as the highest treasure given by God." [42.] However, as mentioned earlier, there was a change in the law from the old to the new (Hebrews 7:12), and Jesus "nailed" the Old Law to the cross (Colossians 2:14); we follow the Law of Christ today. One might ask, "What's wrong with the Ten Commandments? Are these not good, moral commands and principles to govern us today?" In answering this, consider the following comparison of the Ten Commandments with the words of Jesus:[43.]

THE TEN COMMANDMENTS	**JESUS' WORDS**
Exodus 20:3: *"You shall have no other gods before me"*	Matthew 4:10: *"Worship the Lord your God, and serve Him only."*
Exodus 20:4: *"You shall not make for yourself an idol."*	Luke 16:13: *"No servant can serve two masters."*
Exodus 20:7: *"You shall not take the name of the Lord your God in vain."*	Matthew 5:34: *"Make no oath at all, either by heaven, for it is the throne of God …"*

Exodus 20:8: *"Remember the Sabbath day, to keep it holy."*	Mark 2:27–28: *"The Sabbath was made for Man, and not man for the Sabbath, So the Son of Man is lord even of the Sabbath."*
Exodus 20:12: *"Honor your father and your mother."*	Matthew 10:37: *"He who loves father or mother more than Me is not worthy of Me."*
Exodus 20:13: *"You shall not murder"*	Matthew 5:22: *"Everyone who is angry with his brother shall be guilty before the court . . . and whoever says, 'You Fool,' shall be guilty enough to go into the fiery hell."*
Exodus 20:14: *"You shall not commit adultery."*	Matthew 5:28: *"Everyone who looks at a woman with lust for her has already committed adultery with her in his heart."*
Exodus 20:15: *"You shall not steal."*	Matthew 5:40: *"If anyone wants to sue you and take your shirt, let him have your coat also."*
Exodus 20:16: *"You shall not bear false witness."*	Matthew 12:36: *"Every careless word that people speak, they shall give an accounting for it in the day of judgment."*
Exodus 20:17: *"You shall not covet."*	Luke 12:15: *"Be on your guard against every form of greed.*

Where commands or examples of the Old Law, the Old Testament, have been confirmed in the New Testament, they are valid for us today. Notice that many have actually been confirmed as stricter or harder to comply with by Jesus in the New Testament (e.g., condemnation for "looking at a woman with lust" versus actually committing adultery or the same with "extreme anger" versus "murder"). All of the commandments, in fact, have been confirmed in the New Testament as applying to us today, except the fourth, concerning the commandment to observe the Sabbath. Therefore, the position adopted as doctrine by the Lutheran Church is not supported by Scripture.

The Lord's Supper

Communion Service

The Lutheran Church adheres to the doctrine, proposed initially by Martin Luther, that during the distribution of the sacrament, the "substance" of the actual body and blood of Jesus Christ coexists with the "substance" of the emblems of bread and wine (a doctrine commonly known as "consubstantiation"). Current-day Lutherans prefer to call this doctrine a "Sacramental Union" rather than "consubstantiation," as the latter can be confused with "transubstantiation" or a "complete conversion of the elements," as the Catholics and, for the most part, the Orthodox believe.

Lutherans justify the presence of Jesus's actual body and blood as "mixed" with the elements by citing passages such as Matthew 26:26–29 and Mark 14:22–25, where Jesus takes bread, breaks it, and gives it to the disciples and says, "*Take, eat; this is My body.*" Similarly, Jesus gives them the cup and calls it "*My blood of the covenant.*" A further reference is made to 1 Corinthians 10:16–17, where they claim Paul makes it clear that the cup of blessing and the bread are a "participation" or a "sharing" of the body and blood of Christ. [44.]

The abuse of the Lord's Supper, of which Paul warns the Corinthians in 1 Corinthians 11:27 and following, is also suggested to be connected to the issue of Jesus's actual body and blood being present. "So 'real' is this participation in Christ's body and blood, in fact, that (according to Paul) those who partake of the bread and wine 'in an unworthy manner' are actually guilty of 'profaning the body and blood of the Lord'" [44.]

Finally, according to the ELCA's statement from *The Use of the Means of Grace*: "According to the Apology of the Augsburg Confession, Lutheran congregations celebrate Holy Communion every Sunday and festival. This confession remains the norm for our practice (UMG, Principle 35)." [45.] Under "Background" in this source, one reason for participation in the Supper is stated, "The Church celebrates the Holy Communion frequently because the Church needs the sacrament, the means by which the church's fellowship is established and its mission as the baptized people of God is nourished and sustained." [45.] Though many Lutheran congregations observe the Lord's Supper weekly in compliance with this confession, **a large number have chosen to partake biweekly, monthly, or quarterly.** (Since the 1980s, the number of ELCA congregations practicing weekly communion has increased, but only from 20 percent to the **current level of around 50 percent**). [30.] This situation seemingly is the result of the attitudes, consensus, and "cultural influences" of each individual congregation, with reasons for desiring "less frequent communion" being such things as "worshippers coming to the sacrament with less thought or preparation" or the notion that "weekly celebrations of Holy Communion will make the sacrament less 'special'" [45.] In addition, this same source suggests several ways Lutherans might encourage weekly communion within their respective congregations, including teaching the "importance" of same, and experimenting by trying a more frequent observance, then gradually increasing the observances until they become weekly.

The Scriptures are clear that the elements used in the Last Supper were symbolic: "Jesus took **bread** ... and said, 'Take, eat; this is My body ...' Then He took the cup, and gave thanks, and gave *it* to them, saying, 'Drink from it ... for this is My blood of the new covenant ... I will not drink of this **fruit of the vine** from now on ...'" (Matthew 26:26–29). [30.] Jesus refers to the bread (symbolically) as His body and the fruit of the vine (symbolically) as His blood. To argue otherwise is to ignore the fact that the Lord is speaking to His disciples here at a Passover meal; He's instituting a way for them (and, by example, us) to remember His death, which would soon take place "for many, for the remission of sins." He's not offering His actual body or His actual blood for this purpose; the symbols of bread and wine are quite sufficient and, in fact, are God's perfect way for us to remember Him. By not simply reading about the event or even just picturing it in our minds, but rather by taking the emblems, we use all our senses to remember: sight, smell, taste, feelings, and, yes, even hearing, whether we notice the sounds of prayer or song(s) associated with this event, or simply the absence of sound, that we might fully contemplate Jesus's suffering and death on the cross for us.

God so created us that we might remember in this most meaningful way – for He knows how we are apt to forget. Our remembrance is not only affected by how we remember (by partaking of emblems) but also by how *often* we remember. Again, the God who created us knows our limitations for remembering and forgetting. Though Jesus does not note the frequency here, the Scriptures later reveal the Spirit's desire for a "weekly" observance (working through Paul, an example is given in Acts 20:7 that we are to "break bread" and remember our Lord's death on the first day of every week—Sunday).

The Lutheran Church has ignored God's wisdom on this subject (along with their own doctrine—The Augsburg Confession) and rather has catered to the desires of the individual congregations in most of these instances by changing this frequency to a biweekly, monthly, or even quarterly observance, based on man's idea of what would be best (for reasons relating to preparation time and "specialness" of the occasion), not God's instructions. The statement that Holy Communion is celebrated to satisfy the "Church's need for fellowship and to be nourished and sustained" [45] ignores the main purpose – to "Do this in remembrance of Me." We'll see this self-centered attitude moving forward with other denominations, particularly the Presbyterians and Methodists. The method by which this same article instructs or suggests that one "encourage" weekly observance (teaching the importance and gradually introducing a more frequent observance to the congregation) seems to be missing the most important encouragement—God's Word demands it! (Do you think that 'gradual obedience' to Gods Word, with the likelihood that all congregations will not come to 100% obedience here, is acceptable to God?)

The passage in Scripture pointed to as "most clearly" exemplifying the Lord's presence, physically, within the emblems of the Last Supper by Lutherans, is 1 Corinthians 10:16–17. Here Paul asks the following questions: "The cup of blessing which we bless, is it not the communion of the blood of Christ? The bread which we break, is it not the communion of the body of Christ? For we, *though* many, are one bread *and* one body; for we all partake of that one bread."

In response to this, one first must look at the context of this passage; this brief reference to the Lord's Supper is sandwiched between two longer sections of admonition concerning idol worship. It seems obvious that many of the Corinthian Christians were still struggling with this issue—the fact that Corinth was a major seat of idol worship at that time didn't help the situation. In the first thirteen verses of Chapter 10, Paul gives the church members in Corinth a recollection of judgments God levied upon His people, Israel, when they apostatized—which should serve as a warning to His people now that God will not tolerate similar disobedience (continued idol worship, along with, in this case, worship through communion with the Lord). Paul continues in verses 18–22 to point out that "sacrificing" to idols is akin to sacrificing to demons. "You cannot drink the cup of the Lord and the cup of demons; you cannot partake of the Lord's table and the table of demons" (verse 21). God simply will not stand for it!

Returning to his discussion concerning the Lord's Supper in verses 16 and 17, Paul here is telling the Christians that to partake of the Lord's supper is to "commune" with the Lord, share with the Lord, be "one" with the Lord. The same holds true with idol worship; to sacrifice to an idol is to "commune" with that idol, that demon; to share with that demon; to unify with that demon. Paul is not speaking of "sharing or communing" with or in Jesus's actual body and blood; he's drawing a comparison to idol worship—and in so doing, he is stressing the point, as he states in verse 17 of unity in the spiritual body of the Savior. Though they are many, when they remember Jesus this way, they are "one bread" and "one body" in Christ.

Trying to further justify this "real presence" of our Lord in the elements by suggesting Paul's warning in the next chapter of partaking of the supper "in an unworthy manner" (1 Corinthians 11:29) as being directed to those not recognizing Jesus's real body and blood is also without merit. Again, in context, Paul is admonishing the members of coming together to observe the Lord's supper yet treating it as a common meal (verses 17–22) and, worse, exhibiting irrespective attitudes toward one another in the process. The lack of respect or focus on the Lord's supper and its' meaning and significance, is the source of "unworthiness," not an abuse of the recognition of element substance. Whether this situation involved a fellowship meal entered into prior to the observance of the Lord's supper, or simply the observance of the supper only, gone awry, the result is the same—they were not putting proper respect or thought into this solemn event.

Another point that should be noted on this issue concerns the instructions of our Lord as quoted through Paul in 1 Corinthians 11:24, where Jesus, after breaking the bread, states, "Take, eat, this is My body which is broken for you; do this **in remembrance of Me**," and verse 25, where He takes the cup and states, "This cup is the new covenant in My blood. This do, as often as you drink *it,* **in remembrance of Me.**" [30.] "Remembrance" indicates that in later observances of this event, as Jesus is instructing them, He would not *literally* be there with them—not in whole (transubstantiation) or in part (consubstantiation [i.e., "mixed"]), as Lutherans believe.

The account of Jesus's ascension to heaven is yet another consideration. Following His being "taken up … out of their sight," as His disciples watched, the angels commented, "This *same* Jesus, who was taken up from you into heaven, will so come in like manner as you saw Him go into heaven" (Acts 1:9–11). Jesus will indeed return but will return "in like manner" as they saw Him go; the angles did not say, for instance, that He would return "weekly" or "periodically" within the elements of the Supper as a "real" reminder to them!

Finally, as mentioned earlier regarding the Catholic and Orthodox Churches (who believe the elements completely and mysteriously change into Jesus's body and blood, not just "mix with" as held to here), were this really the case, Jesus's body would have to be sacrificed over and over again. However, Hebrews 9:28 tells us Christ was offered only once: "… so **Christ**

was offered once to bear the sins of many. To those who eagerly wait for Him He will appear a second time, apart from sin, for salvation. [30.]

Predestination

The Lutheran Church teaches that God chooses who will be saved before they believe, but not who will be "lost." The LCMS, for instance, states that God "elects" those whom He wishes to bring to faith "from eternity" and that this doctrine is evident from what we read in passages such as Ephesians 1:3–7 and Romans 8:28–30. However, as "evident" as this predestination of the elect or saved may be, this is not the same for the lost; there is "no election by God of wrath" or "predestination to damnation," as God desires all mankind to be saved and to come to a knowledge of the truth, per 1 Timothy 2:4. [47.]

The Scriptures do not teach an "involuntary" election or nonelection by God; this is the Calvinistic doctrine known as "Unconditional Election," which we'll look at more closely in our next Volume (3), Chapter One. For purposes here, addressing the passages cited above as "justification" for this doctrine by the Lutherans will suffice.

In Ephesians 1:3–7, Paul, through the Spirit, is explaining the Biblical nature of "predestination"—that God has chosen His church to be the group of people who will be saved, that God foreknew this from eternity, and this was His will and plan for mankind's redemption (notice that all references here are plural; no particular individual is predestined). That God has not already determined who will be saved (though He is omniscient and foreknows the results of all of mankind's decisions) is evident in several other passages of Scripture, including 1 Timothy 2:3–4: "For this is good and acceptable in the sight of God our Savior, **who desires all men to be saved and to come to the knowledge of the truth**." [30.] How could God have already determined who shall be saved and yet state that He desires all men to be saved? This is inconsistent, which God cannot be, according to Hebrews 13:8. Interestingly, the Lutherans use this passage to justify their doctrine of no predestination to damnation per the above—except they interpret the word "desires" (used in NKJV and NASB; "wants" is the translation used in the NIV) as "God **will have** (KJV) all men to be saved …" The Greek word used here, "*thelo*," means "want, wants, desires"—not "will have," indicating that God has taken decisive action to save mankind but not to condemn them.

A few verses later [from the passages in question (Ephesians 1:3–7)] Paul states in Ephesians 1:13, "In Him you also *trusted*, after you heard the word of truth, the gospel of your salvation; in whom also, having believed, you were sealed with the Holy Spirit of promise" [30.] (We have something to do here—we must hear, trust, and believe, and by indication of other Scriptures, we must also repent, confess Jesus to be the Christ, and be baptized). A few more verses down, Ephesians 2:8–9 states, "For by grace you have been saved through faith, and that not of yourselves; *it is* the gift of God, not of works, lest anyone should boast." "Grace" sums up God's redemptive activity, while "faith" in this passage refers to the response we are to make without thinking we are earning our salvation—to include all we must do (i.e., obedience to the gospel) so we can receive God's offer of salvation in Christ. Romans 5:1–2 further confirms this: "Therefore, having been **justified by faith**, we have peace with God through our Lord Jesus Christ, through whom also we have access by faith into this grace in which we stand, and rejoice in hope of the glory of God." [30.]

In like manner, Romans 8:28 states, "And we know that all things work together for good to those who love God, to those who are called according to *His* purpose." [30.] (We have something to do here as well; we are to "love God," which involves actively obeying His commands; also, we are called according to His purpose. (God's purpose involves obedience to the gospel.) Further light is shed on this in 2 Thessalonians 2:13–14, where Paul tells the Thessalonians, "… because God from the beginning chose you for salvation through sanctification of the Spirit and belief in the truth, to which He called you by our gospel, for the obtaining of the glory of our Lord Jesus Christ. Therefore, brethren, stand fast and hold the traditions you were taught." Paul is admonishing them to stand fast to what they were taught—that through their being "sanctified," or being made holy, by the Spirit, owing to their belief in the truth; being called by the gospel; and responding accordingly, God, in turn, "chose" them for salvation, and granted to them salvation through His grace.

Romans verses 29 and 30 simply extend the thought of verse 28—that by loving God and responding to His call according to His purpose (obedience to the gospel), God, who didn't force us to take these actions, nevertheless foreknew we would do so, and such actions have conformed us to the image of His Son; they have also "justified" our faith, bringing us to a relationship of peace with God through our Lord Jesus Christ. (Romans 5:1ff).

Confession and Absolution

Confession and Absolution

As a carryover from the Catholic and Orthodox traditions, Lutherans incorporate both a public and private "confession" and "absolution" practice into their doctrine. According to a publication by Dr. A. L. Barry, former president of the Lutheran Church–Missouri Synod, entitled *What About ... Confession and Absolution* he had this to say concerning the definition of confession: "Confession has two parts. First, that we confess our sins, and second, that we receive absolution, that is, forgiveness, from the pastor as from God Himself, not doubting, but firmly believing that by it our sins are forgiven before God in heaven." [49.]

He goes on to clarify that in the worship setting, the pastor regularly offers "absolution" to the congregation as a whole, in the name of Christ; while privately, those who are anxious concerning "*particularly troubling*" sins they have committed may come to this same pastor to confess one-on-one and be assured, as they "*hear the words of Christ,* (by the pastor) [27] *I forgive you.*" To encourage these private confession settings, seen as an important function to augment their general confession and absolution announcements from the pulpit, pastors are sworn at their ordinations never to reveal the sins confessed to them.

Concerning the authority that these pastors claim enables them to forgive sin, reference is given to Matthew 16:18, where the "Office of the Keys" is mentioned as giving them the authority to offer for repentant sinners, but to withhold forgiveness from the unrepentant. Relying on this authority, a typical statement one might hear during the worship assembly would be "Upon this your confession, I, as a called and ordained servant of the Word, announce the grace of God to all of you, and in the stead and by the command of my Lord Jesus Christ I forgive you all your sins in the name of the Father and of the Son and of the Holy Spirit." [49.]

As mentioned previously, the New Testament teaches that Christians are to confess their sins to God directly (1 John 1:9) and we are to confess our faults to one another and to forgive one another (James 5:16). No Scripture authorizes a "pastor" of the Lutheran Church (or any other church, for that matter) to pronounce forgiveness of sin, public or private. No man stands between the sinner and Christ, who alone has that authority (Luke 7:48).

This assumed authority, "The office of the keys," is taken directly from Matthew 16:18—a concept discussed and refuted earlier under the Catholic and, particularly, the Orthodox Churches, known as "apostolic succession," where the man Peter is said to be the focus of Jesus's pronouncement, rather than Peter's confession of Christ (the correct interpretation).

Though there are several verses indicating Jesus gave this power to His disciples initially (e.g., John 20:21–23 and Acts 19:18–19), as also discussed earlier, this power or miracle, along with all miracles performed at that time, ceased toward the end of the first century with the death of the last apostle. [When the Word of God was brought into its completeness as the "perfect law of liberty" (James 1:25), miracles ceased (1 Corinthians 13:8–10). Note the use of "will cease," "will fail," and "will be done away." And the time frame was "But when that which is perfect is come" (neuter gender—a perfect thing: the Word of God), [27] then that which is in part will be done away.] Any argument, therefore, that Peter initiated this supposed divine succession cannot be supported by the Scriptures.

Controversial Issues

Woman Pastor

Ordination of Women (Ministers, Elders, Deaconesses)

Whereas both the Roman Catholic and Orthodox Churches as yet do not allow women to serve in formal leadership positions (as elders or deacons), nor do they ordain women as ministers or pastors within the church, the Episcopal and many Protestant churches do. As will be seen in these churches, including the Lutheran Church (ELCA) and many of the spin-offs from this denomination, the acceptance of both women and homosexuals (discussed below) into positions of leadership has been sanctioned.

The ELCA, which was formed in 1988, began ordaining women in 1970 when the Lutheran Church of America ordained the Rev. [5] Elizabeth Platz. The ordination of women today is accepted and noncontroversial within the ELCA. Not all Lutheran churches have gone this route, however; the more conservative arm of the church (and second-largest

Lutheran group), the Lutheran Church–Missouri Synod (LCMS), does not ordain women; nor do they adhere to the position on homosexuality the ELCA has taken.

The first female bishop of the ELCA and second in the world (a bishop governs an entire synod) was elected in 1992—Rev. [5] April Ulring Larson, bishop, ELCA Lacrosse (Wisconsin) Area Synod. As of January 15, 2013, women pastors in the ELCA numbered 3,849, or 23.1 percent of the 16,680 total ordained ministers within the ELCA, with active (nonretired) ministers totaling 32.9 percent.

The issue of gender roles in leadership within the public assembly of the Lord's church is one of much controversy that has only escalated in recent years. The crux of this controversy seems to be several passages in the New Testament where the apostle Paul addresses this issue, first with the Corinthian church in one context and then with the young preacher Timothy in another; along with one other passage in Galatians, which has been misunderstood and misapplied by many. Before examining these Scriptures, however, and to set an overall context, a look at the key verse in the letter from Paul to Timothy is in order—that is 1 Timothy 3:14–15: "These things I write to you, though I hope to come to you shortly; but if I am delayed, I *write* so that you may know how you ought to conduct yourself in the house of God, which is the church of the living God, the pillar and ground of the truth."

Prior to this statement, Paul had just given Timothy instructions of what God desired concerning the roles of men and women within the assembly during worship to Him, along with qualifications of both the leaders (known as elders, also known as overseers, bishops, pastors, or shepherds) and the deacons of the church. What we sometimes forget is that these are not Paul's ideas here; he is speaking as led by God, by the Holy Spirit of God, and as such, these things are timeless (as will be expanded upon a little later). This passage tells us what God truly wants within our worship assemblies—whom He wants to lead, along with the qualifications He desires the leaders to have. It couldn't be clearer.

The passage that gets to the heart of this issue, in this author's opinion, is found in 1 Timothy 2:

> I desire therefore that the men pray everywhere, lifting up holy hands, without wrath and doubting; in like manner also, that the women adorn themselves in modest apparel, with propriety and moderation, not with braided hair or gold or pearls or costly clothing, but, which is proper for women professing godliness, with good works. Let a woman learn in silence (quietness – ASV, NIV; quietly – NASV) with all submission. And I do not permit a woman to teach or to have authority over a man, but to be in silence. (quietness – ASV; quiet – NASV). For Adam was formed first, then Eve. And Adam was not deceived, but the woman being deceived, fell into transgression. Nevertheless she will be saved in childbearing if they continue in faith, love, and holiness, with self-control. (1 Timothy 2:8–15)

Verse 8 of this passage states that only men (the Greek word "*Andros*") are to lead prayers. This is reinforced immediately prior to this in verses one and four, where Paul is addressing the men only. In this context, "*men praying*" would not be limited to prayer only but is representative and would include all acts of worship within the public assembly (i.e., presiding over and distributing the Lord's Supper, leading singing, public speaking, preaching, and teaching). "*Everywhere*" indicates the universal nature of the church, meaning this is to be the rule within all of the Lord's churches everywhere, and "*lifting up holy hands*" is a metaphor for the proper heart, life, and mind of the man leading, who is to be "without wrath or doubting"—no anger or attitude problems toward others or doubting, which would indicate a weak faith. (Other translations, such as the ASV, translate this as "without wrath and disputing," and the NASB translates it as "without wrath and dissension." Either way, the Holy Spirit does not want there to be outside anxiety of this nature inhibiting the one praying).

Women, in 2:9, are to "adorn themselves in modest (Greek – *kosmos* – meaning orderly, decent) [27] apparel, with propriety (dignity, prudence) [27] and moderation (sound discretion, calling for judgment and self-control),[27]" avoiding extremes of immodesty, either overdressing (in an extravagant, showy way, with expensive hair braiding, jewelry, and rich clothing) or dressing with too little body covering (drawing attention). Instead, women are admonished to adorn themselves with good works, which is proper for women professing godliness (2:10).

"Let a woman learn in silence, with all submission" (2:11). This verse, and the next, "And I do not permit a woman to teach or have authority over a man, but to be in silence" (2:12) are two of the most misunderstood passages on this issue. The Greek word for "silence" here, in this context, is "*hesuchios*," which carries a meaning of "quietness," "undisturbing," "still," "quiet," or "tranquility arising from within, causing no disturbance to others." (W. E. Vine) [50] rather than total "silence." The translation becomes important here, as another Greek word for "silence," "*sigao*," means "to keep shut," "to keep closed" of "to hold one's peace"[50.] (i.e., no sound at all)—which is not the word used here in 1 Timothy. However, it is the exact word used in what many consider a parallel passage found in 1 Corinthians 14:34–35: "Let your women keep **silent** [30] in the churches, for they are not permitted to speak; but *they are* to be submissive, as the law also says. And if they want to learn something, let them ask their own husbands at home; for it is shameful for women to speak in church."

The passage in 1 Corinthians is not a parallel passage to 1 Timothy in context or in Greek verbiage. In 1 Corinthians 14, Paul is discussing spiritual gifts and how the Corinthians have been misusing them, particularly in the public assembly, causing confusion and being disorderly. Most of the Chapter leading up to verses 34 and 35 concerns the proper order in which the speaking in tongues, interpretation, prophesying, testifying to a revelation, and teaching are to take place in the assembly. In this context of Paul instructing the men of the congregation on how to function, involving all these activities, he instructs the women to keep "silent" (*sigao*); and concerning the tongues and interpretations, teaching, and the like, should they (the wives) have questions, they are to ask their own husbands at a later time. Paul clarifies this admonition in his subsequent letter to Timothy (in a different context, where he is specifically discussing the roles of men and women in the public assembly, even giving reasons for the same) by using the word "*hesuchios*," or "quietness."

The bottom line here, as mentioned, is that the 1 Corinthian and 1 Timothy passages are not parallel, and the words used for "silence" in each are not the same. It seems unfortunate the word "silence" appears in several translations of 1 Timothy 2:11, such as the KJV and NKJV, as it sends the wrong message. The word "hesuchios" has been translated closer to the original Greek as "quietness" or "quietly" in many of the popular versions (e.g., NASB, ASV, NIV, ESV). As a practical note, if women were to remain completely "silent" in the public assembly, they would not be able to sing in the assembly (Ephesians 5:17–19), nor would they be able to ask questions in a Bible study setting.

Also, 1 Timothy 2:11 states that as women learn in quietness (not total silence), they are to do so "*with all submission*." the Greek word here for "submission" is "*hupotasso*," meaning "To elevate someone over oneself," "Submission by choice," or "a military term of rank." What is being set here, and so often misunderstood, is "priority" as put forth by God, not "superiority," as if dictated by man. Continuing to the next verse, we find the following: "And I do not permit a woman to teach or to have authority over a man, but to be in silence [or quietness]" [27] (1 Tim. 2:12). The Greek words used here include "*didasko*" for "teach," meaning "To give instruction"; and "*authenteo*" for "authority," meaning "To exercise authority on one's own account," "To domineer over," or "to have dominion over." The inspired apostle here does not permit a woman to "teach" (i.e., exercise the official teaching role, whereby the man is subordinated to student status) within the church assembly; nor is she in any other fashion to exercise leadership or "dominion" over a man. In other words, she may not function as an elder or bishop and may not speak publicly as a teacher or preacher in the public assembly of the Lord's church (both of which the ELCA sanctions).

As mentioned, what seems difficult for many to accept here is that God is setting the priority of these roles; it has nothing to do with men exerting their superiority in this matter. That said, as we shall see, many denominations going forward cite one passage in particular in Galatians as support to negate these passages in 1 Corinthians and 1 Timothy, or at least put them in a perspective more amicable toward the women's role; that passage is Galatians 3:26–29: "For you all are sons of God through faith in Christ Jesus. For as many of you as were baptized into Christ have put on Christ. There is neither Jew nor Greek, there is neither slave nor free, there is **neither male nor female**; [30] for you are all one in Christ Jesus.

And if you *are* Christ's, then you are Abraham's seed, and heirs according to the promise."

In the first two and a half chapters of the letter Paul wrote to the Galatian churches, he focused on refuting the Judaizers (an extremist Jewish faction within the church), who were attempting to teach the new Gentile believers that they must obey Jewish law, as well as Christ, in order to be saved. In Paul's concluding remarks to this rebuke, and as a run-up to the above passage, Paul writes, starting in verse 19 of Chapter 3, "What purpose then *does* the law *serve?* It was added because of transgressions, till the Seed should come to whom the promise was made … the Scripture has confined all under sin, that the promise by faith in Jesus Christ might be given to those who believe. But before faith came, we were kept under guard by the law, kept for the faith which would afterward be revealed. Therefore the law was our tutor *to bring us* to Christ, that we might be justified by faith. But after faith has come, we are no longer under a tutor." In this context, Paul is telling the Christians in Galatians 3:26–29 that they are surely no longer under the "tutor of the law" any longer; they have direct access to God the Father through Jesus Christ. (They no longer have to go through a "priest," as in the Old Testament; nor do the women have to go through a male member of the family.) Paul says here every Christian (Jew, Gentile, slave, free, male, female) has a direct vertical path or access to the Father, and that Christians are "Abraham's seed – heirs to the promise," or saved, through Christ. Paul is not discussing gender roles within the church here; the context is that of Old Law vs. New, Old (restricted) access to God vs a New (granted) access for all to God.

Continuing with the analysis of 1 Timothy 2:11–15, there was a divinely intentioned order of creation, and God wants that respected and carried out in the gender roles of His church. Though it is not incumbent upon the Almighty to give a reason for what He inspires men to write, Paul, through the Spirit, gives us two reasons women are not to teach or have authority over men in this instance. First, "For Adam was formed first, then Eve"; and second, "The woman being deceived, fell into transgression." Adam was not deceived, but he sinned; Eve was deceived and sinned (Genesis 3:6–19). Perhaps surprising to some, Paul reaches back to the beginning of time and the beginning of sin as the reason for these restrictions on women, and his doing so indicates that the reasons are not "cultural"—that is to say, for instance, they have nothing to do with the capabilities of women versus men (e.g., a highly educated female professor might be far more qualified to teach, and may do a better job than, say a lower credentialed male counterpart). However, this is not what the Scriptures allow—God's reason, God's priority. Also, by referring to Genesis, it shows these restrictions are not "time-specific" or "place-specific." It's not something that happened in Paul's day and time that is not to be followed in ours, as we live in a modern age where women are accepted as equals. No, Paul makes this timeless and universal in its scope.

Therefore, since Adam was formed first, then Eve, in the order of creation, and since the woman took the lead in introducing human sin into the world, there resulted a penalty of role limitation imposed as a consequence – by God. Women must submit to God's priority assignment, which is neither temporally nor culturally limited. Another explanation as to the entrance of sin into the world was suggested a few years back in a book on this subject entitled *Male Spiritual Leadership* by F. LaGard Smith. [51.] I only introduce this as food for thought, and though it doesn't change the dynamic of what we're discussing here, nor the conclusions drawn, it is an interesting concept. Briefly, Smith suggests it was Adam who—though he was not the first deceived, nor was he the first to take a bite of that apple—he had a responsibility to "stop Eve" from sinning, as her "male spiritual leader"—particularly since he was standing right next to her at the time (Genesis 3:6). I'll let you be the judge of whether this "non-action" on Adam's part constituted a sin of omission. It seems the 1 Timothy passage emphasizes the former, as it states that Eve, being deceived, fell into sin without mentioning Adam other than to say, "He was not deceived."

Finally, 1 Tim. 2:15 states, "Nevertheless she will be saved in childbearing if they continue in faith, love, and holiness, with self-control." This passage is somewhat ambiguous and subject to more than one explanation, particularly as several Bible versions vary in their translation of "she" in this verse. For instance, the singular pronoun "she" shows up in versions such as the KJV, NKJV, ASV, and the ESV, whereas the plural form "women" occurs in the NASB and NIV. This impacts the explanation rather dramatically since, if this is a singular pronoun, "she," it indicates "Eve" is the antecedent noun, meaning "Eve will be saved through her childbearing," carrying the idea that salvation is under consideration (i.e., that she brought the Savior into the world [Genesis 3:15–16]). If, on the other hand, the plural form, "women," is confirmed here, it could mean the apostle's aim was to say that "childbearing" is a term that stands for the totality of a woman's domestic role. (i.e., that being a wife and mother is the highest ideal of Christian womanhood). In the last phrase, "… if **they** [30] continue in faith, love, and holiness, with self-control," the plural pronoun "they" seems to attach to the women, as Paul mentions in 2:9 (as the only antecedent which makes sense here).

Acceptance of Homosexuals

Though the Lutheran Church–Missouri Synod (LCMS) has taken a more conservative stance and denounced homosexual behavior, the ELCA, since the early 1990s, has welcomed gay and lesbian individuals into the church. When the ELCA General Assembly held in 2007 reaffirmed membership for homosexuals, they announced a policy not to ordain practicing homosexuals. This changed when the 2009 churchwide assembly of the ELCA held in Minneapolis voted 559 to 451 to open the ministry of the church to gay and lesbian pastors and other professional workers living in committed relationships. According to their news release, "the actions here change the church's policy, which previously allowed people who are gay and lesbian into the ordained ministry only if they remained celibate." (ELCA News Service, August 21, 2009) [52.]

Full ratification of these changes was confirmed by the Church council, which met on April 9–11, 2010. The current position of the Lutheran Church is reflected in their candidacy manual as adopted by the Church Council in November 2016 (revised June 1, 2020). Under section 1.8, "Guidelines for People in Same-Gender Relationships," we read the following: "All applicants and candidates shall be treated equitably … When working with an applicant or candidate who is in a same-gender relationship, the candidacy committee will follow the same processes for discernment and evaluation as with all other candidates …" [53.]

Scriptural justification for this position was posted on the ELCA website in an article by John Wickham entitled "The Church and Homosexuality." In this article, Wickham asserts first that certain statements made by Jesus far outweigh any rules and judgments found elsewhere in both the Old and New Testaments, and these judgments must further be evaluated by looking at our Lord's moral principles and comparing these to twenty-first-century Western culture. Those principles, he suggests, are simple: "Love your neighbor as yourself," with reference to passages such as Matthew 19:19 and 33:39, Mark 12:31, and Luke 10:27; "Always treat others as you would like them to treat you," referencing Matthew 7:12; and "Forgive, and you will be forgiven," with reference to Luke 6:37. [54.]

With these principles in mind, Wickham called Jesus an "iconoclast" who broke biblical rules and laws if and when they violated His principles. Examples of this would be His rejection of the "law of revenge" found in Leviticus 24:19–22 (Matthew 5:38–42), as well as His rejection of the death penalty for adultery in Leviticus 20:10–11 (John 8:3–11) and His condoning of violations to remember the Sabbath, as found in Matthew 12:1–8. According to Wickham, "... Homosexual sex doesn't violate Jesus' principles of unconditional love and forgiveness any more than heterosexual sex does ... Because Jesus always judged cultural and biblical rules and laws using his principles of love and forgiveness, and rejected biblical rules that violated those principles, his followers are obligated to do the same ..." [54.]

When we look at other passages of Scripture—particularly Paul's "moral standards" concerning women's behavior and dress codes, along with homosexual behavior—these cannot be "blindly followed"; they first must be filtered through the principles of Jesus. Then there's the issue of culture; Paul's condemnation applied to a first-century culture, which most Christians today simply reject. In addition, most Christians today accept divorce and remarriage, despite Jesus's judgment that this is adultery per Matthew 19:3–9: "Christians forgive and accept it because allowing a second or third chance is the loving thing to do." [54.]

Romans 1:18 and following state God's disapproval and condemnation of homosexuality in no uncertain terms. To get around this obvious condemnation, several "Scriptural justifications" have been offered, which are very telling as to the tolerance and attitude given this subject by the ELCA. These examples warrant a closer look. Such phrases as "Jesus was an iconoclast (one who attacks established or cherished beliefs or institutions)

[27] as he applied these principles (His so-called moral principles) [27] of love and forgiveness, and He broke biblical rules and laws when they violated his principles" and "Homosexual sex doesn't violate Jesus' principles of unconditional love and forgiveness any more than heterosexual sex does" - couldn't be further from the truth.

The first of these so-called "violations" concerns Jesus's reference to Leviticus 20:10–11 as recalled in Matthew 5:38–42: "You have heard that it was said, 'An eye for an eye, and a tooth for a tooth.' But I tell you not to resist an evil person. But whoever slaps you on your right cheek, turn the other to him also ..." This passage is spoken of above as "the law of revenge," which Jesus supposedly rejected. This was not a law of revenge but rather a law of mercy. God's purpose for setting this law was to limit vengeance—make the punishment fit the crime, as it were—which apparently was not being done in society at that time.

Therefore, Jesus's admonition in this passage to turn the other cheek, and the ones to follow to give of one's coat, and go the extra mile were gestures of love and mercy following this line of thinking (not at all rejecting "His principals"). Paul refers to this mercy again in Romans 12:20–21 (also recorded in Proverbs 25:21, 22): "If your enemy is hungry, feed him, if he is thirsty, give him drink; for in so doing you will heap coals of fire on his head. Do not be overcome by evil, but overcome evil with good." It seems there's an outcome being sought by God here—one of reflection to those causing harm, that they may in fact turn and seek the God of mercy by these actions.

The next supposed "Biblical violation," that Jesus rejected the death penalty for adultery in Leviticus 20:10–11 by His statement in John 8:3–11, can be explained in a similar fashion. Though the Jewish leaders were using the woman strictly as a trap against Jesus (if He stopped their stoning, He would be accused of violating Moses's law, and if He allowed it, He could be reported to the Romans, who didn't let the Jews carry out their own executions (John 18:31); without limiting the severity of or penalty for her "crime," Jesus evoked a response from the crowd by showing His compassion and forgiveness for the woman, with His statement "He who is without sin among you, let him throw a stone at her first." (Verse 7).

Finally, the accusation that Jesus "condoned violations of the commandment to remember the Sabbath," as recorded in Matthew

12:1–8, can be explained even within the text itself. Jesus first addressed the Pharisees' inconsistency by not condemning David for a similar infraction, as they saw it when David and his companions needed sustenance, entered the Temple, and ate the showbread on the Sabbath (1 Samuel 21: 1–6). Not excusing this, Jesus went on to explain the heart of the matter: the Sabbath was a day of rest and worship to God. He quoted words these Pharisees had heard before from Scriptures such as 1 Samuel 15:22–23, Psalm 40:6–8, Isaiah 1:11–17, and Hosea 6:6 ("I desire mercy [compassion], [27] and not a sacrifice")—words that support the actions of His disciples that day (after all, they were picking grain for food, not harvesting for profit).

Jesus's final statement that He was the "Lord of the Sabbath" certainly must have infuriated these self-righteous Pharisees; however, the Scriptures reveal that though they refused to acknowledge that He was the Creator, He set up the Sabbath in the first place. Jesus owed no man an explanation of His authority to set aside Jewish tradition and emphasize His loving nature and compassion by this exercise. This was by no means a violation of previous Biblical mandates.

It should be noted that comments such as "Jesus was an iconoclast as he applied these principles of love and forgiveness, and **broke biblical rules and laws** [30] when they violated his principles" and "**Homosexual sex doesn't violate Jesus' principles** [30] of unconditional love and forgiveness any more than heterosexual sex does" [54] are outrageous and show to what extent some within this denomination are willing to go to accommodate what they wish to do. Make no mistake, these are man's ideas to justify what otherwise is God's condemnation of such practices. In addition to the above refutation of these comments on a logical, Scriptural basis, these comments attacking our Lord can be refuted on an even higher level—that of the integrity of the Scriptures themselves and our Lord's relationship to those Scriptures.

The Spirit, through Paul, tells us, "All Scripture *is* given by inspiration of God, and *is* profitable for doctrine, for reproof, for correction, for instruction in righteousness, that the man of God may be complete, thoroughly equipped for every good work" (2 Timothy 3:16–17). This passage is often used to defend the idea that the Scriptures, as God's revelation, are complete and are all one needs to "be thoroughly equipped for every good work." As we have already seen a violation of this passage (where additional revelation has been added), and will see others looking at other denominations, here we can point to this passage to confirm the Scriptures are consistent, that they do not contradict themselves, and certainly that our Lord cannot "break Biblical rules" or dismiss some portion of Scripture for the sake of another. The honor Jesus paid to the Old Testament can also be seen in His statement recorded in Matthew 5:17-18, "Do not think that I came to destroy (or contradict) [27] the Law of the Prophets. I did not come to destroy but to fulfill. For assuredly, I say to you, till heaven and earth pass away, one jot or one tittle (stroke of the pen) [27] will by no means pass from the law till all is fulfilled."

Jesus Christ is God; He cannot lie or mislead (Titus 1:2; Hebrews 6:18). In fact, Jesus is the Word: "In the beginning was the Word, and the Word was with God, and the Word was God" (John 1:1). As such, it becomes blasphemous to even suggest our Lord is capable of being inconsistent with Himself! Certainly, Jesus can be identified as being connected to the written revelation of God both in the Old Testament (for instance, Psalm 119:11: "Your word I have hidden in my heart, that I might not sin against You") and as indicated even here in John 1 as the revelation or gospel given to mankind: "In Him was life; and the life was the light of men" (John 1:4). However, in our context here, it seems befitting that our Lord, the Word, is also identified as our Creator (John 1:3), with a direct connection to His natural revelation. Though this revelation has been "clearly seen, being understood by the things that are made" (Romans 1:20), individuals characterized with this particular sin "are without excuse, because although they knew God, they did not glorify *Him* as God, nor were thankful, but became futile in their thoughts, and their foolish hearts were darkened" (Romans 1:20–21).

Abortion

St. Paul's Lutheran Church
Allentown, PA

The Evangelical Lutheran Church in America (ELCA) is the first denominational body we've looked at so far to endorse a "pro-choice" view on this subject. As will be seen moving forward, many liberal and mainline denominations have taken this position. A "social statement" was adopted by more than a two-thirds majority at the second biennial Churchwide Assembly of the ELCA, held in Orlando, Florida, August 28, 1991. Following is a summary statement as confirmed at this meeting, and it continues to be confirmed to this day: "A developing life in the womb does not have an absolute right to be born, nor does a pregnant woman have an absolute right to terminate a pregnancy ('Abortion,' p.2) … as a community supportive of life … 'Abortion ought to be an option only of last resort'" [55.]

In a more detailed explanation of the statement, section IV, "Guidance in Making Decisions Regarding Unintended Pregnancies - B: Ending a Pregnancy," the Lutheran Church stated several reasons for sanctioning induced abortion. These included when continuation would present a physical threat to the woman when both parties did not "willingly" participate in sexual intercourse (i.e., rape or incest), and circumstances when it has been determined the developing fetus is "extremely abnormal" and will likely result in severe suffering or possible death of the infant. The one exception to abortion cited by this ruling was the church's opposition to ending life when a fetus has developed enough to live outside the woman's uterus—even with the aid of "reasonable and necessary technology." [55.]

Prevention of unintended pregnancies was also addressed under section V of this statement. Here it was stressed that attempts to prevent unintended pregnancies were crucial, and the church is willing to provide guidance and assistance as necessary to make available such things as contraceptives and for voluntary sterilization to be considered. Addendum A was offered for approval, stating that they "oppose induced abortion as a method of birth control"; however, this was defeated. In other words, the ELCA currently approves of abortion as a means of birth control. [55.]

Finally, concerning government regulation of abortion and societal attitudes, the ELCA agrees the government has a legitimate role in regulating abortion; the church's role is to encourage its members to participate in public debate when and where possible, seeking to "shape attitudes and values that affirm people in whatever circumstances they find themselves," while respecting those from whom they differ. [55.]

Once again, the more conservative Lutheran Church–Missouri Synod (LCMS) does not agree with the ELCA on this matter and holds abortion to be wrong except to save the life of the mother. [56.]

Concerning the issue of abortion, the ELCA once again has tempered God's Words, which condemn this act to end the life of a developing child (an act of murder) with its own interpretation, first defining the "societal/legal rights" of both the unborn child and the mother (as neither having "an absolute right" to be born or to terminate), then proceeding to define at least four circumstances where abortion can and should be acceptable, as they see it. These four "exceptions" include a "clear threat to the physical life of the woman," "if the pregnancy occurs when both parties do not participate willingly in sexual intercourse," "circumstances of extreme fetal abnormality," and during term, opposing the practice only "when a fetus is developed enough to live outside a uterus with the aid of reasonable and necessary technology."

God's commandment to mankind from the beginning, as confirmed by Jesus in the New Testament, is "You shall not murder" (Matthew 19:18). He goes even further in condemning the anger leading up to this act as already committing the sin of murder in one's heart (Matthew 5:21–22). We further learn from both science and Scripture that "life" begins at conception. From a medical point of view, immediately upon fertilization of the egg, the human zygote begins pairing chromosomes and dividing, and at seventy-two hours it has formed at least sixteen cells, constituting an embryo. The process of development from zygote to embryo to fetus is a "living" process; "life," from this perspective, begins at conception. (Unfortunately, human laws have currently not clarified "life" at this stage as a "person" or "human life"). God, on the other hand, disagrees. James 2:26 states, "The body without the spirit is dead." Therefore, the corollary to this is also true: if the body is living, the spirit must be present. So, when does the human spirit enter the body and thereby bring into existence a human being? Consider the following:

- "Thus says the Lord, who stretches out the heavens, lays the foundations of the earth, and **forms the spirit of man within him**" [30] (Zechariah 12:1).
- "As you do not know the **how the spirit comes to the bones in the womb** [30] of a woman with child, so you do not know the work of God who makes everything" (Ecclesiastes 11:5, RSV).
- "Before I formed you in the womb I knew you; before you were born **I sanctified you**" [30]. (Jeremiah 1:5).
- "For You formed my inward parts; You covered me in my mother's womb. I will praise You, for I am fearfully *and* wonderfully made; Marvelous are Your works, and ***that* my soul knows very well** [30] …" (Psalm 139:13–16).

Many other passages can be cited—including some from the New

Testament, such as Galatians 1:15 and Luke 1:39-44 - indicating that God formed mankind's spirit within the womb, and God recognizes "life," as a "person," a "human being made in His Image" even within the womb as He is forming an individual from conception.

The excuses used by the Lutheran Church to allow abortion cannot be reconciled with Scripture—certainly not as birth control or during early-stage development, or even in the circumstances of a "willing or unwilling" cause of pregnancy. As difficult as other decisions may seem to be, even the jeopardy of the mother or some abnormality of the baby does not excuse the taking of innocent life, according to God.

The seriousness of how God views this subject can be seen in passages such as Exodus 21:22–25, where Old Testament law issues mandates for "accidental injury" to an unborn baby, with punishment ranging from a fine for no injury to "life for life" should the infant die. If God views accidental harm to an unborn child in this fashion, imagine how He views abortion—a deliberate act of murder to an innocent unborn child. In addition, consider God's statements in the following passages:

> **Do not kill the innocent** [30] and righteous. For I will not justify the wicked. (Exodus 23:7).
>
> These six *things* the Lord hates, Yes, seven *are* an abomination to Him: A proud look, a lying tongue, **hands that shed innocent blood** [30] … (Proverbs 6:16–17).

The Scriptures speak very clearly concerning all of these issues, condemning all three: the ordination of both women and homosexuals to the ministry of the Lord's church, and abortion. The justification of these issues by the Lutheran Church (and others) comes from the same line of reasoning—a "cultural" one. It's not that these denominations are unaware of the condemnation of such practices or behaviors in the Scriptures, but rather, they no longer accept the authority of the Scriptures today. (Paul spoke in that day and time, and we live in a different day and time, a different culture where these things no longer apply.) The fact that the Holy Spirit inspired Paul, and thus God sanctioned these words with no time limit, seems to make little difference here.

Referring back to the ELCA comments concerning homosexuality—statements covering Paul's "moral standards" concerning women's behavior and dress codes, along with homosexual behavior—not being "blindly followed," but first being filtered through the "love our neighbor only" principles of Jesus, and a direct reference to the issue of culture (Paul's condemnation applied to a first-century culture, which most Christians today simply reject) bear out this cultural bias.

Using church doctrine as a platform to effect societal norms, as the Lutheran Church has and continues to do, is also not sanctioned by Scripture. As will be discussed with other denominations, including the Methodist Church (in Volume 3), who are active in this area, there are no Scriptures in the New Testament that teach a Christian is to attempt to reform the social structures in which he or she lives. We are to pray to God concerning the world, including "kings" (1 Timothy 2:1–4), and Christians can assist those in distress (James 1:27), and we are certainly commissioned to preach the good news of Christ to all men (Matthew 28:18–20)—but no mention of attempting to change society.

Ecumenism

"Ecumenical" is defined as "*of the world*," and "ecumenism" as "the principles or practice of promoting cooperation or better understanding among differing religious faiths" (*Webster's New World Dictionary*). [57] A more in-depth study of ecumenism among churches is included in the fifth volume of this set, under the topic "Ecumenical Movement." For purposes here, a brief look at recent efforts by the Lutheran Church in this area will suffice.

Early Lutherans denounced division of the church and avoided ecumenical fellowship with other denominations, believing such activities would invite such division and that churches should not share communion or exchange pastors if they do not agree upon doctrine. Though some of the more conservative Lutherans still hold this view, more moderate-to-liberal Lutherans are now willing to share communion and allow preachers from other denominations into their pulpits.

The goal of the Evangelical Lutheran Church in America (ELCA) in the area of ecumenism, is "full communion" with other denominations of diverse doctrine for the sake of "unity." Following is a definition of "full communion" from "*The Vision of the Evangelical Lutheran Church in America*" on the subject:

> "For the Evangelical Lutheran Church in America, the characteristics of full communion and theological and missiological implications of the Gospel that allow variety and flexibility. These characteristics stress that the Church act ecumenically for the sake of the world, not for itself alone. They will include at least the following, some of which exist at earlier stages:

1. A common confessing of the Christian faith.
2. A mutual recognition of Baptism and a sharing of the Lord's Supper, allowing for joint worship and an exchangeability of members.
3. A mutual recognition and availability of ordained ministers to the service of all members of churches in full communion, subject only but always to the disciplinary regulations of the other churches.
4. A common commitment to evangelism, witness, and service.
5. A means of common decision-making on critical common issues of faith and life.
6. A mutual lifting of any condemnations that exist between churches.

> We hold this definition and description of full communion to be consistent with Article VII of the Augsburg Confession, which says, "for the true unity of the church it is enough to agree concerning the teaching of the Gospel and the administration of the sacraments." [58.]

The ELCA has been actively involved in ecumenical dialogues with several denominations in recent years and has established "full communion" / "fellowship" with several denominations under these guidelines, including the Moravian Church, the Episcopal Church, the Presbyterian Church (USA), the Reformed Church in America, the United Church of Christ, and the United Methodist Church. In addition, the international ecumenical organization - the Lutheran World Federation (LWF), of which the ELCA is a member, established some commonality with the Roman Catholic Church in 1999, when these two denominations entered into agreement with their "*Joint Declaration on the Doctrine of Justification.*"

Bilateral conversations, or dialogue, is currently underway with several other denominations in addition to the Roman Catholic Church, as mentioned above; these include the African Methodist Episcopal Church, the Christian Church (Disciples of Christ), the Mennonite Church USA, and the Orthodox Church.

In addition, the ELCA in this country is active in several ecumenical associations, as illustrated below. (A more detailed description is available online under "Conciliar Relations." [59.]

World Council Of Churches

Lutheran World Federation

National Council of Churches

Churches Uniting in Christ

Church World Service

Christian Churches Together

Ecumenism in the twenty-first century is greatly responsible for overall attitudes espousing "unity-in-diversity" among different churches and the common appearance that all churches are essentially the same. While unity is a desirable goal, it is important that the unity is indeed the unity that God desires for His people according to passages such as 1 Corinthians 12:12–28 and Ephesians 4:1–6 (unity of and within Christ's church and between its members and Him, as denoted in Volume One, Chapter 2 of this series), not a form of unity between denominational churches (which is foreign to the New Testament).

As mentioned earlier, the reader is referred to Volume 5 of this series for a more complete examination and Scriptural response on this subject under the topic "Ecumenical Movement."

Worship Service

Most Lutherans place great emphasis on a liturgical approach to worship services, a carryover from their Catholic roots. In fact, when compared to a Catholic Mass, the Lutheran service comprises many of the same elements. A definition of liturgy is "Prescribed forms or ritual for public worship in any of various Christian churches." [57.] These "prescribed forms" are usually instructions or guides written and sanctioned by the denomination and are used by the clergy of that denomination to lead the congregation in public worship.

Several "liturgical guidelines" (both in prescribed text and practice as well as in song selection) have been instituted by the Lutheran Church, including *The Lutheran Book of Worship*, *The Lutheran Service Book*, *The Evangelical Lutheran Worship*, *Lutheran Worship*, and *Christian Worship*, to name a few. These guides spell out precise order and substance for each worship service.

Trinity Evangelical Lutheran Church of Latrobe, Pennsylvania (a typical ELCA congregation), lists under "Leadership – Pastors and Staff" - Pastor Jason Felici as Senior Pastor, Pastor Jess Felici as Senior Pastor, Debbie Morley as Director of Music, Kathe Houck and Barb Miller as Secretaries, and Lori Rolla as Financial Secretary. Their worship service times and announcements are listed in their "Trinity News" letter; the following are portions of this letter dated October 22, 2023: Within the calendar block – these are some of the events that are scheduled: Sunday (22nd) at 8:15 Holy Communion, 9:30 Sunday School, 10:45 Holy

Communion, 12:15 Drive Thru Communion. Tuesday (24th) at 7:00 p.m. Handbells. Wednesday (25th) at 6:30 p.m. Line Dancers, 7:00 p.m. Choir. Saturday (28th) at 11:00 a.m. Confirmation Rehearsal, 5:30 p.m. Spoken Holy Communion. Under the announcement for "Reformation and Confirmation," this is stated, "Mark your calendars and join us at the 10:45 service on next Sunday, October 29, as we celebrate the Confirmation of (five individuals) as these young adults make public affirmation of their faith, we witness the fulfillment of the promises made in their baptism." [60.]

Old Lutheran Church
Singel, Amsterdam, Netherlands
Worship Service

Following is an outline of Trinity's (liturgical) worship service as posted for Saturday, October 21, 2023, at 5:30 p.m. and twice on Sunday, October 22, 2023 (8:15 and 10:45 a.m.): [60.]

- **Prelude, Silent Prayer, Welcome, and Announcements**
- **<u>The Gathering</u>**
    - **The Confession of sins** (offered in unison by the congregation)
    - **The Absolution** was announced by the pastor, assuring the congregation of forgiveness – "In Christ, you are already and always forgiven, Amen."

    - **A Gathering Hymn: Greeting followed by singing of the Kyrie.**
    - **Prayer of the Day** - A **prayer** is offered by the pastor on behalf of the congregation.
- <u>**The Word**</u>
    - **First Reading** - A reading from the **Old Testament**
    - A portion of a **Psalm** (Interactive Reading – Pastor/ Congregation)
    - **Second Reading** from the **New Testament**, followed by a hymn to welcome the Gospel Reading.
    - **Reading from the Gospel.**
    - **Sermon** - Pr. Jess Felici preaches **a sermon** based on one of the day's Bible readings.
    - **Hymn of the Day** is sung.
    - **The Apostles' or the Nicene Creed** is recited as a confession of a common faith in the Triune God – this day the **Apostles Creed** was recited (all the congregation repeated in unison).
    - **Prayers of thanksgiving and intercession** are offered, followed by **"The Peace"** which is offered.
- <u>**The Meal**</u>
    - **Gathering of** Gifts – An offering is taken up for the mission of the church and for those in need.
    - **Offertory (Hymn)** is sung followed by an **Offering Prayer.**
    - **Great Thanksgiving** (Hymn) is sung, followed by another hymn.
    - **Thanksgiving at the Table** – The Pastor offers a prayer ahead of Communion.
    - **The Lord's Prayer** – Recited in unison by the congregation.
    - **Invitation to Communion** – A Pre-Communion hymn is sung.
    - **Distribution of Communion** – The following notes are made: "We believe our risen Lord Jesus is truly present in the bread and wine of Holy Communion and we extend our Lord's invitation to all who are baptized to share in this meal. Please come down the center aisle, take a cup from the tray and gather at the altar rail. Receive the host into your hand.

Wine will be poured into your cup. The Communion wine is gluten-free. Gluten-free wafers are available upon request. For those unable to receive wine, communion cups with water are available ..." [60.]

Table Blessing/Prayer After Communion – These prayers are offered by the Pastor following the distribution of Communion.

- **The Sending**
  - Service concludes with **a Blessing, a Sending Hymn, and a Dismissal** by the Pastor.

Beginning in the 1970s, many of the Lutheran Churches began holding "contemporary" worship services for the purpose of evangelical outreach (usually as a second service in addition to the liturgical service). Today many of those churches have gone to only a contemporary service as a preference of the congregation. Because it is said that Martin Luther contemporized the worship service for his community, these congregations see their actions as in keeping with "Confessional Lutheranism" (per Augsburg Confession, Article VII).

Congregations are encouraged to bring their services into a more "contextually (culturally) sensitive" position: "We call on all churches to give serious attention to exploring the local or contextual elements of liturgy, language, posture and gesture, hymnody and other music and musical instruments, and art and architecture for Christian worship – so that their worship may be more truly rooted in the local culture." [61.]

According to a statement concerning the purpose of Lutheran worship by the former president of the Lutheran Church–Missouri Synod, A. L. Barry, entitled 'Lutheran Worship: 2000 and Beyond,' "We know that God's Word and His holy Sacraments are His precious gifts to us ... The main purpose of Lutheran Worship is to receive these gifts from God ... Our Lutheran Confessions explain this truth as follows: 'The service and worship of the Gospel is to receive good things from God.' (Apology to the Augsburg Confession, Article IV.310). [62.]

In addition to the style and stated purpose of worship, and as mentioned in the organizational section of this denomination, individual pastors are in charge of individual congregations, including worship proceedings and protocol. These pastors must complete special training and formal education (most having substantial theological educations, including a working knowledge of the Greek and Hebrew languages). Pastors can marry and have families, and with the exception of the more conservative movements, female pastors are encouraged. Elders and deacons are defined as ordinary Christians assigned to "assist" the pastor in his responsibilities.

The duties and positions of elders and deacons in the Lutheran Church are basically one and the same. According to The Lutheran Church–Missouri Synod, under the frequently asked question topic "*What is the role of elders in a congregation?*" the word "elder," as used in the Bible per passages such as Acts 14:23; 1 Timothy 5:17–19; Titus 1:5–9; and 1 Peter 5:1–4, refers to those who hold the "pastoral office." This is to be distinguished as being a different position from the "humanly defined office of elder" (also referred to by some as the "deacon" position), whose meaning is not uniform throughout the synod; these elders keep the church's constitution and bylaws, and though their office is not equal to those of biblical elders (whose office is defined as being divinely instituted and indispensable to the church), these elders are nonetheless vital to the church in assisting the pastor in making certain decisions, helping him with visitations, with the distribution of the Lord's supper, and in other ways as needed to help a congregation and pastor maintain a healthy relationship. [63.]

One final aspect of Lutheran worship involves church music. Most Lutheran worship services have a musical program to enhance their services. A group has been established in Valparaiso, IN to train potential musicians and musical leaders to assist in this area – The Association of Lutheran Church Musicians (ALCM). Their online title page states, "Music is a vital expression of Lutheran worship. The church's song takes many forms and is expressed in many ways. By sharing the knowledge, experience and passion that honor our heritage and inspire our future, ALCM nurtures and equips those who lead music in worship. ALCM offers practical education programs and diverse resources through conferences, publications, and fellowship to serve musicians of all types – from paid professionals to volunteers. By connecting servant leaders to one another and by cultivating their musical gifts, ALCM supports worshipping communities in the proclamation of the gospel." [64.] The ALCM defines their members as organists, pianists, choir directors, instrumentalists, praise band and instrumental ensemble leaders, and handbell directors." [64.]

There are many aspects of Lutheran worship that conflict with the Scriptures. A simple reading of the Text reveals the five basic acts of worship God desires, according to His Word. (Refer to "Worship Activities of the Church" in Volume One, Chapter 2 of this series). Comparing Scripture to the above, we find the following:

- No "liturgical" format is indicated—certainly no "liturgical guidelines" to be used as an instruction manual on order or substance of worship. There is no congregational confession of sin, nor absolution of same by a priest (as only God knows the heart and can forgive sin). There are no additional authorized materials to the Bible (i.e., the creeds).
- The Lord's Supper is to be observed weekly, on Sunday only, per Acts 20:7—not Saturday, or any other time when it might be more convenient. In addition, some of the Lutheran congregations observe "periodically" (e.g., on the first and third Sunday of every month). This also is a violation of the Scriptures. The Supper is to be observed by partaking of the bread and the cup – the above example seems to option the bread and offer water for the cup – both are unauthorized in Scripture.
- The "purpose" of worship is not "to receive God's gifts" or for "God to serve us"; the "purpose" of worship is first and foremost to follow New Testament commands and examples in replicating the acts of worship as God desires, fulfilling God's purpose for us, in order to be pleasing to Him. (Acts of worship include singing, praying, remembering Jesus's death in observing the Lord's Supper (properly), listening to His Word, and giving as we have prospered.) Secondly, worship allows us to give thanks, glorifying our God through Jesus Christ: "And whatever you do in word or deed (including worship), [27] *do* all in the name of the Lord Jesus, giving thanks to God the Father through Him" (Colossians 3:17).

We come to bow down to our Creator, to truly "worship" Him as He desires!

- The organizational structure of the church, as outlined in Scripture, does not single out a "pastor" to rule the congregation. Nor are elders to be understood as "Biblical elders (i.e., pastors) versus "lay-elders" - relegated to an "advisory" position to this lone pastor. "Church Councils" elected to make decisions are also not sanctioned in Scripture. God's plan is simple: His Son, Jesus Christ, is to be head of the church universal: "He is the head of the body, the church ..." (Colossians 1:18). Within each local church, He is also the head, and a plurality of elders meeting the qualifications as listed in Scripture (1 Timothy 3 and Titus 1:5–16) are to be appointed to oversee each local congregation. (Acts 14:23, 20:28, Titus 1:5–7, 1 Peter 5:1–5).

  In addition, deacons are described in the Scriptures with similar qualifications required as those of elders (e.g., "Let deacons be the husbands of one wife, ruling *their* children and their own houses well." (1 Timothy 3:12); however, they are not the same as elders, who are to be overseers or shepherds of the congregation (1 Timothy 3:1). Deacons are typically appointed by (and subject to) the elders (with the support of the congregation) to work in the various ministries as needed by the local congregation, as servant leaders. The preacher is certainly an important member of the congregation; however, unless he is also appointed as an elder, he does not lead it! God, in His wisdom, set up a plurality of elders to lead—for a reason – the Lutheran Church ignores this.

  In the New Testament days, preachers of the gospel were not "pastors" of the congregation (unless appointed to this position), and religious titles, such as "Father" and "Reverend," were not used and in fact, were condemned by Jesus (Matthew 23:8–10).

- No musical instruments can be seen in New Testament worship—only "singing and making melody in the heart" (Ephesians 5:19 and Colossians 3:16).

The Good Shepherd Lutheran Church (LCMS)
Inglewood, CA

Questions to Consider

There are several aspects of Lutheran doctrine that could be raised in a conversation with one involved in this denomination. Perhaps the first question could be to inquire whether your counterpart is aware of the various historical doctrines held to be authoritative by their denomination in addition to the Bible. I suspect very few will answer in the affirmative here. (This question, by the way, could be asked of many denominations, as most hold to extra-Biblical doctrines that very few current-day parishioners are aware of; if they are aware, they tend to give little credence to this.)

This question becomes important since many of these earlier statements and confessions held to be binding on Lutherans today are in direct contradiction with each other as well as the Scriptures. Many Lutherans, for instance, have heard of Martin Luther but are unaware of his teachings or that these teachings are held in such high esteem and sanctioned as authoritative by Lutherans today.

There are two questions one might ask that seem crucial to introducing an element of doubt concerning the validity of this denomination. The first concerns justification by "faith alone"—the central precept of Lutheran doctrine today. (The Lutheran World Federation, as recently as 1999, came to an agreement with the Roman Catholic Church over this issue with their

Joint Declaration on the Doctrine of Justification). Martin Luther believed in "faith alone," but as mentioned earlier, Luther's view of "faith alone" was different from what is understood or taught today in the Lutheran Church. Luther meant a faith alone or apart from "works," not a faith alone apart from water baptism, which he felt was essential to salvation. With this in mind, the following question could be posed:

1.) **How can the modern Lutheran reconcile his or her current understanding of "faith alone" (baptism as nonessential for salvation) as authoritative and at the same time profess (whether he or she is aware of it or not) the necessity of water baptism espoused by Luther as also authoritative?**

The simple answer is that one cannot reconcile this. It is contradictory to claim baptism is both essential and nonessential concerning salvation. As suggested in the "Authority of the Lutheran Church" section above, once you abandon clear Scripture, which in itself claims that no "additions or subtractions" are to be made to God's Word (e.g., Proverbs 30:6, Revelation 22:18–19, 2 John 9–10), you violate those very same Scriptures. In addition, the Bible claims to be the *only* authority we are to follow (2 Timothy 3:16–17, Jude 3, 2 Peter 1:3).

Several documents can be offered up in support of the above statement, both of which are listed under "Adult Baptism;" the first is Luther's statement affirming the necessity of baptism, as contained in his *Large Catechism*, held today as authoritative per the constitutions and bylaws of both the ELCA and the LCMS: "Baptism is no human plaything but is instituted by God Himself. Moreover, it is solemnly and strictly commanded that we must be baptized, or we shall not be saved, so that we are not to regard it as an indifferent matter, like putting on a red coat." [21.]

A second set of documents supporting the opposite idea (that baptism is nonessential) comes from official statements by both the LCMS and ELCA:

- "The LCMS does not believe that baptism is ABSOLUTELY necessary for salvation. The thief on the cross was saved (apparently without baptism), as were all true believers in the Old Testament era. Mark 16:16 implies that it is not the absence of baptism that condemns a person but the absence of faith" [22] (Baptism and Its Purpose, 2004). (LCMS website).

- In Kyle Butt's book *What the Bible Says about the Lutheran Church*, he references an ELCA response to the question "*What must a person do to become a Christian?*" This extremely short answer is given: "Jesus said, 'Those who believe in me, even though they die, will live, and everyone who lives and believes in me will never die' (John 11:25–26)." [24.]

The Scriptures are crystal clear on this subject, however:

> "He who believes **and** [30] is baptized will be saved." (Mark 16:16)·
>
> "Truly, truly, I say to you, unless one is born of water and the Spirit he cannot enter into the kingdom of God." (John 3:5 NASB)

The above reference to John 11 is taken out of context to suggest "belief" only is required; "Those who believe in Me" here encompasses all Jesus has commanded one must do to be saved summed up in the word "believe," including what He said in Mark 16:16 and John 3:5 concerning baptism. Even these passages presuppose an understanding that one must obey the other requirements of repentance (Luke 13:3) and confession (Romans 10:9) to be saved. As a side note, Luther also insisted baptism is to be by immersion, which also aligns with Scripture (see the argument under this section above), whereas current ELCA and LCMS positions allow any form (sprinkling, pouring, or immersion).

A second question is related to the first and has, in fact, already been postulated under the heading of "Infant Baptism" in the text above, whereby the Lutheran Church has sanctioned several conflicting doctrines. This question is open-ended, but for the Lutherans, it cannot be answered without violating one of their doctrines:

2.) Why do you baptize infants?

The likely answer will be: "to remove their inherited sin." (Original sin argument). This we have refuted very simply earlier – Adam's consequential sin (death) he did pass on to us, however, his guilt sin he did not. None of us are responsible for our father's sin (Ezek. 18:20; Deut. 24:16).

The Book of Concord states infants are "possessed by the devil" and must be baptized to be saved (Again, original sin argument). In addition, it states that infants are included in Christ's mandate to "baptize all nations" - Matthew 8:19 (this we refuted since you cannot "make disciples" of infants – part of the same verse). The modern-day Lutheran Church claims to accept these teachings but then says there are other ways to be saved that do not include water baptism (i.e., God creating faith in a person's heart via the Holy Spirit, even the heart of an infant), however, baptism, they claim, is "God's gracious way of washing away our sins - even the sins of infants - without any help or cooperation on our part."

If the Lutheran Church claims to believe that in baptism God washes away sins, how, then, can it claim that baptism is not "ABSOLUTELY" necessary for salvation? Once again, the simple answer is that it can't. (Refer to the LCMS statement above from *Baptism and its Purpose 2004*, which confirms this position.) [31.] The Lutheran position on baptism is confused and stands in serious contradiction.

As stated earlier, infant baptism is dismissed by the Scriptures on many levels. One must "hear and understand" (Romans 10:14), "believe" (Romans 10:10–11, John 3:16), "repent" (Luke 13:3; 24:46–47), and "confess" (Romans 10:9) prior to baptism. An infant is incapable of doing any of these. The idea that God creates faith or belief in the heart of an infant doesn't work here – even if belief is somehow instilled by God – an infant must still have "heard and understood," "repented," and verbally "confessed" prior to being baptized! You decide.

In addition, the state of an infant is not in jeopardy according to Scripture. Jesus attested to the innocence of infants: "Assuredly, I say to you, unless you are converted and become as little children, you will by no means enter the kingdom of heaven. Therefore whoever humbles himself as this little child is the greatest in the kingdom of heaven. Whoever receives one little child like this in My name receives Me" (Matthew 18:3–5, also

Luke 18:16–17). Jesus indicates here that if anyone desires to enter the kingdom of heaven, they must be like a little child. If little children have sin against them that requires baptism, how can it be that Jesus presents a child as an example of one who would enter? Jesus did not claim this child needed or was baptized. The conclusion is clear – infants and little children are sinless/innocent.

Conclusion

The Lutheran Church is filled with many kind and sincere people who believe that they are members of the true church that Jesus bought with His blood. However, their origin, organization, and basis for authority, including their many man-made doctrines, stand in opposition to the New Testament, as well as conflicting with each other on numerous points.

- The Lutheran Church uses the name of Martin Luther, who protested and split from the Roman Catholic Church in 1517. The New Testament teaches of one church only, to be named after and belonging to our Lord, Jesus Christ.
- The Lutheran Church teaches that baptism is both essential and nonessential to salvation, (with the current view centering on the latter), whereas the New Testament teaches that a person must be immersed in water as the final act of his or her salvation process.
- The Lutheran Church teaches that texts and documents in addition to the Bible are "authoritative" and "binding"; the New Testament teaches that only God's Word is authoritative and binding.
- The Lutheran Church teaches that a lone pastor is to be the head of a congregation; the New Testament teaches that each congregation is to be headed by Christ, and overseen by a plurality of pastors or elders, who are responsible for the spiritual decisions of that congregation.

The Lutheran Church cannot be the church of Christ established on Pentecost as recorded in Acts 2.

SUMMARY

In Volume 1, Chapter 2, we looked at the church of Christ—the Lord's church as described in the New Testament—not as one denomination out of many, not as a denomination at all, but as a group of individuals obeying the gospel and following the teachings of Jesus. These individuals then were identified as His church—the church Jesus established—the one and only church of our Lord, the *church of Christ.*

This church of Christ was then used as the benchmark for truth, supported entirely by the Scriptures, to compare with the Catholic Church in the following chapter of Volume 1, and here it has been used to compare with the Orthodox, Episcopal, and Lutheran Churches, including comparisons on organization, recognized authority, primary beliefs and doctrines, baptism as it relates to salvation, worship activities, and the like.

To reiterate from the last volume, prior to summarizing the comparisons between the Lord's Church and the denominations in this volume, a clarification from Scripture concerning the singularity of the Lord's church is in order:

One Church

- "***There is* one body**" (Ephesians 4:4). [30.]
- Christ is the Savior of that body: "… as also Christ is head of the church; and He is the Savior of the body" (Ephesians 5:23).
- Thus, Christ is the Savior of one body.
- The body is the church: "the working of His mighty power which He worked in Christ … And He put all *things* under His feet, and gave Him *to be* head over all *things* **to the church, which is His**

body, the fullness of Him who fills all in all" (Ephesians 1:19–23); [30.] "**He is the head of the body, the church**" (Colossians 1:18) [30.]

- o Thus, Christ is the Savior of one singular church—His Church.

Denominations, on the other hand, were founded by mankind, born initially out of false teaching and apostasy from within the Lord's church, to satisfy the "itching ears" and will of man over the will of God. Most denominations we see today are the direct result of reformation efforts, whose purpose (far from being the "eternal purpose of God") was to "reform" from Catholicism initially, then, as doctrinal disagreements became unbearable, to separate from each other, forming yet other denominations—not to adhere to what God established and outlined in Scripture, but to change doctrine and to worship God as men saw fit.

In this volume, we saw the Eastern Orthodox Church split from the Western Roman Catholic Church in AD 1056—this over organizational differences as one friction point; also, the Church of England, or Anglican Church (known as the Episcopal Church in the United States), split from Catholicism in 1534 when King Henry VIII declared it free from any ties to Rome. This result, at least in part, was a result of the personal relations of King Henry being unacceptable to the pope at the time. Finally, the Lutheran Church pulled away from Catholicism in 1517 as the first Protestant denomination to do so, as a result of the many irreconcilable differences Martin Luther had with the pope.

Organization of Christ's Church

The organization of the Lord's church, as it has been arranged by God per the Scriptures is as follows:

- o Jesus as head (Daniel 7:14, Matthew 16:18, Colossians 1:18, Ephesians 1:22), with no man or group of men serving as head of Christ's church.
- o Apostles served under the Lord; their teachings, along with other inspired writings, are the authority of Christ given to the church for all ages (the Bible). There are to be no successors to the apostles after New Testament times. (Ephesians 4:11–16).

- Each local church was independent and autonomous, designated to be under the oversight of a plurality of elders (other names for which are "pastors," "bishops," "shepherds," and "overseers" (Acts 11:30, 14:23, 20:28, Titus 1:5–7, 1 Peter 5:1–5). (No conventions, synods, or councils were to rule over multiple congregations.)
- Preachers of the gospel were not "pastors" of the congregation unless appointed to this position; religious titles (e.g., "Father," Reverend") were not used; in fact, they were condemned by Jesus Himself (Matthew 23:8–10).

Versus

Organization/Hierarchy of Denominations Arranged by Mankind

- **Orthodox:** Patriarch of Constantinople or "First among Equals" over patriarchs governing large areas with dioceses over archbishops governing a portion of a country and metropolitans governing large cities – these over bishops with "sees" including multiple churches over parish priests or presbyters who govern individual congregations, over deacons over subdeacons over the laity.
- **Anglican (United Kingdom):** The Archbishop of Canterbury (Spiritual Head) over thirty-nine provinces worldwide over the General Convention over provincial archbishops (within the UK border) over bishops over dioceses over parishes or churches who elect vestries who select and are over preachers or rectors who are over the laity.
- **Episcopal (United States):** The Church is headed by a U.S. General Convention divided into two legislative bodies – the House of Bishops and the House of Deputies – overseen by a primate or presiding bishop. The convention makes policy for nine provinces (shadow partners with the Anglican Commune) – acting independently, each with a synod and archbishop, these over 110 dioceses each with a presiding bishop, the dioceses are over parishes or churches (six minimum) each who are controlled

by a vestry who select a rector or preacher who is over the laity of each congregation.

- **Lutheran:** ELCA, LCMS, and WELS Synods ruled by bishops with secondary synods or districts ruled by bishops over multiple congregations. Synods and district synods appoint pastors to local congregations, who preside over them.

(Note: No Scriptures are quoted here, as none support these organizational structures.)

Authority of Christ's Church—The Bible Only

- Christ's church uses the Old and New Testaments as the only authoritative guide for governing belief and practice (the Old Testament providing basic principles to emulate, the New Testament revealing Christ's instructions to live by) (Galatians 1:6–9; 1 Thessalonians 2:13; 2 Timothy 2:15; Acts 17:11; 2 Peter 3:16).
- Written by some forty men over sixteen hundred years, these sixty-six books are the product of the Holy Spirit, who empowered these men to pen only what God wanted written (2 Samuel 23:2; 1 Corinthians 2:9–13; 2 Timothy 3:16–17; 1 Peter 1:10–12; 2 Peter 1:20–21), having brought to their remembrance all things Jesus taught, and wanted to preserve for our benefit. (John 14:26).
- The Bible, every word, thus being verbally inspired by God, is inerrant and all-sufficient. (2 Timothy 3:16–17). It is also the complete and final revelation of God for all time (2 Peter 1:3; 2 Timothy 3:16–17; Jude 3; Acts 20:27).

Versus

Authority of the Denominations—Adding to God's Word

- o **Orthodox:** Bible + Holy Tradition, ecumenical councils, apostolic succession, Apocrypha.
- o **Episcopal:** Bible + creeds, tradition/reason/apostolic succession, Book of Common Prayer.
- o **Lutheran:** Bible + Book of Concord, creeds, confessions, catechisms.

(Note: We are not to "add to" or "take away from" God's Word (Revelation 22:18–19; Proverbs 30:5–6).

Worship Activities of Christ's Church, According to Scripture

Emulating the first-century Christians per Christ's / The Holy Spirit's instructions, we observe five acts of worship on the first day of every week (Sunday) (Acts 20:7):

- o First, Christians met to partake of the Lord's Supper, consisting of bread and fruit of the vine as symbols of the body and blood of Christ offered on the cross, in remembrance of His death. (Matthew 26:26–29; 1 Corinthians 10:16–21; 11:20–34).
- o Second, the early church engaged in prayer together (Acts 2:42; 1 Timothy 2:1–8).
- o Third, they sang religious songs together "making melody from the heart" (Ephesians 5:19, Colossians 3:16). Congregational singing was unaccompanied by musical instruments, and the use of choirs, soloists, and such was unheard of.

- o Fourth, they participated in Bible study, either by reading the Scriptures or as preached by a preacher or teacher. (1 Timothy 4:13; 2 Timothy 4:1–4; Titus 2:15).
- o Fifth, they pooled their money on the first day of the week as a treasury from which the Lord's work could be carried out. (1 Corinthians 16:1–2).

In addition to the above five acts of worship outlined in Scripture, Paul gives Timothy further guidelines concerning the roles of men and women, as well as the qualifications of all the leaders (elders and deacons) he, and ultimately the Holy Spirit, expects to be observed within the worship assembly of the Lord's church: "These things I write to you … that you may know how you ought to conduct yourself in the house of God, which is the church of the living God, the pillar and ground of the truth" (1 Timothy 3:14–15).

Versus

Worship Activities of the Denominations, According to Man's Ideas:

- o **Orthodox:** transubstantiation, chrismation, veneration of saints, confession/absolution by clergy, Old Testament services/liturgy.
- o **Episcopal:** transubstantiation, women bishops, remission of sin by clergy, confession/absolution by clergy, instrumental music.
- o **Lutheran:** presiding lone pastor, formal liturgy/creeds, ordination of women bishops and ministers, consubstantiation, instrumental music.

Membership to Christ's Church:

The simple plan of salvation, as explained in Scripture, and which has been offered to everyone, is the "entrance portal" to Christ's church. A person does not "join" Christ's singular, universal church; as he or she is obedient to the gospel, God Himself "adds" that person to the church (Acts 2:41). Following are the five steps to salvation and requirements for membership in Christ's church:

- **Hear the gospel**: "For whoever calls on the name of the Lord shall be saved. How then shall they call on Him in whom they have not believed? And how shall they believe in Him whom they have not heard ...? So then faith *comes* by hearing, and hearing by the word of God" (Romans 10:13–17).
- **Believe Jesus is the Christ, the Son of God**: "God has made this Jesus, whom you crucified, both Lord and Christ. Now when they heard *this*, they were cut to the heart" (Acts 2:36–37). "Believe on the Lord Jesus Christ, and you will be saved" (Acts 16:31).
- **Repent of your sins**: "What shall we do? Then Peter said to them, 'Repent, and let every one of you be baptized'" (Acts 2:37–38). "The time is fulfilled, and the kingdom of God is at hand. Repent, and believe in the gospel" (Mark 1:15). "Unless you repent, you will all likewise perish" (Luke 13:3).
- **Confess the name of Jesus as Lord**: "If you confess with your mouth the Lord Jesus and believe in your heart that God raised Him from the dead, you will be saved. For with the heart one believes unto righteousness, and with the mouth confession is made unto salvation" (Romans 10:9–10).
- **Be baptized (immersed) for the forgiveness of your sins**: "Be baptized in the name of Jesus Christ for the remission of sins" (Acts 2:38). "So he commanded the chariot to stand still. And both Philip and the eunuch went down into the water, and he baptized him" (Acts 8: 38). "Arise and be baptized, and wash away your sins, calling on the name of the Lord" (Acts 22:16). "Jesus answered, 'Truly, truly, I say to you, unless one is born of water and the Spirit, he cannot enter into the kingdom of God'" (John 3:5 NASB).

Versus

Entrance Requirements Set Up by Mankind

- **Orthodox:** Baptism into the Orthodox Church (usually as an infant), then to Christ, chrismation by a priest (through the Holy Spirit, when of age).
- **Episcopal:** Baptism and salvation through the church (usually as an infant), confirmation when of age to confess Jesus, and Lord's Supper three times per year (minimum).
- **Lutheran:** Completion of classes on Lutheran doctrine or catechism, baptism (sprinkling or pouring).

Christ's Church - View on Baptism

One last category needs to be looked at comparing what Scripture attests versus what denominations today teach and practice, that is the category of baptism. The New Testament clearly defines baptism as the vehicle through which a person's sins are forgiven by coming in contact with our Lord's own blood:

- "Without shedding of blood there is no remission" (Hebrews 9:22).
- "To Him who loved us and washed us from our sins in His own blood" (Revelation 1:5).
- This point of contact is the water of baptism, not simply a confession of faith: "Or do you not know that as many of us as were baptized into Christ Jesus were baptized into His death?" (His blood - Romans 6:3).
- "Repent and let every one of you be baptized in the name of Jesus Christ for the remission of sins" (Acts 2:38).

Baptism is thus the "dividing line" between being lost and being saved:

"Baptism now saves you … through the resurrection of Jesus Christ" (1 Peter 3:21 NASB).

Baptism is the point where sins are "washed away" (Acts 22:16) and where "we were all made to drink into one Spirit" (where the Holy Spirit enters) (1 Corinthians 12:13).

Versus

Baptism as Altered by Man's Idea of What God Will Accept

- **Orthodox:** not essential, faith only, member entrance, infant baptism accepted.
- **Episcopal:** not essential, entry into church / saved through the church, infant baptism accepted.
- **Lutheran:** not essential, faith only (changed from the time of Luther), infant baptism accepted.

Volume 3 of this series will begin with an examination of Calvinism, as this theology has had such a wide-ranging influence on denominations past and present. From there we'll examine four additional denominations—two from the Lutheran / Calvinist branch, those being the Presbyterian and Anabaptist Churches, and two from the Anglican / Episcopal branch, being the Methodist Church and the Salvation Army. Following this third volume will be an appendix entitled "Transmission of the Scriptures," wherein we'll explore some of the challenges presented by transmitting God's Word over time, as well as answer some of the criticisms associated with this process, in an effort to bolster the credibility of God's Word, in the face of this criticism.

APPENDIX

THE TRANSLATION OF THE SCRIPTURES

An issue many have raised, casting doubt (as some would see it) upon the words of Scripture as the sole source of truth against denominational error, has to do with the process of translating the Scriptures from the original autographs, and the transmission of these words through time. This appendix will deal with the first of these - translation issues, and we'll look at aspects of transmission in the appendix of our next Volume (3). Though the Holy Spirit originally imparted God's Words to the inspired writers, these critics would say the words have been altered in some cases owing to the many human translations and copies that have been handed down through the years to the present time. With this mindset, the claim that a particular verse in the Bible disagrees with a corresponding denominational doctrine is often offset by the thought that current translations could be a distortion of the original meaning (coupled with a watered-down view of inspiration itself, as was discussed in the appendix following Volume 1 [i.e., thought, or partial inspiration]), thus the argument for Biblical accuracy is dismissed altogether.

This appendix will attempt to address doubts on the subject by presenting evidence supporting the fact that the words we now have recorded in our Bibles are essentially the same words as originally penned by the inspired writers, given certain identifiable variances due to man's attempt to translate and record the Divine Scriptures over the years. The following analysis is by no means exhaustive on this subject but is intended to briefly introduce the reader to some of the challenges facing the early translators and, once again, to put forth evidence supporting the accuracy of current-day translations.

> "The grass withers, the flower fades, but the word of our God stands forever." (Isaiah 40:8)

> "Heaven and earth will pass away, but My words will by no means pass away." (Mark 13:31)

From the prophecies of Isaiah made in 675 BC to the words of our Lord spoken shortly before the New Testament was written around AD 30, we have the assurance from God that His word, His Holy Scriptures (Old and New Testaments) have not been, nor will they ever be, lost. Furthermore, God expects us to read His Word and "rightly divide" its contents per Paul's admonition to Timothy and by application to all Christians everywhere: "Be diligent to present yourself approved to God, a worker who does not need to be ashamed, rightly dividing the word of truth" (2 Timothy 2:15). This statement alone stands against many, if not most, denominational teachings, that put forth the premise that the ordinary Christian is incapable of correctly discerning God's Word—of "rightly dividing the word of truth" on his or her own—without the help of an "institution," a more learned and "ordained" group of clergy. (The Berean Christians who "searched the Scriptures daily" is another example that refutes this idea. [Acts 17:11]).

The first thing we need to understand is that the original writings, or "autographs," as penned by inspired men and recorded on stone, clay, or leather (Old Testament) and later on papyrus, parchment, and vellum (New Testament), have all been lost or destroyed. Therefore, everyone today is dependent upon a translation from those originals.

Much of the following information has been condensed from the book *The Bible Translation Controversy*, expanded edition, authored by Wayne Jackson.[1.]

A translation is simply the rendition of the original text (Hebrew, Greek, or Aramaic) into one's native language. Everyone, unless he reads the biblical languages and has access to the earliest writings, is dependent upon a translation.

There are several factors that influence translations:

- o Determination of the best Greek text to translate from (New Testament)
- o Theology and philosophy of the translators
- o Grammatical difficulties in translating

Determination of the "best" Greek text generally involves the acceptance of one of three methods:

1. **The critical method**: A majority of scholars adhere to this method today. It involves a comparison of ancient Greek manuscripts, early translations, quotations, and internal evidence to try to restore as precisely as possible the originals; the earliest sources are assumed to be the most reliable.
2. **The Majority Text method**: The best Greek text is determined by counting manuscripts, though some may have been discovered more recently. One problem with this method, as some see it, is that many of the manuscripts have been traced to a "common ancestor" [2.] thus, lowering the number previously supposed.
3. **The *Textus Receptus* method**: This method is based on a small group of relatively late manuscripts. A problem with this method is that in at least a dozen places, the text is not supported by any other known Greek text.

The theology of the translators is another factor influencing the finished product—What is the translator's attitude toward the Scriptures? The majority of translators of the KJV, ASV, and ERV, for instance, had a high regard for the Divine origin of the Bible, where any "liberal" influence was reflected mainly in footnotes. This can be compared to the translators of the RSV, where all nine were of the "liberal wing of scholarship." [3.]

Along with this, the philosophy (or "rules of engagement") of these translators must be taken into consideration. Three terms have identified these approaches. The first is **Formal Equivalence (FE) translation.** Here an attempt is made to translate "the words and nuances of the original text" [4] as literally as possible, word for word (provided clarity is conveyed into English).

This was the attitude or philosophy of the KJV, ERV, and ASV translators. The ASV translators stated their aim was to "bring the plain reader more closely into contact with the exact message of the sacred writers." [4.]

The second approach is **Dynamic Equivalence (DE) translation.** This mindset attempts to translate the meaning of the text in free idiomatic English without as much regard to the exact wording of the original text (thought for thought). One of the dangers of this philosophy is that translators may choose to paraphrase what they think the Greek text is trying to convey if they feel the literal is too obscure. D.A. Carson, a defender of the DE method once admitted, "this attitude can lead to all sorts of freedoms with respect to translation … it is no doubt true that the closer one stands to the 'loose end [of the FE/DE spectrum – WJ], the greater the chances of subjective bias." [5.]

Finally, the more contemporary approach are the **Paraphrase versions** (i.e., The Living and Message Versions). Here the emphasis is on translating the ideas of one language into another in the most reader-friendly fashion, with less concern about using the exact words of the original.

The below chart depicts translation comparisons on a scale from word-for-word to thought-for-thought approaches, with the farther right-hand versions being closer to paraphrase approaches.

Translation Comparison Chart

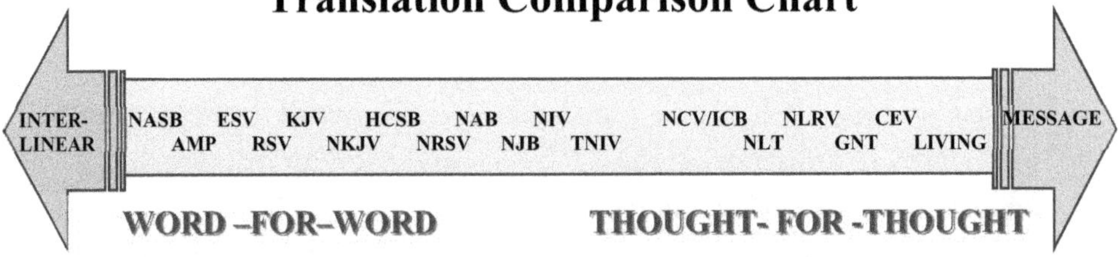

NASB	New American Standard Bible (1971; update 1995)	NIV	New International Version (1984)
AMP	Amplified Bible (1965)	TNIV	Today's New International Version (NT 2001, OT 2005)
ESV	English Standard Version (2001)	NCV	New Century Version
RSV	Revised Standard Version (1952)	NLT[1]	New Living Translation (1st ed. 1996; 2nd ed. 2004)
KJV	King James Version (1611; significantly revised 1769)	NIrV	New International reader's Version
NKJV	New King James Version (1982)	GNT	Good News Translation (also Good News Bible)
HCSB	Holman Christian Standard Version (2004)	CEV	Contemporary English Version
NRSV	New Revised Standard Version (1989)	Living	Living Bible (1950). Paraphrase by Ken Taylor. Liberal treatment of 'blood.'
NAB	New American Bible (Catholic, 1970, 1986 (NT), 1991 (Psalms)		
NJB	New Jerusalem Bible (Catholic, 1986; revision of 1966 Jerusalem Bible)	Message	The Message by Eugene Peterson (1991-2000s)

The following Bible version table by Mark Hoffmann and Bruce Terry further describes the literalness of the major versions. This table is followed by recommendations by these authors. [8.]
(https://docs.google.com/document/d/1-u-5nvjpFDQIMAEc7zTqM8lZLqqC3Eo2h6FEsR1z06g/edit?usp=sharing) (mgvhoffmann / CrossMarks.com)

A 'Literal' > Paraphrase Scale of English Bible Versions

- Literal (1-2) > Idiomatic (3-4) > Dynamic (5-6) > Paraphrase (7-8) > Commentative (9-10) scale based on Bruce Terry's evaluation with additions by mgvh
- Note: a "1" would be a word-for-word interlinear version

Abbr.	Bible	Lit>Dyn	Notes
ASV	American Standard Version, 1901	2	aka Amer. Revised Version; based on KJV > ERV
ERV	English Revised Version, 1881/1885	2	aka Revised Version; revision of KJV
LEB	Lexham English Bible, 2012	2	from Logos/Faithlife
LSB	Legacy Standard Bible	2	in KJV, ASV, NASB tradition
NWT	New World Translation, 1961	2	coheres to Jehovah's Witness doctrine
YLT	Young's Literal Translation, 1862/1898	2	
AMP	Amplified Bible, 2015	2.5	
DRA	Douay-Rheims 1899 American Edition	2.5	Roman Catholic translation of Vulgate
KJV	King James, 1611/1769	2.5	
LAM	Lamsa Holy Bible from Ancient Eastern Mss 1933	2.5	translation of Syriac Peshitta
NASB	New American Standard Bible 1977>1995>2020	2.5	
NKJ	New King James Version, 1982	2.5	revision of KJV
ESV	English Standard Version, 2007 update	3	revision of RSV
JPS	Jewish Publication Society Tanakh, 1917	3	

NRSV	New Revised Standard Version, 1989	3	update of RSV
NRSVue	NRSV Updated Edition, 2023	3	update of NRSV
RSV	Revised Standard Version, 1952	3	
NABRE	New American Bible Revised Ed., 2010	3.5	revision of NAB
CSB	Christian Standard Bible, 2017	4	revision of HCSB
HCSB	Holman Christian Standard Bible, 2000	4	
NET	NET Bible, 1996 > 2005 update	4	
NAB	New American Bible, 1970, 1986	4	
NIVUK	New International Version (UK), 1978	4.5	
NIV	New International Version (US), 1984 > 2011	4.5	2011 ed. is compromise update of 1984 & TNIV
TNIV	Today's NIV, 2002	4.6	updated NIV w/ gender-neutral language
ISV	International Standard Version, 2011	5	
JB	Jerusalem Bible, 1966	5	Roman Catholic; reliant on French Bible de Jérusalem
MOF	Moffat's A New Translation	5	NT only
NEB	New English Bible, 1961, 1970	5	
NJB	New Jerusalem Bible, 1985	5	update to JB based on Hebrew and Greek
REB	Revised English Bible, 1989	5	revision of NEB
CEB	Common English Bible, 2011	5.5	-intended as more readable option to NRSV
GW	GOD'S WORD Translation, 1995	6	
NCV	New Century Version, 1986, 1991, 2007	6	based on English Version for the Deaf
NIrV	New International Reader's Version, 1996	6	simplified version of NIV
NLT	New Living Translation, 1996…2005	6	motivated by LB but indep. and based on Heb/Gk
TEV	Today's English Version, 1966-1976	6	aka Good News Bible (GNB)
Voice	The Voice, 2012	6.5	literary, artistic; screenplay format for dialogue
CEV	Contemporary English Version, 1995	7	updated replacement for TEV/GNB/GNT

MIT	MacDonald Idiomatic Translation Bible	8	
PNT	Phillips' The New Testament in Modern English	8	
MSG	The Message	9	Eugene Peterson's translation/ paraphrase; attends to Heb/Gk
LB	Living Bible, 1971	9.5	paraphrase based on ASV
CPV	Cotton Patch Version, 1968-1973	10	loose paraphrase using American South dialect

Recommended Versions to Consult and Compare
(By Mark Hoffmann and Bruce Terry)

From the **FORMAL / LITERAL** group (0-2.5 on scale):

- LEB, LSB, or NASB: Use one of these to have a literal translation that is 'transparent' to original language.
- KJV: Besides being a classic, this will also highlight use of the *Textus Receptus* (~Majority Text)
- DRA: Useful to see if anything is unique in Latin Vulgate tradition

From **IDIOMATIC** group (3-4):

- ESV: Non-inclusive language; not a particularly elegant translation, but it is becoming a standard for 'evangelical' churches.
- TNK: for Old Testament; Important to get this Jewish perspective based on Masoretic Text
- NRSV / NRS Vue: Standard study text; widely used.
- CSB: Widely used in
- NET: Main importance is to check tc (=text critical) and tn (=translation note) notations

From **IDIOMATIC-DYNAMIC** group (4.5-5.5):

- NIV (2011) or TNIV: NIV is widely used in Protestant churches.

- CEB: Ecumenical translation; intended to replace NRSV for liturgical reading.
- NJB: Provides insight into Roman Catholic perspective.

From **FUNCTIONAL / DYNAMIC** group (6-7.5):

- NLT: Useful dynamic translation but can reflect (conservative) theological biases.
- TEV or CEV: Helpful to see how to translate at a simpler reading level.

From **PARAPHRASE** group (8-10):

- MSG: Peterson did work closely with the Greek/Hebrew; there are some unfortunate phrasings, but he mostly gets things right and highlights where there is an interpretive issue.

Finally, there are grammatical difficulties that arise in translating from Greek into English, which make an absolute literal word-for-word Bible translation almost impossible. For instance, the word order of Greek differs from that of English. Take, for example, 1 Corinthians 16:8–9; the literal Greek for these verses reads: "I shall remain but in Ephesus until the Pentecost. Door for to me has been opened great and effective and opponents many." The literal word-for-word translation of Matthew 1:18 would look like this: "Of her having been betrothed of the mother of him of Mary to Joseph before to come together them she was found in womb having the Holy Spirit."

Sometimes the literal Greek translation would make no sense to an English reader. For instance, the rendering of Luke 3:14: "They were asking and him and soldiering saying, what shall we do and we? And he said to them, none shake through nor fig-shine, and be satisfied with boiled food bought of you."

Another unintelligible rendering would be 2 Corinthians 9:10: "The one and chorus-leading seed to the sowing and bread into food a chorus he will lead."

Another problem is consistency—for instance, the query directed to Paul in Acts 17:18 by some philosophers in Athens would read, "What would this seed-picker say?" The original Greek term "*spermologos*" is more clearly rendered as "babbler" or "gossiper" in this verse.

In other instances, the consistency of the same Greek word may not be practically translated in all occurrences. The Greek word "*spanchnon*" literally means "entrails or intestines." In Acts 1:18, when the body of Judas "falling headlong, he burst open in the middle and all his entrails (*spanchnon*) gushed out." This same word, "spanchnon," was also used by the Greeks to describe the seat of human emotion; therefore, it is best to translate Philippians 1:8 as "I long after you all with the *affection* of Christ Jesus" (ASV, NKJV, KSV), rather than "in the *bowels* of Christ" (KJV).

Manuscripts were written in two styles, uncial, and cursive, with uncial being the older and more important. The typical uncial style would comprise no spaces, no punctuation, all capitals, and broken words to keep exact columns. One would have to know literally where a word starts and ends to translate perfectly. For instance:

PAULASERVATOFJESUSCHRISTCALLEDTOBEANAPPOSTLE ...

According to Dr. Eugene of the American Bible Society, "A literal translation, no matter how much admired and desired, would be unintelligible. A word-for-word rendition with Greek grammatical constructions would be more awkward than an interlinear and convey as little sense."

A good translation will strive for balance, staying as close to the original text as possible, while expressing clearness of meaning. Considering the aforementioned factors, it's apparent that no perfect version can be claimed, and there are bound to be disagreements among sincere Bible students concerning the various versions, all of which contain at least some translating error. The following section will discuss several of the more popular versions in this light.

Translating Errors of Several Popular Versions

(The following critique was extrapolated predominately from Wayne Jackson's work *The Bible Translation Controversy*, expanded edition.)[1.]

The King James Version (KJV) of 1611

The publication of the King James Version in 1611 was a landmark event in the history of the English Bible; for many years it maintained an unquestioned supremacy as *the* translation to rely on. That said, it should be noted that the KJV rests on a weak textual base, especially with reference to the Greek text for the New Testament. The translators simply did not have at their disposal the many manuscripts which are now known, including the Vatican, Sinaitic, Alexandrian, and Ephraim Manuscripts.

The KJV also employs many archaic words whose meanings are in many cases misunderstood or misleading. For instance, "allege" is used for "prove," "allow" for "approve," and "prevent" for "precede." The King James Version also contained the Apocrypha (discussed previously as uninspired writing). The current-day version has undergone numerous revisions; however, the following discrepancies persist:

1. Genesis 1:6 states, *"And God said, Let there be a* ***raqia***[6] (literally, "expanse") [6.] *in the midst of the waters."* The KJV renders *"raqia"* as "firmament," which was a carryover from the Greek Septuagint and later the Latin Vulgate indicating a "solid vault heaven" (that supported the waters above). However, the Hebrew term does not mean that which is *firm*, and the translation is inaccurate.
2. The KJV refers to the "unicorn" (Numbers 23:22) and the "satyr" (Isaiah 13:21). Both are errors, as the Hebrew refers to a wild ox rather than a unicorn and a wild goat, not a mythical satyr. These have been corrected in the NKJV.
3. The KJV renders Acts 2:47 as follows: *"And the Lord added to the church daily* ***<u>such as should be saved</u>****."*[6.] However, the Greek "*tous sozomenous*" is a present-tense participle denoting *"the being saved ones."* (The thought is not that God has already determined who should be saved and, hence, added them to the church). This

rendering accommodates Calvinism and is inaccurate. This has been rendered more accurately in the NKJV as "*those who were being saved.*"

4. In Acts 3:19 the KJV renders the term "*epistrepsate*" as "*be converted*" (passive form), suggesting humankind is passive toward salvation. Thus, conversion is totally an act of God (Calvinistic idea) to which humankind must yield. The verb, however, is active, not passive. The ASV renders this term as "*turn again,*" indicating that humankind must respond to the Lord of his own free will in order to be saved.
5. Galatians 5:17 in the KJV states, "*For the flesh lusteth against the Spirit, and the Spirit against the flesh: and these are contrary the one to the other; so that ye* ***cannot*** [6] *do the things that ye would.*" The Greek term "*poiete*" is in the present subjunctive and should not be rendered "cannot," suggesting man is utterly incapable of right conduct except by supernatural influence—again, a Calvinistic notion. This is corrected in the NKJV.
6. The KJV translators added "if" to Hebrews 6:6, where the Greek has no contingency indicated; this seems to have been added so as not to contradict the "once saved, always saved" doctrine. In addition, the KJV adds "*any man*" to Hebrews 10:38, again not in the original text, for similar reasoning.
7. Mark 6:20 in the KJV states that Herod put John the Baptist in prison and "*observed him.*" The actual translation is "*For Herod feared John, knowing that he was a just man and an holy, and observed him ...*" However, what is meant here is that he kept him safe. The NKJV translates this as "*For Herod feared John, knowing that he was a just and holy man, and he protected him.*"
8. The KJV fails to preserve some of the distinctions within the Greek text—for instance, the rendering of "hell" for both "Hades" and "Gehenna." By making this mistake, the translators have death and hell being cast into the lake of fire in Revelation 20:14 rather than death and Hades. There is a distinction between Hades and hell, as analyzed earlier in my examination of the creeds of the Anglican / Episcopal Church.

9. The KJV translators obscured the meaning of the Greek term "*baptizo*" (immerse) by anglicizing the original term (making a hybrid word from Greek and English), thus allowing "sprinkling," "dipping," "pouring," and the like to also describe this word. This seems to have been deliberately done for theological reasons. The word remains universally mistranslated today. For example, Acts 2:38 should read from the Greek, "*Then Peter said unto them, repent, and be immersed every one of you.*"

The American Standard Version (ASV) of 1901

Guy N. Woods has called the ASV of 1901 "On the whole, the finest of all English Versions of the New Testament in popular use today." Following are a few discrepancies, however:

1. The ASV relegates "*Gods only begotten*" (John 1:18) to a footnote, while putting "*The only begotten Son*" in the text. The best textual evidence, however, agrees with the former, emphasizing the Lord's deity.
2. In John 9:38, concerning the man whose sight Jesus miraculously restored, the apostle wrote, "*And he worshipped him*" (referring to Christ). The ASV puts a footnote to this describing "worshipped" as follows: "The Greek word denotes an act of reverence, whether paid to a creature (as here) or the Creator (see 4:20)." This is a totally radical comment and is unwarranted.
3. The ASV renders Matthew 28:1 as "*late on the Sabbath day, as it began to dawn toward the first day of the week*" *the two Mary's came to the garden tomb and found it empty,* (thus implying Christ arose on Saturday rather than Sunday). But the Greek term "*opse*" means "after," not "late on," hence, "after the Sabbath." [7.]
4. The ASV (along with the KJV and NKJV) is incomplete in its rendering of 1 Corinthians 16:2, in that it fails to accurately translate the Greek "*katamian sabbatou,*" leaving out "every"—as "on the first day of *every* week," indicating the New Testament church assembled and contributed *each* and *every* Lord's Day.

The Revised Standard Version (RSV) of 1946 / 1952

1. The RSV renders the Hebrew word "*almah*" in Isaiah 78:14 as "young woman," while the KJV and ASV render it correctly as "virgin." The RSV thus puts Matthew in the awkward position of arguing for the "virgin" birth from an Old Testament text that doesn't teach it!
2. The RSV renders Acts 3:21 as "*establishing*" instead of the correct translation "*restoration.*" (Millennialism bias is evident here, as "establishing" fits a one-thousand-year reign of Christ on earth better than "restore everything," referring to Christ's second coming and Last Judgment against sin).
3. In Acts 10:43, the RSV has "*does what is right*" instead of "*works righteousness*" or "*believes.*" Many people "do what is right" (morally) but never submit to God's plan of salvation.
4. The RSV translates the present participle form "*hyparchon,*" meaning "existing," in the past tense in Philippians 2:6, implying that after His incarnation, Jesus was no longer in the "form of God"—an obvious mistake.

The New English Bible (NEB) of 1970

One scholar claimed the NEB represented the "freest tampering with the biblical text of any version yet to appear." Following are several examples of this "tampering":

1. The narrative concerning the tower of Babel account (Genesis 11) begins, "*Once upon a time ...*" (indicating it as questionable historical fact).
2. The woman's "seed" (the Messiah) is removed from Genesis 3:15.
3. Speaking of Joseph and Mary, the NEB renders Matthew 1:18 as "*Before their marriage, she was found with child,*" versus the virgin birth affirmation "... *with child before they came together.*"
4. The NEB twice changes "*virgin*" to "*girl*" in Luke 1:27.
5. In Acts 20:7, "*the first day of the week*" is changed to "*Saturday night.*"

6. The "*tongues*" of 1 Corinthians 12:10 is changed to "*ecstatic utterances*" (favoring Pentecostalism).

The New American Standard Bible (NASB) of 1963 / 1970

The New American Standard Bible was designed to replace the ASV. Though it exhibits some improvements, it is not flawless. Following are a few noted errors:

1. The NASB reflects the premillennial bias of its translators in passages such as Galatians 6:16: "*And those who will walk* (after the supposed 1000-year reign)[6] *by this rule, peace and mercy be upon them.*" Most translations render this as "*And as many as walk …*" Also see Mark 13:30 (footnote "race") and Revelation 5:10: "*You have made them to be a kingdom* [6] *and priests to our God.*" Most translations render this "*And have made us a kingdom and priests to our God.*"
2. The NASB has Jesus saying, "*Do not think that I came to abolish the law*" (Matthew 5:17), which is a contradiction of Ephesians 2:15. A better translation would be "*to destroy the law.*"
3. In Galatians 3:26, the NASB has "*For you are all sons of God through faith in Christ Jesus.*" In the Greek text, a definite article precedes "faith"—thus, "the faith" is to be emphasized here (the gospel system, not one's personal faith). The text is better rendered as "*You are all sons of God, through faith, in Christ Jesus.*"
4. The NASB follows the mistake of the RSV in translating Philippians 2:6 with the past tense verb "existed."

The New International Version (NIV) of 1973 / 1978

As one of the most popular versions, the NIV translators sought more than a word-for-word translation. According to Jackson, they felt free to modify sentence structure to make it more "readable." Errors noted within the NIV include the following:

1. The NIV renders Psalm 51:5 as David saying, "*Surely I have been a sinner from birth*" (totally unjustified and supportive of the Calvinistic doctrine of original sin). Most versions—the NASB, for instance—render this as "*I was brought forth in iniquity, and in sin my mother conceived me.*" The text stresses that David was brought into a world of sin rather than that he was a sinner from birth. Also, in Romans 7:18, "*flesh*" becomes "*sinful nature*" (another allusion to original sin).
2. 1 Peter 3:21, as translated in the NIV, suggests salvation may come prior to baptism since baptism is the "*pledge of a good conscience.*"
3. The NIV mistranslates 1 Corinthians 13:10, suggesting that miraculous gifts will continue until "*perfection comes,*" rather than "*when the perfect* (complete thing – neuter gender)[6] *comes,*" referring to the completed revelation or Scripture.
4. The NIV renders Acts 2:27 (translated by most versions as "*hades*") as "*grave,*" while in Matthew 11:23 the same term is translated as "*the depths*"—a wrong concept, per Jackson.

The New King James Version (NKJV) of 1985

The publishers of the New King James Version acknowledge that this edition is not an entirely new translation, but rather its aim was to be a "continuation" of the King James Version with a modernized language style. The translators chose a stricter word-for-word philosophy as opposed to paraphrasing, and this version leaves out the old style "thee," "thou," and "thine," opting for the more modern "you," "yours," and so on.

The translators of the NKJV elected to use the less popular Majority Text as their basis for the work, conceding that many of the Greek manuscripts employed are of later vintage (none being earlier than the fifth century AD) and that they were going against the belief of most scholars that the Majority Text is not the most accurate. That being said, the differences noted between the Majority Text and Critical Text are not all that significant from a doctrinal point of view.

The NKJV attempts to change not only the older-style language of its predecessor but also several of the discrepancies heretofore mentioned (under the KJV section). However, there are a few of these discrepancies the translators did not alter, as listed below:

1. The NKJV continues to translate (incorrectly) the Greek word "*raqia*" as that which is "firm" in Genesis 1:6: "Then God said, "*Let there be a firmament in the midst of the waters.*" (See point 1 in the KJV section above for critique.)
2. Acts 3:19 in the NKJV keeps the passive form of the Greek "*epistrepsate*" ("be converted"): *"Repent therefore and be converted, that your sins may be blotted out,*" indicating that man is passive toward salvation—an incorrect translation.
3. The Calvinistic influence is also not removed in this updated version, either in Hebrews 6:6 (the contingency "if" being again added) or in Hebrews 10:38 (where "*any man*" [KJV] is only altered to "*anyone*" [NKJV]), with both verses accommodating the "once saved, always saved" doctrine.
4. As with most translations, the NKJV maintains that "*baptizo*" is not exclusively "immersion," as indicated by the Greek; thus, the term is anglicized to "baptize" with a modern connotation, allowing for several methods of water application in addition to immersion (sprinkling, pouring, and so forth).

CONCLUDING REMARKS

Concerning the various Bible translations on the market today, one should choose, for one's personal study, a good and solid translation that attempts to convey as precisely as possible God's inspired Word, considering the aforementioned discrepancies of some of the more popular versions. As mentioned previously, there is no perfect translation out there.

In addition, no person should be labeled as either "liberal" or "conservative" simply based on which translation they choose. One's soundness is not dependent so much on the translation as on what one teaches from whatever translation is used. If one teaches error and attempts to prove it from a corrupt rendering of their version, they must be opposed.

Christ and His inspired men frequently quoted from the Septuagint (LXX), the Greek translation of the Hebrew Old Testament (though it can be argued that the Hebrew was a far superior text). The reasoning for this has more to do with reaching the multitudes with the message of Christ (as the LXX was the "common" Bible of the people at that time) than having the most "correct" translation. The Septuagint contains many errors, even incorporating the uninspired apocryphal books, however, our Lord and His disciples never taught truth from any of these corrupted sections.

As will be discussed in Volume 5, under our study of the Jehovah's Witnesses, one could take their version (the New World Translation) and read from it Acts 2:38 ("*Repent, and let each one of you be baptized in the name of Jesus Christ for forgiveness of sins*") and be doctrinally sound. Though this version contains errors in many places, here it does not, and here one could teach the truth using their version (which has value in reaching certain people or groups).

Though certainly it can be said that not all translations are of equal value (including some of the more modern paraphrase versions, where much liberty has been taken with the text, such as Clarence Jordan's Cotton Patch Version), in the final analysis, translation selection is a matter of Christian liberty, given the cautions cited above.

TOPICAL INDEX

BIBLIOGRAPHY

Arakaki, Robert. 2014, "Concerning Eternal Marriage." Orthodox Reformed Bridge. https://blogs.ancientfaith.com/orthodoxbridge/concerning-eternal-marriage.

Archives of the Episcopal Church. "Acts of Convention: Resolution #1997-A053, Implement Mandatory Rights of Women Clergy under Canon Law; Ordination of Rev. Margaret Lee." https://episcopalarchives.org/cgi-bin/ENS/ENSpress_release.pl?pr_number=101910-05.

Berzonsky, Fr. Vladimir. 2004. "One Shepherd, Many Flocks." Orthodox Church in America. https://oca.org/reflections/berzonsky/one-shepherd-many-flocks.

Berzonsky, Fr. Vladimir. "Apostolic Succession: Thoughts in Christ." http://oca.org/reflections/berzonsky/to-qualify-as-an-apostle.

Berzonsky, Fr. Vladimir. 2007. "Thoughts in Christ—Deesis." http://oca.org/reflections/berzonsky/deesis.

Berzonsky, Fr. Vladimir. "Thoughts in Christ—Most Precious Promise." http://oca.org/reflections/berzonsky/the-most-precious-promise.

Bishop Gene Robinson. https://www.britannica.com/biography/V-Gene-Robinson.

Book of Common Prayer. http://www.episcopalchurch.org/files/book_of_common_prayer.pdf.

Bratcher, Dennis. "The Voice 'Low Church and High Church." Christian Resource Institute. http://www.crivoice.org/lowhighchurch.html.

Breck, Fr. John. 2010. "Life in Christ—Baptism in Christ." http://oca.org/reflections/fr.-john-breck/baptism-in-christ.

Breck, Fr. John. 2007. "Life in Christ—Why do we still fast?" http://oca.org/reflections/fr.-john-breck/why-do-we-still-fast.

Breck, Fr. John. "May We Pray for the Departed?" http://oca.org/reflections/fr.-john-breck/may-we-pray-for-the-departed.

Breck, Fr. John. "On Preaching Judgment (Part 1)." http://oca.org/reflections/fr.-john-breck/on-preaching-judgment-part-1.

Breck, Fr. John. "Salvation is Indeed by Grace." http://oca.org/reflections/fr.-john-breck/salvation-is-indeed-by-grace.

Orthodox Church in America. "Sources of Christian Doctrine: The Councils." www.oca.org/orthodoxy/the-orthodox-faith/doctrine-scripture/sources-of-christian-doctrine/the-councils.

"Daily Cycles of Prayer." https://oca.org/orthodoxy/the-orthodox-faith/worship/the-daily-cycles-of-prayer.

Damick, Fr. Andrew Stephen. "Holy Tradition." https://www.oca.org/orthodoxy/the-orthodox-faith/doctrine-scripture/sources-of-christian-doctrine/tradition.

"Divine Liturgy." https://oca.org/orthodoxy/the-orthodox-faith/worship/the-divine-liturgy.

"Divine Services–Archpriest Seraphim Slobodskoy, The Church Building and its Arrangement." http://www.fatheralexander.org/booklets/english/church_services.htm.

"Doctrine, the Symbol of Faith, Man." Orthodox Church in America. http://oca.org/orthodoxy/the-orthodox-faith/doctrine/sources-of-christian-doctrine/man.

Ecumenical Councils of the Orthodox Church. http://www.orthodoxchristian.info/pages/Ecumenical_Councils.htm.

"Episcopal Church Suspended from Anglican Communion." Jan. 14, 2016. http://www.premier.org.uk/News/UK/PRIMATES-MEETING-OUTCOME-Episcopal-Church-suspended-from-full-participation-in-Anglican-Communion "Eucharists."

"Fathers of the Church." https://www.osvnews.com/2019/01/21/fathers-of-the-church-part-1–the-greek-or-eastern-fathers; https://www.oca.org/orthodoxy/the-orthodox-faith/doctrine-scripture/sources-of-christian-doctrine/the-fathers.

Short Summaries of the Ecumenical Councils; (https://churchmotherofgod.org/articleschurch/articles-about-the-orthodox-church/2259-short-summaries-of-the-ecumenical-councils.html)

The First Ecumenical Council: (http://www.goarch.org/ourfaith/ourfaith8062) ; (https://www.goarch.org/-/the-first-ecumenical-council) ; (https://www.oca.org/orthodoxy/the-orthodox-faith/church-history/fourth-century/the-first-ecumenical-council).

The Canons of the Eastern Orthodox Church (First Council): (https://sites.google.com/site/canonsoc/home/canons-of-the-ecumenical-councils/i-nicaeanum-325)

The Second Ecumenical Council: (http://www.goarch.org/ourfaith/ourfaith8065); (https://www.oca.org/orthodoxy/the-orthodox-faith/church-history/fourth-century/the-second-ecumenical-council).

The Canons of the Eastern Orthodox Church (Second Council): (https://sites.google.com/site/canonsoc/home/canons-of-the-ecumenical-councils/i-constantinoplitanum-381)

The Third Ecumenical Council: (http://www.goarch.org/ourfaith/ourfaith8066); https://www.oca.org/orthodoxy/the-orthodox-faith/church-history/fifth-century/third-ecumenical-council.

The Canons of the Eastern Orthodox Church (Third Council): https://sites.google.com/site/canonsoc/home/canons-of-the-ecumenical-councils/council-of-ephesus-431

The Fourth Ecumenical Council: http://www.goarch.org/ourfaith/ourfaith8067; https://www.oca.org/orthodoxy/the-orthodox-faith/church-history/fifth-century/the-fourth-ecumenical-council.

The Canons of the Eastern Orthodox Church (Fourth Council): https://sites.google.com/site/canonsoc/home/canons-of-the-ecumenical-councils/council-of-chalcedon-451-1

The Fifth Ecumenical Council: http://www.goarch.org/ourfaith/ourfaith8068; https://www.oca.org/orthodoxy/the-orthodox-faith/church-history/sixth-century/the-fifth-ecumenical-council.

The Canons of the Eastern Orthodox Church – The Anathemas Against Origen (Fifth Council): https://sites.google.com/site/canonsoc/home/canons-of-the-ecumenical-councils/ii-constantinoplitanum-553-1

The Sixth Ecumenical Council: http://www.goarch.org/ourfaith/ourfaith8069; https://www.oca.org/orthodoxy/the-orthodox-faith/church-history/seventh-century/the-sixth-ecumenical-council.

The Canons of the Eastern Orthodox Church – The Definition of Faith: https://sites.google.com/site/canonsoc/home/canons-of-the-ecumenical-councils/iii-constantinoplitanum-680-681

The Quinisext or Trullan Council (Canons): http://www.intratext.com/IXT/ENG0835/

The Seventh Ecumenical Council: http://www.goarch.org/

ourfaith/ourfaith8071; https://www.oca.org/saints/lives/2019/10/13/70-commeration-of-the-holy-fathers-of-the-seventh-ecumenical=council.

The Canons of the Eastern Orthodox Church (Seventh Council): https://sites.google.com/site/canonsoc/home/canons-of-the-ecumenical-councils/ii-nicaeanum-787

"Fifth Ecumenical Council." http://www.goarch.org/ourfaith/ourfaith8068.

"First Ecumenical Council." http://www.goarch.org/ourfaith/ourfaith8062.

"Fourth Ecumenical Council." http://www.goarch.org/ourfaith/ourfaith8067.

"Frequent Communion." www.catholic.com/encyclopedia/frequent-communion.

"Full Communion Partners / In Dialogue Partners." https://www.episcopalchurch.org/ecumenical-and-inter-religious-relations.

General Convention 1976. "Ordination of Women approved." http://www.episcopalchurch.org/library/glossary/ordination-women.

Greek Orthodox Archdiocese of America. "House of God." https://www.goarch.org/-/house-of-god-inside-an-orthodox-church?inheritRedirect=true.

Greek Orthodox Archdiocese of America. "The Holy Eucharist." https://www.goarch.org/-/the-holy-eucharist?inheritRedirect=true&redirect=%2Fliturgy.

Greek Orthodox Archdiocese of America. "The Sacrament of Holy Unction by the Right Reverend Michael D. Jordan." http://www.st-seraphim.com/unction.htm.

Greek Orthodox Archdiocese of America. “The Sacrament of Holy Unction: Holy Wednesday Afternoon and Evening, Holy Unction.” https://www.goarch.org/holyunction.

Hainsworth, Fr. John. “Antiochian Orthodox Christian Archdiocese of North America, Infant Baptism: What the Church Believes.” http://www.antiochian.org/content/infant-baptism-what-church-believes.

“Hierarchy of Bishops.” http://www.astudyofdenominations.com/doctrines/positions/#bishops.

Hoffmann, Mark and Terry, Bruce; “English Bible Versions” - A Table of Literal > Paraphrase Scale of Bible Versions; mgvhoffmann CrossMarks.com; (https://docs.google.com/document/d/1-u-5nvjpFDQIMAEc7zTqM8lZLqqC3Eo2h6FEsR1z06g/edit?usp=sharing

“Holy Tradition.” https://holyapostles.org/holy-tradition.

“Holy Trinity in Christian Life.” OCA. http://oca.org/orthodoxy/the-orthodox-faith/doctrine/sources-of-christian-doctrine/the-holy-trinity-in-christian-life.

“Homosexual Resolutions: Salt Lake City, UT: Episcopal Church House of Bishops Passes Gay Marriage Resolutions.” https://www.virtueonline.org/salt-lake-city-ut-episcopal-church-house-bishops-passes-gay-marriage-resolutions.

Jackson, Wayne. 2012. *A New Testament Commentary.* Christian Courier Publications.

“King of Peace—Walk through a worship service.” http://www.kingofpeace.org/walkthrough.htm.

Longer Catechism of the Orthodox, Catholic, Eastern Church. http://www.pravoslavieto.com/docs/eng/Orthodox_Catechism_of_Philaret.htm.

Longhenry, Ethan. “A Study of Denominations—Eastern

Orthodoxy." http://www.astudyofdenominations.com/denominations/orthodoxy/#sthash.exdLEYS5.dpbs.

Luther, Martin. *Life of Luther*, 289.

Miller, Dave. 2006. *Piloting the Strait—A Guidebook for Assessing Change in the Churches of Christ.* Pulaski, TN: Sain Publications.

"On this Rock I will build my church—Q & A." http://oca.org/questions/history/on-this-rock-i-will-build-my-church.

Orthodox Christian Information Center. "The Doctrine of the Orthodox Church: The Structure of the Church, Clergy and Laity." http://orthodoxinfo.com/general/doctrine2.aspx.

Orthodox Christian Information Center. "Where Can One Go in an Orthodox Church?" http://orthodoxinfo.com/praxis/holyspace.aspx.

Orthodox Church in America. "Original Christian Church; Question and Answer." http://oca.org/questions/history/the-original-christian-church.

Orthodox Church in America. "Original Sin, Q & A." http://oca.org/questions/teaching/original-sin.

Orthodox Church in America. "Questions & Answers about Orthodoxy, Sinlessness of Mary" http://www.oca.org/QAPrintable.asp?ID=116.

Orthodox Church in America. "Questions and Answers, Questions of the Sacraments." http://oca.org/questions/sevensacraments/questions-on-the-sacraments.

Orthodox Church in America. "Spirituality; Orthodox Spirituality, The Sacraments." http://oca.org/orthodoxy/the-orthodox-faith/doctrine/sources-of-christian-doctrine/the-sacraments1.

Orthodox Church in America. "Spirituality, The Kingdom of Heaven,

Heaven and Hell." http://oca.org/orthodoxy/the-orthodox-faith/doctrine/sources-of-christian-doctrine/heaven-and-hell.

Orthodox Church in America "Symbol of Faith, Eternal Life." http://oca.org/orthodoxy/the-orthodox-faith/doctrine/sources-of-christian-doctrine/eternal-life.

Orthodox Church in America "Volume II – Worship; The Divine Liturgy, Prothesis." https://www.oca.org/orthodoxy/the-orthodox-faith/worship/the-divine-liturgy/prothesis.

Orthodox Church in America "Volume II – Worship; The Divine Liturgy, Offertory: Great Entrance." https://www.oca.org/orthodoxy/the-orthodox-faith/worship/the-divine-liturgy/offertory-great-entrance.

Orthodox Church in America "Volume II – Worship; The Divine Liturgy, Love and Faith." https://www.oca.org/orthodoxy/the-orthodox-faith/worship/the-divine-liturgy/love-and-faith.

Orthodox Church in America "Volume II – Worship; The Divine Liturgy, Eucharistic Canon: Anaphora." https://www.oca.org/orthodoxy/the-orthodox-faith/worship/the-divine-liturgy/eucharistic-canon-anaphora.

Orthodox Church in America "Volume II – Worship; The Divine Liturgy, Epiklesis." https://www.oca.org/orthodoxy/the-orthodox-faith/worship/the-divine-liturgy/epiklesis.

Orthodox Church in America "Volume II – Worship; The Divine Liturgy, Remembrances." https://www.oca.org/orthodoxy/the-orthodox-faith/worship/the-divine-liturgy/rememberances.

Orthodox Church in America "Volume II – Worship; The Divine Liturgy, Our Father." https://www.oca.org/orthodoxy/the-orthodox-faith/worship/the-divine-liturgy/our-father.

Orthodox Church in America "Volume II – Worship; The

Divine Liturgy, Communion." https://www.oca.org/orthodoxy/the-orthodox-faith/worship/the-divine-liturgy/communion.

Orthodox Church in America "Volume II – Worship; The Divine Liturgy, Thanksgiving." https://www.oca.org/orthodoxy/the-orthodox-faith/worship/the-divine-liturgy/thanksgiving.

Orthodox Church in America "Volume II – Worship; The Divine Liturgy, The Benediction and Dismissal." https://www.oca.org/orthodoxy/the-orthodox-faith/worship/the-divine-liturgy/benediction-and-dismissal.

Orthodox Church in America. "Worship; The Church Building." https://oca.org/orthodoxy/the-orthodox-faith/worship/the-church-building/church-building.

Orthodox Church in America. "Worship, The Sacraments, Baptism." http://oca.org/orthodoxy/the-orthodox-faith/worship/the-sacraments/baptism.

Orthodox Church in America. "Worship, The Sacraments, Chrismation." http://oca.org/orthodoxy/the-orthodox-faith/doctrine/sources-or-christian-doctrine/chrismation.

Orthodox Church in America. "Worship, The Sacraments, Holy Eucharist." http://oca.org/orthodoxy/the-orthodox-faith/worship/the-sacraments/holy-eucharist.

Orthodox Church in America. "Worship, The Sacraments, Holy Orders." http://oca.org/orthodoxy/the-orthodox-faith/doctrine/sources-of-christian-doctrine/holy-orders.

Orthodox Church in America. "Worship, The Sacraments, Marriage." http://oca.org/orthodoxy/the-orthodox-faith/worship/the-sacraments/marriage.

Orthodox Church in America. "Worship, The Sacraments,

Penance" http://oca.org/orthodoxy/the-orthodox-faith/doctrine/sources-of-christian-doctrine/penance.

Papadakin, Aristeides. "History of the Orthodox Church—Heresies and Ecumenical Councils." https://www.goarch.org/-/history-of-the-orthodox-church?inheritRedirect=true.

"Quinisext or Trullan Council (Canons)." http://www.intratext.com/IXT/ENG0835.

"Resolutions against Racism: Archbishops Desmond Tutu and Ted Scott, RE: Apartheid in South Africa." http://www.episcopalchurch.org/search/site/apartheid?page=4; http://www.episcopalchurch.org/search/site/apartheid percent2520Ted percent2520Scott.

Rev. Ellen Barrett. https://www.lgbtran.org/Profile.aspx?ID=226.

"Rule of Fasting in the Orthodox Church by Father Seraphim (Rose) of Platina." http://orthodoxinfo.com/praxis/father-seraphim-rose-fasting-rules.aspx.

"Second Ecumenical Council." http://www.goarch.org/ourfaith/ourfaith8065.

Seventieth General Convention of the Episcopal Church. 1991. "The Removal of Racism from the Life of the Nation." https://www.episcopalarchives.org/cgi-bin/acts/acts_search.pl.

Seventy-Fourth General Convention. "Resolution 2003–C051." http://www.episcopalarchives.org/cgi-bin/acts/acts_resolution.pl?resolution=1991–A104.

Seventy-Sixth General Convention. "Referred to racism as sin (2009–A142)." https://episcopalarchives.org/cgi-bin/acts/acts_topic_search.pl?topic=Racism.

"Short Summaries of the Ecumenical Councils." https://

churchmotherofgod.org/articleschurch/articles-about-the-orthodox-church/2259–short-summaries-of-the-ecumenical-councils.html.

"Sixth Ecumenical Council." http://www.goarch.org/ourfaith/ourfaith8069.

The Episcopal Church. "Authority, Sources of (in Anglicanism)." Accessed 9/14/18. https://www.episcopalchurch.org/glossary/authority-sources-of-in-anglicanism.

St. John the Baptist Greek Orthodox Church, Carmel-by-the-sea, CA; "Receiving Communion"; https://www.stjohn-monterey.org/our-faith/communion.

"Teachings of the Orthodox Church." www.goarch.org/ourfaith/ourfaith7062. (Rev. Fr. Thomas Fitzgerald)

"The Divine Services", Seraphim Slobodskoy; May 22, 2020, May 29, 2020; The Church Building and Its Arrangement.

https://maximologia.org/2020/05/22/the-divine-services-by-seraphim-slobodskoy/

"The Priest is Responsible for the Eucharist." www.catholic.org/featured/headline.php?ID=274.

"The Trinity, Q & A." http://oca.org/questions/teaching/the-trinity.

"Third Ecumenical Council." http://www.goarch.org/ourfaith/ourfaith8066.

Thompson, Bert, and Brad Harrub. 2003. *Investigating Christian Evidences – A Study Course.* Montgomery, AL: Apologetics Press.

"Tradition in the Orthodox Church." www.goarch.org/ourfaith/ourfaith7116.

Ware, Timothy. "The Orthodox Church—Faith and Works, Q & A." The Orthodox Church in America. http://oca.org/questions/teaching/faith-and-works.

"Why Do We Use Communion Spoons?"; Fr. John Whiteford, News, Comments, & Reflections; 3/28/2016; https://orthochristian.com/91947.html...

Butt, Kyle, MA, "*What the Bible says about the Lutheran Church*", Apologetics Press, Inc. Montgomery, Alabama 36117-2752; 2005.

Rose Publishing, Inc., 2005 Research, Inc.; PowerPoint: *"Denominations Comparison – Lutheran Church"* www.rose-publishing.com

Stork, Theophilus (1858), *The Life of Martin Luther and the Reformation in Germany* (Philadelphia, PA: Lindsay and Blakiston).

Webster's New World Dictionary, 3rd College Edition, 1988, Simon & Schuster, Inc., pg.1358

The Lutheran Church – Missouri Synod: Brief Statement of the Doctrinal Position of the Missouri Synod, Adopted 1932, "*Of the Holy Scriptures*" pp. 1 (https://www.lcms.org/about/beliefs/doctrine/brief-statement-of-lcms-doctrinal-position)

ELCA – Synods (https://www.elca.org/About/Synods)

ELCA – "Almost 61 Million Lutherans in the World" (https://elca.org/News-and-Events/2731)

The Lutheran World Federation – A Communion of Churches; LWF membership represents over 77 million Christians in the Lutheran tradition in 99 countries across the globe; (https://www.lutheranworld.org/content/member-churches)

Lutheran Church – Missouri Synod (https://www.britannica.com/topic/Lutheran-Church-Missouri-Synod)

The Lutheran Church Missouri Synod; About the President; (https://www.lcms.org/about/leadership/president/biography)

The Lutheran Church Missouri Synod; Partner Church Bodies; (https://www.lcms.org/how-we-serve/international/partner-church-bodies)

Wisconsin Evangelical Lutheran Synod Church, United States; (https://www.britannica.com/topic/church-Christianity)

WELS 2016 District Conventions; (https://wels.net/wels-2016-district-conventions/)

WELS, What We Believe – Doctrinal Statements; (https://wels.net/about-wels/what-we-believe/doctrinal-statements/#toggle-id-8)

WELS, History – Leadership; (https://wels.net/about-wels/history/leadership/)

WELS, Who We Are – Synod Administration; (https://wels.net/about-wels/who-we-are/#toggle-id-23)

ELCA – "*Constitutions, Bylaws, and Continuing Resolutions of the Evangelical Lutheran Church in America*", Adopted April 30, 1987, Edition current April 2018; "*Introduction*", pg. 9;

Chapter 2 – "Confessions of Faith" (2.07).

LCMS – The Lutheran Confessions – What are the Lutheran Confessions? (https://www.lcms.org/about/beliefs/lutheran-confessions)

Belief and Practice – The Lutheran Church – Missouri Synod, *"What About … The Difference Between the ELCA and the LCMS."*; (https://www.lcms.org/about/beliefs)

Kolb, Robert, and Timothy J. Wengert, eds. *The Book of Concord: The Confessions of the Evangelical Lutheran Church.* Minneapolis, Minnesota: Fortress Press, 2000.

Evangelical Lutheran Church in America; Model Constitution for Congregations of the Evangelical Lutheran Church in America; Chapter 9 – *The Pastor*, C9.02 (Constitutions, Bylaws, and Continuing Resolutions of the Evangelical Lutheran Church in America, Edition current as of September 2011 – Model Constitution for Congregations, Chapter 9).

Evangelical Lutheran Church in America; Constitutions, Bylaws, and Continuing Resolutions of the Evangelical Lutheran Church in America – as adopted by the Constituting Convention of the ELCA (April 30, 1987 and as amended (through the Twelfth (2011) – Church wide Assemblies of the ELCA; Chapter 7 – *Ministry*; 7.31.13 (Preparation and Approval) Sections c and d; p. 28.

LCMS Frequently Asked Questions, Doctrinal Issues – Baptism, "*Baptism and its purpose*" Doctrine – Baptism (pdf). https://www.lcms.org/about/beliefs/faqs/doctrine#baptism)

Belief and Practice – The Lutheran Church – Missouri Synod; Faith Alone, SOLA FIDE. (https://www.lcms.org/about/beliefs)

Luther's Large Catechism Fourth Part: Of Baptism #6; *Book of Concord: The Confessions of the Evangelical Lutheran Church* (2000), Robert Kolb and Timothy Wenger teds, trans. Charles Arand, Eric Gritsch, et al. (Minneapolis, MN: Fortress Press).

LCMS Frequently Asked Questions, "Baptism and its Purpose"; "Why do Lutherans use the "Sprinkle" method for Baptism?", (http://www.lcms.org/faqs/doctrine#baptism)

The Use of the Means of Grace – A Statement on the Practice of Word and Sacrament, Adopted for Guidance and Practice (by the) Evangelical Lutheran Church In America; Part 2 – *Holy Baptism and the Christian Assembly – Water is Used Generously*, 26 / 26A.

LCMS Frequently Asked Questions, Doctrinal Issues – Baptism, "*Why baptize infants*" (pp. 13); Infant Baptism History (pp 7). Doctrine – Baptism (pdf). https://www.lcms.org/about/beliefs/faqs/doctrine#baptism

Longhenry, Ethan, "A Study of Denominations" / *"Lutheranism"*,

(http://www.astudyofdenominations.com/denominations/lutheranism/#sthash.LjtzBdvS.dpbs)

"Comparison of Old Testament with the Words of Jesus"; Life Application Study Bible, New American Standard Bible – Updated Edition, Zondervan, 2000, pg. 137, *"Jesus and the Ten Commandments"*

The Lutheran Church – Missouri Synod: Frequently Asked Questions, The Lord's Supper, *"Q: What verses in Scripture can be cited that teach "that BOTH bread and wine AND Christ's true body and blood" are present in the Lord's Supper?"* (https://www.lcms.org/about/beliefs/faqs/doctrine)

ELCA, Worship Resources: Frequently Asked Questions -*Why and how do we move to weekly communion*?(http://download.elca.org/ELCA%20Resource%20Repository/Why and how do we move to weekly Communion.pdf? ga=2.26852669.1423621492.1586812801-1359316336.1586812801)

The Lutheran Church – Missouri Synod: A Brief Statement of the Doctrinal Position of the Missouri Synod; *"Of the Election of Grace"*, Sect. 35 & 37. (www.lcms.org/doctrine/doctrinalposition#electionofgrace)

Miller, Dave, Ph.D., "Piloting the Strait, A Guidebook For Assessing Change In Churches of Christ"; Eighth Printing, 2006; Sain Publications, Pulaski, TN.; "Are We Saved By Grace Alone?, pp. 307–313.

Belief and Practice – The Lutheran Church – Missouri Synod, Beliefs and Practices; *"What About … Confession and Absolution."*; http://www.lcms.org/about/beliefs

ELCA Roster Database, Prepared by ELCA Research and Evaluation, Feb. 2013; "Fact Sheet About Ordained Women" (elca.org)

ELCA News Service, August 14, 2005; ELCA Assembly Celebrates Women In Ministry;

(http://www.elca.org/News-and-Events/5525?_ga=2.21599480.259335174.1534855905-1707630997.1534615193)

Belief and Practice – The Lutheran Church – Missouri Synod, Beliefs and Practices; *"What About … The Ordination of Women to the Pastoral Office"*; http://www.lcms.org/about/beliefs

Male Spiritual Leadership, by F. LaGard Smith; Published by 21st Century Christian, 1998.

Belief and Practice – The Lutheran Church – Missouri Synod, *"What About … Homosexuality"* (http://www.lcms.org/about/beliefs)

ELCA News Service, August 21, 2009 – "ELCA Assembly Opens Ministry to Partnered Gay and Lesbian Lutherans (09-CWA-34-CA); (https://www.elca.org/News-and-Events/6587)

ELCA – Candidacy Manual, Adopted by the Church Council November 2016 (revised June 1, 2020); Section 1.8: *Guidelines for People in Same-Gender Relationships.* (ELCA.org – pdf)

ELCA "*The Church and Homosexuality*"; John Wickham, 08/01/2004; (http://www.elca.org/JLE/Articles/742?_ga=2.259396617.261821120.1534856161-593350227.1534606020)

Belief and Practice – The Lutheran Church – Missouri Synod, *"What About … Abortion"*; http://www.lcms.org/about/beliefs

ELCA – Faith and Society, PDF – Social Teaching Statement adopted by majority vote at Churchwide Assembly of ELCA meeting in Orlando, FL, August 28 – Sept. 4, 1991; "Abortion"; *Social Statement Summary* PDF; Section IV: "*Guidance in Making Decisions Regarding Unintended Pregnancies*" (http://elca.org)

"*Abortion and the Bible*" by Dave Miller, Apologetics Press, (www.apologeticspress.org)

"*The Origin of the Soul*", Lesson 7; Apologetics Press Intermediate Christian Evidences Correspondence Course – Bert Thompson, Ph.D. and Eric Lyons, M. Min.

ELCA – Ecumenism*: "The Vision of the ELCA*" (PDF); (http://www.elca.org)

ELCA – "*Conciliar Relations*": Christian Churches Together; Church World Service; Churches Uniting in Christ; Lutheran World Federation; National Council of the Churches of Christ; Would Council of Churches; *Joint Declaration on the Doctrine of Justification'* (Roman Catholic Church); (http://www.elca.org)

ELCA – Ecumenism: "Bilateral Conversations"; (http://www.elca.org)

Trinity Evangelical Lutheran Church, Latrobe, Pa; Worship Services / Worship Bulletin (Oct. 17, 18, 22, 2020 / Leadership and Staff; (https://trinitylatrobe.com/worship-bulletin/)

Nairobi Statement on Worship and Culture: 6. Challenge to the Churches https://worship.calvin.edu/resources/resource-library/nairobi-statement-on-worship-and-culture-full-text)

"Lutheran Worship 2000 and Beyond", *Seven Theses on Lutheran Worship,* by Dr. A.L. Barry,

Board of Elders – Holy Cross Lutheran Church, Arlington, TX; (http://www.lcms.org/document.fdoc?src=lcm&id=885)

Lutheran Church-Missouri Synod, February 1998; (Thesis I: "The Main Purpose of Lutheran Worship Is to Receive God's Gifts"; (http://www.lcms.org/lutheran-worship-2000-and-beyond)

The Lutheran Church of Australia, "How Lutherans Worship / The Lutheran Worship Service – "God, the Center of Worship"; Music in the Church. (https://www.lca.org.au/about-us/how-lutherans-worship/)

The Lutheran Church, Missouri Synod - Frequently Asked Questions – Worship & Congregational Life - "*What is the role of elders in a congregation?*" (http://www.lcms.org/faqs/worship#elders)

Butt, Kyle, MA, "*What the Bible says about the Lutheran Church*", Apologetics Press, Inc. 230 Landmark Drive, Montgomery, Alabama 36117–2752; 2005 (pg.18).

Luther's Large Catechism Fourth Part: Of Baptism #6; *Book of Concord: The Confessions of the Evangelical Lutheran Church* (2000), Robert Kolb and Timothy Wenger teds, trans. Charles Arand, Eric Gritsch, et al. (Minneapolis, MN: Fortress Press).

LCMS Frequently Asked Questions, Doctrinal Issues – Baptism, "*Baptism and its purpose*" (pp 2); "*Why baptize infants*" (pp. 13); Infant Baptism History (pp 7). (https://www.lcms.org/about/beliefs/faqs/doctrine) - Doctrine – Baptism (pdf).

Jackson, Wayne; "*The Bible Translation Controversy – Expanded Edition*"; Stockton, CA; (http://www.christiancourier.com)

English Bible Translations: "*English Bible Translations – Rated on a scale of 1 to 10 as to Literalness*". https://docs.google.com/document/d/1-u-5nvjpFDQIMAEc7zTqM8lZLqqC3Eo2h6FEsR1z06g/edit?usp=sharing

ENDNOTES

INTRODUCTION

1 Apologetics Press, Inc.; 230 Landmark Dr., Montgomery, AL 36117-2752; www.apologeticspress.org

CHAPTER 1 – THE ORTHODOX CHURCHES

1 Rose Publishing, PowerPoint, "Denominations Comparison," (2005), RW Research, Inc., "Distributions US/World."

2 "First among Equals" or *'primus inter pares'* (Latin), indicates the supreme spiritual leader. The current (2023) primus inter pares for the Eastern Orthodox Church worldwide is Archbishop Bartholomew I of Constantinople. (https://en.wikipedia.org/wiki/Bartholomew_I_of_Constantinople)

3 "Continuity of faith" - Teachings of the Orthodox Church; Rev. Thomas Fitzgerald - https://www.goarch.org/-/teachings-of-the-orthodox-church)

4 "Reverend [sic]" or "Rt. Reverend" – the author disagrees with the title per Matthew 23:9.

5 OCA; "The Original Christian Church"; Question and Answer. https://www.oca.org/questions/history/the-original-christian-church

6 Apostolic Succession: 'Thoughts in Christ' by Fr. Vladimir Berzonsky, "To Qualify as an Apostle"; (http://oca.org/reflections/berzonsky/to-qualify-as-an-apostle)

7 Tradition in the Orthodox Church; Dr. George Bebis; 8/13/98; www.goarch.org/ourfaith/ourfaith7116

8 () Added by the author for clarity.

9 Jackson, Wayne; "Man of Sin" – 2 Thessalonians 2:3-4; *"A New Testament Commentary"*, 2nd Edition, 2012, Christian Courier Publications; pp. 443

10 10. **Bold** or underline added by the author for emphasis/clarity.

11 "What the Early Church Believed: Bishop, Priest, and Deacon;" Catholic Answers; Holy Orders; Ignatius of Antioch; http://www.catholic.com/tract/bishop-priest-and-deacon; (Letter to the Magnesians 2 [A.D. 110]).

12 Orthodox Church in America, "Vol. 2 – Worship, The Sacraments, Holy Orders"; (http://oca.org/orthodoxy/the-orthodox-faith/doctrine/sources-of-christian-doctrine/holy-orders)

13 "Father [sic]" - the author disagrees with the title per Matthew 23:9.

14 "One Shepherd, Many Flocks," Orthodox Church in America, Fr. Vladimir Berzonsky, Dec. 26, 2004; (https://oca.org/reflections/berzonsky/one-shepherd-many-flocks)

15 OCA; "On this Rock I will build my church;" Q & A – (http://oca.org/questions/history/on-this-rock-i-will-build-my-church)

16 History of the Orthodox Church by Aristeides Papadakin, Ph.D.; "Early Administrative Structure," "Heresies and Ecumenical Councils," and "The Pentarchy"; (https://www.goarch.org/-/history-of-the-orthodox-church?inheritRedirect=true)

17 Greek Orthodox Archdiocese of America; "An Outline of the Orthodox Faith," 8/25/90; (https://www.goarch.org/-/an-outline-of-the-orthodox-faith?inheritRe)

18 OCA; Volume I – Doctrine and Scripture; Sources of Christian Doctrine; "Tradition;" (https://www.oca.org/orthodoxy/the-orthodox-faith/doctrine-scripture/sources-of-christian-doctrine/tradition).

19 Teachings of the Orthodox Church; "Councils and Creed," "Tradition;" Rev. Thomas Fitzgerald - https://www.goarch.org/-/teachings-of-the-orthodox-church.

20 20. OCA; Volume I – Doctrine and Scripture; Sources of Christian Doctrine; "The Fathers;" https://www.oca.org/orthodoxy/the-orthodox-faith/doctrine-scripture/sources-of-christian-doctrine/the-fathers

21 Holy Apostles Orthodox Church; Holy Tradition and the Scriptures; https://holyapostles.org/holy-tradition.

22 Greek Orthodox Archdiocese of America; Tradition in the Orthodox Church; George Bebis, Ph.D. 8/13/98; "The Ecumenical Councils – Acta Concil. II, 1. Sabas" https://www.goarch.org/-/tradition-in-the-orthodox-church

23 Orthodox Church in America; Volume I - Sources of Christian Doctrine: "The Councils;" www.oca.org/orthodoxy/the-orthodox-faith/doctrine-scripture/sources-of-christian-doctrine/the-councils.

24 1 Peter 1:24-25: Isaiah 40:7-8

25 Lightfoot, Neil R., "How We Got the Bible"; 3rd Edition; Baker Books; 2003, "The Canon of the Scriptures", pp 153.

26 The Holy Canons of the Orthodox Church - Including the Jurisdictional Canons and Guidelines of the Exarchate of Nebraska by Rt. Rev. Mar Melchizedek; EAC Publications, 2018; The First Ecumenical Council, "The Canons of the 318 Holy Fathers Assembled in the City of Nicea in Bithynia" (Pgs. 13-16).

27 The Ecumenical Councils of the Orthodox Church; Adapted from an essay by the Late Rev N. Patrinacos; The Second Ecumenical Council; The Nicene Creed – (Councils 1 & 2). http://www.orthodoxchristian.info/pages/Ecumenical_Councils.htm

28 The Holy Canons of the Orthodox Church - Including the Jurisdictional Canons and Guidelines of the Exarchate of Nebraska by Rt. Rev. Mar Melchizedek; EAC Publications, 2018; The Second Ecumenical Council, "The First Council of Constantinople" (Pgs. 17-19).

29 The Holy Canons of the Orthodox Church - Including the Jurisdictional Canons and Guidelines of the Exarchate of Nebraska by Rt. Rev. Mar Melchizedek; EAC Publications, 2018; The Third Ecumenical Council, "The Council of Ephesus" (Pgs. 20-21).

30 Greek Orthodox Archdiocese of America; 8/24/89; The Third Ecumenical Council: (http://www.goarch.org/ourfaith/ourfaith8066)

31 OCA; Volume III – Church History, Fifth Century; The Fourth Ecumenical Council; https://www.oca.org/orthodoxy/the-orthodox-faith/church-history/fifth-century/the-fourth-ecumenical-council

32 The Ecumenical Councils of the Orthodox Church; Adapted from an essay by the late Very Rev N Patrinacos; Fourth Ecumenical Council; (http://www.orthodoxchristian.info/pages/Ecumenical_Councils.htm)

33 The Holy Canons of the Orthodox Church - Including the Jurisdictional Canons and Guidelines of the Exarchate of Nebraska by Rt. Rev. Mar Melchizedek; EAC Publications, 2018; The Fourth Ecumenical Council, "The Council of Chalcedon" (Pgs. 22-27).

34 OCA; Volume III – Church History; Sixth Century; The Fifth Ecumenical Council; https://www.oca.org/orthodoxy/the-orthodox-faith/church-history/sixth-century/the-fifth-ecumenical-council

35 Greek Orthodox Archdiocese of America; The Sixth Ecumenical Council; Published 8/11/85; The Council's Pronouncement; https://www.goarch.org/-/the-sixth-ecumenical-council

36 The Holy Canons of the Orthodox Church - Including the Jurisdictional Canons and Guidelines of the Exarchate of Nebraska by Rt. Rev. Mar Melchizedek; EAC Publications, 2018; The Sixth Ecumenical Council; The Third Council of Constantinople; Quinisext (or Quinisextine) i.e., Fifth-Sixth. (Pgs. 31-61)

37 The Ecumenical Councils of the Orthodox Church; Adapted from an essay by the late Very Rev N Patrinacos; Seventh Ecumenical Council; (http://www.orthodoxchristian.info/pages/Ecumenical_Councils.htm)

38 The Holy Canons of the Orthodox Church - Including the Jurisdictional Canons and Guidelines of the Exarchate of Nebraska by Rt. Rev. Mar Melchizedek; EAC Publications, 2018; The Seventh Ecumenical Council. (Pgs. 62-78)

39 (OCA; Volume I – Doctrine and Scripture; The Symbol of Faith; Man; https://www.oca.org/orthodoxy/the-orthodox-faith/doctrine-scripture/the-symbol-of-faith/man).
40 (OCA; The Trinity; Q and A; https://www.oca.org/questions/teaching/the-trinity).
41 OCA; "Thoughts in Christ" by Fr. Vladimir Berzonsky, The Most Precious Promise; Nov. 27, 2005; (http://oca.org/reflections/berzonsky/the-most-precious-promise)
42 OCA; Volume I – Doctrine and Scripture; The Symbol of Faith; Man; https://www.oca.org/orthodoxy/the-orthodox-faith/doctrine-scripture/the-symbol-of-faith/man).
43 OCA; The Orthodox Faith; Volume I – The Holy Trinity; The Holy Trinity in Christian Life; https://www.oca.org/orthodoxy/the-orthodox-faith/doctrine-scripture/the-holy-trinity/the-holy-trinity-in-christian-life).
44 Ware, Timothy, The Orthodox Church, pp. 219
45 OCA; Volume I – Doctrine and Scripture; The Symbol of Faith; Eternal Life; (http://oca.org/orthodoxy/the-orthodox-faith/doctrine/sources-of-christian-doctrine/eternal-life)
46 J.W. McGarvey (no date), The Fourfold Gospel (Cincinnati, OH; Standard), p. 487.
47 OCA; The Orthodox Faith; Faith and Works, Q & A (http://oca.org/questions/teaching/faith-and-works)
48 'Life in Christ' by Fr. John Breck, Salvation is Indeed By Grace (http://oca.org/reflections/fr.-john-breck/salvation-is-indeed-by-grace)
49 OCA; Work of the Church; 'Life in Christ by Fr. John Breck, On Preaching Judgment (Part 1); July 2, 2002; (http://oca.org/reflections/fr.-john-breckWork of the /on-preaching-judgment-part-1)
50 Purgatory; St. Basil the Great – "Prayers for Pentecost" https://www.ccel.org/s/schaff/encyc/encyc09/htm/iv.v.xcvi.htm
51 OCA; Work of the Church; "May We Pray for the Departed?"; Life in Christ, by Fr. John Breck; (http://oca.org/reflections/fr.-john-breck/may-we-pray-for-the-departed)
52 Orthodox Church in America, Volume IV – Spirituality, The Kingdom of Heaven, Heaven and Hell (http://oca.org/orthodoxy/the-orthodox-faith/doctrine/sources-of-christian-doctrine/heaven-and-hell)
53 Lugger, John; "Denominations: From God Or Man? (Volume One)"; Re-published May 8, 2024, by AuthorHouse; Chapter 3 – The Roman Catholic Church, "The Authority of the Roman Catholic Church," The Apocryphal books – Pgs. 159-165.

54 Jackson, Wayne, "A New Testament Commentary," 2nd Edition, 2012, Christian Courier Publications; (2 Timothy Chapter 1, (15-18) Examples – Bad and Good, pp. 463, 464.

55 OCA, "Life in Christ" by Fr. John Breck, Jan. 1, 2010, Baptism in Christ (http://oca.org/reflections/fr.-john-breck/baptism-in-christ)

56 OCA, Volume II – Worship, The Sacraments, Baptism (http://oca.org/orthodoxy/the-orthodox-faith/worship/the-sacraments/baptism)

57 The Longer Catechism of the Orthodox, Catholic, Eastern Church, Article X on Baptism, #291–295 (http://www.pravoslavieto.com/docs/eng/Orthodox_Catechism_of_Philaret.htm#ii.xv.iii.i.p41)

58 Antiochian Orthodox Christian Archdiocese of North America, *Infant Baptism: What the Church Believes* – by Fr. John Hainsworth (http://www.antiochian.org/content/infant-baptism-what-church-believes)

59 Lugger, John; "Denominations: From God Or Man? (Volume One)"; Re-publication by AuthorHouse May 8, 2024. Appendix – "Defending the Inspiration of Scripture; "Internal Evidence – Scientific Foreknowledge - Medicine" (pp. 356-357).

60 Orthodox Church in America, Volume II – Worship, The Sacraments, Chrismation (http://oca.org/orthodoxy/the-orthodox-faith/doctrine/sources-or-christian-doctrine/chrismation)

61 Orthodox Church in America, Volume II – Worship, The Sacraments, Holy Eucharist (http://oca.org/orthodoxy/the-orthodox-faith/worship/the-sacraments/holy-eucharist)

62 OCA, Volume II – Worship, The Sacraments, Penance (http://oca.org/orthodoxy/the-orthodox-faith/doctrine/sources-of-christian-doctrine/penance)

63 Orthodox Reformed Bridge; Concerning Eternal Marriage, Robert Arakaki, May 16, 2014; (https://blogs.ancientfaith.com/orthodoxbridge/concerning-eternal-marriage/)

64 Orthodox Church in America, Volume II – Worship, The Sacraments, Marriage (http://oca.org/orthodoxy/the-orthodox-faith/worship/the-sacraments/marriage)

65 Greek Orthodox Archdiocese of America, The Sacrament of Holy Unction: Holy Wednesday Afternoon and Evening, "Holy Unction" (https://www.goarch.org/holyunction)

66 Greek Orthodox Archdiocese of America, The Sacrament of Holy Unction by the Right Reverend Michael D. Jordan (http://www.st-seraphim.com/unction.htm)

67 Orthodox Church in America, Volume II – Worship, The Sacraments, Holy Orders (http://oca.org/orthodoxy/the-orthodox-faith/doctrine/sources-of-christian-doctrine/holy-orders)

68 Orthodox Christian Information Center, The Doctrine of the Orthodox Church: The Structure of the Church, "Monasticism" (http://orthodoxinfo.com/general/doctrine2.aspx)

69 OCA; "May We Pray for the Departed?"; Life in Christ, by Fr. John Breck; (http://oca.org/reflections/fr.-john-breck/may-we-pray-for-the-departed)

70 OCA – Questions & Answers about Orthodoxy, "Sinlessness of Mary" (http://www.oca.org/QAPrintable.asp?ID=116)

71 OCA, "Thoughts in Christ" by Fr. Vladimir Berzonsky, Feb. 11, 2007, "Deesis" (http://oca.org/reflections/berzonsky/deesis)

72 Greek Orthodox Archdiocese of America; History of the Orthodox Church, Aristeides Papadakis, Ph.D., "The Iconoclastic Crisis" (https://www.goarch.org/-/history-of-the-orthodox-church?inheritRedirect=true)

73 Lugger, John; "Denominations: From God Or Man? (Volume One)"; Re-publication by AuthorHouse May 8, 2024; Chapter 3 - "The Roman Catholic Church, The Worship of Mary – Fourth Century AD, Mary, the "Mother of God" (pgs. 302-304).

74 Orthodox Church in America, "Life in Christ" by Fr. John Breck, March 1, 2007, "Why do we still fast?" (http://oca.org/reflections/fr.-john-breck/why-do-we-still-fast)

75 The Divine Services – Archpriest Seraphim Slobodskoy, The Church Building and its Arrangement (http://www.fatheralexander.org/booklets/english/church_services.htm)

76 "The Divine Services – The Clergy and Their Sacred Vestments; https://www.fatheralexander.org/booklets/english/church_services.htm.)

77 OCA; The Orthodox Faith; Volume II – Worship; The Divine Liturgy – The Divine Liturgy; https://www.oca.org/orthodoxy/the-orthodox-faith/worship/the-divine-liturgy/the-divine-liturgy

78 OCA; The Orthodox Faith; Volume II – Worship; The Divine Liturgy – The Divine Liturgy; https://www.oca.org/orthodoxy/the-orthodox-faith/worship/the-divine-liturgy/the-divine-liturgy

Prothesis: https://www.oca.org/orthodoxy/the-orthodox-faith/worship/the-divine-liturgy/prothesis

Blessed is The Kingdom: https://www.oca.org/orthodoxy/the-orthodox-faith/worship/the-divine-liturgy/blessed-is-the-kingdom

Great Litany: https://www.oca.org/orthodoxy/the-orthodox-faith/worship/the-divine-liturgy/great-litany

Antiphons: https://www.oca.org/orthodoxy/the-orthodox-faith/worship/the-divine-liturgy/antiphons

Small Entrance: https://www.oca.org/orthodoxy/the-orthodox-faith/worship/the-divine-liturgy/small-entrance

Epistle: https://www.oca.org/orthodoxy/the-orthodox-faith/worship/the-divine-liturgy/epistle

Gospel: https://www.oca.org/orthodoxy/the-orthodox-faith/worship/the-divine-liturgy/gospel

Fervent Supplication: https://www.oca.org/orthodoxy/the-orthodox-faith/worship/the-divine-liturgy/fervent-supplication

Offertory: Great Entrance: https://www.oca.org/orthodoxy/the-orthodox-faith/worship/the-divine-liturgy/offertory-great-entrance

Love and Faith: https://www.oca.org/orthodoxy/the-orthodox-faith/worship/the-divine-liturgy/love-and-faith

Eucharistic Canon: Anaphora: https://www.oca.org/orthodoxy/the-orthodox-faith/worship/the-divine-liturgy/eucharistic-canon-anaphora

Epiklesis: https://www.oca.org/orthodoxy/the-orthodox-faith/worship/the-divine-liturgy/epiklesis

Remembrances: https://www.oca.org/orthodoxy/the-orthodox-faith/worship/the-divine-liturgy/rememberances

Our Father: https://www.oca.org/orthodoxy/the-orthodox-faith/worship/the-divine-liturgy/our-father

Communion: https://www.oca.org/orthodoxy/the-orthodox-faith/worship/the-divine-liturgy/communion

Thanksgiving: https://www.oca.org/orthodoxy/the-orthodox-faith/worship/the-divine-liturgy/thanksgiving

Benediction and Dismissal: https://www.oca.org/orthodoxy/the-orthodox-faith/worship/the-divine-liturgy/benediction-and-dismissal

79 OCA: The Orthodox Faith; Volume II – Worship; The Diving Liturgy; Love and Faith; https://www.oca.org/orthodoxy/the-orthodox-faith/worship/the-divine-liturgy/love-and-faith

80 OCA; The Orthodox Faith; Volume II – Worship; The Divine Liturgy; Epiklesis; https://www.oca.org/orthodoxy/the-orthodox-faith/worship/the-divine-liturgy/epiklesis

81 OCA; The Orthodox Faith; Volume II – Worship; The Divine Liturgy; Communion; https://www.oca.org/orthodoxy/the-orthodox-faith/worship/the-divine-liturgy/communion

82 Greek Orthodox Archdiocese of America; Liturgy and Worship; The Holy Eucharist by Rev. Thomas Fitzgerald; https://www.goarch.org/-/the-holy-eucharist

83 St. John the Baptist Greek Orthodox Church, Greek Orthodox Metropolis of San Francisco; Carmel by the Sea, CA; Our Faith - Receiving Communion; https://www.stjohn-monterey.org/our-faith/communion

84 OCA: The Orthodox Faith; Volume II – Worship; The Divine Liturgy; Love and Faith; https://www.oca.org/orthodoxy/the-orthodox-faith/worship/the-divine-liturgy/love-and-faith
85 OCA; The Orthodox Faith; Volume II – Worship; The Divine Liturgy; Eucharistic Canon: Anaphora; https://www.oca.org/orthodoxy/the-orthodox-faith/worship/the-divine-liturgy/eucharistic-canon-anaphora
86 OCA; The Orthodox Faith; Volume II – Worship; The Divine Liturgy; Epiklesis; https://www.oca.org/orthodoxy/the-orthodox-faith/worship/the-divine-liturgy/epiklesis
87 Pinedo, Moises, "What the Bible says about the Catholic Church;" Apologetics Press, 2008; Chapter 2 – The Papacy, "Was Peter a Pope?" / "Who was Peter?'" (Pgs. 38-48).

CHAPTER 2 – THE EPISCOPAL CHURCH

1 The Anglican Domain; About Our Church; Church History; http://anglican.org/church/ChurchHistory.html
2 "Reverend / Most Reverend [sic]" - the author disagrees with the title(s) per Matthew 23:9.
3 The Book of Common Prayer; Historical Documents; Articles of Religion 867 (VI); https://www.bcponline.org
4 A Study of Denominations by Ethan Longhenry; Anglicanism/Episcopalianism; "The Book of Common Prayer"; https://www.astudyofdenominations.com/denominations/anglicanism/
5 An Episcopal Dictionary of the Church; Glossary of Terms; Authority, Sources of (in Anglicanism); https://www.episcopalchurch.org/glossary/authority-sources-of-in-anglicanism/
6 An Episcopal Dictionary of the Church; Glossary of Terms; Hooker, Richard; https://www.episcopalchurch.org/glossary/hooker-richard/
7 An Episcopal Dictionary of the Church; Glossary of Terms; Scripture; https://www.episcopalchurch.org/glossary/scripture/
8 Lugger, John; "Denominations: From God Or Man? (Volume One)"; Re-published by AuthorHouse May 8, 2024. Appendix – "Defending the Inspiration of Scripture; "The Canon of the Scriptures" (pp. 340-341); "Internal Evidence – Scientific Foreknowledge" (pp. 352-358).
9 Huston, Diann (Former member of the Church of Christ on Fishinger Road, Columbus, OH); deceased; Devotional forwarded by her daughter, Amber Huston, August 11, 2023.
10 National Academy of Sciences; "Teaching Evolution and the Nature of Science;" National Academy Press, Washington, DC; 1998; Pg. 5.

11 Thompson, Bert, Ph.D.; "The Case for Creation;' 1986; "The Laws of Probability;" Apologetic's Press; Pgs. 1-6
12 Morris, Henry M., Ph.D.; "The Twilight of Evolution;" Baker Books, Grand Rapids, MI., 1963, Pg. 26.
13 Bales, J.D., and Clark, R.T., "Why Scientists Accept Evolution;" 1966; Grand Rapids, MI.' Baker Books.
14 Watson, D.M.S.; "Adaption,"; Nature, 1929; page 223.
15 Thompson, Bert, Ph.D.; "The Case for Creation;" 1986; Apologetic's Press; "The Law of Biogenesis," Pg. 39; Kirk, David; (1975), *Biology Today* (New York: Random House).
16 Miller, Jeff, Ph.D., "Science vs. Evolution;" Apologetics Press, 2013; "The First and Second Laws of Thermodynamics" "The First Law;" pgs. 18-19.
17 Miller, Jeff, Ph.D., "Science vs. Evolution;" Apologetics Press, 2013; "The First and Second Laws of Thermodynamics" "The Second Law;" pgs. 20-21
18 Thompson, Bert, Ph.D.; "The Case for Creation;' 1986; "The Laws of Probability;" Apologetic's Press; Pg. 68.
19 Thompson, Bert, Ph.D.; "The Case for Creation;' 1986; "The Law of Cause and Effect;" Apologetic's Press; Pg. 31.
20 Miller, Jeff, Ph.D., "Science vs. Evolution;" Apologetics Press, 2013; "Genetics vs Evolution;" "Creating Information; A Prerequisite for Evolution;" Pg. 107.
21 Webster's New World Dictionary of American English; Third College Edition; Div. of Simon & Schuster, Inc.; 1988; CR 1991. (Definition of "logic").
22 Huse, Scott M.; "The Collapse of Evolution;" 3rd Edition, "The Geologic Column;" pgs. 55 57; Baker Books, 1997; Grand Rapids, MI; Distributed by Apologetic's Press.
23 Huse, Scott M.; "The Collapse of Evolution;" 3rd Edition, "Biology" "The Trilobite Eye;" Pg. 27; Baker Books, 1997; Grand Rapids, MI; Distributed by Apologetic's Press.
24 Gish, Duane T.; "The Amazing Story of Creation from Science and the Bible;" Institute for Creation Research, California, 1990, p. 104.
25 Shawver, Lisa, "Science News;" 1974; 105:72.
26 Levi-Setti, Riccardo; "Trilobites;" 1993, Pgs. 57-58.
27 Eldridge, Niles; (As quoted in "Ellis" – 2001, pg. 49.)
28 National Academy of Sciences; "Teaching Evolution and the Nature of Science;" National Academy Press, Washington, DC; 1998; Pg. 4.
29 National Academy of Sciences; "Teaching Evolution and the Nature of Science;" National Academy Press, Washington, DC; 1998; Pg. 56.
30 "The Scientific Case for Creation" by Bert Thompson, Ph.D.; Apologetics Press, Montgomery, AL; 1995; Chapter 4 (pgs. 31-38).

31 All comments in parentheses in the entire discussion of 'evolution,' both mixed into and aside from quoted text, are this author's comments/opinions. (Except for direct reference quotes).

32 Sarfati, Jonathan, Ph.D., F.M., "Refuting Evolution;" Master Books; First printing: May 1999, Seventh printing: October 1999; Follow-up Sequels, by Jonathan Sarfati, Ph.D., F.M., with Mike Matthews – "Refuting Evolution 2"; Master Books; First Printing: October 2003, Third Printing May 2003; And the Sequel "Refuting Evolution 2, Updated and Expanded;" Creation Book Publishers, P.O. Box 350, Powder Springs, GA 30127; Third edition: November 2013.

33 1662 Book of Common Prayer; Church of England – The Apostle's Creed; Original Text: "He went down into hell" [https://upload.wikimedia.org/wikipedia/commons/4/49/The_Book_of_Common_Prayer.pdf] – Pg. 273 (PDF) / Pg. 262 (Original Text); 1st revision: "He descended into hell" (Still the standard in Anglican doctrine, sourcing Roman Catholic Standard [https://www.catholic.org/prayers/prayer.php?p=220]; Also Episcopal Source per Glossary [https://www.episcopalchurch.org/glossary/apostles-creed-the/]; 2nd revision (2000 BCP) Episcopal Doctrine: "He descended to the dead;" The Episcopal Church, "What We Believe" "The Creeds" [https://www.episcopalchurch.org/what-we-believe/creeds/].

34 The Episcopal Church – "What We Believe" The Creeds; The Apostles' Creed; The Nicene Creed. [https://www.episcopalchurch.org/what-we-believe/creeds/].

35 Jackson, Wayne, "A New Testament Commentary," 2nd Edition, 2012, Christian Courier Publications; 1 Corinthians 8: (4-6) – Things Sacrificed to Idols; page 316.

36 Something Happened When I Prayed, by Dan Winkler; 2020; D & D Publishing, Huntington, TN; ESV used for text unless otherwise noted; Lesson 3, pages 19-20.

37 Pinedo, Moises, (The Pope, the Papacy, and the Bible), Apologetics Press, Inc., (2005), https://apologeticspress.org/the-pope-the-papacy-and-the-bible-626/

38 Longhenry, Ethan, "A Study of Denominations," Positions of Authority – Statement of Belief; A Hierarchy of Bishops; https://www.astudyofdenominations.com/doctrines/positions/#bishops

39 Longhenry, Ethan, "A Study of Denominations," Roman Catholicism, I: Authority; Apostolic Succession: https://www.astudyofdenominations.com/denominations/catholicism1/#apostolic

40 An Episcopal Dictionary of the Church; Glossary of Terms; Authority, Sources of (in Anglicanism; https://www.episcopalchurch.org/glossary/sacramentals/

41 The Episcopal Church – What We Believe; Core to Our Beliefs; The Sacraments; https://www.episcopalchurch.org/what-we-believe/

42 The word "be" was added by this author, as the statement omitted.

43 The Episcopal Church – What We Believe; Holy Baptism – Celebrating Baptism; https://www.episcopalchurch.org/what-we-believe/baptism/
44 An Episcopal Dictionary of the Church; Glossary of Terms; Baptism; https://www.episcopalchurch.org/glossary/baptism/
45 An Episcopal Dictionary of the Church; Glossary of Terms; Baptismal Covenant; https://www.episcopalchurch.org/glossary/baptismal-covenant/
46 An Episcopal Dictionary of the Church; Glossary of Terms; Baptismal Regeneration: https://www.episcopalchurch.org/glossary/baptismal-regeneration/
47 An Episcopal Dictionary of the Church; Glossary of Terms; Renewal of Baptismal Vows: https://www.episcopalchurch.org/glossary/renewal-of-baptismal-vows/
48 An Episcopal Dictionary of the Church; Glossary of Terms; Baptismal Feasts; https://www.episcopalchurch.org/glossary/baptismal-feasts/
49 Lugger, John; "Denominations: From God Or Man? (Volume One)"; Chapter Two – The Church of Christ; "One Church," (pgs. 56-61); Re-published by AuthorHouse May 8, 2024.
50 Lugger, John; "Denominations: From God Or Man? (Volume One)"; Re-published by AuthorHouse May 8, 2024. Chapter Two – The Church of Christ; "The Establishment of the Church of Christ," (pgs. 31- 50); Reference to "Hardeman – Bogard Debate, Little Rock, AR; April 19-22, 1938; "The Establishment of the Church." Gospel Advocate, Nashville, TN. (https://www.gospeladvocate.com)
51 The Episcopal Church – "What We Believe"; "The Eucharist, Holy Communion"; https://www.episcopalchurch.org/what-we-believe/communion/
52 Lugger, John; "Denominations: From God Or Man? (Volume One)"; Re-published by AuthorHouse May 8, 2024. Chapter Three – The Roman Catholic Church; "The Holy Eucharist (Communion)"; (pgs.212-224).
53 An Episcopal Dictionary of the Church; Glossary of Terms; Nicene Creed. https://www.episcopalchurch.org/glossary/nicene-creed/
54 () Added by the author
55 Jackson, Wayne, "A New Testament Commentary," 2nd Edition, 2012, Christian Courier Publications; John, Chapter 6 – (41-58, "Discourse on the Bread of Life;" (pgs.156-157).
56 An Episcopal Dictionary of the Church; Glossary of Terms; Eucharist. https://www.episcopalchurch.org/glossary/eucharist/
57 An Episcopal Dictionary of the Church; Glossary of Terms; Eucharistic Elements. https://www.episcopalchurch.org/glossary/eucharistic-elements/
58 Webster's New World Dictionary; Third Edition; 1988, Simon & Schuster, Inc. "Communion" (Pg. 282).
59 Spicer, Paul PH.D.; Email sent to author September 3, 2023.
60 An Episcopal Dictionary of the Church; Glossary of Terms; Sacramentals. https://www.episcopalchurch.org/glossary/sacramentals/

61 Lugger, John; "Denominations: From God Or Man? (Volume One)"; Re-published by AuthorHouse May 8, 2024. Chapter Three – The Roman Catholic Church; Primary Beliefs and Doctrines; The Sacrament of Confirmation (Pgs. 206-212); Auricular Confession/Sacrament of Penance (Pgs. 224-230); The Sacrament of Matrimony/Celibacy (Pgs. 251-270); The Sacrament of Holy Orders (Pgs. 167-178); The Sacrament of Extreme Unction (Pgs. 246-251).

62 An Episcopal Dictionary of the Church; Glossary of Terms; Confirmation. https://www.episcopalchurch.org/glossary/confirmation/

63 An Episcopal Dictionary of the Church; Glossary of Terms; Reconciliation of a Penitent. https://www.episcopalchurch.org/glossary/reconciliation-of-a-penitent/

64 An Episcopal Dictionary of the Church; Glossary of Terms; Confession of Sin. https://www.episcopalchurch.org/glossary/confession-of-sin/

65 Lugger, John; "Denominations: From God Or Man? (Volume One)"; Re-published by AuthorHouse May 8, 2024. Chapter Three – The Roman Catholic Church; Primary Beliefs and Doctrines; Auricular Confession/Sacrament of Penance (Page 227).

66 Lugger, John; "Denominations: From God Or Man? (Volume One)"; Re-published by AuthorHouse May 8, 2024. Chapter Three – The Roman Catholic Church; Primary Beliefs and Doctrines; Indulgences (Pgs. 236-246).

67 An Episcopal Dictionary of the Church; Glossary of Terms; Marriage. https://www.episcopalchurch.org/glossary/marriage/

68 An Episcopal Dictionary of the Church; Glossary of Terms; Celebration and Blessing of a Marriage. https://www.episcopalchurch.org/glossary/celebration-and-blessing-of-a-marriage/

69 Based on the OT 'Law of Witnesses' (Deuteronomy 19:15)

70 An Episcopal Dictionary of the Church; Glossary of Terms; Ordination. https://www.episcopalchurch.org/glossary/ordination/

71 The Book of Common Prayer, According to the use of The Episcopal Church; Church Publishing, Inc, New York; Gregory Michael Howe, Custodian of the Standard Book of Common Prayer, January, 2007; On-line, PDF; "Preface to the Ordination Rites", Pg. 510. https://www.episcopalchurch.org/wp-content/uploads/sites/2/2021/02/book-of-common-prayer-2006.pdf

72 The Book of Common Prayer, According to the use of The Episcopal Church; Church Publishing, Inc, New York; Gregory Michael Howe, Custodian of the Standard Book of Common Prayer, January, 2007; On-line, PDF; The Examination (Bishop - pp. 517-520). https://www.episcopalchurch.org/wp-content/uploads/sites/2/2021/02/book-of-common-prayer-2006.pdf

73 An Episcopal Dictionary of the Church; Glossary of Terms; Apostolic Succession. https://www.episcopalchurch.org/glossary/apostolic-succession/

74 An Episcopal Dictionary of the Church; Glossary of Terms; Historic Episcopate. https://www.episcopalchurch.org/glossary/historic-episcopate/
75 An Episcopal Dictionary of the Church; Glossary of Terms; Ordination of Women. https://www.episcopalchurch.org/glossary/ordination-of-women/
76 An Episcopal Dictionary of the Church; Glossary of Terms; Extreme Unction. https://www.episcopalchurch.org/glossary/extreme-unction/
77 An Episcopal Dictionary of the Church; Glossary of Terms; Ministration to the Sick. https://www.episcopalchurch.org/glossary/ministration-to-the-sick/
78 An Episcopal Dictionary of the Church; Glossary of Terms; Original Sin. https://www.episcopalchurch.org/glossary/original-sin/
79 An Episcopal Dictionary of the Church; Glossary of Terms; Salvation. https://www.episcopalchurch.org/glossary/salvation/
80 An Episcopal Dictionary of the Church; Glossary of Terms; Soteriology. https://www.episcopalchurch.org/glossary/soteriology/
81 An Episcopal Dictionary of the Church; Glossary of Terms; Righteousness. https://www.episcopalchurch.org/glossary/righteousness/
82 Lugger, John; "Denominations: From God Or Man (Volume One)"; Re-published by AuthorHouse May 8, 2024. Chapter Three – The Roman Catholic Church; Primary Beliefs and Doctrines; The Sacrament of Baptism/Salvation; Original Sin (Pgs. 193-198).
83 Paraphrased comments and quotes by the author.
84 Lugger, John; "Denominations: From God Or Man (Volume One)"; Re-published by AuthorHouse May 8, 2024. Chapter two – The Church of Christ; "Terms of Admission to Membership in Christ's Church;" (Pgs. 85-90).
85 Miller, Dave, Ph.D., *"Piloting the Strait, A Guidebook For Assessing Change In Churches of Christ";* Part IV – The Specifics of Change; Chapter 29, "Embracing Denominationalism;" IV. "Are We Saved By Grace – Alone?" (Pgs. 311-312); Eighth Printing, 2006; Sain Publications, Pulaski, TN.
86 Jackson, Wayne, "A New Testament Commentary," 2nd Edition, 2012, Christian Courier Publications; Luke Chapter 17; (20-21) The Coming Kingdom; (Pages 124-125).
87 Defending the Faith Study Bible (NKJV); Apologetics Press; 2019; Primary Writers: Kyle Butt, M.A., M.Div.; Eric Lyons, M.Min.; Dave Miller, M.A., M. Div., M.A.R., Ph.D.; Jeff Miller, M.S., Ph.D.; Commentary, Mark 9:1 (Pgs. 1815-1817).
88 Lugger, John; "Denominations: From God Or Man (Volume One)"; Re-published by AuthorHouse May 8, 2024. Chapter Three – The Roman Catholic Church; Primary Beliefs and Doctrines; "Veneration of Images and Relics" (Pgs. 270-276); "The Worship of Mary – Fourth Century AD" (Pgs. 277-304).
89 An Episcopal Dictionary of the Church; Glossary of Terms; Veneration. https://www.episcopalchurch.org/glossary/veneration/

90 An Episcopal Dictionary of the Church; Glossary of Terms; Veneration of Saints. https://www.episcopalchurch.org/glossary/veneration-of-saints/
91 An Episcopal Dictionary of the Church; Glossary of Terms; Mary the Virgin, Mother of Our Lord Jesus Christ, Saint. https://www.episcopalchurch.org/glossary/mary-the-virgin-mother-of-our-lord-jesus-christ-saint/
92 An Episcopal Dictionary of the Church; Glossary of Terms; Hail Mary. https://www.episcopalchurch.org/glossary/hail-mary/
93 An Episcopal Dictionary of the Church; Glossary of Terms; Veneration of the Cross. https://www.episcopalchurch.org/glossary/veneration-of-the-cross/
94 An Episcopal Dictionary of the Church; Glossary of Terms; Cross. https://www.episcopalchurch.org/glossary/cross/
95 Pinedo, Moises 2008. "What the Bible Says about the Catholic Church." Apologetics Press.
96 Apologetics Press, On-line Article - from January 2021 Reason & Revelation periodical;

"Homosexuality: Society, Science, & Psychology (Parts 2 & 3); by Jeff Miller, Ph. D.

https://apologeticspress.org/homosexuality-society-science-and-psychology-part-2-5909/

https://apologeticspress.org/homosexuality-society-science-and-psychology-part-3-5925/
97 St. John's Episcopal Church, Jackson, WY. https://www.stjohnsjackson.org/worship/
98 St. John's Episcopal Church, Jackson, WY.; Bulletin Sunday, Sept. 24, 2023. https://www.stjohnsjackson.org/uploads/images/sept-24-2023-10am_500.pdf
99 Lugger, John; "Denominations: From God Or Man (Volume One)"; Re-published by AuthorHouse May 8, 2024. Appendix: "Defending the Inspiration of Scripture" (Pgs. 333-358); Chapter Three – The Roman Catholic Church - "Apostolic Succession" (Pgs. 140-160; 167-178; 219; 247-249).

CHAPTER 3 – THE LUTHERAN CHURCH

1 "Indulgences" - https://www.catholic.com/encyclopedia/indulgences#VII._BASIS_OF_THE_DOCTRINE.
2 The 95 Theses of Martin Luther; Author: Martin Luthor; Bulletin Inserts.org; Articles 27, 50, and 51. https://bulletininserts.org/the-95-theses-of-martin-luther/#:~:text=27.,forever%20along%20with%20their%20teachers.
3 Stork, Theophilus (1858), The Life of Martin Luther and the Reformation in Germany; (Philadelphia, PA: Lindsay and Blakiston).

4 Webster's New World Dictionary, 3rd College Edition, 1988, Simon & Schuster, Inc., Definition of "Synod;" (pg. 1358).

5 "Reverend [sic]" - the author disagrees with the title per Matthew 23:9.

6 Evangelical Lutheran Church in America; Constitutions, Bylaws, and Continuing Resolutions of the Evangelical Lutheran Church in America – as adopted by the Constituting Convention of the ELCA (April 30, 1987, and as amended (April 2018) – Church-wide Assemblies of the ELCA; Chapter 7 – Ministry; (Standards for Ministers of Word and Sacrament) 7.30/7.31.02 (Sections a. and b.); (Preparation and Approval) 7.31.03 (Sections a - g); pgs. 28-29. https://download.elca.org/ELCA%20Resource%20Repository/Constitutions Bylaws and Continuing Resolutions of the ELCA.pdf?_ga=2.48425382.1665186178.1695935161-1784036654.1695926433

7 Lugger, John; "Denominations: From God Or Man? (Volume One)"; Re-published by AuthorHouse May 8, 2024. Chapter Three – The Roman Catholic Church; Primary Beliefs and Doctrines; Primary Beliefs and Doctrines; The Sacrament of Holy Orders (Pages 167-178).

8 The Lutheran Church – Missouri Synod: Brief Statement of the Doctrinal Position of the Missouri Synod, Adopted 1932, "Of the Holy Scriptures;" #1. (https://www.lcms.org/about/beliefs/doctrine/brief-statement-of-lcms-doctrinal-position#holy-scriptures)

9 The Lutheran Church – Missouri Synod; Statement of Scriptural and Confessional Principles; VI – Confessional Subscription. https://www.lcms.org/about/beliefs/doctrine/statement-of-scriptural-and-confessional-principles#VI (Underlining words by author).

10 Evangelical Lutheran Church in America; Constitutions, Bylaws, and Continuing Resolutions of the Evangelical Lutheran Church in America – as adopted by the Constituting Convention of the ELCA (April 30, 1987, and as amended (November 2022) – Church-wide Assemblies of the ELCA; Chapter 2 – "Confessions of Faith" (2.07). https://download.elca.org/ELCA%20rce%20Repository/Constitutions Bylaws and Continuing Resolutions of the ELCA.pdf (Bold/underlining words by author).

11 Evangelical Lutheran Church in America; Constitutions, Bylaws, and Continuing Resolutions of the Evangelical Lutheran Church in America – as adopted by the Constituting Convention of the ELCA (April 30, 1987, and as amended (November 2022); Introduction – Secretary Sue E. Rothmeyer, August 12, 2022. https://download.elca.org/ELCA%20Resource%20Repository/Constitutions Bylaws and Continuing Resolutions of the ELCA.pdf

12 WELS, What We Believe – Doctrinal Statements; (https://wels.net/about-wels/what-we-believe/doctrinal-statements/#toggle-id-8) (Underlining of words by author)

13 Barry, Dr. A.L., Past President, The Lutheran Church – Missouri Synod; What About – The Difference Between the ELCA and the LCMS? https://files.lcms.org/file/preview/L8e2Gjt87rWqodPoNpfP5lMUXuhzitFK

14 LCMS, About, Beliefs, Frequently Asked Questions – 2nd Question: "What are the main differences between The Lutheran Church – Missouri Synod and the Evangelical Lutheran Church in America (ELCA)? https://www.lcms.org/about/beliefs/faqs/denominations#elca-differences

15 Evangelical Lutheran Church in America; Constitutions, Bylaws, and Continuing Resolutions of the Evangelical Lutheran Church in America – as adopted by the Constituting Convention of the ELCA (April 30, 1987, and as amended (November 2022); Model Constitution for Congregations; Chapter 9 – Rostered Minister (C9.02. – Page 221). https://download.elca.org/ELCA%20Resource%20Repository/Constitutions_Bylaws_and_Continuing_Resolutions_of_the_ELCA.pdf

16 Evangelical Lutheran Church in America; Constitutions, Bylaws, and Continuing Resolutions of the Evangelical Lutheran Church in America – as adopted by the Constituting Convention of the ELCA (April 30, 1987, and as amended (November 2022); ELCA Constitution; Chapter 7, Ministry; Section 7.31.03. Preparation and Approval, (c., and d.) Page. 29. https://download.elca.org/ELCA%20Resource%20Repository/Constitutions_Bylaws_and_Continuing_Resolutions_of_the_ELCA.pdf

17 (Culture) - added by the author for clarity.

18 The Lutheran Church Missouri Synod; Belief and Practice - Being "Lutheran;" Faith Alone. https://www.lcms.org/about/beliefs

19 About the ELCA; What We Believe; ELCA Faith Tradition; What should I know about the ELCA faith tradition? What do Lutherans believe? https://www.elca.org/About/What-We-Believe/ELCA-Faith-Tradition?_ga=2.195752548.919961667.1696343003-1784036654.1695926433

20 Joint Declaration of the Doctrine of Justification, by the Lutheran World Federation and the Catholic Church; Section 3 - The Common Understanding of Justification, Sub-sections 15 & 16; Section 4.1 – Human Powerlessness and Sin in Relation to Justification, Sub-section 21. https://download.elca.org/ELCA%20Resource%20Repository/Joint_Declaration_on_the_Doctrine_of_Justification.pdf?_ga=2.154517232.919961667.1696343003-1784036654.1695926433

21 Luther's Large Catechism Fourth Part: Concerning Baptism #6; *Book of Concord: The Confessions of the Evangelical Lutheran Church* (2000), (Page 457); Robert Kolb and Timothy Wenger teds, trans. Charles Arand, Eric Gritsch, et al. (Minneapolis, MN: Fortress Press). https://files.lcms.org/file/preview/51843C79-B65E-4225-8B44-40CFE12C86E5

22 LCMS Frequently Asked Questions, "Baptism and its Purpose"; "Can you please clarify the Lutheran view of Baptism and its purpose? 2004; (http://www.lcms.org/faqs/doctrine#baptism)

23 The Use of the Means of Grace – A Statement on the Practice of Word and Sacrament, Adopted for Guidance and Practice (by the) Evangelical Lutheran Church In America; Part 2 – *Holy Baptism and the Christian Assembly – Water is Used Generously*, 26 / 26A. (Page 32). https://download.elca.org/ELCA%20Resource%20Repository/The_Use_Of_The_Means_Of_Grace.pdf?_ga=2.160251709.1098881710.1696522413-1784036654.1695926433

24 Butt, Kyle, MA, "*What the Bible says about the Lutheran Church,*" Appendix A –"What About the Thief on the Cross?"; "What must a person do to become a Christian?" Apologetics Press, Inc. 230 Landmark Drive, Montgomery, Alabama 36117-2752; 2005.

25 Lugger, John; "Denominations: From God Or Man? (Volume One)"; Republished by AuthorHouse May 8, 2024. Chapter Three – The Roman Catholic Church; Primary Beliefs and Doctrines; The Sacrament of Baptism/Salvation; Mode of Baptism (pgs. 198-205).

26 Carrell, Gene M., Minister, Church of Christ, Columbus, Ohio, "*The Lutheran Church*" (Teaching Outline), March 2007.

27 Added for clarity by the author

28 The Book of Concord, The Confessions of the Lutheran Faith; The Large Catechism; Holy Baptism, "Of Infant Baptism;" Sections 49, 50, 51, 52, & 53. http://old.bookofconcord.org/lc-6-baptism.php

29 LCMS Frequently Asked Questions - Doctrine, **"How does faith play a role in infant Baptism? Is faith later taken care of when the child is confirmed?"** https://www.lcms.org/about/beliefs/faqs/doctrine#faith

30 Emphasis (Bold or Underline) added by the author.

31 LCMS Frequently Asked Questions - Doctrine, "*Baptism and its purpose*" (pp 2); "Why do Lutherans baptize infants;" https://www.lcms.org/about/beliefs/faqs/doctrine#why

32 Just and Sinner, Infant Faith, Oct. 24, 2012; http://justandsinner.blogspot.com/2012/10/infant-faith.html

33 LCMS Frequently Asked Questions, Doctrinal Issues – Baptism, "*Baptism and its purpose*" (pg. 2); "Can you please clarify the Lutheran view of Baptism and its purpose? Does the child become a Christian when baptized?" https://www.lcms.org/about/beliefs/faqs/doctrine#purpose

34 LCMS Frequently Asked Questions – Doctrinal Issues – Baptism; "Infant Baptism History (2 pages); Q: "You say that infant baptism is ONE way of salvation. Since this practice was unknown in the New Testament or even the early Catholic Church, it is speculative. The Bible says that repentance is a

prerequisite for faith. I repented at five, so it can be early but not in someone's arms." (Pg. 7). https://www.lcms.org/about/beliefs/faqs/doctrine#history

35 Concordia Lutheran Church, "Why Should We Baptize Infants?" "The third objection: But infants can't have faith!" https://www.con35.cordiajt.org/sermons-resources/concordiajt.cfm

36 Lugger, John; "Denominations: From God Or Man? (Volume One)"; Re-published by AuthorHouse May 8, 2024. Chapter Three – The Roman Catholic Church; Primary Beliefs and Doctrines; The Sacrament of Baptism/Salvation; Original Sin (Pgs. 193-198).

37 Pinedo, Moises; Apologetics Press; Infant Baptism; https://apologeticspress.org/infant-baptism-2709/a

38 Jackson, Wayne, "A New Testament Commentary," 2nd Edition, 2012, Christian Courier Publications; Matthew (Chapter 18 – Verses 1-6); "Who is the Greatest in the Kingdom," (Page 41).

39 Lenski, R.C.H., "Commentary on the New Testament – The Interpretation of St. Matthew's Gospel;" Henderson Publishers, Inc.; First Printing – August 1998; Matthew 18:4 (Pg. 683; Matthew 18:6 (Pg. 687).

40 Boles, H. Leo; "A Commentary on The Gospel According to Matthew;" Gospel Advocate Co., Nashville, TN. 37202; 1979; Matthew 18:6-9 (Pg. 370).

41 Lugger, John; "Denominations: From God Or Man? (Volume One"; Re-published by AuthorHouse May 8, 2024. Chapter Two – The Church of Christ; One Church; (Page 57); Appendix, Internal Evidence – Scientific Foreknowledge, Medicine (pgs. 356-357).

42 LCMS – The Lutheran Confessions – The Large Catechism; Conclusion of the Ten Commandments; Sections 311 (pg. 40) and Section 333 (page 42). (https://www.lcms.org/about/beliefs/lutheran-confessions)

43 "*Comparison of Old Testament with the Words of Jesus*"; Life Application Study Bible, New American Standard Bible – Updated Edition, Zondervan, 2000, pg. 137, *"Jesus and the Ten Commandments"*

44 LCMS – Frequently Asked Questions – Doctrine; The Lord's Supper; "Where in the Bible does it say Christ's body and blood are present at Communion? / What verses in Scripture can be cited that teach "that BOTH bread and wine AND Christ's true body and blood" are present in the Lord's Supper? (https://www.lcms.org/about/beliefs/faqs/doctrine.)

45 ELCA, Worship Resources: Frequently Asked Questions - *Why and how do we move to weekly communion*? Background and Practice; (http://download.elca.org/ELCA%20Resource%20Repository/Why_and_how_do_we_move_to_weekly_Communion.pdf?_ga=2.26852669.1423621492.1586812801-1359316336.1586812801)

47 The Lutheran Church – Missouri Synod: A Brief Statement of the Doctrinal Position of the Missouri Synod; "*Of the Election of Grace*", Sect. 35 & 37. (www.lcms.org/doctrine/doctrinalposition#electionofgrace)
48 Miller, Dave, Ph.D., *"Piloting the Strait, A Guidebook For Assessing Change In Churches of Christ";* Eighth Printing, 2006; Sain Publications, Pulaski, TN.; "Are We Saved By Grace Alone?" (pp. 311-312.)
49 Belief and Practice – The Lutheran Church – Missouri Synod, Beliefs and Practices; "*What About … Confession and Absolution.";* http://www.lcms.org/about/beliefs https://files.lcms.org/file/preview/l3ND8hgL23tzCJWPm4SC3ED1bArI5kSb
50 Vine, W.E., "An Expository Dictionary of New Testament Words, with their Precise Meanings for English Readers;" First published 1940. 16th impression 1966; Fleming H. Revell Company. ["Silence" – 1 Tim. 2:11 ("hesuchios") vs 1 Cor. 13:34-35 ("sigao")]
51 *Male Spiritual Leadership,* by F. LaGard Smith; Published by 21st Century Christian, 1998.
52 ELCA News Service, August 21, 2009 – "ELCA Assembly Opens Ministry to Partnered Gay and Lesbian Lutherans (09-CWA-34-CA); (https://www.elca.org/News-and-Events/6587)
53 ELCA – Candidacy Manual, Adopted by the Church Council November 2016 (revised June 1, 2020); Section 1.8: *Guidelines for People in Same-Gender Relationships.* (ELCA.org – pdf)
54 ELCA "*The Church and Homosexuality*"; John Wickham, 08/01/2004; (http://www.elca.org/JLE/Articles/742?_ga=2.259396617.261821120.1534856161-593350227.1534606020)
55 ELCA – Faith and Society, PDF – Social Teaching Statement adopted by majority vote at Churchwide Assembly of ELCA meeting in Orlando, FL, August 28 – Sept. 4, 1991; "Abortion"; *Social Statement Summary* PDF; Section IV: "*Guidance in Making Decisions Regarding Unintended Pregnancies*" https://download.elca.org/ELCA%20Resource%20Repository/AbortionSS.pdf?_ga=2.129870476.122685347.1698358395-1784036654.1695926433
56 Belief and Practice – The Lutheran Church – Missouri Synod, "*What About … Abortion*"; http://www.lcms.org/about/beliefs https://files.lcms.org/file/preview/3jxAHFLmb96aR7yvu0wDH3vzk2dpXVGC
57 Webster's New World Dictionary of the American Language – College Edition; The World Publishing Co., Cleveland and New York.
58 ELCA – Ecumenism: "*The Vision of the ELCA*" (PDF); (http://www.elca.org) https://download.elca.org/ELCA%20Resource%20Repository/The_Vision_Of_The_ELCA.pdf?_ga=2.122611723.122685347.1698358395-1784036654.1695926433 (Last Page).
59 ELCA – "*Conciliar Relations*": Christian Churches Together; Church World Service; Churches Uniting in Christ; Lutheran World Federation; National

Council of the Churches of Christ; Would Council of Churches; *Joint Declaration on the Doctrine of Justification* (Roman Catholic Church); https://www.elca.org/Faith/Ecumenical-and-Inter-Religious-Relations/Conciliar?_ga=2.88402971.122685347.1698358395-1784036654.1695926433

60 Trinity Evangelical Lutheran Church, Latrobe, Pa; Worship Services / Worship Bulletin (Oct. 22, 2023 / Leadership and Staff; https://storage2.snappages.site/G2T66P/assets/files/Pentecost-21-October-22-2023.pdf ; Trinity News, Oct. 22, 2023; https://storage2.snappages.site/G2T66P/assets/files/Trinity-News-October-22-2023.pdf

61 Calvin Institute of Christian Worship for the study and renewal of worship; Nairobi Statement on Worship and Culture Full Text: 6.1 - Challenge to the Churches. (https://worship.calvin.edu/resources/resource-library/nairobi-statement-on-worship-and-culture-full-text)

62 "Lutheran Worship 2000 and Beyond", *Seven Theses on Lutheran Worship,* by Dr. A.L. Barry, Board of Elders – Holy Cross Lutheran Church, Arlington, TX; https://unite-production.s3.amazonaws.com/tenants/holycrosshrco/attachments/332201/LutheranWorship2000Beyond.pdf

63 The Lutheran Church, Missouri Synod - Frequently Asked Questions – Worship & Congregational Life - "*What is the role of elders in a congregation?*" (http://www.lcms.org/faqs/worship#elders)

64 Association of Lutheran Church Musicians (ALCM), Valparaiso, IN. https://alcm.org

APPENDIX

1 Jackson, Wayne; "*The Bible Translation Controversy – Expanded Edition*"; Stockton, CA; (http://www.christiancourier.com)

2 Jackson, Wayne; "*The Bible Translation Controversy – Expanded Edition*"; Stockton, CA; Chapter 3 – The Underlying Text, (Pg. 6). (http://www.christiancourier.com)

3 Stroop, J. Ridley (no date), "What Shall We Do with the New Bible?" (Nashville, TN: Stroop); pg. 23.

4 Jackson, Wayne; "*The Bible Translation Controversy – Expanded Edition*"; Stockton, CA; Chapter 4 – "The Translator's Theology and Philosophy," (Pg. 9). (http://www.christiancourier.com)

5 Carson, D.A. (1979), "The King James Version Debate" (Grand Rapids, MI: Baker); Pg. 89.

6 Bold, underlined, or Parenthesis – added for emphasis by the author

7 Arndt, William F. and F. W. Gingrich, (1967), "A Greek-English Lexicon of the New Testament and Other Early Christian Literature (Chicago, IL: University of Chicago Press); pg. 606.

8 Table of "A 'Literal' > Paraphrase Scale of English Bible Versions," Followed by Recommendations; Mark Hoffmann and Bruce Terry; (https://docs.google.com/document/d/1-u-5nvjpFDQIMAEc7zTqM8lZLqqC3Eo2h6FEsR1z06g/edit?usp=sharing); (mgvhoffmann/CrossMarks.com)

Milton Keynes UK
Ingram Content Group UK Ltd.
UKHW010914070724
445144UK00009B/61/J